MW00380202

Confederacy of Ambition

William Winlock Miller and the
Making of Washington Territory

Confederacy of Ambition

William Winlock Miller and the Making of Washington Territory

William L. Lang

UNIVERSITY OF WASHINGTON PRESS

Seattle and London

Copyright © 1996 by the University of Washington Press
Printed in the United States of America

Library of Congress Cataloging-in-Publication Data

Lang, William L.
    Confederacy of ambition : William Winlock Miller and the making
of Washington Territory / William L. Lang.
        p.   cm.
    Includes bibliographical references and index.
    ISBN 0-295-97502-4 (alk. paper)
    1. Miller, William Winlock, 1822–1876. 2. Politicians—Washington
(State)—Biography. 3. Pioneers—Washington (State)—Biography.
4. Washington (State)—Politics and government—To 1889.   I. Title.
F891.M545L36   1996
979.7'03'092—dc20
    [B]   96-8932
                                                            CIP

The paper used in this publication meets the minimum requirements of
American National Standard for Information Sciences—Permanence of
Paper for Printed Library Materials, ANSI Z39.48-1984.

For Annie and four westering families:

the Palmers and Johnstons of Oregon

and the Waddoups and Calls of Utah

Contents

Preface

The idea for this biography originated with Pendleton Miller, the grandson of its subject. Knowing the general contents of his family's papers, especially William Winlock Miller's rich political and business correspondence, Pendleton Miller believed that a biography of his grandfather could shed new light on Washington's territorial history. He was steeped in this history from family stories and the assiduous manuscript and book collecting that his brother, Winlock William Miller, Jr. (1908–1939), had pursued, which resulted in an impressive library of Pacific Northwest Americana. Much of that collection, which included a sizable cache of Miller family papers, was donated to Yale University and became a central part of the Western Americana collection at the Beinecke Rare book and Manuscript Library. For more than two generations, scholars in Pacific Northwest and western history have benefited from the Miller family's sense of history and generosity.

Aside from the large gift of papers to Yale, however, the family still had thousands of items, books, maps, paintings, photographs, and other memorabilia that reflected three generations of political and economic life in the Pacific Northwest. The most voluminous and most intriguing were the personal papers of William Winlock Miller. During the late 1980s, Pendleton Miller decided to donate these papers to the University of Washington. What is curious about the two collections, however, is the lack of a discernable pattern of division. A letter written one day, which can be found in the Beinecke archives, might be matched by a reply the following day that is in the University of Washington archives. When the two collections are combined, the resulting corpus presents a fairly thorough documentation of W. W. Miller's public life, and a considerable amount of his private one as well.

In 1989, after Pendleton Miller's death, Elizabeth Carey Miller went forward with her husband's plan to donate the papers to the University of Washington and to pursue a biography of the family patriarch. Betty Miller had long been associated with the University of Washington primarily as a benefactor and specialist contributor to the university's school of horticulture. Her generosity had made a horticultural library possible. A recent family gift has also established an endowed chair at the university's law school. But more than this, Betty Miller was also an internationally recognized authority on Pacific Northwest native plants and had created one of the great personal horitcultural gardens at her home in The Highlands, north of Seattle.

As anyone who knew Betty can attest, when she set her mind to do something she did not relent until it was accomplished. Her extraordinary work in beautification of the Chittenden Locks and several major highways in the Seattle area are examples of her determination to make things happen. She approached the Miller biography project with the same enthusiasm, energy, and most intelligent interest. With the sage advice of Frank Minton, and working with Robert E. Burke of the university's history department and Don Ellegood and Julidta Tarver of the University of Washington Press, Mrs. Miller sought a historian with a record of sound scholarship and writing ability to undertake the project. The family papers donated to the university's archives had been expertly catalogued and were ready for use, so all that needed to be done was select a historian.

I include these details here because my work on this project brought me into contact with a most remarkable woman, and it is not too much to say that this biography is in many respects the result of her commitment to the primacy of solid scholarship as a fulfillment of her husband's vision. In one of our early meetings, she asked if I intended to pursue all available sources. I answered that a biography practically compelled an author to track down every bit of information pertaining to the subject, especially if the inner life could be exposed. She assented and took the conversation one step further by challenging me to find out what made W. W. Miller tick. Why had he come west? How had he made his money? And why, perhaps, had he married Mary McFadden? Nothing will embarrass, she bluntly offered, and she did not care if the book sold more than a few copies: she wanted the book to be true to the record and to be unimpeded by any considerations. She pledged not to intrude, and she was true to her word, for as she read early drafts of each chapter she offered reactions and engagingly listened to my assents and dissents. The completed book is the better for those conversations.

The discoveries I made enroute began with the surprising richness of family materials in the Beinecke Library archives. What most of us thought was primarily official correspondence turned out to be at least half-related to family affairs, thereby shedding more light on Miller's activities. In those researches and others, I have racked up considerable debts to archivists and librarians, the best of whom contribute to the quality of books in ways only authors can know. At the University of Washington Manuscripts and Archives Division, Karyl Winn guided me to the most important collections and took a very gratefully received personal interest in the project. Janet Ness, of the same department, helped make the finding of materials practically problem-free.

At Yale University, George Miles went out of his way to aid my research and helped broaden my search for relevant materials. He also shared information on the original Miller bequest to Yale and the history of the Miller papers at the Beinecke, while making my stays in New Haven more pleasant. In Illinois, Cheryl Schirnning at the Illinois State Library and Lowell Voelkel at the Illinois State Archives alerted me to several sources I surely would have missed.

Closer to home, at the Washington State Library in Olympia, Jeanne Engerman and Gayle Palmer gave me the benefit of their knowledge of Olympia materials. Eb Geisecke and Drew Crooks also pointed me to important sources for Olympia history. I owe a special debt of gratitude to Mary Ellen Meryhew, Harvey Steele, and Steve Waterson of the U.S. Customs Service for graciously allowing me to use un-archived historic documents housed in the Customs Service offices in Seattle and San Francisco. At the Seattle Federal Records Center, Joyce Justice helped me locate the most important federal records to chart Miller's official business correspondence. Wayne Larson and David Hastings at the Washington State Archives in Olympia spent several sessions with me and dug out important legal documents pertaining to Miller's land acquisitions. I am especially grateful to historians Julie Eulenberg of Seattle and Shanna Stevenson of Olympia for freely shar-ing their research with me and keeping me from making several errors.

In the course of researching and writing this book, I collected other debts from friends and historians who endured hearing about Miller, his foibles, and my pursuit of him. Carol Zabilski, Associate Editor of *Pacific Northwest Quarterly,* read portions of the manuscript, gave me her usual keen reading, and gave friendly advice. During many evening conversations, Carol and Ivan Doig endured my tales about pursuing Miller and then gave great counsel on writing the story and setting things out straight. Kent Richards of Central Washington University, Isaac Stevens's biographer and expert on Washington territorial his-tory, read the entire manuscript and kept me from errors, while alert-ing me to nuances in territorial political history. David Alan Johnson of Portland State University and Robert E. Burke of the University of Washington also gave me critical readings of the manuscript and sound advice on how best to structure the Miller story.

With three historian friends I had ongoing discussions about regional history, biography, our craft, and sundry other subjects. I want to acknowledge my debt to them out of both professional camaraderie and deeply held friendship. To Bill Robbins of Oregon State Univer-sity, Tom Edwards of Whitman College, and Bob Bunting of Fort Lewis College—thanks for the good talk, good arguments, and challenging ideas that made me think a little harder. And this book also owes much to Julidta Tarver, my editor at the University of Washington Press, who has been part of this from the beginning and took a much appreciated personal interest in its completion.

One person, above all, has a personal imprint on this book. Her sensitive but pointed critiques of my scribblings and her loving support have made this book better than I could have hoped. Being married to the perfect editor is a writer's dream, but I am the more fortunate because Marianne Keddington-Lang is an even better partner in life than she is an editor.

Confederacy of Ambition

William Winlock Miller and the
Making of Washington Territory

CHAPTER 1

Young Man to the Frontier

The desire of prosperity has become an ardent and restless
passion in their minds, which grows by what it feeds.
Alexis de Tocqueville, *Democracy in America*, 1835

In late March 1850, twenty men maneuvered their oxen-
pulled wagons into a casually formed train on the road leading west
out of Beardstown, Illinois, ready to begin a months-long journey to
Oregon and California. William Winlock Miller, a twenty-eight-year-
old teacher who had already spent one season in California, had agreed
to captain the train, which included three of his brothers, two uncles,
and more than a dozen others. The men were young, most of them
younger than Miller, and all had little idea what lay ahead of them
beyond the Missouri River and west along the Great Platte River Road.
The news of gold discoveries, which had lured Miller and twenty-five
thousand other argonauts west over the trail in 1849, had created a
nationwide sensation that nearly doubled the overland traffic in 1850.
Heading west from the Beardstown ferry on the Illinois River, Miller
led the wagon train to Independence, Missouri, where the men out-
fitted themselves and joined the throng headed west, driving their ox
teams sometimes several abreast on the trail.[1]

The men left Beardstown in high spirits. Some declared California as their destination, dreaming of riches from the goldfields, while others had Oregon and its fertile valleys on their minds. We can only conjecture why the Miller brothers painted Oregon on their wagons, but it is likely that William had already discovered that fortune could be very fickle in California. The alluring descriptions of Oregon, which they had been reading for nearly a decade in letters home from displaced Illinois emigrants, also may have tempted and persuaded them to relocate to a land of fecundity and promise, a place, as one correspondent wrote, that was "more like Palestine than anything I have ever seen."[2]

Oregon pulled hard on people in Illinois. A national drumbeat for Oregon settlement had built up momentum during the 1840s, and throughout the decade newspapers in central Illinois peppered their columns with "News from Oregon" epistles, many written by former residents.[3] Teacher and printer George Goudy from nearby Jacksonville sent back enthusiastic descriptions of Oregon after his emigration in 1849. He advised readers of the *Illinois Daily Journal* to turn north off the California Trail and come to Oregon, where the land was bountiful beyond imagination. The trek was not onerous, Goudy wrote, and "there was more to be feared from the Californians than Indians— they would steal our cattle if we did not watch them closely." Rice Dunbar, a Beardstown farmer, wrote from Oregon in 1847 that Oregon had "the best wheat . . . that I ever saw in any country." Dozens of other correspondents praised everything from the fertility of the soil to the healthfulness of the climate. "The sick get well here," another Illinoisan put it in 1847, adding "the man with a broken constitution may recover his health and his physical energies."[4]

As alluring as reports on Oregon or the golden promises of California mining might have been, however, Miller and his compatriots would not have undertaken the arduous journey west if there had not been a "push," a reason for leaving. The push came from the local economy and social conditions in Beardstown, which had only partially recovered from the national economic depression that had rocked the town a decade before. Founded in 1829 when Thomas Beard had selected the site of a recently vacated Kickapoo Indian village on the Illinois River, Beardstown had considerable advantages. Located at the head of navigation on the Illinois River, eighty-eight miles from the river's junction with the Mississippi, Beardstown had quickly become a central supply point for Springfield and other inland prairie towns that had grown rapidly by the mid-1820s after Indian land titles had been extinguished and surveys conducted. The discovery of coal seams at nearby Bluff Spring and the establishment of a major ferry across the Illinois stimulated additional settlement. By 1837, the town had platted three additions and its wharf accommodated a steady line of steamboats ferrying goods north from St. Louis. Two large gristmills, a major sawmill, a distillery, and a hog market made it the "pork capital" of Illinois. At the close of the decade, Beardstown seemed poised for even more growth, but the extended waves of a national depression reached the area, washing away its confidence and stunting its growth.[5]

Beardstown rebounded during the early 1840s when thousands of land-hungry settlers crossed the Illinois River at the struggling community to claim newly opened lands in Iowa. The town gleaned profits by outfitting those westbound travelers and shipping goods in the opposite direction to Springfield and other settlements in central Illinois. Still, Beardstown could not realize its potential. It benefited from river traffic but lacked improved roads, putting it at a disadvantage to towns that supplied the faster-growing communities near Springfield. The Beardstown-Springfield route, which one traveler described as "the worst of all the muddy roads that ever were traveled," was often impassable when the rains came, stalling commercial traffic and isolating the Beardstown market. By the mid-1840s, local entrepreneurs recognized their vulnerability and agitated for a state-chartered plank road. With no support from the legislature and too short of capital to finance the project without a bond-offering charter, the town had to wait until the summer of 1850 before work could begin on the road.[6]

As Miller's wagon train prepared to leave Beardstown, local boosters were still promising better times ahead and proclaiming their town both progressive and energetic. But just weeks after the men's departure, the newspaper's editor admitted that even with recent improvements Beardstown had justifiably been "associated with the horrible phantoms of poverty, bankruptcy, disease and death."[7] The dark legacy of those problems and a sputtering local economy probably had impelled Miller and his cohorts to seek brighter horizons. Little prevented them from going. Of the men known to have been part of the wagon train, none was deeply invested in Beardstown. Three had tried their hand at farming, one had been a partner in two dry goods stores, and another had held a minor appointed office. Only one owned any land, all were single, and all were young—the oldest was thirty and the youngest was still a teenager. They all had good reasons to accept the risk for the chance to find wealth and a better future.[8]

For the Miller brothers, moving to improve their condition seemed to be as much family heritage as personal decision. The family's peripatetic course had begun two generations earlier, during the fulsome years following the Revolutionary War when thousands of families had moved west from the Tidewater and Piedmont regions to the lush valleys of Kentucky, Tennessee, and Ohio. Miller's father, William Miller, made that journey as a child sometime before 1800, when his family moved from Virginia to Greensburg, Kentucky, a small settlement on the Green River in the west-central section of the state. Growing up in Greensburg, William Miller attended school episodically, apprenticed in carpentry as a teen, and worked at the trade for several years. In 1815, at the age of twenty-seven, he married twenty-five-year-old Martha Elkins Winlock, also a transplanted Virginian. By 1822, when Martha Miller gave birth to William Winlock, the couple's family had grown to include five children, three girls and two boys. Miller's modest earnings as a carpenter either failed to provide for his family, or he saw what looked like a better life. Sometime after 1820, he left his trade and purchased a small hotel in Greensburg.[9]

Miller prospered in the hotel business, but evidently he wanted better opportunities. In 1827, he moved the family to St. Louis, where he bought another hotel and operated it for two years before moving again, this time to central Illinois. Settlers had been moving into the state's prairie regions throughout the 1820s, and as the population grew so did opportunities for service businesses. Miller settled into Springfield on the Sangamon River, where he purchased a hotel and tavern with quarters large enough to house his family, which now included seven children. Three years later, in 1832, the Millers moved again, this time some thirty miles west to Jacksonville. The family remained in Jacksonville for a decade, the longest residency any of the Miller children enjoyed during their youth, before they made their move to Beardstown in 1843. In each place, save Beardstown, William Miller operated a tavern or hotel and was well known as a convivial hotelier.[10]

The family's transiency was not unusual. Not unlike other Americans who moved into the Ohio and Mississippi valley frontiers during the early nineteenth century, the Millers acted on both an optimistic urge to move and a pessimistic reaction to disappointments. All new places held some appeal, while all old places had flaws. Alexis de Tocqueville captured that way of life best when he described the inhabitants of Illinois in 1831 as ultimately unsatisfied itinerants who moved regularly for gain, "to ameliorate it [their condition] still more; fortune awaits them everywhere, but not happiness." They were, as Tocqueville put it, "constantly seeking to acquire property, power, and reputation."[11] For William Winlock Miller, his father's itinerancy made risk-taking and moving to improve one's condition seem natural, familiar, and perhaps even predictable.

Young Miller got more from his father than an example of the beatitudes of frontier itinerancy. In Springfield, William Miller had stepped forward when the call for volunteers went out at the onset of the so-called Black Hawk War. As settlers like the Millers took up lands in the lower Rock River valley, Sauk Indian leader Black Hawk resisted leaving the tribe's village near the mouth of the river. After an initial challenge from Illinois militia in 1831 and a retreat across the Mississippi River, Black Hawk gathered forces and returned to the Rock River area in the spring of 1832, determined to win back his people's lands. Miller and citizens in Springfield, Jacksonville, New Salem, and other prairie settlements filled the volunteer ranks and prepared to push Black Hawk out of Illinois.

Miller first enrolled in a regiment of infantry militia organized in

Sangamon County in 1831; but when the confrontation between military forces and the Indians under Black Hawk seemed imminent, he transferred to a spy battalion, which quickly elected him its captain. It was while he was in charge of his gang of two hundred spies, searching out the Indians' locations, that Miller met and marched with Abraham Lincoln, another Sangamon County man who had also transferred to a spy battalion during the war.[12] Miller participated in few actual battles. Late in the war, however, he commanded a regiment in a strenuous pursuit of Indians who crossed the Wisconsin River and fled toward the Mississippi, only to be caught in a bloody battle at the Bad Axe River, which effectively ended the war. Back home in Springfield, the volunteers recuperated and later accepted the plaudits of citizens at a "great ball" at Miller's hotel, where the volunteers were feted. "The attendance was enormous," the press reported; "it included the flower and chivalry of the state."[13]

The Miller children surely witnessed the celebration and must have been impressed by their father's heroic stature. He had achieved a modest level of recognition in the community, and his camaraderie with other citizen soldiers guaranteed a steady visitation at his hotel. Even after the family moved to Jacksonville, "Major Billy Miller"—as his cohorts called him—continued to host gatherings of militiamen who celebrated the "victories" they had achieved in the Black Hawk War. The war had created a group consciousness that compelled many volunteers to remain organized as militia units, even though they had to furnish their own uniforms, guns, and equipment. In 1836, more than three hundred of these veterans came to Miller's hotel in Jacksonville, where the Major set a table loaded with partridge, venison, turkey, and quail. One of the dozens of toasts was a huzzah for Miller: "Our host, Major Billy Miller—in himself a host for hospitality and good cheer! In the camp, or at the board, you'll find him at his post, with a carving knife or sword, as a hero or a host."[14]

For a decade or more, local politicians and men of influence gathered at Miller's hotel to discuss affairs and enlarge their circle of influence. They were Whigs in a time of increasingly Democrat-dominated politics. In those frequent meetings, men like Richard Yates, soon to be elected to the state legislature as the lone Whig in a Democratic county, made lifetime alliances.[15] The meetings and discussions that took place downstairs from the Miller family residence must have drawn the attentions of the teenage William Winlock Miller. Overhearing their talk and watching his father's cronies, Miller would have received a workable apprenticeship in the adult male world of fighting in the Indian wars, frontier economics, and, above all, politics. We can only speculate at what lessons he might have drawn or how well he integrated this learning with his formal schooling, but the activities at Miller's hotel in Jacksonville had to have left some strong impressions.

Like other youngsters in Jacksonville, William Winlock Miller's formal schooling consisted of six or seven years of periodic classes, sometimes from instructors only a few years older than himself. In 1825, only seven years after statehood, Illinois passed a school law that provided for county schools; but creating school districts, giving qualifying examinations for teachers, and regulating curriculum were left to the counties. Until the early 1840s, when the legislature passed more progressive public school legislation, most local communities supported private subscription schools to bolster existing public schools. In Jacksonville, where Illinois College was established in 1830, Miller grew up in a community that took an especially strong interest in education. Although Miller may not have been too attentive in grammar school—one of his comrades remembered years later spending "truant hours" with Miller at a local swimming hole—his attitude had changed by the time he attended Illinois College. It is likely that Calvin and George Goudy, brothers who had reputations as superb teachers at the college, sparked Miller's interest in scholarship; and it may well have been George Goudy who first suggested to Miller that he take up teaching as a profession.[16]

It is uncertain which or how many years Miller attended Illinois College, but by 1845 he had accepted a teaching position in Bluff Spring. Located about four miles east of Beardstown on the main road to Springfield, Bluff Spring had been settled in the early 1830s, primarily because of its rich coal deposits. It had grown quickly, and by the mid-1840s the combination of agriculture, coal mining, and local industries provided the town with a relatively stable economy. In Bluff Spring, as in other Illinois towns in the 1840s, a committee of local leaders chose their children's teachers from a list of young men and women who had passed an exam and received a teaching certificate. Miller presented his credential to the Bluff Spring committee and passed muster, but it is likely that a personal connection was as responsible for his getting the job. Judge John A. Arenz of Beardstown, an important Cass County political leader and early investor in Bluff Spring, was a family friend and Miller's future brother-in-law.[17]

At Bluff Spring, Miller taught students at several grade levels, all in common, instructing them in arithmetic, English grammar, geography, history, and orthography. His students ranged in age from twelve to eighteen, and most had advanced to at least the ninth grade. Evidently, Miller used approved texts, such as McGuffey's *Rhetorical Guide* and *Reader* series, but he also introduced his students to Shakespeare, English poets, and classical literature, principally to instruct them in moral values and the worth of education. One former student later admitted to not being attentive enough and missing valuable lessons. Another apologized for laziness, calling Miller "the faithful teacher" and himself "the wayward pupil." Miller must have had high standards and expectations, as the apologetic pupil later wrote him: "you drilled into me long ago at Bluff Spring schoolhouse" Edward Young's poetic lines "'We take no note of time/But from its loss.'" For Miller, looking back years later, "everything pertaining to my humble career as teacher at Bluff Spring" had given him "pleasant recollections" and a sense of accomplishment.[18]

While the distant memory of his "humble career" might have given Miller some pleasure, he may well have felt other emotions in 1849 as he reflected on his humble pay and the even humbler prospects of teaching. Years later, he admitted that he had struck out for the California goldfields because he could not "timidly agree to be a 'nothing' in the world." Miller's ambition, if not his fear of being insignificant, crashed headlong into the economic realities he faced in Beardstown. His decision to leave Bluff Spring, Beardstown, his family, and all he had known in his twenty-seven years was not impetuous. His foray

YOUNG MAN TO THE FRONTIER   11

to California the year before had introduced him to a life so different from the one he had known that it must have been compelling, if not irresistible. As much as could be expected, Miller went west with his eyes open.

There is also evidence that poor health may have compelled Miller to leave Illinois, where fevers had often become nearly epidemic. Evidently, Miller's health suddenly had declined in 1847 or 1848, but it is unclear how serious his malady was or exactly what he had contracted. He suffered from relatively poor health throughout his entire adult life, but there is no evidence that a degenerative condition or other disease attacked him in 1848. Whatever his ills before and during the trip west, by 1853 he claimed his health had substantially returned and he felt robust and energetic. Still, on at least two occasions in later years he mentioned health as a factor in his emigration. His symptoms—physical weakness, depression, fevers—suggest a range of possibilities, perhaps including rheumatic fever or a blood disease.[19]

Regardless of the relative mix of reasons for his emigration, Miller never second-guessed his decision to leave Illinois or admitted to any feelings of uncertainty. He headed up the wagons in 1850 and pointed them west along the road to Independence. Heading northwest, the party intercepted the Platte River Road and traveled west on the south bank of the Platte River to Fort Laramie, nearly 650 miles from Independence. There they crossed the North Laramie River and continued west through South Pass, where they probably used the Sublette Cutoff on the way to Fort Hall on the Snake River, a strategic post that had been built in 1834 by Nathaniel J. Wyeth, earliest of the Oregon Trail adventurers. Fifty miles west of Fort Hall, the Beardstown men branched left, taking the California Trail and rolling by City of Rocks, across the Great Basin on the north bank of the Humboldt River.

California was the destination of most of Miller's wagon train, even though the *Beardstown Gazette* had warned its readers to avoid rushing to California. "The acquisition of such abundance," the paper predicted, "will, in the end, be a public calamity." The *Gazette*'s caveat did not faze the California-bound members of the party. At the next major fork, they split from Miller's group, turned, and followed the

Humboldt into the Sierra Nevada mountains. After nearly four months on the road, the gold-seekers were eager to reach their destination and frictions had developed among the men—some of it directed at William Miller's leadership—which may have added a wagon or two to the group headed for California. Crossing the mountains, they headed down one of several routes to the placer streams west of the range. Some remained for a season, others for a few years before returning to Illinois, and one of Miller's brothers stayed in the goldfields until his death. But William Miller, his brothers Robert and Edmund, and a few others left the Humboldt trail, turned northwest, and followed an emigrant track that Jesse Applegate had marked out just four years earlier. The Applegate Trail took the Miller brothers' party north to the Siskiyou Mountains in southern Oregon and into the Rogue River Valley, where some Willamette Valley settlers, disappointed California miners, and new emigrants had established some fledgling settlements.[20]

The men drove their oxen-pulled wagons north into the Willamette Valley. After several days of traveling, they turned east and ascended the Santiam River to a ferry crossing nine miles above the Willamette River. The Santiam landscape had a familiar and appealing feel to it. More than any other place Miller and his companions had seen on the overland trek, this looked like the stream-cut prairies of central Illinois. There was more elevation to it, and the timbered uplands, where Indians had not burned back the forest, did not look like Illinois, but the luxuriant prairie grasses in the lowlands and the fertility of the soil attracted them. And like Beardstown, the small settlements along the Santiam were isolated from the center of population, the old mission settlement at Salem, eighteen miles to the northwest. Still, why Miller chose the Santiam over other places in the Willamette Valley is unclear. He may have known or known about two Beardstown-area families—the Campbells and the Treadways—who had recently migrated there. He may have stopped there because Santiam City was the first settlement the men struck heading north. Or perhaps Miller simply liked the look and feel of the place.

William Miller, Robert Miller, Edmund Miller, Fred Nolte, John

Shearer, and perhaps two or three others—seven wagons in all—wheeled into Santiam City in late July or early August 1850. Three small settlements had grown up on the Santiam during the late 1840s: Syracuse on the south end of Milton Hale's ferry, Santiam City on the north bank, and Jefferson some two miles farther up the river. The nascent town of Jefferson had developed near a cluster of farms that the Jesse Looney, Frederick Steiwer, Hiram Johnson, and James Bates families had claimed under land laws passed in 1844 by the Oregon Provisional Government.[21] Robert and Edmund Miller and John Shearer stayed no more than a week or two at Santiam before continuing up the Willamette Valley to Fort Vancouver, the old Hudson's Bay Company post on the Columbia River. They worked as day laborers at Vancouver to re-provision themselves and then headed south to California to try their luck. But California gold still did not lure William Miller or Fred Nolte. They decided to stay.[22]

Miller liked the community, no doubt in part because several families took an immediate interest in his experience as a teacher. Within a month of his arrival, Miller was offered a contract to teach sixteen children in a school that had just been organized at the conjunction of the Johnson and Looney farms. It may have seemed ironic to him that he had prodded oxen for more than twelve hundred miles, suffered the discomforts of the trail, and bickered with some of his train members only to take up practically where he left off: herding a group of teenagers through lessons in arithmetic, grammar, and history. Ironic or not, teaching at the Jefferson school was his ticket to a new country.[23]

The Santiam settlements had grown up in isolation, distant from the nearest supply sources in Oregon City and relatively cut off even from Salem. During the early years, in the mid-1840s, settlers had little more than a barter economy, based primarily on agriculture and stock-raising. Conditions did not improve until the legislature approved construction of a road connecting Salem and Marysville (later Corvallis). The key link in this Willamette Valley arterial was a ferry across the Santiam River, which made the Santiam settlements an important way station on the only road that connected Oregon

City and Salem to the Umpqua and Rogue river valleys in southern Oregon. By 1850, the population of Santiam City, Jefferson, and Syracuse numbered more than one hundred. Thrown on their own resources, neighbors helped each other, tending stock, building fences and barns, and providing community services. "The neighbors shared with each other," one former resident remembered, "and at butchering time the meat was always divided among them." On festive occasions, they held "celebrations and had big community dinners in the grove—even put on home talent shows."[24] Because Miller taught children from ten Jefferson-area families, he came into immediate contact with the core group of earliest residents, especially the Looney and Steiwer families.

Jesse Looney, who was nearly fifty years old in 1850, and his wife Ruby had emigrated from Tennessee to Oregon with his brother William's family in 1843. They had joined a wagon train that included the Applegate, Waldo, Nesmith, and Gaines families, all pioneers who would figure prominently in Oregon politics by mid-century. The Looneys spent their first winter at Whitman Mission before rafting their goods down the Columbia River and heading south into the Willamette Valley. Leaving his family in Salem, Looney rode south looking for the right place for his large family, which included eight children. He filed a claim on the Santiam in 1844, put up a large barn, raised horses and cattle, and operated a sizable farm. When a stage line chose a route through Jefferson, Looney's became the stage stop where horses were changed. In 1849, Looney's eldest daughter, Susan, brought another recent emigrant into the extended family when she married Frederick Steiwer, a Prussian-born farmer who had filed a claim near the Looneys. Miller became an unofficial member of the Looney-Steiwer clan and was especially close to the Steiwers. Frederick and Susan named one of their sons Winlock in Miller's honor.[25]

In the classroom, Miller had the same success he had enjoyed in Bluff Spring. Students later confided to him that he had been their best teacher, that he had taught them more than the required lessons. "I have not learned so well," John Looney wrote Miller in 1852, "as when I went to you." But teaching did not sustain him. He had left Illinois in part because teaching school had not made him feel significant; it did not match his ambition. In Oregon, even if the landscape and teaching might have given him pleasant reminders of Bluff Spring, he clearly wanted another kind of life. Besides, Miller's situation in Oregon made him think differently about teaching, regardless of his success. For one thing, his teaching job at Jefferson was short-term, governed by a contract specifying that classes be held for only one term, sixty days during the fall. For another, his students ranged in age from nine or ten to eighteen, and he held classes in a large, rough-hewn log structure with "a big fireplace at each end to heat the building." And more important, he received a lower wage. Even though the community compensated him with furnished lodging and an allowance for board, his pay was unattractive—seven dollars per pupil per term, when carpenters earned $2.50 per day.[26]

Money—his lack of it or his desire to acquire it—figured prominently in Miller's estimation of his life at Jefferson. What wealth there was on the Santiam in 1850 came principally from trade, either in agricultural products or livestock. Although conditions had improved since the mid-1840s, when hard currency was extremely scarce and wheat was an official medium of exchange, coin was still scarce in the Oregon countryside. In most communities, mill owners and merchants were the most likely to have cash and often served as unofficial bankers. In Jefferson, Jesse Looney, Hamilton Campbell, and Jacob Conser had capital to lend out. Looney had the largest landholdings and the largest extended family in the area, all of whom were relatively prosperous farmers. Conser had invested in Syracuse and Santiam City, built a gristmill and sawmill in partnership with Napoleon Evans and E. E. Parrish, and held an interest in the ferry. Campbell had emigrated from central Illinois and brought money with him to invest. By reputation, he was considered wealthy.[27]

Miller had something in common with all of them, especially Conser and Campbell, who had both come from Illinois. Like Miller, Conser had made the overland trek in his late twenties—he was four years older than Miller—and he had a keen interest in politics, both in Illinois and Oregon. Campbell had come from near Beardstown, and it was through him that Miller got his first business opportunity in Oregon. In February or March 1851, Campbell, Miller, and another central Illinois migrant, B. R. Biddle, joined in a stock-raising partnership. At Campbell's urging and with promises of good opportunities in the cattle business, Biddle had earlier packed up his family and journeyed to Oregon from Cass County. Once in Oregon, Biddle had engaged in some cattle dealing and then enthusiastically had agreed to join Campbell in a cattle-raising venture in 1851.

The reputedly prosperous Campbell, who had three children under Miller's tutelage in the fall of 1850, proposed to trail 2,000 cattle from California into southern Oregon. In partnership, Campbell, Biddle, and Miller, plus a fourth investor—a man named Ralston—planned to build up a ranch and "trading establishment in the Umpqua Valley," where the stock would be pastured and readied for sale in the newly discovered goldfields along the Rogue River. Each of the partners pledged $1,000 to finance the ranch, which they hoped would do a brisk business with miners headed to the strikes. Biddle and Miller also agreed to each give Campbell their own notes for $900—payable in four years at 6 percent interest—for 500 head from the herd.[28]

The plan relied on Campbell getting the stock to the Umpqua and Biddle finding willing buyers. Evidently, only Campbell put any cash up front. He apparently carried most of the burden, even agreeing to post Biddle's share of the trading post investment. Where Miller would have gotten his portion of the investment is unclear. He may have had access to money from Illinois, although there is no evidence that he did, or he may have enlisted Conser as a silent investor. Conser himself might well have offered Miller his financial support at the very beginning. Whatever the source of Miller's proposed investment, it turned out that he never had to pony up any cash or sign a promissory note for the cattle. Even before Miller had left the Santiam in midsummer of 1851, the partnership agreement had begun to unravel. Miller later confided to Biddle that "a business connection with men in whom I had so little confidence was unpleasant to me." He may have backed out of the whole affair by the fall of 1851. By the following spring, Miller had divorced himself from the enterprise and the partnership had descended into disagreement.[29]

The villain in the business turned out to be Campbell, who Biddle later described as a "black hearted hypocritical scoundrel that justly deserves the hisses and contempt of every honest man." Campbell had delivered no more than 800 or 1,000 head to the Umpqua, had sold 140 head to Ralston on the sly, and may have traded cattle for horses. "There was not anything carried out as intended," Biddle later confessed to Miller, admitting that he felt personally sorry that Miller got nothing from the effort. "The ranche," he reminded Miller, "was to have been yours," but "there was no ranche established."[30]

For his part, Miller wanted no compensation, if in fact he had any coming, and he wanted no part of a court case Biddle had launched against Campbell. Miller had written to Biddle that he considered Ralston a "western blackleg" and that he had lost confidence in Campbell because he had "failed to comply with his promises and written contract."[31] With that in mind, Miller counseled:

> I would not do Campbell the least harm if I had it in my power. I am a firm believer in the doctrine that man is punished for his sins in this World and I think Campbell will not be an exception to the rule.[32]

Miller knew Campbell better or judged him better than Biddle had. By late 1852, Campbell had been completely discredited in Jefferson and was considered a "d__n blackguard," as one of Miller's correspondents put it. Little more than two years later, Campbell was thrown on hard times, "struggling like a drowning man" with his son-in-law trying to save him. Finally, he fled to California to escape his creditors.[33]

Unlike Campbell, Miller left the Santiam community on good terms, with strong friendships, and even beloved by his students and their parents. Again, there may have been some "push" that prompted Miller to leave; but not unlike his father, he acted more from the promise of opportunity elsewhere and the need for change than from a dissatisfaction with his circumstances. He could have remained in Jefferson, but little held him there. He owned no real estate and was still unmarried, although even in his few months on the Santiam he had found mutual interest with some of the young women in the area. A little more than a year after he left, Frederick Steiwer reminded Miller of his amorous relationships in Jefferson, suggesting that he return and pursue the women he had left behind. "Bill if you want to get married," Steiwer wrote, "com over. The Biddle gals will take your ey. Tha can wigel too."[34] But romance and marriage fell a distant second to Miller's prime interest: finding a better situation in Oregon. He sought "property, power and reputation," as Tocqueville had put it, but he had few means to acquire them. So far, his friendships in Oregon had introduced him to men of good will and some means, inserted him into a comfortable community, and entangled him in a stillborn business. It was a mixed legacy and provided no certain path to a career. To secure that, Miller reached back to Illinois and the political heritage of his youth.

Miller came to Oregon a firm advocate of the Whig party, as much through inheritance as well-considered belief. His father's loyalty to the Whig banner had been consistent and visible, and Miller had regularly voted Whig in Illinois before emigrating west.[35] But political allegiance at mid-century was not rigid or structured. Political parties relied less on ideology and more on adherence to general tendencies that bonded together coalitions of pragmatically inclined interest groups. Loyalty to the policies and personal image of the parties' principal leaders often became a more important test of membership than belief in any specific political idea. Whigs followed Henry Clay's views, which emphasized a predilection for protecting property rights and state-supported economic development. Democrats adhered to the viewpoints expressed by Andrew Jackson and his heirs, who generally supported smaller property owners and smaller government. But in the wake of Congress's acceptance of the Wilmot Proviso in 1846, which outlawed slavery in the western territories to be acquired through the Mexican War, the issues of slavery and states' rights divided both parties. Passage of the Compromise of 1850, which brought California into the Union, had quelled some of the divisiveness, but both parties were in traumatic flux at the beginning of the decade.[36]

Miller left Illinois as a Whig who had lived most of his life in predominantly Democratic counties. He believed in the righteousness of Henry Clay's vision of American development and feared the populist inclinations of the Democrats. In his chosen new home, he again lived in a place dominated by Democrats. As a fellow Illinois emigrant to Oregon, David Logan, had written home in 1851: "This is no place for a Whig."[37] Nonetheless, Miller's political connections were Whig, the Whigs had the White House and control of patronage in the territories, and Miller was looking for a main chance. That chance came in March 1851, when President Millard Fillmore signed a certificate of appointment naming William W. Miller surveyor and inspector of revenue for the Port of Nisqually in Northern Oregon.[38]

It took months for the news to reach Miller on the Santiam in Oregon. When he did get word, it came from unofficial sources—his brothers-in-law in Beardstown, John McDonald and Horatio Rew. For Miller, it was a natural line of political communication. McDonald and Rew were active Whigs who had some standing in state politics and kept close connections with their man in Washington, Representative Richard Yates. Yates served his constituents well, especially by attending to local patronage. He also kept watch on Illinois Whigs who had federal positions in Washington, D.C., protecting them when necessary and in return receiving information and influence in governmental departments. Yates had special ties to the Miller family. Not only had he begun his political career in the circle of men who frequented Major Billy Miller's hotel and tavern in Jacksonville, but he also had relied on local support from Judge John Arenz, a Beardstown civic leader, and Sylvester Emmons, publisher of the *Beardstown Gazette*. Both had married into the Miller family.[39]

Emmons was the more important of the two Miller in-laws, and he probably offered Miller more political advice and influence than Arenz did. A lawyer who had converted to the Mormon faith, Emmons had emigrated to Hancock County, Illinois, in 1843, where he joined Joseph Smith's Nauvoo community on the banks of the Mississippi River, north of Quincy. Within months of setting up practice in Nauvoo, however, Emmons became angered at Smith's theocratic policies.

Joining a group of like-minded dissenters in 1844, Emmons published the anti-Mormon newspaper, the *Nauvoo Expositor,* on June 7, which pilloried Smith and included potentially libelous stories about his reported sexual practices. Smith retaliated by destroying Emmons's press, which eventually landed Smith in the Carthage, Illinois, jail, where a mob attacked and shot Smith and his brother dead.[40]

While Brigham Young and other Mormon leaders regrouped in Nauvoo, Emmons fled the town and his adopted community. He moved southeast about one hundred miles to Beardstown, where he continued his legal practice and established the *Beardstown Gazette* in 1845. Stridently Whig and virulently anti-Mormon, the *Gazette* became a vehicle for Emmons's intemperate rejection of Joseph Smith's theology and a powerful component of the Whig's political machinery in Cass County. By 1849, Emmons had been elected to a judgeship and also served as postmaster for Beardstown. So, in 1847, when he married Elizabeth Miller—the closest in age to William among the Miller children—he brought the Millers even more into the center of the Whig tent. With two Whig judges and a prominent lawyer as in-laws, a strong connection with Yates, and his father's friendship with Abraham Lincoln, Miller's Whig connection ran deep.[41]

Two Illinois Whigs in Washington, D.C., claimed credit for Miller's appointment in Oregon. Richard Yates surely had a direct role in persuading the Fillmore administration to give an Illinois supporter the office; but Josiah Lucas, a Miller family friend who had a high post at the Land Office, also claimed to have "procured" the job. For his part, Miller was unsure who had actually acquired the office for him and knew no other details of the process.[42] Those pursuing the appointment had begun the hunt even before February 1851, when Congress had decided to create a new port of entry in Oregon, the first north of the Columbia River.

Oregon Territorial Delegate Samuel Thurston, a Democrat, had lobbied the Whig administration for *his* choice when he first heard of the possible creation of the Port of Nisqually district. First he suggested Michael T. Simmons, one of the earliest settlers in Olympia, on the southern tip of Puget Sound. But Secretary of the Treasury William

Meredith had said no to Thurston and had "demanded the names of two Whigs." In reply, Thurston "told him no," as he explained to a friend, but said that he "would divide the spoils with him." Still, the secretary refused to budge. The Whig party, he informed Thurston, would control the spoils. In his typical fashion, Thurston then wrote the secretary a pompous and blistering letter, warning him of what would happen if he rejected Thurston's compromise suggestions: "I told him [he] would raise a fire that would burn out root and branch all the Whigs in Oregon." Given that Oregon was predominantly Democratic, with few Whigs to "burn out," his threat must have sounded a bit hollow.[43]

While Thurston was brandishing his political saber, Miller's political allies successfully stole the march and acquired the position for him, a Whig who had solid Illinois credentials. Nonetheless, Miller's appointment as a Whig was hardly a triumphant victory in Democratic Oregon. He took up his office, then, at some political disadvantage, with only his previous residency in Oregon as a partial saving point. By 1851, however, Miller had made friends in Northern Oregon— some of them Democrats—so when he prepared the required $1,000 bond, Puget Sound residents Michael T. Simmons, Hugh A. Goldsborough, and Edmund Sylvester stepped forward to sign a guarantee of his character.[44] By late July, Miller had moved from the Santiam to Salem, where he prepared to leave for Olympia, the freshly platted town where the Treasury Department had sited the new port of entry. He had read of his appointment in the *Oregon Spectator,* and perhaps he had also heard the news directly from the paper's editor, George Goudy, Miller's former teacher from Jacksonville, but still no official confirmation had reached him. In a quandary, he sought the advice of John P. Gaines, the Whig governor of Oregon, who presumably had regular and direct communication with Washington. Gaines advised him not to wait but to get on his way to Olympia and let the official letters catch up with him.[45]

Miller arrived in Olympia on August 1, 1851, the first federal official to take up a position in Northern Oregon, that portion of Oregon that two years later would become Washington Territory. He went with almost no knowledge of his duties, without an official letter or document confirming his position, and with no regulations or other paraphernalia of office. He knew the post paid $1,000 per year; and, with opportunities for mercantile investments and other business opportunities, it would likely "be worth 3 or 4,000 a year," as his brother-in-law had informed him in April. That was a significant improvement over his wage as a teacher in Jefferson, but more important, his appointment as surveyor of customs at the Port of Nisqually instantly made him one of the participants in the making of Washington Territory. It launched him on a career path that took him further than his father had aspired and well beyond his own hopes. From the moment he arrived at Olympia to take up his duties, Miller ceased being a "nothing in the world" and began to fulfill his ambitions.

CHAPTER 2

In the Government's Service

*I know that men sometimes play green and it is always
a strong game but this finessing is not always necessary
when you are complete master of the subject before
you. . . . Never let your fire be drawn but keep your own
counsel and your judgment to yourself.*
Josiah M. Lucas to William W. Miller, 1855

As he headed north down the Willamette River in 1851,
William Miller had little idea of what lay ahead of him. He knew that
his new position as surveyor of customs had attracted many job-
seekers, perhaps for the salary or maybe the recognition, even standing, it might bring, but he had only the barest knowledge of its
requirements and protocol. He had almost no image of Olympia, no
intimation of what the place Congress had selected for the new port
might be like, who had settled there, or what kind of community they
had created. But as he later confessed, because he could only "depend
on his own exertions" to make his way in life, he had not hesitated to
embrace another risk and move from the Santiam.[1] He had stepped
out again on the itinerant track his family experience had endorsed,
but this time it would be different. Although he could not have

23

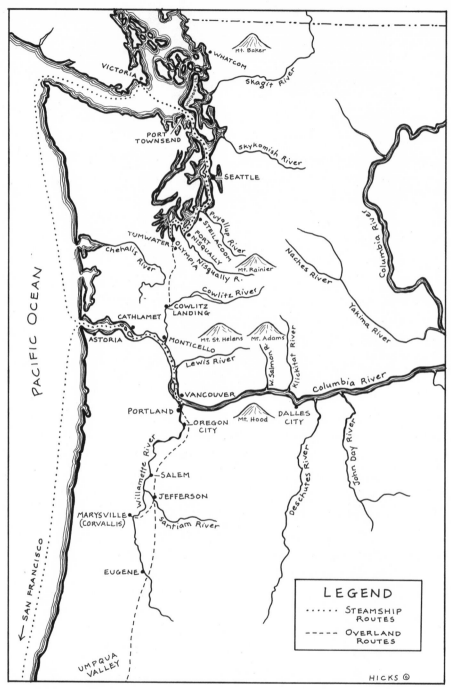

Map 1. William Miller's Oregon Country

known it as he traveled north in the last days of July, Olympia would be his home for the rest of his days.

For a man born, raised, and familiar with inland prairies and river valleys, living at the saltwater port of Olympia must have required adjustment from the first day. Lying at the tip of Budd Inlet, a long finger of Puget Sound that pointed south toward the Cowlitz Plains and the distant Columbia River, the town had been hacked out of a thick forest environment less than two years before Miller arrived. Even by Oregon Country standards, Olympia was raw. The settlers had barely cleared the land—"A dog couldn't get through the woods," one early resident later claimed—and roads were virtually nonexistent. The area's first non-Indian settlers, Edmund Sylvester and Levi Lathrop Smith, had staked claims in 1846 at the mouth of the Deschutes River, in part because other Americans had already settled at nearby New Market (present-day Tumwater) the year before and in part by whim. "I do not know what attracted my attention this way," Sylvester later confessed, "except I was destined to settle here."[2]

The Puget Sound and Cowlitz Plains had not drawn many men like Sylvester previous to the mid-1840s. Most of the overland migrants had headed south of the Columbia to the Willamette Valley, where Methodist missionaries had created a thriving community in the late 1830s. The valley's fertility pulled the emigrants away from the gravelly soils to the north, and the hegemonically powerful Hudson's Bay Company, headquartered at Fort Vancouver since 1825, discouraged American settlement north of the Columbia. The HBC had long considered the northern portion of Oregon as its domain, investing heavily in Fort Nisqually, its port on Puget Sound, and in an extensive farming operation at Cowlitz Plains. The company had encouraged settlement in the area by its own retired employees, but most had chosen instead to settle in the Willamette Valley or the Tualatin Plains south of the Columbia. Some retired HBC men had settled along the lower Cowlitz River, however, and a few Americans had ventured north of the river before 1846, when the Oregon Treaty gave the United States control of the disputed territory all the way north to the 49th Parallel.

The most important American settlement party, one led by Ken-

tuckian Michael T. Simmons, had come west in 1844 and had paused
for a season on the north bank of the Columbia upriver from Fort
Vancouver. With advice and aid from Chief Factor John McLoughlin
at the fort, Simmons headed north in 1845, crossing the Lewis and
Cowlitz rivers to the Deschutes, not far from its mouth on Budd Inlet.
Simmons had scouted the area earlier and had selected the falls of the
Deschutes because of its potential for waterpower. The settlers took
a series of claims, calling their settlement New Market. By late 1847,
Simmons had enlisted eight partners—including Maine-born Edmund
Sylvester—in building a sawmill at the falls, the first on Puget Sound.[3]
Other settlers had made claims in the area, including John Jackson,
who had come in 1844 and homesteaded near the HBC farming operations on the Cowlitz, and George Washington Bush, a black settler
who had steered north to British-dominated territory in 1845 because
Oregon's Provisional Government had passed a Black Exclusion Law
that outlawed African American settlement south of the Columbia. A
large settlement of HBC farmers had come from the Red River country in 1841, but fewer than ten families remained in the Puget Sound
region by the late 1840s. Not until after passage of the Oregon Treaty
did more settlers take up land north of the Columbia. By 1848, enough
of them had moved in to prompt HBC complaints with U.S. authorities that Americans had illegally squatted on company lands. But even
with the increasing settlement, the population north of the Columbia remained small. What headstart they had toward some growth
quickly dissipated in 1849 when news of the gold strike in California
swept the Oregon Country, taking two thousand or more settlers—
including Sylvester and other Cowlitz men—along in a stampede south
to find gold. By 1850, only 280 Americans were clustered in widely scat-
tered communities, existing in a kind of semi-isolation with only unim-
proved traces connecting them.[4]

Ironically, Olympia was a product of that gilded enthusiasm. After
one season of trial in the goldfields, Sylvester headed back to Oregon
with other disappointed miners in the last days of 1849. Not eager to
retrace his overland route, Sylvester sailed north on the brig *Orbit*, a
ship he had purchased in San Francisco with three other partners.

Sylvester's *Orbit*, the first American commercial ship to sail into Budd Inlet, dropped anchor at the mouth of the Deschutes in January 1850. Back at his claim, where he "found things just as I had left them," Sylvester transformed his homestead into a townsite. In the company of Isaac N. Ebey, Benjamin F. Shaw, Michael T. Simmons, Charles H. Smith, and a few others, he agreed to lay out the town on his land and name it Olympia.[5]

By the time Miller arrived, some eighteen months later, much had changed. Simmons had purchased the *Orbit* from his partners and sent it back to San Francisco with lumber from the New Market mill. He then stocked his new store at Olympia with the mercantile goods the ship brought back from California. Olympia had acquired a post office, and Simmons had been named postmaster.[6] The incidental commerce with Fort Nisqually, the HBC post north of Olympia on Puget Sound, had grown with the population. Ships had begun carrying timber to Victoria, California, and Hawaii, and perhaps a dozen or more houses lined the waterfront. There was even talk of creating of a new Oregon county.[7]

Despite its growth and optimism in 1851, Olympia remained isolated, something Miller found out when he made his trip north. Leaving the mid-Willamette Valley, he traveled on a newly constructed wagon road to Oregon City and then by river to Portland, a new city that had been platted only a few years before and had just been granted a charter from the territorial legislature. At Portland, where a deep enough anchorage made it the head of navigation on the Willamette for seagoing vessels, steamboat service had been initiated a year before. At a cost of about ten dollars, Miller booked passage down the Willamette and Columbia rivers to the mouth of the Cowlitz.[8]

The Cowlitz River ran west from the Cascade Mountains and turned south at Cowlitz Plains, thirty-seven miles from its conjunction with the Columbia. A natural water arterial north to the prairies, the Cowlitz had served Chinook-speaking Indians for hundreds of years as a main travel route and had been adopted by HBC men, traders, and northbound settlers as the cheapest and easiest overland route to Puget Sound. Hiring Indian canoeists at the mouth of the

Cowlitz, Miller traveled upriver to Cowlitz Landing, where the river took its sharp turn east. At the landing, he began the last leg of his trip, resting at John Jackson's homestead way station and then proceeding by horseback via the Cowlitz Portage northwest to Fort Nisqually. The portage—a crude road with no bridges across streams and no ferry at the Nisqually—had been developed in the early 1840s by HBC to connect its farms on the Cowlitz with Fort Nisqually.[9]

It was the other way to Olympia, the sea route, that had necessitated the creation of a customs district and Miller's new post. Sea commerce in the southern part of Puget Sound began in earnest in 1833, when HBC established Fort Nisqually to dominate the northern fur trade. The fort, located about fifteen miles north of Budd Inlet hear the mouth of the Nisqually River, constituted the only port on Puget Sound. Described in 1843 as "an enclosure of fir logs, on an average, eighteen feet high" with "a store for trading in furs and several small buildings," the fort served as the main shipping point for the Puget Sound Agricultural Company, the HBC's subsidiary that operated large farms at Cowlitz Plains and Nisqually after 1840. The Cowlitz farm and other similar operations at HBC forts in the Columbia River Basin supplied the company's posts and Russian-American Company posts with foodstuffs. In 1847, for example, HBC shipped more than seven tons of wool, nearly two thousand sheepskins, and hundreds of cowhides and horns to London.[10] Manufactured goods from England, trade with the Russian-America Company in Alaska, commerce with other HBC posts in the region—especially Fort Victoria on Vancouver Island—and shipments to and from Hawaii made Fort Nisqually a busy port. After the 1846 treaty, that sizable commercial traffic took place in newly decreed American waters, which soon came under the purview and control of the United States Customs Service.[11]

From the standpoint of American merchants in southern Puget Sound, Miller's arrival could not have come any too soon. During the preceding half dozen years, enforcement of American customs regulations in Puget Sound had created conflict between the Hudson's Bay Company and the Americans. The Sound's labyrinthine waterways made surveillance difficult, but even more problematic was the loca-

tion of the nearest customs office at Astoria at the mouth of the Columbia River, far to the south. Smuggling in Puget Sound, which had
become a cottage industry, bedeviled American customs agents and
sometimes led to conflicts with HBC shippers. For American shippers,
the conditions were unsettling, for they not only shipped in goods from
American ports but also both purchased merchandise from HBC and
competed against it.

If customs officials applied the revenue laws to HBC shipments—
the 1846 Walker Tariff had specified 30 percent duties on most imported
consumer goods—there was a considerable difference in retail prices.
If violations occurred and ships were detained, however, then either
receiving merchandise or shipping it out could be delayed for weeks.
The *Cadboro*, for example, was sequestered in port for customs infractions in 1850 for more than two months. Both HBC and American
businessmen on Puget Sound operated in an economically circumscribed arena. What affected one affected all. This was especially the
case for Michael Simmons and many of his associates. Simmons had
long done business with HBC Chief Factor William Tolmie, including bartering services and renting out the *Orbit* to haul the company's
produce. Thomas Glasgow, sometime inspector of customs in Puget
Sound for Customs Collector John Adair in Astoria, often sold Tolmie
lumber. Speaking for his own interests and others entangled with HBC,
Simmons petitioned for a new customs district both to rationalize
commerce and to ensure some protection for trade through the
enforcement of revenue laws.[12]

In part, then, Miller had been sent to Nisqually because local
American interests had requested help, but the situation also had
broader implications than the fortunes of Olympia's nascent merchants. It was part of the aftermath of the Oregon Treaty of 1846.
Although the treaty had allowed HBC to retain its lands, installations,
and trading privileges in the territory south of the 49th Parallel, and
even though most American settlers were favorably disposed toward
the company, occasional disagreements and frictions between Oregonians and HBC interests had created a contentious situation. Some
of it focused on land policies and trading practices, but much of it

revolved around HBC dominance of the sea trade in Northern Oregon. Samuel R. Thurston, Oregon's first territorial delegate and an anti-HBC politician, lobbied Congress and the James K. Polk administration to create a customs district for Oregon in part to hold HBC accountable to U.S. revenue laws (as specified by the treaty). Congress satisfied Thurston's request in 1848 by choosing Astoria, Oregon, as the first customs office on the Pacific Coast. Even though the gold rush would soon make California ports the busiest on the Pacific, it made sense in 1848 to select Astoria, the oldest non-Indian settlement in Oregon and the gateway to inland transportation. In the spring of 1849, Polk's choice for collector of customs, John Adair of Kentucky, arrived at Astoria ready to administer the nation's revenue laws.[13]

Adair's aggressive application of law exacerbated an already uneasy situation and set in motion a chain of events that resulted in declaring Nisqually a port of delivery in January 1850 and establishing the Port of Nisqually in February 1851. Adair had been in Astoria just a few weeks in mid-April 1849 when he detained the HBC's *Columbia* in the harbor and levied duties on all goods in the ship's hold destined for resale, including items bound for Vancouver Island, north of the 49th. Company officials cried foul and appealed to Washington, complaining that the United States had no legal basis for taxing goods shipped to ports in British territory. The government agreed and rescinded the duties, but the *Columbia* incident proved to be a harbinger. The next year, customs officials seized the British ship *Albion* as it loaded spars near Dungeness Spit in violation of a trading regulation. Within weeks, officials detained and searched the *Cadboro* at Nisqually, brusquely informing HBC Chief Factor William F. Tolmie of several violations of the revenue laws. Tolmie "made several remonstrances against [t]his proceeding but with[ou]t effect." In these and other incidents, U.S. customs officials rendered a squeaky tight reading of the laws and often overstepped their authority. Washington later overruled local officials, but the immediate effect at Nisqually was to put the Hudson's Bay Company on the defensive.[14]

By May 1850, harassment of HBC commerce had become customs policy. Delegate Thurston, who had made diminution of HBC influence in Oregon his personal goal, finally prevailed on Secretary of the Treasury William M. Meredith to require all British vessels sailing to Nisqually to clear customs at Astoria, forcing all ships from Victoria on a 350-mile detour and two dangerous crossings over the Columbia River bar. While this regulatory decree sparked HBC complaints and diplomatic correspondence between London and Washington, it also added stimulus to Michael Simmons's request for a customs district on Puget Sound. The local Olympia petition aside, it was also clear that requiring HBC ships to go to Astoria for clearance did not solve all of the problems in Puget Sound. Collector Adair in Astoria still had to patrol the Sound to prevent smuggling and enforce the laws, as he reminded the Treasury Department in early 1851.[15] He urged the department and pleaded with Thurston to create a new customs district.[16] Congress responded in February 1851, but the new district did not become a reality in Olympia until Miller arrived in early August.

What Miller knew about the immediate history of customs enforcements on Puget Sound and the conflicts between customs and the HBC is unclear. The *Oregon Spectator* had publicized the ship seizures, and it is likely that Oregon Governor John Gaines had discussed the HBC question with him before Miller went to Olympia.[17] If Miller had any predispositions on the situation before arriving in Olympia, however, he kept them to himself. It is clear that he had no specific instructions from the Treasury Department, but that was not uncommon. The Customs Service had expanded rapidly during the previous two decades, and many collectors and deputy collectors had no training or even information when they took over their posts. In most isolated regions, such as Puget Sound, communications between local customs officials and Washington, D.C., were unpredictable, so collectors and surveyors tended to operate on their own.[18] It is likely that Miller got most of his information about conditions on the Sound—and opinions about conflicts with HBC—from Simmons, Edmund Sylvester, Isaac Ebey, and H. A. Goldsborough, men who had vested interests in commerce and who conducted business with Tolmie at Nisqually. Goldsborough, for example, was friendly with HBC and hoped that the new district would make shipping easier and less costly. Several months before Miller's arrival, he had written Tolmie, offering to secure legislation favorable to HBC commercial interests.[19]

Miller quickly made acquaintance with Goldsborough, Simmons, Ebey, and others who had supported the creation of the new customs district, and several of the men were sufficiently impressed to sign his bond. Miller may have been willing to serve their interests, but he was hamstrung. Simpson P. Moses, President Millard Fillmore's choice for collector, had not yet arrived, and until he did Miller could do nothing. The collector had to swear him into office, and Miller could not fulfill any of his functions as surveyor without Moses's direction and approval. Worse, Miller had no forms or official seals and no means of approving or disapproving inspected cargoes. Judging from his letters to the Treasury Department, Miller felt a combination of frustration and confusion. At the same time, he seemed not to be too concerned about his fate. Writing his brother in late August, Miller tersely told him that the position paid modestly but it "takes no time."[20]

Just weeks later, however, Miller's job became complicated and time-consuming. James Douglas, HBC factor and soon-to-be governor of Vancouver Island, queried Miller from Fort Nisqually on September 9, requesting that the *Cadboro* be cleared to land goods directly at the fort rather than sailing the extra distance to Olympia. Miller faced two problems. If he acceded to Douglas's request, he would cut a technical but important corner in the regulations—all shipments were supposed to come directly to the Port of Entry before proceeding to a port of delivery. More serious, Miller felt he had no authority to act on *any* request. As he explained to Douglas, Collector Moses still had not arrived and all Miller could do was

> inform Gen. John Adair, Collector at Astoria, and if he will empower me to act by appointing me a Temporary Inspector I will take great pleasure in accommodating you, otherwise I must decline having anything to do with the matter.[21]

Miller took his federal responsibility seriously, and he had wisely taken a prudent, almost cautious, line. He offered to help Douglas, but declined to act illegally. Tariff and excise tax returns, in an era without corporate or personal income tax, brought in the majority of federal revenue, and the Treasury Department expected customs collectors to vigilantly levy duties and fines. Miller adhered to the law, sometimes in an almost officious manner, knowing that failure to collect duties meant less revenue for the government and perhaps a threat to his own salary. In the *Cadboro* case—his first—Miller had waded into a murky situation that offered no clear alternatives. If he inspected the ship and approved its landing at Fort Nisqually, his action would give the intercourse legal standing. If he refused, then the ship might still land its cargo and he would fail to assign and collect duties. Writing Adair for advice, Miller hoped that the collector could keep him out of harm's way, but Adair's reply gave little comfort. Adair had no more authority over the Port of Nisqually than "the Collector of New York," he wrote, and he could not give any official instructions or convey any special dispensations or powers on Miller. Nonetheless, he advised:

> All vessels of all nations have the right to enter at the Port of Olympia. Now it is a port of entry inviting the commerce of the world, and it would be violation of the comity of nations to detain such vessels within the harbor.[22]

If it were he, Adair continued, he would inspect the *Cadboro* and send it on its way. Adair had no doubt "it would be sanctioned by the Secretary of the Treasury."

Miller ignored Adair's counsel, fearing the consequences, but the complaints from HBC officials did not diminish. The company's men, understandably, were unsure who was in charge and where to appeal. Adair had assured Douglas, a man known for his parsimony and penchant for detail and control, that Miller could let the vessel go about its business if he wanted. "In this emergency I have ventured to advise Mr. Miller," Adair wrote Douglas, "the case being simple and clear to my mind. If I were in his place I certainly would not detain [the ship] if I could not take the responsibility of clearing any vessel." There was the quandary again and no solution in sight. Chief Factor

Tolmie then tried sorting the conflict out, brusquely telling Miller: "We now await your arrival [at Nisqually] . . . and should it be inconvenient for you . . . hope you will fill up the necessary forms and send them by return of bearer." Miller replied in measured terms, reminding Tolmie that he could do nothing without a directive from Collector Moses and that Adair had no authority to relieve Miller of his responsibility.[23]

Surely feeling buffeted, Miller sought advice and instructions directly from Washington. As he explained to the new treasury secretary, Thomas Corwin, two ships lay at anchor in the harbor, one of them trying to load a shipment of wool and agricultural products from Cowlitz for shipment to Victoria. Miller had appealed to the district attorney of Oregon for an opinion, he explained, but he wanted approval to act in the collector's behalf until Moses arrived. The "inconvenience to local citizens is significant," Miller informed Corwin, and more emigrants were arriving weekly. The portent for Miller was obvious: He would be put in this position time and again unless Moses arrived soon. The relief Simmons and his associates had hoped to receive with the new port of entry seemed to have nearly evaporated.[24]

Miller finally received approval to conduct business as a proto-collector. He inspected and cleared ships, collecting more than four thousand dollars in duties during November 1851, but he remained in a very compromised situation. From the Treasury Department's perspective, Miller had yet to perfect his office. No bond had been received in Washington, and Miller still had not taken an oath of office. In the meantime, Miller conducted business from Olympia, traveling the fifteen miles by land and twenty-five by water to Nisqually—often by canoe—whenever inspections and clearances were required. It made better sense, and was required by his appointment, to reside at Nisqually, but Miller could find housing only in Olympia. Plus, the men who most wanted the customs office on the Sound lived and did business in Olympia.[25]

If Miller's life as the first federal officer in Northern Oregon had been difficult since August, his situation became even more uncom-

fortable once Simpson P. Moses arrived in late November. An aggressive Ohio lawyer, Moses had gone to Washington for personal consultations with the Treasury Department soon after his appointment.
There he learned something about the affairs on Puget Sound, but
whether he received any specific instructions to apply more pressure
to HBC commerce is unclear. Whatever the source of his vigilant attitude toward HBC—and some historians have speculated it was for
personal gain or to ingratiate himself with local anti-HBC men—
Moses quickly became the company's nemesis. He had taken his time
getting to Olympia, traveling leisurely with two of his brothers, A. B.
and A. J. Moses, and Pennsylvania lawyer Elwood Evans. Treasury
Department officials later concluded, a Miller confidant put it, that
Moses was "peddling trinkets etc. whilst on his way." But once on the
scene in Olympia, the collector wasted no time putting pressure on
the company.[26]

On his way to Olympia, Moses had met with a group of anti-HBC
settlers at Cowlitz, who presented him with a petition attacking HBC
trading practices and demanding action. At Olympia, where Moses
administered Miller's oath of office, he told his surveyor how he
intended to conduct the customs office and end British evasion of revenue laws. Moses made arrangements to contract with Michael Simmons for use of his store's second floor as a customs office—a space
Miller had been using for several months—and directed Miller to organize an exploring expedition. Moses wanted Miller to take a small crew
in the customs cutter and explore the southern Sound, from Olympia
past Nisqually and north to Commencement Bay, scouting as many
coves and bays as possible for evidence of revenue law violations.[27]

On the evening of November 21, Miller put into the Sound in the
face of a driving rain, commanding a crew that included Elwood Evans,
A. B. Moses, four Indians, and a group of Olympia men—H. C. Wilson, A. M. Poe, Theo Dubosy, and Enoch Fowler. "Having run day and
night from the time of leaving Olympia"—without a letup in the rain—
until reaching Commencement Bay, they surveyed the settlements,

calling at the Indian huts and making inquiry of the Indians as to whether they had seen any English or boats of any kind in Puallub [Commencement] Bay recently. They promptly answered in the negative.

"Before returning I considered it my duty," Miller reported, "to examine the pack trails" to see if any "afforded for secretly introducing foreign goods into the interior of the country." He split up his party, taking Moses and Evans with him overland to Fort Steilacoom and sending the rest with the cutter. Slogging his way through the wetlands to the Nisqually River and north again to Steilacoom, Miller found no evidence of smuggling other than "vague reports of Indians" trading with men on a foreign vessel in the Strait of Juan de Fuca. The expedition had cost nearly two hundred dollars, Miller reported to Moses, but had come up empty.[28]

If the report disappointed Moses, he kept it from Miller. It probably made little difference anyway, because the day after Moses received the report events unfolding at Fort Nisqually gave him an opportunity to flex customs office muscles and contest HBC trading activities. On November 27, 1851, the *Beaver*, steaming from Fort Victoria on Vancouver Island with the *Mary Dare* in tow, dropped anchor at Nisqually Landing. Chief Factor W. F. Tolmie and his assistant, Edward Huggins, came on board, greeted the passengers, and took them to the fort. The *Beaver*'s passengers—HBC Factor John Work, his wife Josette, three of their children, and the sister of another HBC official, James Birnie—convivially shared news from Victoria, exchanged mail, and enjoyed Tolmie's hospitality. Passengers unloaded and the ships proceeded up the Sound to Olympia, where customs officers would officially clear the ships and cargo for landing at Nisqually.[29]

Miller, along with Temporary Deputy Collector Evans and two deputized agents—Isaac N. Ebey and A. J. Simmons—boarded the vessels and began a routine inspection, comparing the ships' manifests against their cargoes. As surveyor, Miller directed the inspections, and before long he discovered several technical violations, the type that Moses had clearly instructed him to cite and treat with appropriate action.[30] H. A. Goldsborough, a passenger on the *Beaver* and witness to the proceedings, called the "entire transaction as pitiful trifling and utterly unworthy of official action," but Miller took his orders seriously and called forward Captain Charles Stuart, informing him that the customs service had to seize his vessel for revenue law infractions.[31]

The charges against Stuart and his counterpart on the *Mary Dare* included failure to deliver their manifests and concealing trade goods with intent to escape customs duties. In the case of the *Mary Dare,* it was 230 pounds of sugar—destined for Tolmie's personal pantry— that qualified as contraband. U.S. law prohibited importation of sugar in shipments of less than 600 pounds. The ship also concealed two dozen more scythes than listed on the manifest. The *Beaver* had further violated regulations because it had anchored at Nisqually, had allowed Tolmie aboard, and had let the passengers go ashore before coming to Olympia.[32] Moses allowed the officers and crew to leave the ship, although he assigned deputized customs men to stay on board and keep the cargo holds sealed, but the ships remained in the harbor, prohibited from discharging cargo or leaving port. Tolmie took Mrs. Work and Rose Birnie to Olympia to retrieve their luggage, which they had not taken with them from the *Beaver* at Nisqually. In the meantime, Miller took responsibility for securing and detaining the ships, Moses brought official charges against the HBC vessels to Oregon District Court Justice William A. Strong at Cathlamet, and Tolmie fired off dispatches to James Douglas in Victoria.[33]

Moses acted self-righteously confident. The bit in his mouth, he held hard to line, accusing the British of deceit and holding Stuart personally liable. For their part, Tolmie and Douglas denied each accusation and questioned the legality of the entire action. Both litigants were at the far end of their respective governments' line of communications, and their forum was William Strong's residence at Cathlamet on the Columbia. The Yale-educated Strong had to rule on the case, which really boiled down to two issues. Had the HBC ship captains violated any revenue laws, and were the customs officials justified in seizing the vessels? On December 12, not trusting the speed or security of communications to Cathlamet, Moses sent Miller as his personal representative to visit Strong and explain the conditions of the seizure.

Tolmie and Douglas had claimed that the American detention of the *Beaver* and the *Mary Dare* was wholly fabricated, that the captains were unaware of the regulation specifying clearance first at Olympia, and that Captain Stuart had explained to Miller and Evans that he did not have sufficient fuel to steam the extra miles to Budd Inlet. Speaking for Moses, Miller told Strong that both captains had previously commanded American vessels and knew the laws well and had sailed the Sound in a "manner designed to evade detection." Strong listened and took it under advisement.[34]

By the first of the new year, the ships had been in detention for nearly six weeks, at great inconvenience to HBC. The potential damage, Douglas had warned Tolmie in mid-December, could be devastating. But the often imperious Douglas saved his venom for Moses, whose conduct he labeled as "scandalous." By late December, when he knew more of the details, Douglas admitted "that our own proceedings have not been so prudent and circumspect," but that still did not justify the attack Moses had leveled.[35] Behind the scenes, Douglas informed HBC Governor George Simpson, and protests found their way to Washington. In Northern Oregon, however, Miller continued to carry Moses's mail by enlisting David Logan, his Illinois family friend in Portland, to represent the customs service in court. Douglas directed Tolmie to secure an Oregon lawyer as well, and Simon B. Mayre of Portland was retained as counsel. The case was scheduled for hearing in Olympia, the first to be heard in newly created Thurston County. Ironically, because of limited steam packet departures from Portland, Judge Strong, Miller, Tolmie, and the two lawyers traveled together north to Olympia. None of them later repeated the conversations they had on that voyage, but it is clear that both sides in the controversy wanted a quick resolution. Nearly three months of contention had sufficiently established Moses's enforcement credentials, and HBC officers desperately wanted their ships out of detention.[36]

On January 19, 1852, John Work and Tolmie rode to Olympia to give their depositions to Judge Strong. Once again, Tolmie protested the seizure and the Americans' attempt to hold Captain Stuart liable. Stuart's predicament worried Tolmie sufficiently that two days later he authorized the captain's use of a canoe at Nisqually so he might make an escape to Victoria. But when Judge Strong rendered his ruling on January 22, both sides claimed a victory. Despite Miller's testimony that the 1799 revenue law governing sugar imports applied, Strong ruled that Moses had erred in seizing the ships. Still, the judge did confirm other violations and approved the fines. Tolmie registered yet another protest, promising to appeal to the secretary of the treasury, even as he posted a bond for the release of the *Beaver* and the *Mary Dare*. On January 25, Tolmie, John Work, and the crew steamed back to Nisqually on the *Beaver*, pleased that the crisis had passed and relieved that Captain Stuart had taken flight in time to elude receipt of an arrest warrant, which Alonzo Poe had tried to serve.[37]

Moses had lost his bid to punish HBC for its "duplicitous actions," as he had written Judge Strong, but he had not taken out the bit yet. With the *Mary Dare* ready to unload its cargo at Nisqually and take on agricultural products for shipment to Victoria, Moses instructed Miller to seize all trade goods in the ship's hold and warehouse them under a customs seal. Identifying the extra scythes as justification, Moses inflicted an additional penalty and assigned Miller the job of enforcement. Tolmie would not stand for it. Confronting Miller at HBC's Nisqually beach storehouse, Tolmie challenged the whole business and demanded specific reference to the revenue laws. An embarrassed Miller had to back down and agreed the regulations did not support seizure of the entire store of goods. "Half a day's work lost to wagon & oxen & cart," Edward Huggins wrote in the fort's journal, "on account of the above foolish transaction."[38]

The foolishness continued. This time the target was the *Beaver*. Moses wrote Miller on February 6: "The 'goods in the trade room' as per outward bound manifest of the steamer 'Beaver' you will cause to be landed and warehoused under seal of the U.S. at your port." The ships could leave port, but Moses had determined that HBC would not escape some punishment beyond the penalties assigned in Strong's verdict. Moses took HBC to task for applying its own valuations to trade goods rather than have them inspected at Olympia. As Moses warned Tolmie, "you have not seen proper to comply" and "the law will not allow vessels to enter at and clear from any other than the Port of Entry."[39] Why Moses turned the screw an extra notch is unclear. He may have suspected that higher authorities would bargain away the court verdict, as in fact they did, but he may also have been playing to the demands of local anti-HBC extremists. A public meeting had been held in Steilacoom within two weeks of the verdict, where an agitated crowd had passed strongly worded resolutions calling for a wholesale divestiture of HBC lands and suggesting that the company had bribed Judge Strong. In one resolution, the assembled crowd profusely thanked Moses for his vigilance and courage.[40] Regardless of Moses's standing and the importance of enforcing revenue laws, Miller began to feel uneasy about the policy and its consequences. In one instance, Moses had Miller inspect some linens that had been mistakenly included in a case containing other goods.[41] As the pursuit of technical violations continued, Miller sought better relationships with HBC men at Nisqually.

Not being at Nisqually had become more than an inconvenience for Miller. Shuttling back and forth between Olympia and Nisqually not only made his job more difficult, but it also had begun to take a toll on his health. After the release of the *Beaver* and the *Mary Dare,* Miller sought out Tolmie and talked him into partitioning one end of the beach storehouse at Nisqually to serve as a makeshift office and dwelling. Just days after their confrontation at Nisqually beach, HBC workmen began work on Miller's storehouse room. By early March 1852, Miller had moved, physically distancing himself from Moses and attaching him to the Nisqually community.[42]

During the next few months, Miller subtly but steadily also detached himself from Moses's policies. Precisely when he began either to better appreciate the HBC side in the customs disputes or to question the utility of Moses's tactics is uncertain, but it is clear that by early summer 1852 Miller had become a minor advocate for HBC complaints. In July, he wrote Secretary of the Treasury Thomas Corwin that HBC should not be forced to sail to Olympia before discharging cargo at Nisqually. The port of entry, Miller explained to Corwin, was called Nisqually, which referred to the Nisqually Landing at Fort Nisqually and not to Olympia. The heaviest burden of commerce came to Nisqually Landing, and going the fifty extra miles to Olympia and back unnecessarily extended the voyages. Miller also reminded Corwin that during his months as the lone customs officer he had allowed HBC vessels to proceed directly to Nisqually without checking in at Olympia. "I have yet to learn," Miller continued, "that the interests of the Revenue have been prejudiced thereby."[43]

Miller proposed a solution. If the surveyor had a place of residence at Nisqually, he argued, HBC ships could be inspected at Nisqually Landing and obviate the "loss of time and money suffered by the Hudson's Bay Company" that resulted in sailing to Olympia. If the department did not object, Miller continued, he had already contracted with HBC Factor Tolmie to have a separate residence constructed at Nisqually, which HBC would rent to Miller at a reasonable cost. "I have taken the responsibility to act in the matter without instructions," he explained, because of the "great personal inconvenience and injury to my health" from traveling on the open water in all climates. Miller had received Tolmie's agreement in two letters posted on July 15 at Fort Nisqually. One included a prominent thank you to Miller for "uniformly and promptly" attending to duties at Nisqually, coupled with Tolmie's promise to build a house "as soon as sawmill lumber can be obtained for the purpose." The arrangement, which Miller had not discussed with Moses, amounted to a quid pro quo, a deal that Miller had engineered on his own.[44]

Having set this plan in motion, Miller told Moses of both his arrangement with Tolmie and his appeal to Corwin. He had agreed to rent the new building at Nisqually for one year without prior approval, Miller reported, adding, "I am in hopes you will represent this matter to the Department at Washington that no blame may attach to me."[45] Miller was not worried about reaction at the Treasury Department—he had been in direct correspondence with Corwin for two months—it was Moses who concerned him. Miller's thinly disguised manipulation probably was not lost on the collector; and as HBC workers built the house at Nisqually throughout the following several months, Miller found himself more and more in conflict with

Moses.[46] Moses held the line on the requirement that HBC clear all ships at Olympia, although he did allow Victoria-bound vessels carrying *only* agricultural products to leave directly from Nisqually. But Moses made that dispensation an unofficial one.[47] Miller had argued the point with Moses in August, writing that the great majority of the company's ships came to Nisqually in ballast from Victoria and required no inspections. More disturbing to Miller, Moses had waved off a customs violation by the American brig *John Davis*, even though Miller had presented clear evidence of the captain's evasion of the 1799 Revenue Act. Although he restrained from uttering it, Miller began to view Moses as a capricious and prejudicial official.[48]

By October 1852, after workmen had completed his Nisqually dwelling, Miller had become even bolder in his advocacy for temperate application of revenue regulations on HBC commerce. On Tolmie's behalf, first suggesting it to Moses and then writing directly to Treasury, Miller asked if just the captains of HBC vessels could proceed to Olympia with their manifests to secure official clearance. The whole business, Miller wrote, boiled down to common sense. Neither the customs service nor HBC benefited from the placement of the port of entry at Olympia. Furthermore, most smuggling in Puget Sound, Miller wrote Secretary Corwin, came from the "petty carrying trade," not from the ships of thirty tons or more that were covered under the 1799 Revenue Act. Indians ferried most of this trade in canoes, Miller explained, "which will easily carry two tons." There were so many engaged in the trade, he warned,

> it will be impossible for the revenue officer to board the numerous canoes, which can be seen going to and from any point and almost at any time. If importations are suffered thus to be made when a canoe shall be found with dutiable goods on board, the person in charge can easily inform the officers that he was on his way to the Port of Entry to duly enter his boat and if not boarded which ninety nine cases out of a hundred could not possibly be done, the canoe would land the cargo at any place they pleased in this cargo district and thus the revenue would be defrauded.[49]

Moses agreed and soon wrote Corwin, expounding on the foolishness of originally siting the port of entry at Olympia. "I have kept officers of customs constantly afloat in every kind of weather in open boats," Moses proudly reported, but the region simply could not be covered from Olympia. It made better sense to locate the port of entry at Port Townsend in Admiralty Inlet, the entrance to Puget Sound.[50]

Complicating and surely influencing Miller's judgment of Moses were two additional problems. Miller had known for some time— probably from Tolmie—that Moses had demanded and accepted petty bribes from HBC officials to facilitate ship clearances. James Douglas had written Tolmie in early 1853 that some forty barrels of flour and thirty barrels of salmon should be given to Moses at no charge. Moses had made it clear, Douglas explained, "that a gift of that kind will not be unacceptable, and to refuse it might expose us to inconvenience and trouble."[51] While it may have been a common procedure among some customs officials to accept gifts from ship's captains or businessmen, this arrangement put Miller in an even more uncomfortable position as he increasingly pleaded the HBC's case on regulations.

More troubling for Miller, however, was his own financial situation. Since his arrival in Olympia in August 1851, Miller had worked without receiving his salary. Although he had submitted his account vouchers as required, no pay came from the Treasury Department, at first because of his unofficial status and later because of Moses's inaction. Miller had complained to Moses in July 1852, pointing out "that no portion of my salary has been paid since my entrance upon duty." Moses ignored this and other letters, pleading that his office had no funds and Miller had to seek his salary in Washington. Miller applied pressure through Josiah M. Lucas, his Illinois friend at the Land Office who had helped the surveyor's appointment in 1851. Lucas had seen the accounts and assured Miller that Treasury knew about Moses and the situation in Olympia. "I will see that you shall not suffer," Lucas promised Miller, "as I have a host of friends in all the departments . . . all of whom are willing to do me any reasonable favor."[52]

Despite Lucas's assurances, the Treasury Department took a cautious approach, informing Miller in mid-January 1853 that he should ask Moses for the correct forms to forward his account to Washington. When Miller queried Moses about the forms, he again got no response. Even after Miller went to the collector's personal residence in Olympia, Moses brushed him off, telling him he was too busy to respond. "As I had reasons for believing that Collector Moses did not intend to promptly forward [my] accounts," Miller wrote a customs official in frustration, he had sent duplicates of his accounts to Washington. Miller's suspicions grew when he caught Moses fabricating a story about the office accounts in reports to the Treasury Department. When confronted and asked pointedly if he would honor Miller's own account, Moses replied that "he had no public funds on hand and could not do it . . . [and] would make no promise to do so."[53]

Moses pleading poverty must have galled Miller, considering that two months earlier the collector had ordered him to man his boat "during the ensuing winter, so as to be ready for service at any moment," admitting that there might not be money enough to pay the incurred costs. When Miller sent in his quarterly report in February, he reminded Moses that he had kept the boat in operation "entirely out of my own pockets," and he wondered how long Moses expected these conditions to prevail.[54] His patience nearly exhausted, Miller took his complaints directly to the commissioner of customs, perhaps believing what Lucas had offered about Moses: "I think that Moses is not pure gold, to say the least." Miller informed the commissioner that he had kept the Nisqually office operating with his own funds and had not complained to Washington, but he could not stand by and let Moses cheat other customs employees. "I have reason to believe," Miller accusingly wrote,

> that the Collector of this District is in the habit of taking blank receipts and receipts at much higher rates than were actually given, etc., etc. from boatmen and others. I take this precaution in order that the innocent may get their pay and that the interest of the government may be protected at this Port.[55]

No doubt, Miller's whistle-blowing did not endear him to Moses, who likely heard about the charges. Miller may have actually confronted

Moses in person about payment to the boatmen and Indians employed by the customs office. Earlier, he had been bold enough to write the collector a stinging criticism of Moses's brother, A. Benton Moses, charging him with inattention to duties and sloppy work. This chapter of the tempest concluded when Moses finally forwarded Miller's accounts with a note asking Treasury to speed payment, but it was too late to mend the rift between surveyor and collector. Disagreement over policies, personal friction, and distrust had cleaved whatever corporate unity existed. Besides, in the spring of 1853, both men faced the political axe. The Democrats had put their man in the White House in March, and as Whig appointees Moses and Miller were certain to be out of office soon.[56]

The new administration made its predictable sweep, appointing John Davis as governor of Oregon and replacing Collector Moses with Isaac N. Ebey. But even with Moses gone there lingered an image of malfeasance and perhaps even corruption. Miller continued to request his back pay, which now amounted to more than three thousand dollars; and many of Miller's friends, especially those who had either worked for Moses or had disagreeable dealings with him, came forward with accusations.[57] Ebey wrote the Treasury Department that Moses had defrauded practically everyone on Puget Sound. "He has swindled anyone here," Ebey claimed,

> who has had anything to do with him from the wealthy citizen who rented him the Custom House [Michael Simmons] down to the poor blind Hudson's Bay servant who boarded his boatmen at Nisqually.[58]

As Ebey calculated it, Moses owed Simmons more than fifteen hundred dollars in promised rent and had kept two town lots he had extracted from Simmons in the bargain.[59] Within a year, and under the opposition party's administration, the Treasury Department sent J. Ross Browne, its crack agent, to Puget Sound to investigate.

Worse than Ebey's charges against Moses was a scurrilous attack on the collector's character. Alonzo Poe, one of Moses's erstwhile employees, referred to him as "old circumcision" in a letter to Miller in 1853, about the time that charges against Moses began to surface. Moses "will go out of office with a perfect whoop," Poe wrote. "The old Rabbi has received notice to give up possession of Simmons' building." Poe's ugly anti-Semitic defamation was misplaced, for Moses was not Jewish, but his bigotry stands as a suggestive measurement of Moses's unpopularity. How broadly Poe's characterization circulated or was shared by others, including Miller, is unclear, but there is no question that Miller, Poe, and Ebey collectively despised the ex-collector.[60]

Once in office as collector, Ebey wasted little time in reorganizing the district, even though Moses at first would not surrender his accounts. The new collector appointed his good friend and business partner, A. M. Poe, as inspector of revenue in northern Puget Sound. He tried to retain Miller as surveyor of customs at Nisqually, but he knew it would be difficult to keep a Whig in office. He argued vigorously for Miller because, as incredible as it seemed to Ebey, Washington had appointed Simpson Moses's brother, A. Benton Moses, to the surveyor's post. Writing to President Pierce, Ebey railed that no worse selection could have been made. Not only was Benton Moses incompetent and perhaps as stained as his brother, but he also had been "the retailer of all the low slanders that were concocted and put in circulation against your Excellency prior to the election."[61] Despite this information, Pierce did not change the appointment. Ebey accepted the decision, but he made his own local correction and appointed Miller as his deputy collector.[62]

Miller had not been eager to continue in the Customs Service, but he agreed to accept the deputy collectorship as a favor to Ebey and Poe, who both wanted Miller to manage the customs district's accounts. During his tenure as surveyor, he had earned their respect as a man of dependability, sharp business acumen, and strict honesty, and he had endeared himself to other customs employees by helping them recover wages Moses had failed to pay. Miller also accepted the position as a political hedge, because he was still trying to secure full payment of his surveyor's salary from the Treasury Department. The office paid eight dollars per day—about two thousand dollars per year—

which was not an inconsiderable sum. But the economic benefits of the job probably interested Miller less than its political implications.[63]

The connection between Miller's political life in government service and his personal life, as a recent migrant to the Oregon Country and a nascent businessman, had less clarity than he desired in 1853. In so many ways and despite his participation in some of the more important political and economic events on Puget Sound, he had not yet made a life for himself. If he planned on remaining in the country, Miller knew as well as he knew anything that he had to find a place in the local economy and society.

CHAPTER 3

Making a Life

*With a trembling hand and for the first time in my life
I undertake to address a Lady. . . . it will afford me the
most exquisite pleasure to call on you at such times
during the short period you will remain here, as may
suit your convenience.*

Miller to Letitia Work, July 22, 1853

From the time he left Illinois, Miller had pursued two
images of himself. The more aggressive one pictured an upright but
ambitious adventurer, a man who pursued his dreams and made his
wealth by hard work and intelligence. The other, less compulsive portrait set him in a bucolic scene with family and friends in the fore-
ground and community as backdrop. The two images would dominate
his life, sometimes creating enormous conflict while at others seem-
ing almost conjoined. In 1853, however, the images were more sketch-
like in Miller's mind, and he gravitated toward the more concrete of
the two, the one with immediacy and substance.

Opportunism figured largely in Miller's original acceptance of the
customs job in 1851, and to some extent it guided his actions during
his tenure. Always efficient in his work and associations, Miller
embraced the adage that "time is money." Considering that the cus-

toms surveyor's job "takes no time," as he explained to his brother in 1851, he expected to pursue opportunities as he found them. By mid-1852, the Thurston County tax list reveals how far and how quickly Miller's ambition and energy had taken him. Only five men in the county had larger holdings. He listed $2,800 in taxable real and personal property. One year later, Miller's worth topped $6,000.[1]

He began his business activity at Olympia almost as soon as he arrived by assisting storekeeper Michael Simmons. Isaac Ebey and Simmons had purchased the *Orbit* from Edmund Sylvester in early 1850, intent on engaging in the coasting trade between San Francisco and Puget Sound. Their first cargo included 35,000 feet of plank lumber, 400,000 cedar shingles, and hundreds of bushels of potatoes. On the return, the *Orbit* shipped in goods from two principal San Francisco firms, Foster Sewall & Company and Treadwell & Company. The goods—which stocked Simmons's store and were sold to other investors—included items as varied as slide rules, harmonicas, cologne, a gothic clock, patent leather shoes, parasols, and kegs of nails. Perhaps in trade for using Simmons's upper floor as a temporary customs office, Miller handled the store's account books.[2]

By mid-1852, Miller was entwined in the growing Olympia economy, serving as a broker and buyer for Simmons, an intermediary between government agencies and suppliers, and a source of cash. In Puget Sound's cash-scarce economy, Miller was among a handful of men who had either cash or access to it. In short order, he became a lender and creditor, using both his own money and the resources he managed for Simmons. In August 1853, Miller lent Edmund Sylvester $800 at 4 percent interest per month on a six-month note. Six months later, he had eight other men on his books, some paying as much as 5 percent per month, including H. A. Goldsborough, who borrowed nearly a thousand dollars at 10 percent per annum. By late 1854, Miller carried more than seven thousand dollars in loans on his books.[3]

Miller knew how to make money, as other Olympia residents quickly recognized. But how and where he had developed this talent are obscure. There is no evidence that he had engaged in business in Illinois. School teaching had been his trade. Still, he must have had some knowledge of commerce and general economic conditions in Illinois. He had observed his father's struggle in the hotel business and local shopkeepers sharping for trade in Beardstown, and it is likely he accepted the Whig party's economic views, especially Henry Clay's preachments on the importance of internal improvements to frontier farming communities. He no doubt knew that business conditions could and did change quickly and that fortune was often fickle.

Miller had lived in Beardstown during the 1830s and 1840s, when the town had prospered. Among a gang of ambitious Illinois towns, Beardstown had capitalized on its river port—the busiest on the much traveled Illinois River—but after the Mexican War changes in market conditions, a paucity of capital, some transportation improvements that benefited rivals, and dwindling immigration had stalled the town's growth. The boosters' promises had evaporated; and though Beardstown had survived by serving an immediate agricultural hinterland, it had failed to become a robust trading center. The rendering of that flat economic horizon, which defined Miller's Illinois, had impressed on him the importance of regional development and the realities of inter-town competition. The conditions also had propelled him west.[4]

Regardless of how much Miller knew about economic conditions in Illinois and how eager he may have been, he needed a substantial talent to garner his initial successes. One of his acquaintances called him "the greenest man about trade that he ever saw," hardly a testimonial to Miller's bargaining skills. But he had a gift for comradeship. His easiness with other men combined with a keen-eyed ability to estimate their abilities and intentions. The former trait made him an attractive business partner, while the latter kept him cautiously skeptical of all business propositions. Miller had learned to base his evaluations on what men did, not what they promised. He watched how they attended to their obligations, whether they knowingly withheld information from associates, and how true they were to their agreements.[5]

The world Miller inhabited in Olympia in 1853 was a commercial frontier. Men like himself, who had come hoping to find a beachhead

William Winlock Miller **(1822–1876)**. In 1852, when this daguerreotype was taken in Olympia, Miller had been Surveyor of Customs for less than one year, but he had already begun to invest in commerce and to build a network of friends, including Edmund Sylvester, Michael T. Simmons, Isaac Ebey, and other early businessmen of the south Puget Sound region. (UW14328)

William Miller (**1788–1863**). William Winlock Miller's father was a model of western itinerancy. Born in Virginia in 1788, he married in Kentucky in 1815, moved to Missouri in 1827, and finally settled in Beardstown, Illinois, in 1829. He had the reputation as a garrulous innkeeper, who prided himself on his participation in the Black Hawk War against Upper Mississippi River Indians and on his friendship with Abraham Lincoln. (UW15751)

Martha Elkins Winlock Miller (1790–1856). A Virginian by birth, Martha Winlock married William Miller in 1815 and gave birth to eight children between 1815 and 1830. She bemoaned the emigration to the West of her sons William and Richard, and she never gave up hope that they would return to Illinois. The rest of her children all settled in Beardstown or within one day's travel of her home. (UW15750)

Richard Thomas Miller (1828–1873). William Miller's troubled brother pursued riches in the goldfields of California, Nevada, and Idaho. He never succeeded in finding a paying vein, but he acquired government positions, made influential friends, and nearly became a major political figure in northern California. Although he finally abandoned his itinerant lifestyle, married, and fathered two children, he died a premature death from alcoholism in Silver City, Idaho. (UW15759)

Mary Worthy Miller. Mary Worthy married Richard Miller in 1869 in Idaho, hoping to help him save himself from the degradation he had suffered in California and Nevada mining towns. Miller's premature death left her with two children and an unwanted dependency on William Miller's benevolent support. (UW15760)

Alonzo Poe, William Miller, Isaac Ebey. These three men became fast friends through their work for Simpson P. Moses, the Collector of Customs at the Port of Olympia. Ebey became one of the early settlers in Olympia and later homesteaded a farm on Whidbey Island, where he remained active in politics during the 1850s until his death at the hands of Indians in 1857. Poe worked at several government jobs in Olympia during the 1850s and was one of the principal organizers of the movement to create Washington Territory. (UW14329)

William Winlock Miller (1822–1876). By the mid-1860s, when this carte de visa was taken, Miller had invested in transportation, milling, and real estate in Washington Territory, but he also had become interested in San Francisco. During the late 1860s, Miller purchased real estate in the City by the Bay and invested in California gold and banking stocks with some intentions of moving there. (UW15764)

Winlock Miller (1870–1963). Winlock Miller, eldest son of William Miller, aided his mother in managing the Miller family properties after his graduation from Yale University in 1892. After his mother's death in 1927, Winlock Miller continued to manage the family estate and devote himself to community service, including a several-decade-long membership on the University of Washington's Board of Trustees. (UW15748)

Pendleton Miller (1872–1910). The second son of William Winlock Miller, Pendleton was barely school age when this photograph was taken in Seattle. He went to private school in Belmont, California, with his older brother Winlock, and to Yale University in 1890. At the time of his unexpected death in 1910, Pendleton had been helping to manage the Miller family properties. (UW15761)

Obediah B. McFadden (1814–1875). O. B. McFadden came to Oregon in 1853 as associate justice of the Washington Territory Supreme Court. In 1858, he became chief justice of the territorial supreme court, and in 1872 he won election as territorial delegate from Washington. As a prominent lawyer and wheelhorse in the Democratic party, McFadden wielded consideral political influence in the territory. (UW15756)

Thornton F. McElroy. T. F. McElroy began his newspaper career in Washington as Whig editor of *The Columbian* in Olympia. He transferred his loyalties to the Democratic party by the mid-1850s and supported the Union cause during the Civil War. By the 1870s, McElroy was part of Miller's loyal cadre of Democrats who helped manage the party's foot soldiers at election time. (UW15754)

Edward Furste. Edward Furste was one of Miller's steadfast political workers in the Washington Territory Democratic party. Owner of the *Pioneer
and Democrat*, Furste used his paper's columns to do battle with opposing Whig and Republican sheets. Furste was the compiler and publisher
of extensive documents in 1857 that attempted to defend Governor Isaac
Stevens in the martial law controversy. (UW15758)

Frank Clark. Clark was one of the most vocal opponents of Isaac Stevens during the 1856 martial law controversy and a political manipulator from Steilacoom, who, according to one associate, had "either too much low cunning or not enough." (UW15769)

Fred Steiwer. A native of Prussia, Steiwer was one of several successful farmers on the Santiam River, where William Miller spent two seasons before taking a federal position in Olympia as surveyor of Customs. Steiwer introduced Miller to local businessmen and aided him in joining in an ill-fated partnership in livestock trading in 1851. (UW15768)

Susan Steiwer. Steiwer took a strong liking to William Miller when he taught school for a group of families in Jefferson, Oregon, in 1851. For several years after Miller left the Willamette Valley community, Steiwer corresponded with him, giving him news of local events and urging him to return and make a home there. (UW15767)

Benjamin Franklin Shaw. Shaw was one of the early settlers in the south Puget Sound area. He served as interpreter for Governor Isaac Stevens at the Medicine Creek Treaty council in 1855 and later as a leader of the Washington Territory Volunteers in a fateful and disreputable attack on an Indian village in the Grande Ronde Valley in 1856. During the 1860s, Shaw was a sometime business partner with William Miller in transportation schemes. (UW15753)

Josiah Lucas. Pictured here in 1865 in Washington, D.C., Lucas was William Miller's most important political confidant outside Washington Territory. Posted in Washington for much of the 1860s, Lucas kept Miller informed on important shifts in national political power and advised him on policies that would reward his interest. (UW15755)

Elwood Evans. An ambitious lawyer who had met William Miller in the employ of customs collector Simpson Moses, Evans was also a friend of Isaac Stevens but opposed the governor during the martial law controversy. Evans joined the Republican party and served as secretary of the territory during the Lincoln administration, although he was suspected of consorting with Copperheads and of generally being too friendly with Democrats. (UW15757)

for future wealth, boosted its potential just as an earlier generation had in the Mississippi Valley. "The Northern portion of Oregon is much more valuable than I had expected," Isaac Ebey had written his family in 1850,

> a very desirable location for those who want to make money. . . . The prices in San Francisco all range to twenty five per cent up than the prices paid for the same articles on the Columbia river. A Man can now make more money in Oregon than he can in California. . . . [6]

In letters home to family and friends, Miller and his friends often knowingly exaggerated the wealth to be made, but they were true to their enthusiasms, engaging in the economy with optimism and a sense of common destiny. To a large extent, they felt they were part of a group effort, that their success depended on accommodation and a willingness to enhance opportunities for all.

Miller embraced the idea that he and his fellows were partners in a larger enterprise. A limited number of them scratched up commerce and competed for advantage, and they recognized the benefits government protection and investment could bring. As a consequence, the line between public and private affairs tended to blur, creating an overlapping of responsibility and opportunity. Miller often found himself inhabiting both worlds. Exactly how he managed to juggle his official duties as a customs man and his business activities is not clear, for while he enforced government revenue laws and levied duties he also participated in the principal import business in Olympia. As he helped seize ships and pursued smugglers, he lent ship's captains and merchants venture capital for commercial endeavors. Due in large measure to his fortunate mediating role in local sea commerce, Miller could aid businessmen and also build up a sizable store of capital, making him a valuable resource for everyone.[7]

Where and how he made his first sizable investments give us some insight into his method and tactics. In February 1852, only a few months after arriving on the Sound, he extended his business arrangement with Simmons to include a serendipitous partnership. The details of the partnership are unknown, but it is clear that Miller took on the financial burden, while Simmons's assets seemingly provided genuine collateral. Miller negotiated purchase of an Olympia town lot with a house and outbuildings. Town founder Edmund Sylvester, who held a lien on the property, helped facilitate the sale. Miller agreed to pay $600 in three installments, with the final payment due in July. Within weeks, however, he had arranged to lease the house and buildings back to Sylvester for a minimal rent. Miller's payments, in effect, financed Sylvester's original loss, while Sylvester got some immediate use and Miller and Simmons acquired the property.[8]

Miller's method, if it can be called that, incorporated three strategies that would stand him well over the next two decades. He chose his investments as much from the failures of others as from venture opportunities. He conservatively advanced money to men who either could provide additional opportunities through their political and financial associations or represented a secured risk. Finally, he did business with friends and developed friendships through business. Miller was conservative to the core, almost the opposite of a stereotyped frontier bonanza investor. He generally avoided speculations and schemes, and when he did bite on them he often rued his decision. Because he trusted his own instincts above all others and chose to invest in other people's risks, he made money and became land wealthy through secured debt foreclosures. The chalk line of his financial acumen—and more important than his business method—was his attention to detail and consistent focus on the numbers in his ledger book.

Miller's 1853 account book records only two loans, one a small amount to a local resident, the other a sizable advance—$800—to Edmund Sylvester. There is no hint about Miller's financial resources, no paper trail that charts how he acquired sufficient capital to easily lend $800, even if he did charge 4 percent per month in interest.[9] It is likely that he made some of his money by investing in cargo shipments and making small loans while he worked his customs job. But in the spring of 1852 he had also made another investment of sorts, when he agreed to run the Tumwater Sawmill. The operation of the mill hung in jeopardy in March 1852, because the multiple owners were in disagreement over their roles in the business and even if the mill should remain open. Miller proposed to operate the mill, which meant taking over the books, while the partners sorted out their quarrels.[10]

For operating the mill in the interim, Miller received an undisclosed portion of the mill's receipts, pending the solution of the suit. Miller did not record the amount and it is unclear how long he operated the mill, but the experience must have encouraged him to pursue industrial investment. In April 1853, he agreed to enter a new mill-owning partnership. Along with Hugh A. Goldsborough, Michael Simmons, and Wesley B. Gosnell, Miller formed a company—Skookum Mill—to build a sawmill on Gosnell's Donation Land Claim on Hammersley Inlet north of Olympia. Gosnell contributed the land as his portion of the investment, while Miller provided $900 in cash to finance construction. In effect, Miller sponsored Goldsborough and Simmons, specifying a three-installment repayment schedule to coincide with the planned completion of the mill in February 1854. He waived any profits from the enterprise but rewarded himself with a full one-quarter ownership in the company, including the land.[11]

In the Skookum Mill enterprise, Miller pursued nearly the same strategy he had employed in the purchase of Olympia property in 1852. He fronted the mill's investment, required repayment, and placed most of his risk in the overall success of the business, knowing that if additional investment were necessary he could advance funds as private loans to his partners. And that is precisely what happened. The mill constructed, Goldsborough and Simmons appealed for more cash and indebted themselves for an additional $900 in February 1854. Miller now had his partners on his own account ledger, while the Skookum Mill, plagued by construction and production accidents, struggled to make a profit.[12] The enterprise did not prosper, whether due to poor mill management or other conditions, so the partnership broke apart in mid-1855. Miller ended up with one-quarter of a failed company and its debts. But he made the best of a poor business decision by negotiating the dissolution of the partnership and delivering full ownership and attendant liabilities to Simmons. Miller ducked the debt, while he continued to hold the promissory notes Simmons and Goldsborough had signed.[13]

Miller's sense, perhaps even instinct, for business increasingly drew him into the affairs of other men in Olympia. In the process of lending money to them, he had to inquire into their affairs and sometimes suffer their failures and transgressions. During the early 1850s, it was not uncommon for his debtors to request help in collecting a debt due them or to ask Miller to facilitate another loan with a third party. In late 1853, a debtor suggested that Miller help him sell his property to satisfy the debt. In another instance, a borrower who had been cheated by a co-investor sought relief from Miller, asking him to help out in his loss by joining him in yet another investment scheme.[14] In these and other situations, Miller played the role of honest and reliable broker, always mindful of his own interests and never acting without taking full measure of the situation and the men involved. Nonetheless, he genuinely tried to further the fortunes of men he trusted, believing that their advance benefited the commonwealth.[15]

Miller's economic interests knew few bounds. He purchased town lots in Olympia, acted as a broker for men wishing to buy land, and invested in livestock trading. In 1852, he assisted financially in the establishment of the *Columbian,* the first newspaper published north of the Columbia. The following year he nearly entered into business with Ebey to supply livestock to the military at Fort Steilacoom. He was an eager investor who passed up few opportunities without at least some investigation, in some ways the personification of the frontier entrepreneurial stereotype. Yet he operated cautiously, avoiding commitments that might compromise his freedom to act. His natural conservatism, born of his own timidity and even a degree of shyness, became a strength. He agreed with and followed the advice of his Illinois friend, Josiah Lucas. "We are often thrown off our guards, through various causes . . . ," Lucas would write Miller in 1855, "we get to believe that we are 'keen, wide awake' and that it takes a smart fellow to entrap us."[16]

Miller had moved swiftly into local business, especially once he lost his Customs Service post. How much wealth he had in 1853 and 1854 is difficult to gauge, but he had enough cash to lend out more than $1,000 by year's end and carried an additional $5,267 in loans during 1854. By January 1855, Miller had $6,762 in loans outstanding on his account book; eight months later, the amount had increased to $8,554. Given Miller's conservatism, it is likely that he had assets in excess of twenty thousand dollars by 1855. Although he continued his partnership with Hugh A. Goldsborough and Michael Simmons in the sawmill venture, Miller had discovered that loaning money at interest was the surest and fastest way to wealth in Olympia. By the mid-1850s, he enjoyed a reputation as a sound and even remarkable businessman. He had become, as one of his correspondents put it, "the moneyed man of Olympia."[17]

Miller's economic success, however, was only one side of his image of a productive life. As satisfied as he seemed, he also longed for family and community. He had focused on economics first because he accepted it as primary and sustaining, the essential aspect of any measurement of the good life. But from the time he left Illinois, he had wrestled with what family meant to him and what responsibilities he had to the rest of the Millers. Even his decision to remain in Oregon, when his brother and other relatives pursued chance in the California goldfields, suggested that Miller sought more a replication of an Illinois farm community in the West than an El Dorado. There is no doubt that his desire for success on the frontier played a major role in his decision to remain in Oregon, but it was also perhaps the safer course. On the Santiam and in Olympia, Miller found familiar, permanent-looking institutions and developing communities. In another sense, his choice veered toward the radical, suggesting that he might not return to Illinois and his family, that he was prepared to reject his home.[18] As he made clear to his brother Richard in 1851, Miller suffered from homesickness and he reeled from making a choice between the West and Illinois. Yet, he could not just return home. He would not go back before he had achieved a high and visible measure of success. Perhaps more revealing of his attitude about family was his habit of comparing his position and wealth against that of John Arenz and Sylvester Emmons, his brothers-in-law who held judgeships in Illinois. In response to a letter that referred to the amount of money Miller hoped to make, another well-fixed brother-in-law, John McDonald, replied that based on Miller's figures he lagged behind economic conditions in Illinois.[19]

Regardless of his investment in Puget Sound, Miller's connection with home was still strong in the fall of 1852, when his mother wrote him about the premature death of McDonald from typhoid fever. She reminded her son that he should not consider Oregon his home, that Illinois and the family remained his legitimate place:

> William I do not know that I ever heard anything that struck me so force-fully. Last night I could not sleep for thinking about you. Was I never to see you again my Son come home you do not know how bad we want to see you. If you have not made as much money as you want or not come home you can make a living hear [sic].[20]

Despite his mother's pleas and her suggestion that he come home to help his sister Dorothy run the mercantile business his father had built, Miller did not seriously consider going home in 1852. He still held his Customs Service post and had just begun to see the fruits of loaning his capital to Olympia businessmen. He waited on more success before contemplating a return.

By the mid-1850s, a family dialogue of sorts developed between the Miller households in Illinois and the new Washington Territory. Increasingly, the Beardstown folk became more curious about Miller's life on Puget Sound, especially whether it was sufficiently remunerative to justify his long absence from home. From Illinois, his sisters' husbands—John Arenz and Sylvester Emmons—boasted to Miller that their investments in the Beardstown area were finally paying off handsomely, reminding him what might await him if he returned home. The measurements were economic, but the call home was emotional.[21] From Olympia, Miller kept his family informed about his life but gave them few details. Still, he must have boasted that he had made some money and acquired a measure of position, because Arenz wrote an affirming note of recognition in 1855 that seemed to confer the family's blessing on Miller's business affairs. "It affords us all great pleasure," Arenz wrote, "to learn that you have succeeded so well that honor and riches are in your possession."[22]

During his first years on Puget Sound, conservative and radical ideals pulled Miller first one way and then another. At times the emotional pull home to Illinois nearly overwhelmed him, while at others he seemed determined to create a new home for himself on the frontier. He and his brother Richard played a nonconformist role in the family by staying out west longer than their Illinois kin preferred. Miller's conservative tendencies suggested returning home, but his ambition demanded that he attain some measure of accomplishment. He confessed to Richard in 1853 that it was "altogether doubtful" he would "ever return to Illinois." In reply, the younger Richard touched his conservative side, writing that perhaps they should both go home to be with their parents and be true to familial duty:

> William, our parents are growing very old. They have now nearly perhaps quite finished their "three score years and ten" the allotted time of man.[23]

The pull from home was strong. Even the family's African-American housekeeper pleaded with Miller to return home. "I think you had better come home," Martha "Pentecost" Miller wrote in 1855, "and not just be gone to make complaints as though you had just got there."[24] The risk-taking and ambition-driven side of Miller's character, the impulses that had taken him to the frontier in the first place, resisted these sentimental arguments. Ironically, it was an emotional impulse from an unexpected quarter that inspired Miller to make a new home on Puget Sound and to take his greatest risk. He seemed to abandon his conservative business sense when an affair of the heart fully captured him. More powerful than the emotional pull from Illinois, Miller's attraction to a woman on Puget Sound prompted him to pursue a most impetuous path.

Miller's relationships with women in Illinois had been a bit uncertain. He had female friends, perhaps even romantic attachments, but he may have been clumsy or timid around women. In his correspondence with friends in Bluff Spring and Beardstown, he mentioned several women who may have been intimate friends, but he seemed ambivalent about pursuing romance. In reply, a friend warned him not to dally too long in Oregon:

> Peggy sends both arms full of love to you. She says if you don't come in one year you will be too late as she is determined on getting married.[25]

Other friends kept him informed about marriages among his old acquaintances and hinted that a few women were still available. "She is a very firm girl," George Ropp wrote to him in Oregon about one of the women Miller had earlier fancied, "and I think if you come over soon you can drive your stake where ever you want to that is to say you can get her."[26]

Despite his occasional references to women, it is unclear whether Miller actually had much experience in sexual matters. Off and on during his twenties his health had been poor, and there is evidence that he was shy. "Speaking of love angels," his brother wrote him in 1854, "have you not come across something yet in human shape that you thought looked very much like an angel or are you still as you were when you left home afraid to look at anything that wears petticoats?"[27] Once in Oregon, Miller had few if any relationships with women. There were few opportunities on the Santiam, and there were reportedly only two "ladies" in Olympia when he arrived.[28] But in 1853, two years after he had come to Puget Sound, Miller met Letitia Work, twenty-two-year-old daughter of HBC Factor John Work and his Metis wife, Josette. It was a fateful meeting, stimulating Miller's emotions and causing him to uncharacteristically throw off some of his conservatism. For the first time, he was in pursuit of a woman.[29]

Miller's romantic interest was the daughter of one of HBC's most important officers in the Oregon Country. Born in County Donegal, Ireland, in 1792, John Work had been raised in a farming family and worked in agriculture before emigrating to North America in his teens as a Hudson's Bay Company man. He had been assigned to posts in Lower Canada and in the Rockies before he came to the Columbia in the 1820s and had led some of the most important HBC expeditions into the Snake River country, southern Oregon, and northern California. His wife Josette, daughter of Pierre Legace and a Cree woman, raised ten children in HBC forts as far-flung as Fort Hall in Idaho and Fort Simpson in Alaska. Letitia, the couple's third child, was probably born in June 1831 at or near Fort Hall. By the time William Miller met her, Letitia had lived at Fort Vancouver, Fort Simpson, and Fort Victoria, and she had been educated at the Willamette Mission in Salem, Fort Vancouver, and Fort Victoria. She had moved with her family to Victoria in 1849, where they were part of a large settlement of HBC traders, agriculturalists, craftsmen, and laborers.[30] She frequently went by canoe from Victoria to Fort Nisqually to visit her sister Jane, the wife of William F. Tolmie. It was on one of those visits in 1853 that Miller met Letitia and apparently fell in love at first sight.[31]

Miller was not Letitia's only suitor. At first stymied by his shyness and insecurity, Miller had friends inquire about her interests, her receptiveness, and who else might have a chance with her. He discovered that the captain of the *Mary Dare* had already approached Work about his daughter, and that Edward Huggins, Tolmie's assistant at Fort Nisqually, had also taken a strong interest.[32] Miller stewed and let trepidation dominate him for months. After an awkward intercession on his behalf by Tolmie had failed to get Letitia's favorable attention, Miller tried to write her. He drafted two letters. One he sent, and one he held for himself. Letitia received the one that read:

> With a trembling hand and for the first time in my life I undertake to address a Lady. You will therefore pardon the awkwardness of expression. Since I had the pleasure of first seeing you, my admirations of your charms and just esteem for your sense, taste, and worth have increased with every interview. . . . it will afford me the most exquisite pleasure to call on you at such times during the short period you will remain her, as may suit your convenience.[33]

In the letter he did not or could not send, Miller exposed more of himself and his feelings, revealing how deeply he had plunged and how desirous he had become. Beginning with a description of a night of frivolity at a local tavern, "where everyone seemed to be enjoying themselves in the highest degree," Miller composed his plea:

For me the scene had no charms. My feelings were all with one who was not present. And now I find myself at my table giving utterance to the feelings of my heart by writing thus to the absent one—yourself. . . . Miss Letitia if you only knew the secret workings of my heart, you would find that my timidity was produced by my love [and] admiration of you. . . . Oh! Miss Letitia do you remember an evening long since when I was in your company but for a few minutes[?] Since that evening you have had more influence over my feelings than all others together. . . . if a visit from me would be agreeable to you it will give me infinite pleasure to call on you at the 'Fort.' . . . I have then only left me in conclusion to assure and reassure you of the honesty and purity of my intentions and of the firm and unwavering affection of your devoted lover.[34]

Bound up in anxiety over a perceived rejection, Miller was unsure what to say and, worse, what to do. Writing to Tolmie for advice, Miller confessed that he had been too timid and had probably sent her the wrong message: "The Lady may think that I have been trifling with her. Not so." It was insecurity, perhaps even embarrassment, he explained to Tolmie, that had made him stumble. "Had I have had a fortune to have laid at her feet I might have acted far bolder in the matter than I have," he confessed, "but I had no fortune. She had a happy home and I was unwilling to ask her to quit that home until I was certain I could take her to one as good." More revealingly, however, Miller confessed:

To accomplish this I was willing to quit my old associates up and give up the idea of ever returning to my relatives. I thought by taking the claims on this Island [Whidbey Island] of which I have so often spoken and by concentrating all of my little means upon that one place and engaged in farming, merchandizing, there is hardly a better spot on the Sound.[35]

What had drawn him so strongly to Letitia that he eagerly contemplated changing his course, that he was, in fact, "willing to quit my old associates"? In his unsent letter, he described her "modesty of deportment" and her "total freedom from the silly affectations of the society" that Miller had known. It first brought admiration, he wrote, "and then for the first time in his life to love." Miller repeated to Tolmie how deeply he held his feelings, explaining "that I was drawn towards her first by her own charms and good sense." But then he added another reason, one he could not have written to Letitia. "Secondly," he disclosed, "by the mean prejudice which bad characters, who were themselves in my respect so far beneath her seemed or pretended to entertain towards her."[36]

Miller's reaction to the prejudice against Indian and mixed-blood women—which had increased on the frontier as more and more white women came to the new settlements—drove his feelings hard. He planned to take her to Whidbey Island, Miller confided to Tolmie, where he could protect her from "a prejudice which some of the meaner characters here and many on her own Island [Vancouver] pretend to entertain." Whidbey Island offered a respite from discrimination, because, as Miller hoped, "the population of that Island would be mostly Americans from the Eastern states, a population who would entertain no prejudice against the Lady." Naive as Miller's assumptions about the new emigrants' social values might have been—in so many cases these were the very people who held prejudicial views—it suggests that Miller's compassionate feelings and his obvious disgust at the insults she endured informed at least a part of his passion.[37]

How much these sentiments reflected any broader questioning of Olympia society is difficult to gauge. Promising to break off with his friends may have referred to the character of some narrow-minded men in his group, such as Alonzo Poe. Many HBC men had married Indian or mixed-blood women in the Red River country and in Oregon, and many of the wives, including Josette Work, participated directly in fur trade operations, keeping their lives connected to both the Indian and non-Indian worlds. After the influx of American settlement, however, attitudes changed, and Indian wives received far less respect and had to bear increasingly prejudicial attitudes. In his confidential and honest discussion with Tolmie, Miller had both exposed his own sensitivities on the subject and seemingly forgotten which world Tolmie represented. Tolmie, after all, had married Letitia's sister and knew better than Miller the painful sting of racist attitudes.[38]

It is also likely that Miller wanted to distance himself from the anti-HBC Americans who had fueled so much bad feeling and had indirectly put Letitia's parents through the contentious *Mary Dare* episode in 1851. In September 1853, Miller wrote Tolmie that he promised "to resign all public employment" and to forgo "whatever her father may give her [that it] may be invested [and] placed beyond my control." He had never been part of the inner HBC circle at Nisqually and he knew how distrustful many of them were toward American officials, but he had established good relationships with Tolmie, Huggins, and others, so he worried that his pursuit of Letitia Work might damage those relationships. "This disappointment," Miller assured Tolmie, "shall in no way alter my regard for yourself and any number of your family." He would rather cease discussing Letitia with Tolmie, Miller confided, than cause injury to their relationship.[39]

Miller continued to hope that Letitia Work would give him a second look, a chance to show her his sincere devotion. But during the following year, all of his entreaties met with rejection. At long last, Tolmie advised him in August 1854: "My sincere advice to you is to banish all thoughts thereof from your mind."[40] Three years later, she married Edward Huggins, Tolmie's successor at Fort Nisqually. To Huggins, it seemed a natural, perhaps even predictable, relationship. They had practically lived in the same house at Nisqually whenever she visited, Huggins remembered, so "an attachment ensued." Both of them were part of the larger HBC family at Nisqually and Victoria, an extended family that did not include Miller. Huggins was also only one year older than Letitia, while Miller was thirteen years her senior. More important, however, Letitia had rejected "several offers she had received from men of standing and wealth," as Huggins later put it, to choose him.[41] In that description there is irony, for Miller had thought of himself as too poor to openly court Letitia. He even tried to dispel any suggestion that he coveted a dowry her father might bestow.

Nonetheless, Miller *was* a man of "standing and wealth," and that had been his ambition ever since arriving in Oregon. He had avidly pursued opportunities, manipulated controversy when he had to, and made business friends of people he may not have embraced otherwise. His life in Oregon was dominated by chasing down the main chance and making something of himself. It had little relationship to the fantasy he spun to Tolmie, of a life on Whidbey Island, tilling the soil, trading merchandise, and keeping his love safe from racial insults. The life Miller had made in Oregon was grounded deeply in business and politics, not affairs of the heart. As much as his emotions in 1853 might have pulled on him, he had already set a course that looked more like the portrait of the ambitious adventurer than the self-satisfied family man.

CHAPTER 4

In Washington Territory

*The great object after all for which many poor mortals
leave their homes [is] . . . improvement of their condition.
It is a laudable effort, provided that nobler qualities of
our nature are not thereby impaired; for nothing is more
contemptible than a man, who values money above all
things. But I have no fear for you on that score.*

John Arenz to William Miller, 1853

William W. Miller had arrived in Olympia in 1851 wear-
ing political clothes. As the first federal officer to take up duties in Oregon north of the Columbia River, he could not have avoided it. It was
politics, after all, that had gotten him to Olympia, and it was politics
that would shape his job. But Miller had not come as a political man;
at least, he did not immediately embrace a political life in Northern
Oregon. Although politics was not a strange arena to him—his sisters had married political men, both Whig judges, and his father had
enthusiastically contributed time and effort in Whig causes—he had
demurred from taking an active part in political work. He seemed to
believe in Whig political goals, which for a generation had emphasized national economic investments and an active government, but
he had never expressed himself as an idealogue or a fanatic. He was

politically temperate and even cautious, hardly the kind of regular party man who soldiered in nineteenth-century political organizations. Because of temperament or perhaps his health, Miller had kept the Cass County political machine at arm's length.

Miller had held steady to his political heritage in Oregon, but he had found few Whigs in the territory and almost no party organization. By 1850, Oregon Democrats heavily outnumbered their opponents and dominated the territorial legislature. They had organized early and successfully drew on an increasing national Democratic strength. Veering away from the aggressively commercial and expansionist wings of the national party, Oregon Democrats emphasized self-sufficiency and local sovereignty. They portrayed themselves as speaking for local producers and family farmers, consistently warning the electorate that the monopolistic Whigs' policies would tie the whole region to an outside political agenda.[1]

Miller, no doubt, heard quite a litany of charges against Whigs while he lived in the midst of a large pocket of Democrats on the Santiam. Still, he stayed solidly within the Whig fold, especially after his appointment to the customs job. Some Oregon Whigs, knowing his connections with Illinois party leaders, tried to enlist him as an ally in bolstering the party in the territory. Although he sidestepped the invitations, he still maintained connections with Whigs in Illinois and Washington, D.C., no doubt hoping to protect himself from political squabbles in Oregon, which increased significantly during the early 1850s. But his protectors could not shield him from political calamities, and Miller soon learned that in Oregon Territory he would have to take care of himself. He began to look at the political landscape more as local Democrats did, seeing local development as more important than national policies and understanding the significance of political self-determination in the territory.

Within fifteen months of arriving in Olympia, Miller had his first lesson in the politics of officeholding and an introduction to the importance of local political organizations. In November 1852, the national electorate endorsed a Democratic administration and turned out the Whigs, who had captured the White House only twice in twenty years and had both of their presidents die in office. Franklin Pierce, a practiced and convivial politician from New Hampshire and compromise Democratic nominee, won a landslide election, capturing 254 electoral votes to opponent Winfield Scott's 42. Sharp political observers had predicted Pierce's win—especially as they watched the national Whig party tear itself apart over the slavery issue, sending its southern members headlong into the Democratic fold—but the size of the victory surprised the nation. What the Democrats' triumph might mean to national political and economic interests was unclear in March 1853, when Pierce took the oath of office, but to political appointees, including those in Washington Territory, it meant a thorough house-cleaning of officeholders.

Miller's benevolent adviser and protector in Washington, Josiah M. Lucas, advised him to duck low, switch to the Democratic party, and get behind fellow Illinoisan Stephen Douglas. A pragmatist with his eyes focused on a troubled political world, Lucas looked at the electoral horizon and saw the Whig party in terminal decline. "The Whig administration do not deserve success," Lucas wrote Miller just after the November 1852 election. "They have shown themselves to be for themselves and a few toadies exclusively." Even the party's erstwhile leader, Lucas offered, should be toppled from his political pedestal: "Dan'l Webster died with self upon his last breath—he was a giant in intellect but a bankrupt in morals."[2]

Miller listened carefully to his adviser, but the Democratic voices in Oregon had already caught his attention. Prominent among his political friends in Northern Oregon was Isaac N. Ebey, pioneer settler of Whidbey Island and aggressive Democratic politician. Just four years his elder, Ebey shared many things with Miller. Like Miller, his family had been peripatetic, moving from Kentucky to Ohio and then to Sangamon County, Illinois, in 1832. Also like Miller, Ebey's father had fought in the Black Hawk War in Illinois and knew Abraham Lincoln. Ebey also came from a large family and had tried his hand at a profession in Missouri before heading west during the late 1840s. But where Ebey had been an aggressive pursuer of the main chance—he had been one of the investors in the *Orbit* in 1850 with Benjamin F.

Shaw and Edmund Sylvester—Miller had been conservative, even cautious. Where Ebey had actively established friendships with businessmen on the Sound to further his political future and had secured appointment as a customs inspector from Collector Moses, Miller had arrived as a political appointee, with his connections distant from the scene. Most important, where Ebey had sought political position from the beginning, Miller had been careful and tentative about joining political circles. Nonetheless, Miller became fast friends with Ebey and Alonzo M. Poe in 1852, and their discussions often included politics.[3]

In part, it was Miller's friendship with Ebey that nudged or even pushed him in the direction of the Democratic party in 1852 and 1853. Ebey had come from Missouri with a strong political sense and drive to match. In a letter to his younger brother in the spring of 1853, he boasted of his prescient move to Puget Sound. "In a large company [of men in Missouri] I put my finger on the map of Oregon," he bragged, "and I said to them here is a 'future state' here is a 'capitol.' The state I pointed to was Northern Oregon, the capitol was where Olympia now stands." Within a little more than a year after settling on Whidbey Island, he won election as one of two representatives in the Oregon Territorial Legislature from Northern Oregon. In 1852, he stood in the front row of politicians urging a break from Oregon and establishment of a new territory north of the Columbia River. By March 1853, as he could write to his brother, "My position here is as fair as I wish it to be," predicting that he might soon be governor or territorial delegate. Whatever political demerits he may have had, Ebey made up for them with a disarming ego.[4]

How readily Miller took to Ebey's style of politics—especially his ego—is uncertain, but there is little question that Ebey gave him a sharp reading of the local political landscape. At first, their common ground was customs work. Miller had met Ebey within weeks of his arrival at Olympia in 1851 and they worked together in November, when Collector Moses had sent them on a surveying mission on the Sound. As early as October, Miller had visited Ebey's farm on Whidbey Island and was corresponding with him about customs matters, economic conditions, and politics.[5] During the following three years, Miller worked off and on with Ebey on customs matters; Ebey served as an inspector in several ship seizure cases involving HBC vessels. He listened to Ebey's Anglophobic railings against HBC, while he worked out his own accommodations with William F. Tolmie and other HBC officials and surely noted the rewards such HBC-bashing brought local politicians like Ebey.

Miller also became friends with Ebey's family, especially his wife, Rebecca. He clearly liked the Whidbey Island cluster of settlers; and by early 1853, when Miller was fairly certain he would be a Whig casualty, he began to consider stock-raising and even settling on the island. In February 1853, Miller agreed to co-sponsor chartering a brig to bring more settlers to the island, with the hope that an increase in families would help build up a strong and stable community. Six months later, he seemed to include himself as one of the new settlers when he wrote to Tolmie, spilling his plans to spirit Letitia Work away from the rough conditions at Nisqually to a new home on Whidbey Island. After his courtship of Letitia sputtered and failed, all talk of his moving to the island ceased.[6]

In politics, Miller and Ebey agreed on a fundamental principles of territorial political life: action taken to improve the territory in practically any manner was an investment in everyone's future gains. Feeling the political winds on the Sound, Miller knew in the spring of 1852 that the combination of antagonism toward HBC and the great distance Northern Oregon settlements were from Oregon City, plus the desires of local political hopefuls, would coalesce into a movement for political independence. Steilacoom surveyor John Chapman's ringing July Fourth oration in 1851, the first call for separation from Oregon, and the Cowlitz Convention in August had already framed the issue. A petition had been sent to Oregon Territorial Delegate Joseph Lane, and rumors flew that Lane would enthusiastically support favorable congressional action.[7]

As a federal official, presumably with political influence, Miller was pulled into the first stirrings of the independence movement when local petitioners asked for his assistance in getting their complaints heard in Oregon City or Washington, D.C. There was little he could do but sign a petition or stand with a local group that might want a post office or other government convenience.[8] By July 1852, Miller had been recognized as a coming political figure with his appointment as deputy marshal by Joe Meek, a staunch Democrat and a principal figure in Oregon territorial politics. What role Ebey and other Northern Oregon Democrats may have played in this appointment is uncertain, but clearly Miller had taken a step toward the Democratic party. His ties to the Whigs were still real, however, and he often asked their advice. Three months earlier, in response to Miller's queries about political activity in Lewis County, William Strong, Whig chief justice of the Oregon Territorial Supreme Court, suggested that Miller go slow, warning him that much of the political pot-stirring for independence and county-splitting were acts of self-promotion by ambitious politicians. Keep your distance, Strong advised.[9]

Miller learned quickly to keep his distance from erratic politicians, but he also learned to be dexterous and to take advantage of opportunities. He tended to measure and trust individuals more than political platforms, prizing personal loyalty well above party regularity. He had learned the importance of strong friendships in Illinois, which made it easy for him in the spring of 1852 to write Democratic Senator Stephen Douglas of Illinois—chairman of the Senate Committee on Territories—urgently pleading for wagon road construction in the territory. But in Oregon it was his personal and political camaraderie with Isaac Ebey that first choreographed his course in territorial politics. Jacob Conser, a Santiam friend who sat in the Oregon legislature with Ebey, confirmed Miller's assessment. In July 1852, Conser counseled Miller to stick tight with Ebey. He was "the right kind of *Democrat*," Conser advised. "I have the utmost confidence in Col. E. as a man, a legislator, and a Democrat."[10]

Miller needed little prodding, but he shied away from a full leap to the Democratic column and continued to hedge his bets by maintaining ties with local Whigs. One of them, fellow Illinoisan David Logan, a Miller family friend and a confidant of Abraham Lincoln, tried to get Miller involved in Whig politics. "The division in the democratic party is still great," Logan wrote Miller in August 1852, "and

promises much good to the Whigs." Evidently dismissive of the rumblings north of the Columbia, for he could not have been ignorant of
the drumbeat for political separation, Logan pressed Miller to join in
the good fight against the Democrats in the next contest for Oregon's
territorial delegate. "We must elect the next delegate," Logan implored,
suggesting that he might make the run himself if Miller would help.[11]

By late 1852, Miller knew he had correctly read the political current,
even if he still hesitated to fully put in with the Democrats. Members
of both parties, including his friends A. M. Poe and Isaac Ebey, had
closed ranks north of the Columbia and had begun a direct march
toward separation from Oregon. The Columbian, an Olympia newspaper published for the express purpose of creating an independent
territory, published its first issue on September 11, 1852, just weeks before
the second independence convention, scheduled to take place on
November 25 at Monticello, near the mouth of the Cowlitz River. Poe,
Ebey, Miller, and several others were the newspaper's first agents, pushing not only the paper but also the idea of separation from Oregon.[12]

In the waning days of the Fillmore administration, after Congress
had received a second petition from Northern Oregonians, those north
of the Columbia got their wish to be separate from their associates
to the south. Before that event, however, William Miller had already
made his transition to the Democratic party, and by late spring he
was living in a new political landscape. President Pierce had appointed
Isaac Ingalls Stevens from Massachusetts as governor of the new territory, Charles Mason of Rhode Island as territorial secretary, and
James Patton Anderson of Mississippi as U.S. marshal. In the top customs position, Pierce broke the pattern of appointing outsiders and
chose Isaac Ebey, who replaced the detested Simpson Moses. Ebey's
vocal criticism of HBC officials may well have influenced the incoming Pierce administration, which knew the settlement of disputes
between settlers and HBC was an important matter.[13]

Miller stayed on the customs staff in an advisory capacity until
August, when Ebey named him "Deputy Collector," even though he
had no authority to make such an appointment.[14] When called upon
to justify the questionable appointment, Ebey put the political reason

first. "Long before his [Miller's] removal," Ebey wrote the secretary of treasury,

> he was known and recognized here as a Democrat as acting with the Democratic Party giving the full measure of his influence, his talents and his money for the advancement of Democratic principles for the election of regularly nominated candidates for office and by assisting pecuniarily more liberally than any other man in this Territory for the establishment of the Democratic Press in this Territory.[15]

Ebey's defense linked three developments that help explain why and how Miller had become central to the Democratic party in the new territory. The *Columbian*, which had been financed with Whig money from Portland and even printed on a press that had been used by T. J. Dryer's *Oregonian*, succeeded in aiding the establishment of Washington Territory. But the national triumph of the Democrats quickly took the luster off the prize; the election meant that they had a Whig paper in a new territory that surely would be controlled by Democrats. By September 1853, a principal backer of the paper, steamboat captain and entrepreneur John C. Ainsworth, began to worry about his investment. Writing to his man in Olympia, Thornton F. McElroy, Ainsworth complained that he was "sorry on the whole that I did not stop it when the [contract] year was out." He had a paper whose purpose had become superfluous. "I have offered the concern to the Democrats for $2500," he informed McElroy, adding,

> I will see the people of Washington Territory damned before I will publish a paper out of my pocket for their benefit. If they want a paper why don't they purchase it? . . . I suppose they are all waiting the arrival of Stephens [*sic*] when matters will be decided according to Gov. Stephens.[16]

Knowing how important the newspaper could be to local politicians, Ainsworth had shopped around for investors and had nearly talked Michael T. Simmons into purchasing the paper. But nothing happened until Governor Stevens arrived in November 1853. Once on the ground in Olympia, the governor quickly set about getting a newspaper to serve as the voice of the Democratic party in the territory. It was not long before investments were made, a significant portion coming from Miller.[17] It is not surprising, then, that the *Pioneer and Democrat*—as the new Democratic paper was called—vigorously defended Miller when complaints were raised in 1854 that as a Whig he should not be retained by the new Democratic administration. "It might be well to have the facts brought in mind," the paper chastised Miller's critics. "[Miller] has acted consistently with the democratic party ever since his residence in the territory."[18]

The newspaper's statement exaggerated Miller's early commitment to the Democrats, but the editor had made his point. By early 1854, Miller had proven himself to be a fully engaged player in territorial politics, and he had aligned himself with the Democrats. In Oregon and Washington territories, the social glue of Democratic politics was a mixture of personal friendships, group identifications, trusted local political institutions, expressed reciprocal loyalties, and an almost communitarian sense of being part of something larger than parochial desires. The personable and eminently trustworthy Miller naturally gravitated to the party's center, where he occupied an important spot in the territory's new and necessarily circumscribed political arena. His activities in 1853 and 1854 took place at one of the most significant political interesections, where money and public opinion and executive power crossed. Without necessarily seeking it, Miller had become a man worthy of attention by Governor Stevens, who could hardly ignore anyone who could muster investments and take the lead in shaping public opinion.[19]

Stevens had known about Miller long before he arrived in Olympia in November 1853. In the spring, the newly appointed governor had written to key political men in the new territory, using a list of names fed to him by Oregon Territorial Delegate Joseph Lane. Miller's name, along with two dozen others, was on that list. How much Stevens actually knew about him is unclear, but what he knew probably came from the system of political networks that oiled the inner workings of national politics. One web of connections took him to Joseph Lane and Senator Stephen A. Douglas, two important Democrats who had figured prominently in the creation of Washington Territory. Douglas, a major contender for the Democratic presidential nomination in 1852 and chairman of the Senate Committee on Territories, had more power with regard to territorial policies than any other politician in the capital. He knew Miller's family in Illinois and he knew about Miller's tenuous customs position on Puget Sound, especially the desire of local Democrats to retain him as surveyor. He also knew that Miller had taken some initiative in local politics, because Douglas had received a personal letter from him in 1852, laying out the need for roads north of the Columbia River and the likelihood that Northern Oregon would petition for separation. In that letter, Miller addressed Douglas in a casual manner, as if Douglas were simply a friend and not a politician who could breathe life into or dramatically terminate the presumptuous political movement.[20]

Miller's political protector in Washington, D.C., Josiah Lucas, had become a Douglas loyalist and had lobbied him on Miller's behalf a number of times in 1853, especially when Miller was trying to pry his salary out of the Treasury Department. Referring to the political jockeying in the spring of 1853 when job-seekers pestered Douglas and others for positions in Washington Territory, Lucas wrote Miller that Douglas would have saved Miller's job at Nisqually "had he been in the city." Douglas would have interceded, Lucas confided because "he feels very kind towards you, for I have heard him so express himself on several occasions." According to Lucas, it was delegate Lane who had ousted Miller and secured the appointment of A. Benton Moses. As Lucas explained, "Lane is the man that done it," but he could not tell Miller why. An ambitious politician, Lane knew that control of patronage was one of his most important political tools, and he used it to punish his enemies and reward his friends, often seeking no other counsel.[21] Lane had struck a political friendship with Stevens, one that would last throughout Stevens's life, and it is likely that he told Stevens about replacing Miller, the erstwhile Whig now turned Democrat, and also about Miller's qualities and position among the territory's Democrats. Writing a a letter of introduction to Miller in April 1853, Stevens seemed to have drawn a sharp bead on Miller from his conversations with Douglas and Lane. In the letter, he emphasized his commitment to road building in the territory, pandering to Miller as a "prominent citizen" who he hoped would aid him and his officers in the great work.[22] That letter began a political friendship that would last until Stevens's untimely death in September 1862.

The text of their nine-year friendship can be summed up in one word: politics. Although Miller often advised Stevens on a range of subjects—not the least was economic policy and personal finance—the chord of strength they tied between each other was political organization and activity. Both considered the Democratic party a bulwark of local and regional interests against what they perceived as a nationalizing force, one that had first worn the Whig garments of Henry Clay's "American System" but soon draped itself in the cloaks of the Republican party's championing of economic development and anti-slavery. Formerly a Clay-following Whig, Miller had come to believe that only the Democratic party could advance the particularistic economic interests of territories like Washington. He worked closely with Stevens and other Democratic activists in the territory to build party machinery that could advance the general interest, while maintaining political control in the hands of a few trustworthy stewards.[23]

Miller counted himself among those stewards by mid-1854, in part because he had provided a source of financial stability and in part because his personality encouraged political teamwork. Those twin contributions—money and political comradeship—kept Miller in the center of Democratic politics throughout his life, but between 1853 and 1855 it is arguable which contribution made him more valuable to the new territory's important men. Miller's financial contributions and his network of friends aided Stevens in knitting together a web of political connections that helped attach a disparate group of politicians to an independent-minded governor. As in all territories, the federally appointed governor had to fashion harmonious relationships with local politicians if he expected to succeed. Although it was Miller's political savvy that made Stevens's success more likely, initially it was his financial acumen that made him most valuable to the new governor.

The foundation of Miller's business sense was his ability to judge men and financial conditions and then to act with prudence. In matters of economics, he could agree with other political men on one cardinal point: what benefited the territory benefited all. With his reputation for careful investments and accounting, Miller served as a broker of sorts, often easing one man's economic plight by advancing a loan or paying off a claim one politician had on another.[24]

Stevens liked and trusted Miller, but more importantly he shared his belief that economic development of any part of the territory constituted good public policy. The governor articulated as much in his first message to the territorial legislature in February 1854, when he laid out an ambitious program that included tasks as disparate as military training and establishing a territorial library. Miller did not record his opinion of Stevens at the time, but he could not have missed the governor's ambitious, almost aggressive tone. And surely he observed that Stevens was not an ordinary politician.

Stevens came to Olympia with unusual credentials. A West Point graduate and military engineer, he had fought in the Mexican War, worked on geodetic surveys, and learned the ways of bureaucratic politics. He had also commanded the northern section of the Pacific Railroad Surveys, which had thrust him into the larger development of the northwest region. As perhaps the person most knowledgeable about the natural resources of the Columbia River Basin and upper Missouri River regions, Stevens became a forceful advocate of economic and political development. In 1860, he would declare to fellow territorials that the Northwest was the crucial region for future United States development. "It is not a fiction," he told them; "the great vision of Columbus" was true right there along the Columbia River.[25]

During his first months as governor, Stevens investigated conditions, including the inadequacy of transportation and mail service, and especially the festering dispute over the valuation of Hudson's Bay Company properties in the territory. His experience in the military had taught him that all policy decisions in the nation's capital were essentially political and that wresting benefits from the federal government required personal lobbying. To "do my part toward the development of the resources of this territory," as he had told citizens the previous

November, Stevens went east in June 1854 to argue directly before congressmen and executive departments. The task was daunting, he confided to Miller from Washington. Too much needed doing and, as he had feared, Territorial Delegate Columbia Lancaster seemed overwhelmed. With his characteristic sense of importance and confidence, Stevens assured Miller he would do what he could to advance the territory's interests.[26]

The governor worked the bureaus and spoke with important policy-makers, but he brought no triumphs back with him when he returned to Olympia in December 1854. The most urgent problem, however, could not be resolved through lobbying in Washington. Stevens also served as superintendent of Indian affairs and had complete control and responsibility in the government's relationships with Indian tribes. Without resolution of Indian land claims, as settlers repeatedly reminded the governor, those who had claimed land under the Oregon Donation Land Act probably could not perfect their land titles.[27]

Addressing the areas west of the Cascades where settlers had congregated, Stevens set about negotiating treaties during the winter of 1854–1855. After completing treaties with Puget Sound Indian tribes, he waited for warm weather before heading east of the Cascades to hammer out agreements with Indians on the upper Columbia and its tributaries, and then farther east to hold councils on the Missouri River in June and July. In all, he completed fifteen treaties, using a forceful strategy that raised a strong arm of power and extended a paternalistic hand of tranquillity. The governor's absence from Olympia had immediate political consequences. He had to leave governmental affairs in the hands of Territorial Secretary Charles H. Mason, thereby lessening his control of political events. More important, he had to forgo any thought of entering a political campaign for territorial delegate in 1855.[28]

Stevens never hid his ambitions well, and it is unlikely that those who had gained his confidence during his first year as governor—including Miller, Mason, and Goldsborough—were unaware that he coveted the delegate's office. But running for office took time and atten-

tion. The political landscape changed each year as more emigrants settled north of the Columbia River, forcing candidates to continually
remake alliances. Campaigning for election as territorial delegate
boiled down to a straightforward strategy: Recruit friends and associates to gather and rally support, first at county nominating conventions and later at the territorial convention. It was politics at the
personal level and full of ambiguities, in part because the weak party
organizations in the territory could do little to collect or hold votes.
The politicians themselves wielded most of the power. Those with
favors to bestow—the officeholders—had the advantage. But during
the winter and early spring of 1855, as potential candidates jockeyed
for a run in the delegate election, Stevens was preparing to conduct
treaty negotiations east of the mountains. He simply could not manage both a political campaign and treaty deliberations.[29]

Miller played the political arena as well or better than others, and
by early 1855 he had moved closer to the governor, advising him on
territorial patronage.[30] Miller also understood, perhaps better than others, that only organized political parties, not officeholders, could provide political stability. In February 1855, he took the lead in organizing
a Democratic club in Olympia, which in effect formally bonded an
already existing coterie of men pledged to Stevens.[31] This embryonic
Stevens clique hoped to put its mark on the emerging party structure
in the territory, but that was hardly certain, for too many Democrats
could object to the governor's policies and create troublesome schisms.
Nonetheless, it was the Stevens group that stood at the power center
of the new party.

Political handicappers in 1855 were hard put to see a sure winner
in the delegate race. Stevens appeared on county convention ballots,
even though it was unlikely he could sustain a campaign. Columbia
Lancaster, who had not dazzled as delegate, could muster little popular support. Isaac Ebey wanted the delegate's job and was sure to run,
but there were those who thought him too ambitious. The previous
year's runner-up, U.S. Marshal J. Patton Anderson, made it clear he
would try again. As a friend to Anderson, a confidant of Ebey, and a
nascent political adviser to Stevens, Miller found himself in an unen-

viable position during the campaign. In March, Ebey began canvassing Puget Sound, hoping that Miller would help his candidacy. He regularly advised Miller on his progress and predicted that if Whidbey Island supported him he would throw himself into the campaign. In Steilacoom, Seattle, and Port Townsend, Ebey thought he had solid support from local politicians Frank Clark, Frank Matthias, Henry Yesler, and Hilory Butler. He predicted that he would beat Stevens on the Sound and that Anderson could win only if he polled very strongly along the Columbia River. As the governor's candidacy flagged, Ebey gained confidence, predicting he would attract disaffected Stevens men. As he wrote his brother in late April, "the main thing with my friends is to stand up without flinching."[32]

Even knowing that Stevens would not pursue the campaign, Miller hesitated to formally endorse another candidate. His strong business and personal relationship with Ebey must have pulled at him, and he surely did not want to be accused of "flinching," but a political cloud had formed over the Whidbey Islander's candidacy. Some Democrats had questioned Ebey's employment of a Whig, A. M. Poe, as a customs agent. Others along the Sound had criticized his handling of customs accounts, even charging Ebey with malfeasance in office.[33] Miller remained loyal to Ebey, but he kept himself at arm's length from his friend's campaign. Although Miller did not publicly support Anderson, he aided the marshal's candidacy by his lukewarm, almost neglectful relationship with Ebey during the campaign. A Mississippi lawyer with the ear of Democrats in the nation's capital, including Secretary of War Jefferson Davis and President Pierce, Anderson also had familial ties to federal officials in Washington Territory—his cousin was Associate Territorial Justice Victor Monroe. As U.S. marshal, Anderson was known throughout the territory, partly because he took the census in 1853 and partly because he was the territory's sole law enforcement officer.[34]

Anderson prevailed in the election, but how much and what Miller did to aid Anderson's campaign is unclear. It is likely that he played some role in the territorial Democratic convention, where Anderson outpolled Ebey. Anderson certainly trusted Miller, for when he left for

Washington, D.C., in October 1855 he left his financial affairs in Miller's hands.[35] But Anderson trusted Miller's abilities even more explicitly in politics. Before and after he took his official position as territorial delegate, Anderson began to rely on Miller's advice and political information, especially in matters related to patronage. Writing from New York in November, on his way to Washington, Anderson discussed political appointments in the territory, emphasizing that Miller be sure to inform him who was and who was not a true and steady Democrat:

> Everything else being equal I always prefer my own friends to those of any other man. . . . I never forget a friend, and thank god, I look upon all good Democrats as friends. A mild and water wishy, washy, poor, pukey pizzerinctum can never command my respect, but it is not so much on account of his opposition to me as to my party.

Regarding Miller's strong suggestion that Benjamin F. Shaw, a friend of Stevens, Ebey, and Miller, get some federal appointment, Anderson replied that he would not penalize Shaw for not supporting him in the election. "The fact that he was not an Anderson man in the last convention does not weigh a straw with me," Anderson wrote, instructing Miller to just give him his best advice.[36]

Miller functioned as Anderson's political sieve in the territory, helping him sort out rumor from fact and advising him on which men deserved favors. Even in defeat, Ebey hoped Miller might aid him in prodding Anderson to seek an increase in his customs salary. After all, Ebey reminded Miller, he had been a good loser and had worked hard for Anderson in the general election. If Miller interceded on Ebey's behalf, and there is no evidence that he did, he failed. Anderson did not lobby for Ebey and, in fact, could not even stop the administration from removing him from office. "I was shocked, I assure you," Anderson wrote to Miller on the news that Ebey would lose his position. "I am puzzled," he continued, adding, perhaps in honor of Miller's friendship with Ebey, "I would like to see someone in it who is a friend to Col. E."[37]

Ebey's removal, which no doubt resulted from his inattention to political business in the territory, was part of a larger shaking and sorting out among territorial Democrats. From the time Washington became a territory, the Democrats huddled around Governor Stevens, but his political style made tight organization difficult. As his biographer, Kent Richards, commented, Stevens was "too individualistic, too volatile, too much oriented to sweeping political designs, and too little interested in the detailed work required to build a political organization." Those who disagreed with Stevens fell into a large anti-Stevens camp, which included Whigs, disaffected Democrats, and men of no settled party affiliation. During the 1855 elections, men who called themselves Free Soil Democrats in Thurston County—often suspected of being Know-Nothings—created dissension and forced the Stevens Democrats to counteract their nativist politics.[38]

For Miller, the wisest course was one of intelligent neutrality, especially when his friends and political allies squabbled. Increasingly during 1854–1855, he moved closer to Stevens without isolating himself from other politicians, especially federal officeholders. By mid-1855, Miller had seven active politicians on his account books, including Governor Stevens, Territorial Secretary Charles H. Mason, and Attorney General John S. Clendenin. He also took on another official position in May 1855, when he accepted Justice Edward Lander's offer to serve as clerk for the 2nd Judicial District of the U.S. District Court in Washington Territory.[39]

In the two years since Washington had become a territory, Miller had moved fully into the ranks of the Democratic party and was known as an adept politician and money manager. The two strengths that had first recommended him to Stevens in 1853 would make him one of the governor's most important allies when war broke out between recalcitrant Indians and the white occupiers of their lands. Miller's political and business savvy would make him the steadiest rudder Isaac Stevens could command when a maelstrom threatened to suck the governor and his political future to the depths in 1856.

CHAPTER 5

Friends in War

*As to myself, I have great regard for Stevens and while I
have scorned to act the sycophant to him when in power
I will not desert him if he should be removed and thereby
should not be able to feed us poor devils any longer.*
W. W. Miller to B. F. Shaw, August 20, 1856

Miller and Governor Stevens forged their chain of allegiance from an alloy composed of nearly equal parts business, politics, and personality. The catalyst in this political metallurgy was the
two men's shared belief in the power and sanctity of friendship, understood as an iron-hard loyalty tempered by a gold-soft judgment of each
other. Just as Miller knew the importance of supporting the governor
and aiding the growth of the Democratic party, Stevens understood
the value of Miller's counsel and increasingly discovered that he was
the truest of his circle and the most valuable. But in late 1854, as the
governor embarked on the most difficult of his political missions in
Washington Territory, it was unlikely that either man fully appreciated how their chainlinks would be tested. No one could have fore-
seen the political and cultural rupture that lay ahead for everyone in
the territory, least of all the participants at the center of the struggle.

The Indian War became the dominant event in early Washington

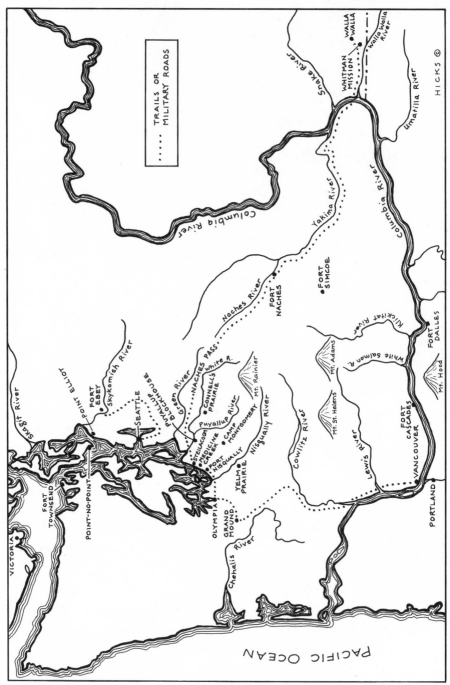

Map 2. Indian-Settler Conflicts, 1856

territorial history, a crucible of cultural identity and purpose for Stevens, Miller, the volunteer warriors, and the citizenry. This cultural drama had begun unfolding decades before Congress created Washington Territory, but in 1854 an urgency seemed to determine events. For Stevens, the urgency lay in extinguishing Indian land titles. Settlers were emigrating to the new territory in larger numbers. They coveted Indian lands and wanted unrestrained access to the region's natural resources. The perceived Indian title problem had percolated to the top of Stevens's agenda, higher even than transportation improvements. He proved just how important it had become during the last days of the year by taking his first ambitious and aggressive steps toward acquiring Indian land in the territory. Sailing north down the Sound in December, Stevens traveled to Medicine Creek near the Nisqually Bottoms, where representatives of Puget Sound Indian tribes gathered in response to his call for a council.

The scenes played out at Medicine Creek followed a script that had been used more than a hundred times before in North America. Representatives of white government selected Native American leaders, called them to council, and then maneuvered them to accept a treaty of "amity and equity," which circumscribed the Indians' freedom and their rights to most of their ancestral lands.[1] At Medicine Creek, Stevens laid out his proposed treaty, aided by interpreter Benjamin F. Shaw, who communicated it in Chinook Jargon, the trade patois of the coastal region.[2] As other treaty negotiators had done before him, Stevens insisted on anointing one leader for each identified tribe, even though it was rare that any individual chief could act for anyone beyond his immediate band. Under the council arbor, Stevens spelled out the document in terse descriptions, brooked little argument from the Indians, and pressed them to sign. There was an implied threat draped behind these discussions that Indians could lose even more land— probably to force—if they did not sign. Indians at the council saw little alternative. They signed, thereby accepting three small reservations in the South Sound region, some payments, and the promise of access to accustomed hunting and fishing grounds. In the exchange, they gave up claim to more than two million acres of Puget Sound land.[3]

The Medicine Creek Treaty set the form and content for more than a dozen treaties negotiated by Stevens at six council meetings held in 1854–1855 with the major tribes in Washington Territory. He held two councils on Puget Sound—at Point No Point and Point Elliott—attempted one at Spokane, and held an enormously important one at Walla Walla. In present-day Montana, Stevens added a treaty council with tribes west of the Continental Divide at Missoula and one with tribes east of the Divide on the Missouri River downstream from Fort Benton. Indians who signed the treaties agreed to accept United States hegemony, to engage in only friendly relations with their neighbors, to abstain from the use of liquor, and to accept other provisions that defined their behavior and what the government would pay for their lands in goods and annuities.[4]

The importance of what took place in those councils, especially at Walla Walla in June 1855, where Oregon Superintendent of Indian Affairs Joel Palmer aided Stevens, cannot be overstated. R. H. Lansdale, a member of Stevens's party, pronounced the Walla Walla treaties

> a good bargain, all things considered, peace—particularly. Many of the Indians were totally averse to treating when they first came here, but the negotiations were well conducted, I think.

The treaty provisions that pleased Lansdale set the context for all subsequent official and many private relationships between Native Americans and whites in the Northwest. From the government's viewpoint, the Indian leaders Stevens had selected at Walla Walla had consigned tribal lands to non-Indian use and settlement. It was an indelible legal bargain, as sacred as any oath, binding the U.S. government as guardians of Indian peoples and equally binding Indian tribes to honor the newly ascribed rights of non-Indians in the region. The treaties were infused with conflicting images. On the one hand, the government and tribes appeared as independent political entities mutually agreeing to contract terms; on the other hand, the government assumed a hegemonic persona that looked on Indian tribes as inferiors and dependents. Regardless of the merits or demerits of specific provisions in the treaties, their completion and the speed of the accomplishment made them harbingers of a future that would be dominated by non-Indian interests and nearly always at the expense of the indigenous people.[5]

Many Indian leaders had recognized the invading whites' juggernaut long before Stevens conducted his treaty-making tour. Especially on the east side of the Cascades, where the Cayuse had attacked the Whitman Mission in 1847 and fought an eight-month war against an army of volunteer soldiers, Native Americans knew that more and more settlers would come and use up more and more of their lands and resources. Yakama and Palouse Indians became more concerned in 1853, when George McClellan met with them while doing survey work for the railroad survey under Stevens's command.[6] By 1855, when Stevens and Palmer were negotiating treaties with the Yakama, Walla Walla, Palouse, and Nez Perce tribes, news of gold discoveries on the Upper Columbia near Fort Colville had been announced, an event certain to attract even more whites to the region. Stevens sent H. R. Crosbie to investigate the rumor, and his report confirmed the richness of the finds. The news troubled Indian leaders, who worried whether treaty agreements could protect them from future conflicts with whites.[7]

Increasingly during the summer, miners caravaned across Yakama, Palouse, Spokane, and Colville lands, and minor frictions turned inflammatory.[8] The killing of several miners by a group of young Yakama warriors in mid-summer unbalanced the tentative agreements struck at Walla Walla, and the killing of Indian Agent Andrew J. Bolon in September unhinged the peace between whites and Indians on the Columbia Plateau. Bolon's death became the trip wire of a war against the Yakama Indians, which widened to engage regular and voluntary soldiers, including William W. Miller, in a two-year conflict that flared in fights on both sides of the Cascades.[9]

When Stevens learned about Bolon's murder, he was engaged in treaty negotiations with the Blackfeet on the Missouri River. In Olympia, Territorial Secretary Charles H. Mason acted in Stevens's absence, issuing a call for volunteer troops to form companies and ready themselves to defend the territory's white settlements. On the west side of the Cascades, where most settlers had believed the nearby Indian tribes were peaceful, a panic raced from settlement to settlement, fed by rumors that an Indian conspiracy threatened to bring wholesale war to all whites in the territory. As volunteer soldiers organized themselves and scrambled to find armaments, Major Gabriel Rains at Fort Dalles ordered a 100-man force under Brevet Major Granville O. Haller to the Yakama country in early October. An unfortunate firefight ensued between Haller's column and Yakama warriors, cutting off any potential discussion of the Bolon murder and enraging Indian leaders, who marshaled more than a thousand fighters and chased Haller back across the Columbia River.[10]

The conflict east of the Cascades was far from William Miller's Olympia, but the shots fired by Haller and his Yakama adversaries reverberated from Toppenish Creek to Puget Sound. The major's ignominious defeat and retreat confirmed the suspicions harbored by Stevens and voiced by the *Pioneer and Democrat* that the regular army had no intention of forcefully punishing the Indian perpetrators or countering the alleged Indian War conspiracy. The citizens of the territory would end up manning their own defense. The army had sent a reinforcement from Fort Steilacoom under Captain Maurice Maloney in late October, but it had turned back before crossing Naches Pass into Yakama country when news from Fort Dalles convinced them they would be outnumbered east of the mountains. On the west side of the mountains, settlers believed rumors that the Indians had combined and that they were sure to attack. Meanwhile, Indians interpreted the war preparations by whites as confirmation that they would all be killed regardless of the treaty guarantees.[11]

While the fear of an imminent Indian attack set Puget Sound communities on edge, the first company of volunteers formed in Olympia. Under the leadership of Judge Gilmore Hays, the volunteers hastily gathered resources and joined up with Captain Maloney's regular army troops, marching off toward Naches Pass in the Cascades. Other Olympians who were perhaps less adventurous—including William W. Miller—joined another volunteer band. Commanded by Captain Charles Eaton and numbering just under twenty men, the "Rangers" had been organized to patrol the nearby region and seek out Leschi, a Nisqually leader who had sometimes agitated for war even though he worked a farmstead near Yelm and had long been regarded as friendly toward whites. Miller served as Eaton's quartermaster and commissary, with the rank of 3rd Sergeant, while his friend A. M. Poe joined up as a soldier. After chasing Leschi and his brother Quiemuth away from their fields, Eaton detailed Miller to Fort Steilacoom for more supplies and pack horses and sent Poe to gather more recruits at Olympia and other settlements.[12] Meanwhile, two of Eaton's men, Lieutenant James McAllister and a settler named Connell, went with two Indians to scout the Puyallup River on October 27. Either from ambush or in a direct exchange of fire, Indian bullets felled the two men. Only days later and near the same place, Sheriff A. B. Moses and Olympia lawyer Joseph Miles, two of Hays's volunteers who were returning as messengers from Captain Maloney's command, ran headlong into an Indian camp on October 31. They precipitated a fight and were killed.[13]

By early November, Mason had authorized four additional companies of volunteers to defend the area south of Olympia to the Columbia River. Olympia and other Puget Sound settlements were in a near panic. "Hell is broke loose," James Tilton wrote George Gibbs from Olympia, "and everybody is excited." In late October, Indians attacked three homesteads on the White River, leaving nine dead and taking several as captives. One week later, Lieutenant William Slaughter lost his life when his troops, along with Gilmore Hays and the Olympia volunteers, tangled with Puyallup, Nisqually, and Klickitat Indians. Stevens had just started back to Olympia from east of the Divide as these conflicts rocked the settlements west of the Cascades. Mason appealed to the regular army for more patrols and began drawing up plans for quartering settlers in stockades and for rounding up noncombatant Indians. More unfounded stories circulated about Indian atrocities and imminent attacks, while citizens built blockhouses and gathered weapons.[14]

Meanwhile, Stevens made his way west to the Coeur d'Alene Mission in late November and then traveled on to Lapwai Mission on the

Clearwater River with an armed guard, where he tried to mend the fractured peace he thought he had created at the Walla Walla Council. Late in December, before going on to The Dalles and Olympia, Stevens met with the Oregon volunteers and a command of Washington volunteers under B. F. Shaw at Umatilla on the Columbia. He also began a strident criticism of the regular army's behavior during the crisis, firing off a series of letters charging that General John Wool, commander of the Department of the Pacific, had purposefully withheld troops. By mid-January, when he arrived back in Olympia, Stevens had also changed roles from treaty-maker to treaty-enforcer and had become determined to control events. As governor, superintendent of Indian affairs, and commander of volunteer forces, Stevens had resolved that the Yakamas and all other tribes who he charged had broken the peace—his "children," as he called all Indians under his supervision as superintendent of Indian affairs—would feel the sting of his patriarchal chastising whip. Contemptuous of General Wool's policies, Stevens moved quickly to expand the volunteer forces Mason had hastily organized during late 1855. He cobbled together a corps of volunteer officers from his trusted associates, while he authorized the organization of citizen troops and the building of blockhouses near Puget Sound settlements.[15]

By the end of January 1856, the territorial legislature had gone on record complaining about the inadequate response of U.S. Army troops and Stevens had willfully taken command of the situation. "I prefer to please myself," Stevens had written his mother the previous summer, adding, "I have determined to carry out my own views in certain matters." In matters of war, as his friends and enemies would soon discover, he had strongly set ideas and he counseled himself.[16] The men closest to him, including Miller, gave him wide berth and accepted his headstrong style, at least in part because of his previous war experience and his command of the Pacific Railroad Survey Expedition. As one of his contemporaries appraised him, Stevens "seemed to be like unto Jackson (A. J.) in his firmness . . . [and] willingness to shoulder all responsibility for his *own* acts." Issuing new orders for volunteer service on February 1, 1856, Stevens disbanded the existing volunteer units and created a three-battalion army. By mid-month, he had selected his primary commanders and had set six-month service terms for volunteer soldiers.[17]

As in any war strategy, Stevens's plan rested heavily on the successful coordination of available resources, which meant the efficient organization of volunteer soldiers and use of materiel gathered from private sources. For the organization of the soldier corps, he selected Territorial Surveyor General James Tilton as adjutant general. For the acquisition and disbursement of supplies, Stevens chose Miller as quartermaster and commissary general.[18]

Although he had served as quartermaster for the First Volunteer Regiment the previous fall, Miller faced a wholly different set of problems as quartermaster for the newly organized Second Volunteer Regiment. To begin with, volunteer companies had been raised in several communities on the west side of the Cascades, from Vancouver in the south to Whatcom in the north. Most included little or no equipage; even mounted battalions had difficulties acquiring enough horses. Further, the selection of volunteer officers by popular vote and the legislature completely bypassed the federal oversight of territorial affairs, breaking with normal procedure and politicizing the territory's militia. Ultimate control of all military operations, including strategy and supplies, rested with Governor Stevens, but his officers often complicated operations because they either had little knowledge of or ignored standard military protocol and organization. Finally, the territorial government had no funds to finance an army, so it used scrip, a pseudo money that was worthless unless redeemed by the U.S. government.[19]

With little hope that General Wool would commit regular troops and materiel to carry the governor's war to the Indians, Stevens established a two-front strategy. On the west side of the mountains, Stevens ordered a defensive policy, including the construction of blockhouses for every four families and regular patrols to keep Puget Sound Indians from threatening settlements and joining with potential allies from the east. To punish the eastside Indians for allegedly breaking the peace, Stevens planned a major campaign in Yakama territory to begin during the spring of 1856. He issued a proclamation on January 23, advising all merchants and farmers that the defense of settlements required their full cooperation with the volunteer forces and that they should sell them goods and services upon request. One week later, he wrote the commissioner of Indian affairs that friendly Indians were under watchful guard and "the people of the whole Sound region are living in block-houses or in their immediate vicinity" to protect themselves. Indians had attacked Seattle on January 26, prompting Stevens to concentrate forces for defense of the town and to appoint Edward Lander commander of a new volunteer company.[20]

Stevens worried that settlers might further panic and fail to join in a common defense. By personally pledging his full energy to the perceived Indian threat and urging settlers not to leave "in our hour of adversity," he demonstrated his resolve and pushed forward with the organization of the volunteer army.[21] All of this Stevens-ordered activity required Quartermaster General Miller to run a sizable supply operation. He soon ran into difficulties. The first source of military materiel should have been the regular army supply depots, but General Wool had ordered his troops not to cooperate with the volunteers. As a result, the congressionally approved allotment of arms for Washington Territory in 1855 had been sent to Vancouver barracks on the Columbia River rather than to Olympia, making it difficult to supply the volunteer companies on the Sound. Miller's best alternative source for military supplies was the Hudson's Bay Company, but as Chief Factor James Douglas in Victoria had informed Tilton in November:

> We are, I confess with sorrow, badly prepared for the exigencies of a state of warfare, there being, at this moment, only one hundred hand of arms in this colony and those are in the stores of the Hudson's Bay Company.

Douglas had promised the company's full suppport to assist "in checking the inroads of the merciless savage," but they could ship only forty guns and three kegs of gunpowder.[22]

Miller faced more difficult supply problems than locating sufficient arms. The building of a dozen or more blockhouses in the Puget Sound area meant securing lumber, nails, and other construction supplies from local sources and transporting them to the sites. Miller first had to find the supplies, but that was often only half of the problem. Convincing merchants to accept government scrip sometimes became the larger obstacle and foiled the bargains. In early February, for example, Miller's assistant quartermaster in Port Townsend, R. S. Robinson, reported making an arrangement with the Puget Mill Company for construction materials and a vessel to transport the supplies up the Sound. Paying in scrip, Robinson explained, meant a hard bargain. "I want you to stand by me in this contract," Robinson forcefully pleaded. "I thought it better to get the supplies though at a very high rate."[23]

From the outset, Miller knew that he had to keep the Quartermaster Corps operating on a fairly tight rein. Reports had to be made, shipments counted and recorded, and all payments entered in accounting ledgers if the territory hoped to recoup the value of the scrip issued for war supplies. Miller directed the purchases of Robinson and five other assistant quartermasters, each assigned to one of the 2nd Regiment's battalions: Robinson with the Northern Battalion at Fort Townsend; Frank Matthias at Seattle; M. R. Hathaway with the Southern Battalion at Vancouver; Warren Gove with the Central Battalion at Steilacoom; Charles S. Weed at the central supply depot in Olympia; and A. H. Robie at The Dalles to supply the planned expedition to eastern Washington.

Miller required quartermasters and other authorized personnel to fill out vouchers and receipts for all purchases of services and merchandise and then file them with his office in Olympia. Quartermasters made most of their purchases under orders from either Miller or Stevens, but commanders in the field also bought horses, supplies, and equipment without prior authorization, paying what they pleased. Miller stood at the apex of this supply and commissary system, coordinating the acquisition and movement of war materiel and accounting for its value and ultimate use. Although he devised a logical and efficient system to keep track of the quartermaster operations—one dictated in large part by the government's accounting procedures—

it proved to be inadequate. Its failures, which bedeviled Miller through-out the war, would create a legacy of fiscal and political troubles.[24]

At the beginning of the war, Miller focused on supporting the gov-ernor's military plan, which emphasized headquartering troops at posts throughout the Puget Sound region and building up a sizable store of materiel at a central depot in Olympia. During the first weeks in February, Miller ordered barrels of flour, tins of coffee, cooking sup-plies, and other goods from Steilacoom merchant Phillip Keach and contracted with HBC Factor W. F. Tolmie at Fort Nisqually for cloth-ing and blankets. He readily got Keach to accept scrip as payment, but Tolmie hesitated. Because he knew Miller and trusted him, Tolmie forthrightly explained his reluctance, openly wondering how likely it was that the government would redeem territorial scrip at full value. "I have been informed," he wrote Miller, "that the authorities at Washington . . . frequently make large deductions on the plea of over-charge on the part of those furnishing goods." The prices Miller offered to pay were too low, Tolmie added, and there was an additional prob-lem. "I have so far acted without authority from headquarters," Tolmie confessed, "and it is in the power of the HBCo to make me person-ally liable for the supplies furnished government, should they disap-prove of my action in the matter."[25]

Miller found his supplies, although not all he desired, from other sources just in time to stock Montgomery's Station, a stop along the old emigrant road and the most strategic post Stevens had ordered to be built.[26] Miller worried about his quartermasters' purchases, warn-ing them not "to allow any extravagant charge, such as would tend to depreciate the value of the scrip," but he put the highest priority on speed. He wanted supplies acquired quickly and shipped even faster. After purchasing eight wagons in early February at Grand Mound, south of Olympia, Miller issued orders to his assistant on the 14th to push forward all shipments to Montgomery's. "Let no wagon come without a load," Miller wrote Charles Weed, "and let them come with-out delay." Four days later, after Miller had noted sluggish progress in gathering supplies for the newly named Fort Montgomery, he barked at Weed: "For God's sake order a large quantity of such articles as the written requisitions call for and ship them . . . tomorrow—let there be no fail."[27]

Miller's short-tempered note reflected the order he had received the same day from Stevens, which directed him to oversee the movement of supplies to Montgomery's and the construction of a ferry across the Puyallup River. The following day, Miller sent out twenty-seven wagons from Yelm Prairie to Montgomery's loaded with flour, clothing, and other supplies. He also sent parties to Muckleshoot, Nisqually, and Steilacoom for additional supplies, while he enlisted settlers to help construct the ferry and blockhouse at the Puyallup. Miller's quick action impressed Stevens, who commended him for "the energy you have manifested in getting the provisions and forage into the field." But the governor rarely paused long for laudations. Noting that everything must be done at once and quickly, Stevens challenged Miller to have all the work done within two days. "Push forward with the train yourself," he admonished, "it is important that the utmost energy characterizes all our movements."[28]

During the last week of February, Miller kept up a feverish pace, even beyond the demands Stevens had placed on him. On February 28, he wrote the governor that two posts had been established. He had also scouted the forks of the Puyallup for grass, secured other forage for animals, and brought up enough supplies for fifty days at a forward post on the Puyallup. Those supplies included 1,350 pounds of flour, 36 barrels of pork, 75 barrels of beef, 1,400 pounds of sugar, 200 pounds of coffee, and 150 pounds of tea. The stores also contained bushels of beans, rice, blocks of hard bread, and other staples.[29] Stevens wanted the stores in place and ready to supply volunteers under Major Gilmore Hays who were trying to corner Leschi's forces, estimated to be four hundred strong. Additional supplies were necessary at the blockhouses, where settlers had been encouraged to stay. In effect, Stevens had Miller and his quartermasters provisioning both tangents of his military strategy at once, the campaigns against the Indians and the defense of the settlements.[30]

The governor's military plan, however, did not work as smoothly or as successfully as he had hoped. His decision to force a military punishment on recalcitrant Indians without the support of the regular army put an enormous strain on the territory. In the Puget Sound region, where Stevens enforced a defensive policy, settlers either abandoned their farms out of genuine fear or followed the government's directive to cloister up in one of the blockhouses. Although a sizable number of Indian raiders threatened settlers, nothing approaching full-scale war conditions ever existed, which prompted some citizens to criticize the sacrifices Stevens had imposed on them.[31] East of the mountains, decisive war-making by Klickitat Indians on the Columbia River in mid-March disrupted the governor's war plans and underscored the inadequacy of the volunteer army's resources.

Supplies and their disbursement were at the heart of Stevens's strategic problems. The volunteer companies were never at full strength. Even in those with larger rosters, soldiers left when they pleased to tend to family duties. Miller even offered supplies to the wives of soldiers if their husbands would remain in the field.[32] When the volunteer companies did not fill out their rosters and guerrilla attacks by Indians compromised wagon trains, Stevens was forced to scavenge the force he had instructed B. F. Shaw to assemble for the planned foray into eastern Washington against the Yakamas, even though Shaw had spent weeks filling his company and gathering supplies. For Miller, the situation became progressively more difficult, especially after the sudden attack on the settlement at the Cascades of the Columbia on March 26, 1856.[33]

Without warning and with devastating psychological and military effect, a combined warrior force of Klickitat and Yakama Indians attacked the settlements at the Cascades of the Columbia, a key geographical point in steamboat transportation on the river. General George Wright and his regulars, with orders to maintain the peace in eastern Washington, were garrisoned at Fort Dalles, forty miles upriver. A sizable cache of military provisions at the Cascades was the target of the attack, which took place the day after Wright's force left the Upper Cascade steamboat terminal for The Dalles. Launching a series of quick strikes and pinning forty settlers in Bradford's Store at the Lower Cascades, the Indians killed fourteen residents and three soldiers in the two-day fight. Using a cannon, Lieutenant Phillip Sheridan's regulars stormed the Lower Cascades on March 28, as Wright and his troops landed at the Upper Cascades.[34]

The events at the Cascades sent a shock wave through the Northwest. Just two weeks earlier, Stevens had congratulated a volunteer force under command of Gilmore Hays for repulsing a combined attack at Connell's Prairie led by Leschi and his Yakama ally, Qualchan. The fierce battle on the Columbia dashed the feelings of optimism that the war would be over soon. Even in Portland, where citizens had thought themselves safe from the war, fright replaced complacency and homeguards were readied. Down the Columbia at the mouth of the Cowlitz, the news of the war created anxiety among the few whites, but Judge Strong and former HBC Factor James Birnie kept close watch on Cathlamet Indians who had familial ties to Klickitat and Yakama villages to prevent them joining in any conflicts. Miller's department came under immediate pressure to increase supplies at Vancouver. He responded quickly, diverting a portion of the stores he had ordered from Portland to supply Shaw's expedition up the Columbia. But the inefficiencies in Vancouver, at least partly the fault of Assistant Quartermaster M. R. Hathaway, soon became a major problem and eventually forced Miller to send Edward Furste, his personal assistant in Olympia, to investigate.[35]

The ability of Miller and the rest of the volunteer army to meet sudden exigencies, such as the attacks on Seattle and the Cascades, had been compromised from the beginning. But an additional distraction in the spring of 1856—one more political than military in character—had unbalanced everyone's confidence and threatened to cripple the government. The acorn of the crisis was embedded in Stevens's blockhouse policy on the Sound. Convinced that some settlers knowingly had aided recalcitrant Indians, Stevens ordered many families with known connections to the tribes—especially former HBC employees living on the Yelm and Muck prairies—to be quartered at Fort Nisqually.[36] Just days after Stevens's order, the firefight on Connell's Prairie on March 10 raised new fears that the warrior bands were freely circulating in the area, prompting Stevens to bring Shaw's forces north from the Columbia to increase patrols. Several settlers on Muck Prairie resisted the relocation order, leading Stevens to suspect that the Indians would receive aid from friendly whites and organize additional attacks. Stevens authorized that force be used, if necessary, to remove the men he deemed dangerous. "You are instructed," Tilton wrote Jared S. Hurd,

> to use every persuasion possible with those suspected persons before resorting to force, but should they resist, you are authorized to employ force, and coerce their [suspected Indian sympathizers] immediate removal. As they occupy that part of the country which is at present a part of the theatre of war, Martial Law of necessity exists there, consequently you may well have no hesitation in enforcing the order to remove all whom you may find in a suspicious locality.[37]

Major H. J. G. Maxon took early action under the governor's orders and arrested several mixed-blood farmers and incarcerated them at Fort Steilacoom. Stevens became convinced that stronger action was necessary, especially after reports that one of the farmers boasted that he "went when and where he pleased without arms . . . [because] the Indians said that they would not hurt the French or English" in the area.[38] Further news that the imprisoned settlers planned to challenge their arrest in territorial court and had secured the services of attorneys William H. Wallace and Frank Clark prompted Stevens to declare martial law in Pierce County.

Stevens had taken a long and deep step into controversy. It is clear he did not anticipate the hostility his actions engendered. As his biographer concluded, the governor probably did not know or give much thought to the legal implications of imposing martial law. He assumed it was within his power as chief executive, that it was an extension of his civil *and* military prerogatives. Others disagreed. The ensuing legal-political battle took on its own life, dominating the governor's already limited attentions and seriously detracting from the territory's support of the war effort.[39]

Among citizens west of the Cascades, the martial law drama nearly overshadowed the larger war story during March, April, and May. In the first act, Stevens removed the mixed-blood prisoners from Steilacoom and held them in Olympia for a military trial, hoping that his officers might find credible evidence against them. Territorial Court Justice Edward Lander took the lead in the second act when he stepped in for an ailing Chief Justice Francis A. Chenoweth. Lander, who one of his contemporaries called "an extra sensitive, nervous, irritable man . . . who could brook superiority from no one," tried to call the court into session in Steilacoom. He assumed that martial law would no longer be in Pierce County once the prisoners had been removed to Thurston County, but Stevens enforced his martial law order and sent armed volunteers to obstruct the opening of court. In the third act, Lander and Stevens traded threats as the judge opened court in early May with an armed protective force ready to face off against volunteers under B. F. Shaw's command. When Lander tried to hold court in Olympia, Stevens extended martial law to Thurston County, forcing another showdown. Lander refused to comply with the governor's order, was put under arrest, and was taken to Camp Montgomery, where he sat incarcerated with the original prisoners. The final act came when a recovered Chenoweth opened court in Steilacoom and issued arrest orders for Shaw and others holding Lander in captivity. Stevens finally relented on May 24, declaring the state of emergency over and revoking his martial law order.[40]

Although his chief responsibility lay in securing and moving supplies, Miller could not stay clear of the martial law fracas. He was one of Stevens's inner circle of officers. More important, he had become the governor's principal political advisor, even if Stevens often ignored his wise counsel. During the earliest stages of the conflict, Stevens wrote a "private" letter to Miller, asking him to review a scathing letter criticizing Stevens that Justice Chenoweth had sent to the attorney general in application for reappointment as chief justice in Washington Territory. The letter, Stevens charged,

> is slandering covertly the people of the Territory. I have carried, in return, the war into Africa as Lander is backing Chenoweth and lending himself to

Chenoweth's insinuations. I include them both in my protest against their re-appointment. Now I want my friends and the democratic party to sustain me. . . . I have taken my ground boldly and decisively and shall not falter in the least.[41]

Miller knew what was at stake in the martial law tussle. While the legal and constitutional disputes inherent in the conflict between the governor's military authority and the territory's judicial purview were important, it was the political game that had the highest stakes. Almost from its inception, Stevens's governorship had been embroiled in military activity, which enhanced his and the Democratic party's political power in the territory. The governor's detractors in the martial law episode may have legitimately disagreed with his actions, but the political motive ruled the day as they openly critiqued Stevens in the opposition press and complained to officials in Washington, D.C., hoping to embarrass and diminish him. George Gibbs and William H. Wallace, two erstwhile Whigs, led the charge. They were joined by Elwood Evans, H. A. Goldsborough, and two Democrats, Frank Clark and Bion F. Kendall, who had already tangled with Stevens or the governor's men and saw this fracas as a means to organize their opposition.[42]

Stevens seemed to almost encourage the fight, as he wrote to Miller, taking the dispute "into Africa." But he had to be careful. Gibbs and Goldsborough, his staunch opponents in the issue, had written the secretary of state, charging Stevens with usurpation of the law and demanding his immediate removal.[43] Even those Democrats who supported Stevens knew that he might have overreached his authority. One loyal Democrat confided to an associate that the governor's action worried him; "the legal gentlemen of this territory condemn Stevens and consider it [martial law declaration] a gross outrage. I think myself, Stevens was rather hasty." He added:

at the same time I say if he had the right and if the public safety demanded Martial Law, then I say he had a right to enforce it, *but* I do not think the emergency of the case would warrant any such course.[44]

As Stevens pursued his headstrong course and the conflict escalated, he began to look over his shoulder and to ask Miller and Shaw for advice.[45] In late May, when a showdown with Chenoweth seemed imminent, Miller collected information for Stevens. Writing from Steilacoom, Charles Weed cautioned Miller that the opposition had organized an armed resistance to the enforcement of martial law and that they planned to occupy Chenoweth's courtroom if necessary. "Let the Governor look out," Weed advised. "I think he had better have the clerk of this county arrested with his books and papers and taken to some other place."[46]

It is unlikely that Miller encouraged Stevens to pursue the course suggested by Weed. There had already been far too much confrontation, and it seemed more and more likely that only a political resolution at the highest levels could extricate the governor from the grip of controversy. Stevens, probably on advice from Miller, wrote Shaw on May 21 that he hesitated, as Warren Gove put it, to "summons the whole county of Pierce to protect the court. . . . I wish to do nothing more than maintain the ground I have taken. . . . " Miller knew that the tunnel of trouble was rapidly narrowing. Any additional action by Stevens would only increase the likelihood that the administration in Washington would act. In late May, as Chenoweth readied to open court, Victor Monroe, whom Stevens had selected to adjudicate the military commission convened at Camp Montgomery to hold trial against the mixed-blood prisoners, covertly warned Miller to be careful what actions he took in Stevens's cause. Miller had authorized an illegal action in the governor's defense, Monroe judged, adding, "In thus volunteering to you my advice I do so as a friend with a view of saving you from trouble."[47]

Miller could not escape the trouble. After opening court, Chenoweth issued a ruling negating Stevens's martial law proclamations and arrested Shaw for refusing to release Justice Lander and the others from custody. Probably with advice from Miller, Stevens abandoned his policy and released the men at Camp Montgomery. The long crisis was over, but Shaw's fate remained unsettled and the planned campaign east of the Cascades waited in abeyance. The situation forced Stevens to beg the court for Shaw's release. On May 28, he enlisted Miller to carry a letter to the court and to argue the governor's case before Chenoweth. There is no official record of what had transpired between Stevens and Miller before the meeting with Chenoweth or what he said to the judge, but Miller secured Shaw's freedom on the promise that he would return to face contempt charges.[48]

Chenoweth would later claim that Miller had divulged that he had strongly advised Stevens against any further challenges to the court. Chenoweth called Miller an "off-hand man" who eagerly did the governor's disagreeable work. Miller let the *Pioneer and Democrat* respond for him. Labeling the charges ridiculous, "a work of the imagination," the paper reminded Chenoweth that Miller "was universally respected" for his magnificent service as quartermaster general. In effect, he was above reproach.[49]

Stevens had extricated himself from a potentially embarrassing showdown at Steilacoom, but the controversy dogged him for more than two years. It became a rallying point for his opponents in the territory, and it left a stain on his political record, creating problems for him in Washington, D.C. As Stevens's political adviser, Miller could not ignore the issue either. In July, Territorial Delegate Anderson warned that the issue had "raised a breeze" in the capital. "We are in a stew," Anderson wrote Miller.

> Cass [Michigan] calls for information [on the issue] in the Senate. The President called at my room (between us) last night. I wasn't in. He left word for me to call and see him this morning at 9 o'clock. It is now 1/4 to 9—I must go—God knows what will be the end of it.[50]

By August, President Pierce and Secretary of State William Marcy had heard a range of accusations against Stevens, including charges that he drank heavily and could be abusive. Further, the charges had become public knowledge outside of Washington Territory when the *New York Times* published letters by Stevens's opponents in the territory.[51]

The *Pioneer and Democrat* continued to defend Stevens in Washington Territory, but the governor's allies could not ignore the damage that had been done. Rumors that the president would remove

Stevens from office circulated freely. Miller hoped the disquiet would at least mellow, but it did not. Writing in late August to his close political associate, B. F. Shaw, Miller confided:

> The news from Washington looks rather gloomy for our little friend I. I. From what [Gilmore] Hays and [J. Patton] Anderson write the chances are even that he will be removed. If he is removed there will be a great sympathy for him here among the honest people of the country—how politicians will act time will determine. . . . As to myself, I have great regard for Stevens and while I have scorned to act the sycophant to him when in power I will not desert him if he should be removed and thereby should not be able to feed us poor devils any longer.[52]

By September, Stevens had abandoned any idea of retaining the governorship and had decided to run for territorial delegate. Miller believed he could win. Writing Shaw in early September, Miller predicted "that the people here are with him stronger than ever." For Stevens's part, he waved good riddance to the flap and told Miller he was prepared to enter a campaign for the delegate spot.[53]

Miller endured the governor's travails in the loyal demeanor that had become his political trademark. Nonetheless, he also faced tribulations and choices in 1856, some personal and some political. Just as the martial law controversy had begun to heat up in the spring of 1856, Miller had his attention jerked homeward to Illinois, when a letter from his sister in Beardstown brought tragic news.

> It is with a sad heart that I sit down this evening to write you the painfull news of the death of our dear Mother. Oh, William how uncertain life is but two weeks ago to-day Ma was in town and I thought I never see her more cheerfull in my life. She spoke often of you and Dick that day and was looking forward to the day with so much pleasure when you would return home.[54]

We can only guess at Miller's reaction to the mournful news. Surely he corresponded with family members in Illinois, and there is record of him writing Richard in California within weeks of their mother's death, but we have no expression of his deepest feelings. The only mention of the event is an appended comment he included in official correspondence to Benjamin Shaw. "I have just heard of the death of my mother," Miller laconically wrote in late June, "and dont feel like writing."[55]

In his notation to Shaw, Miller may have unintentionally expressed his emotional predicament as well as his personal distress. By 1856, after too many years away from Illinois, Miller occupied a kind of familial middle ground that left him feeling both connected to his family in Illinois and increasingly estranged from their lives. The Miller kin struggled to understand why he remained on the far edge of the continent, begging him to come back home. They repeatedly reminded him that he and his brother Richard had been gone far too long. "You may think that you are forgotten by us here or nearly so," one of his sisters wrote in 1855, "but believe me you are not." Despite the pleas, Miller seemed to shrug off the implied guilt as he pursued his life in Washington. His distance from home increased with the onset of the Indian War, when he chose to invest even more of himself in the territory. Nonetheless, when his sister Magdelene wrote him that their mother's death had broken the family's "strongest link," he must have felt great remorse, especially reading his sister's plaintive prayer: "Oh! William may this affliction have the effect that our Heavenly Father undoubtedly designed it should."[56] Miller probably did not see Divine Providence in his mother's death, but surely he felt conflict between his feelings for family and his public responsibilities. His political loyalties to Stevens and to the war effort overwhelmed or displaced his personal distress. He let the pain of his mother's death interrupt him, but only for a time. The day following his terse letter to Shaw he was back at the quartermaster account book and writing memoranda.

Wartime conditions left Miller few choices. Stevens had committed volunteer troops to a major campaign against Yakama Indians east of the Cascades. The governor had made this choice in part because he had become convinced that General George Wright would not punish the Yakamas. He suspected that General Wool was withholding troops for political reasons, but it is unlikely that there were sufficient troops and supplies at federal disposal to mount a major campaign.

In a typically strong-willed manner, Stevens ordered B. F. Shaw to march 175 volunteers over the mountains and challenge the Yakamas.[57]

The governor's marching orders placed an enormous burden on Miller's Quartermaster Corps. He had stockpiled materiel at Camp Montgomery, but the new orders required collection of enough goods from several commands to supply a full depot in Yakama country. That meant a heavy load in processing transfers, purchases, invoices, and vouchers. By mid-June, when Miller's department had sufficient materiel at hand, Shaw turned over the posts on the Puyallup and nearby prairies to the regular army. He crossed Naches Pass and descended into the Yakima River Basin prepared to engage the enemy. General Wright had earlier proposed establishing a permanent fort in Yakama country to maintain peace, but Stevens wanted a more aggressive policy. He hoped to chastise the Indians and then force them to renew their treaty pledges. Shaw agreed and had also become determined to carry a war to the recalcitrant Indians, even though Wright had warned him against it and had refused to promise him aid. When Shaw found no Yakamas to fight, he headed south into Oregon's Grande Ronde Valley, where he stormed a village of Walla Walla, Cayuse, and Umatilla Indians on July 17, killing more than fifty residents and destroying 120 lodges.[58]

Shaw's "victory" set the stage for Stevens's final wartime action. Convinced that he could manufacture a new peace, Stevens called a second Walla Walla Council and set off for eastern Washington Territory in late August. Although the Grande Ronde battle had created great tension among mid-Columbia Indians and one of the governor's pack trains was attacked on his way, Stevens persisted in his plan. But the meetings, held between September 11 and September 18, failed to resolve the divisive issues that had first been discussed in 1855. Stevens gave up the council and prepared to leave, but angry Indians attacked the governor's camp. After a day of episodic fighting, the Indians withdrew and Stevens left for The Dalles under armed guard.[59] Stevens's last efforts as commander of the territory's volunteer forces and as superintendent of Indian affairs had ended ignominiously, with the governor and his men hounded out of Yakama country. The disputes would continue and more battles would be fought until hostilities ceased in 1858.[60]

Stevens had ordered the disbandment of the volunteer forces almost immediately after learning of Shaw's fight at Grande Ronde. Even in his near compulsion to bring the Yakamas and their allies to task for alleged treaty violations, the governor had recognized that continued prosecution of the war made less and less political sense, and Shaw's "victory" provided some justification to declare the war's end. For Miller, though, the disbandment order did not bring much relief. Stevens enlisted him in August to quickly fill a new company to reinforce Shaw's volunteer forces, but more importantly he faced the larger burden of dismantling the volunteer forces. With several large commands still in the field and thousands of dollars in supplies in government storehouses, Miller discovered that ending a war was more difficult than beginning one.

His first directive instructed the quartermasters to begin closing down operations. "You will report in person to this office," Miller wrote his men in mid-July, "for the purpose of making a final settlement of the business of your post." He worried that a casual accounting of their inventory, purchase vouchers, and disbursements might lead to loss of government property. He warned the quartermasters to prevent soldiers from pilfering supplies when they mustered out and to disallow even their keeping full rations. But such general policies beg problems. What about the volunteers who had no means of sustenance and had already contributed their own weapons and equipment to the cause? Did Miller and the governor intend on abandoning their soldiers? Miller argued the case before Stevens, who reluctantly approved the cash purchase of additional supplies by the quartermasters on the assurance that payment would be forthcoming from the Indian Department within sixty days. As it turned out, Congress took years to approve that payment, but in the summer of 1856 Miller had made a good faith effort to support the volunteers.[61]

A better and more important test of Miller's loyalty to the volunteer army came in his oversight of accounts. The chances of a prompt and liberal redemption of the territory's war debt hung in the balance.

By mid-August, Miller had discovered a nest of problems with his quartermasters' accounts, many of them quite beyond their means of control. As one of his principal quartermasters, R. S. Robinson, later explained:

> Frequently my post was thronged with Indians who had been employed in transporting stores . . . all demanding their pay, and always in a hurry, that they might return to their homes . . . [so] it was a matter of economy to the post, for if they remained all night they had to be fed. . . . White men could not be had at any price for scrip to do the business.[62]

In other cases, the volunteer commanders resisted breaking up their units, in part because they had planned on acquiring more goods or had large orders pending when they had been told to disband. In one case, Miller acted with dispatch by sending Charles Weed on board the *A. Y. Trask* to oversee disbandment at Port Townsend and Bellingham Bay and bring back surplus goods.[63]

The most troubled depot was in Vancouver. This was partly because of its proximity to Portland, where the territory purchased sizable amounts of goods, but it was also because Miller's quartermaster at Vancouver, M. R. Hathaway, had bungled his accounts. Reports on Hathaway's sloppy procedures had prompted Miller to send Edward Furste to Vancouver in April for an official inspection. Furste reported "that the affairs of this office are in an awfully bollixed condition." Furste criticized Hathaway's procedures, use of employees, and perquisites, characterizing him as "a God d—n fool, and unfit for the post." Within weeks, Miller had hired M. B. Millard, an experienced businessman from Portland, to take over Hathaway's accounts. By July, Millard had discovered dozens of accounting inconsistencies and "considerable property, horses, saddles, etc. appraised into the [Volunteer] Service at Vancouver which was furnished by citizens aside from those who volunteered." Evidently, the confusion at Vancouver —or perhaps Hathaway's mendacity—resulted in a major supply bottleneck that left the depot with a large amount of surplus war property.[64]

Disposing of accumulated goods presented Miller with an even larger problem than maintenance of accounts. The selling of public property at auction had to be arranged with great care. The potential for difficulties ranged from poorly appraised merchandise to fraud. Bound up in the process was the acceptance and relative value of scrip, the currency of choice in purchasing auctioned goods. Everyone understood that scrip circulated at a discount in relation to coin, in part because it could only be issued for war-related purposes and also because there was a justified fear that Congress would not honor scrip at par when it compensated the territory for war outlays. With this in mind, commanders in the field had often purchased livestock or goods at inflated values, assigning a higher-than-market price on the purchase vouchers that the sellers would later redeem in scrip.[65]

To keep order and control costs, Miller had published a notice in the *Pioneer and Democrat* in late March, informing everyone holding vouchers and other claims that documentation would be required before scrip could be issued. He also instructed officers to be stingy in their valuations. "It has been my uniform practice in settling the war accounts throughout our Territory," Miller wrote a quartermaster in April, "to cut down any account that I thought was exhorbitantly high, before issuing scrip." Miller feared that either liberal appraisals or procedural irregularities could undermine scrip values and compromise the entire Quartermaster Corps, which might jeopardize congressional payment of the war debt. His adviser in the nation's capitol, Josiah Lucas, had cautioned him about these dangers, warning that scrip and voucher accounts would be keenly evaluated by Congress. Miller took his advice and pledged to stay on top of the accounts. In mid-April, reports indicated that Washington Territory scrip was trading as low as 30 cents on the dollar in Portland. One month later, Miller assured nervous officers that the voucher-redemption process would be regular and that there was "no possible chance of their being defrauded." Nonetheless, by August scrip-holders began complaining to him that the value of their vouchers had plummeted and they feared the worst.[66]

The vagaries of discounted scrip aside, Miller worried more about the auctions, where fraud was more likely. On August 1, he publicized the auctions in the *Pioneer and Democrat:*

> To whom it may concern: The public property pertaining to the volunteer organization of this territory will shortly be sold to the highest bidders for scrip signed by the Quartermaster and Commissary General and approved by the Commander in Chief. Persons therefore having accounts against the volunteer organization and who may wish to make purchases of the public property will perceive the necessity for handling in their accounts to the different quartermasters and getting scrip issued on the same without delay.[67]

The auctions became logistical nightmares. Not only did the quartermasters have to collect surplus goods, but each issuance of scrip had to bear the signatures of both Miller and Stevens. At Vancouver, Millard pleaded with Miller to come personally to the auction to facilitate the operation. He rejected the invitation, writing Millard that "it would be extremely inconvenient for me to issue you scrip at Portland." Miller had sixteen quartermasters and agents to oversee, and "if I absent myself to attend to your business, all others must be neglected."[68] Instead, he sent James K. Hurd to help.

Miller believed that he could assure the closest surveillance if he forced all of his quartermasters to bring their vouchers and scrip to him personally. He was intently focused on the conditions of his accounts. As he wrote Stevens in early September, "I think I shall be ready . . . to make any report you may require with regard to the business of my department . . . and I will try and have my accounts so that they will answer any test." There had been a few complaints about policies, which no doubt had troubled Stevens, but no malfeasance had been charged, and the *Pioneer and Democrat* had publicly characterized Miller's operation as "exceptional and efficient."[69]

Both Stevens and Miller knew, however, that the Democratic newspaper's opinion was not the important one. The Quartermaster General's accounts had to pass muster with Congress to guarantee payment of the territory's war debt. In part because J. Ross Browne's investigation of the causes and conduct of the Indian War in Oregon and

Washington had left questions about the reliability of war-related records, Congress authorized a three-member commission in September 1856 to examine the ledgers, muster rolls, and vouchers. The commission scheduled its review of Washington Territory records for spring 1857 in Vancouver. With that meeting in mind, Miller had set a December 26, 1856, deadline for scrip issuance. He spent January and February busily gathering reports from his quartermasters for submission to the commission. Stevens had attempted but failed to get Miller appointed to the commission, no surprise considering that his actions and accounts would be one of the commission's focal points.[70]

Two members of the commission, Lafayette Grover and Rufus Ingalls, an army captain who happened to be Stevens's third cousin, understood and sympathized with the territory's plight. The third member, army Captain A. J. Smith, had no known predispositions. During their investigations, the commission reviewed all account books in detail, noting prices paid for individual services and goods, wages paid out to volunteer soldiers and officers, and the general accounting methods used by Miller and his quartermasters. They compared the amount on vouchers with current market prices, commenting that "irregularities and imperfections were, of course, to be found, but to a lesser extent than might have been anticipated." The commission's report allowed $1,481,475.45 for the Washington volunteer army's expenses, approximately $500,000 higher than Miller's first estimate. The report charged Miller with personal responsibility for more than $187,000.[71]

The commission's report gave Washington Territory and Miller relatively high marks, but it did not assure payment. Some in Congress questioned the entire volunteer military operation and had little interest in rewarding the participants. Stevens argued strenuously that Congress should honor the volunteer effort and pay the debt. He enlisted Oregon Sentor Joe Lane in the fight but still failed to get quick approval. Instead, Congress sent the accounts to the Treasury Department's third auditor, Robert J. Atkinson, a man known to look at all public expenditures as monies to be saved. Atkinson's review treated the territory and Miller's accounts with more skepticism. He criticized

Miller for paying prices "which seem in some instances to be very high," and he questioned the quartermaster general's personal account:

> General Miller's accounts show large amounts for meals and lodging furnished various persons, at generally $1 per meal, without designating the persons. . . . He reports bills for the lodging of wives of the volunteers, at $10 per month.[72]

Atkinson directed most of his criticism at the several quartermasters under Miller's control who he judged had purchased too many goods or paid exorbitant prices. Not surprisingly, Atkinson severely criticized the operations of the Vancouver depot and the auction sale, including a specific reference to M. R. Hathaway, who "retained no accounts showing from whence or whom he received [supplies]." His strongest criticism of Miller charged him with drawing funds simultaneously from two arms of government, the legislature and the volunteer army. Atkinson's charge was true, for the new governor, Fayette McMullin, had continued Miller in the position of quartermaster general while he also took a seat in the territorial legislature. But Atkinson added no charge of malfeasance, and the issue died once Miller and McMullin explained the conditions.[73]

The third auditor's report reduced the claim amounts for both Oregon and Washington by more than half. Congress finally accepted the figures in 1860, thereby ending a long politically charged pursuit of the war debt payment. Throughout the process—and for years afterward—Miller received plaintive letters requesting his help in securing payment for vouchers issued during the war. He stood by the volunteers, writing the Treasury Department on their behalf dozens of times throughout the 1860s and early 1870s. For Stevens, the issue became an albatross. Elected territorial delegate in 1857, Stevens received continual criticism for not getting congressional approval for payment of the territorial war debt.[74]

The Indian War debt issue touched nearly every community in western Washington. Merchants, farmers, and soldiers all needed swift action. They were at the mercy of Congress, and they looked to Miller and other politicians to plead their cases. As thoroughly as any other experience in the young territory's existence, the Indian War had galvanized the population. Miller's management of the Quartermaster Corps had put him at the center of the activity that had bound citizens together throughout the war. His advocacy of the holders of scrip and vouchers connected him even more strongly to his fellow citizens and made him even more valuable to the territory's political establishment. As the war had attracted friends and neighbors into the volunteer companies, it also had provided an additional political focus for the territory. In that respect, Miller fought the war with friends and through it he established a broader foundation for his political and civic activities.

CHAPTER 6

Political Advantages

*I believe in Miller's plan. Give no quarters nor take none.
Let them all go to hell together everyone for himself in
this chase. They say that's Miller.*

J. S. Jaquith to Warren Gove, January 24, 1858

Miller's service during the Indian War underscored a
truth he had already learned: all public decisions are fundamentally
and completely political. Without politics, nothing moves, no change
takes place. Without politics, no one receives rewards and no one risks
personal reputations, futures, or fortunes. For Miller, the martial law
episode and the drawn-out hassle over congressional reimbursement
of territorial war expenses were cases in point. The Indian War had
spawned both problems from necessity, as Miller saw it, but the governor's policies had contained great risks. The political bonfire sparked
by the martial law controversy had singed everyone in Stevens's tight
circle. Its residual smoke hung over the territory, threatening to
suffocate the Democratic party. Also smoldering was the dilatory
redemption of scrip and vouchers, an issue that posed an even larger
threat to Miller and his Democratic colleagues. Although he had kept
himself almost entirely out of the flames, Miller had inhaled enough
fumes to learn anew about the dangers of politics.

Miller knew that political whirlpools spun most furiously at the center, so he had assiduously tried to live at arm's length from the electoral vortex, preferring to organize, influence, and manage political activities from a safer periphery. That was how he had entered Washington Territory's political world in 1853, as a well-heeled and businesslike Democratic party manager. He would stand for elective office only three times, once for the territorial House of Representatives in 1857, again for Territorial Council in 1858, and fifteen years later for mayor of Olympia. He won each time, but his heart was not in electoral politics. The electoral world was too visible a forum for what Miller liked most about politics—the personal connection. He gravitated toward the center of political networks, not toward the center of political maelstroms. His connection and importance to other Democrats stemmed both from his increasing wealth and his personal relationships with active men. He had many of them on his account books either as debtors or as financial partners. In effect, Miller had overlaid his financial and political networks, making nearly all relationships dual in nature and complicated. In Miller's world, election results, party strategies, and ledger accounts co-existed in a natural tabulation of unified purpose that emphasized mutual benefit to all politically loyal men.[1]

The purpose of politics, as Miller saw it, was the advancement of mutual interests and the development of territorial resources. In pursuit of these goals, Miller lived a two-faceted political existence. One side reflected personal relationships, man-to-man arrangements that he measured as straightforward exchanges of promises, risks, and rewards. The other side mirrored his commitment to the territory and its development, his conviction that everyone gained in proportion to their investment and that all received some benefit from *any* improvement of conditions. Partisanship meant something to him— he stayed within the Democratic family throughout his career—but he recognized that spiteful political behavior should be avoided to protect the body politic.[2]

Miller's demeanor matched his political precepts. He was straightforward, even to the point of bluntness, and he expected direct responses to questions and suggestions. Partisanship was a necessity, for without it the territory's meager political resources would resist focus and little would be accomplished. More important, personal loyalty to colleagues and to agreed purposes guaranteed some measure of success. In early 1855, imbued with this pragmatic political philosophy, he joined with other local politicians to form a Democratic Club in Olympia. The club created the local Democratic organization first to protect Olympia's interests in the territory, second to serve as a clearinghouse for territorial and national political information, and finally to solidify personal relationships and their concomitant loyalties.[3]

Isaac Stevens was foremost among Miller's political friends, and Miller expended most of his political energy on behalf of the governor.[4] By the last stages of the Indian War, he had become Stevens's political confessor and an *ex officio* political chief of staff. During the summer of 1856, with the martial law controversy still nagging the governor, Miller chaired the Thurston County Democratic Convention and led the Stevens delegates, who controlled the convocation. Miller and his cohorts served as the governor's inner staff and were widely perceived as a tight gang of political supporters, but they operated from a shifting agenda without much, if any, discipline. They often staged political events, such as the gala they organized in late October 1856 to honor Stevens as commander-in-chief of the volunteers, to publicize their leader's accomplishments. Of necessity, much of their activity focused on Stevens's politics—including his ambitions—rather than on an articulated plan of action. Among the circle of Stevens men, Miller became the political field marshal. By early 1857, he had begun designing Stevens's campaign for territorial delegate and was advising the candidate, especially on patronage and related issues.[5]

Stevens needed little urging to make the run for territorial delegate, an election Miller told him he could win in a walk. With his governorship almost surely scuttled by the martial law controversy, Stevens inclined toward the vagaries of electoral politics and away from the humiliation of dismissal from office. In August 1856, Miller knew that the governor's enemies had nearly succeeded in convincing President Pierce to remove his long-time friend and military colleague from office. Writing from Washington, D.C., veteran politician John Cain warned Miller. "I thought you had better have the information," Cain explained, "but in full confidence . . . your own prudence will tell you the importance of not letting it become publick at least by the friends of the Gov."[6]

For months, Miller had known that the political horizon would be stormy. In April, Josiah Lucas, Miller's politically savvy friend from Illinois, had cautioned him that the governor's reputation in the nation's capital had skidded. To Miller's description of Stevens as a "dashing young fellow," Lucas had retorted that he was "sometimes 'otherwise,'" a clear reference to reports of the governor's excessive drinking. Lucas warned Miller: "I should not select him as a 'fitting' man to engineer a canoe, if she had freight aboard to the value of six bits." Be wary, Lucas added, of too tight a connection with Stevens, urging Miller to make stronger connections with national rather than territorial politicians.[7] But Miller understood much better than Lucas did that territorial political rewards rarely came from national politicians or national contests. The "winning" and the "gain" were tied tightly to local developments, and in Washington Territory nearly all Democratic activities were tied to Isaac Stevens's future. Electing him territorial delegate, Miller knew, could bring himself and his circle of friends significant opportunities and rewards. To that end, during the spring of 1857, Miller orchestrated the governor's candidacy, calling on men from the volunteer officers' corps to carry their commander's campaign in county conventions throughout the territory.

The political lay of the land in Washington Territory, however, had been altered significantly by the martial law affair and the failure to get quick congressional action on the territory's Indian War debt. In early 1857, former Whigs, some of Stevens's political opponents, and other dissidents helped spawn the territory's Republican party and its voice, the *Washington Republican*. The *Pioneer and Democrat* pumped the governor's electoral bid by enlisting support from Indian War veterans and castigating the opposition as unpatriotic.[8] In Seattle, as Franklin Matthias informed Miller in April, the Democratic County Convention offered a resolution condemning Stevens's actions during the war as "subversive of Democratic principles calculated to lead to tyranny and oppression." The situation in Clark County seemed little better. "The people are with him," an informant wrote Miller, "but there is so much political juggling among the democracy that there is no telling how it will result."[9]

The jugglers came under control at the territorial Democratic Convention in May, when Miller and convention chairman Edmund Fitzhugh, who owed his secure position as an Indian agent to Stevens, engineered a unanimous ballot victory for their man. Stevens had no serious opposition within the party and the Republican nominee, Alexander Abernethy from Monticello, had little support except in Clark County and along the lower Columbia River. Although the election was probably never in doubt, Miller and other Stevens supporters wanted more than a simple victory in the July polling. They hoped for a definitive mandate. If Stevens expected to successfully lobby Congress on behalf of the territory—and not incidentally the interests of his supporters—he had to erase the blot on his reputation in Washington, D.C. As Lucas had informed Miller, members of the U.S. Senate were "down upon Stevens" and "against entrusting anything to him."[10]

Miller enlisted Stevens supporters to stump the territory with the candidate during June. The governor's opponents, especially on the Sound, tried to entice Democratic bolsters to support Abernethy. Stevens took the threats seriously and committed himself to a rigorous schedule of speeches in communities from the Sound south to the Columbia and east to Walla Walla. Olympia lawyer and orator Selucius S. Garfielde, volunteer army officer H. J. G. Maxon, and Supreme Court Justice Obediah McFadden joined Stevens in the canvass for votes, each speaking plainly and unapologetically for his candidacy. Stevens was ebullient, writing Miller in mid-June that he expected to sweep Clark County—his opponent's backyard—and "to approach unanimity" in other Columbia River counties, from Pacific to Walla Walla. The opposition continued to wave the martial law flag, but voters probably worried less about the governor's legal transgressions than his ability to squeeze Indian War repayments out of Congress. As one

Stevens loyalist wrote Miller: "We ask no quarter in the fight and give none. . . . Let them foul mouthed slanderers sail on the Sound the votes of the people will cram the line down their throughts [*sic*] by the result of the election." Nonetheless, whether they voted for Stevens or against the "slanderers," the electorate gave him a landslide victory with winning tallies in every county but Pierce, where the governor's martial law dictates had been most vehemently resisted.[11]

Miller's own political capital had been high throughout the spring of 1857. J. Patton Anderson had even urged him to petition the Democratic party to have his name put forth as Stevens's replacement. Anderson himself had already been suggested for the post—his name had been actually submitted to President Buchanan—but he had begged off, saying, "I could be of no earthly benefit to the people of the Territory as Governor, except to prevent a worse man from getting it." Anderson hoped to get Miller, or perhaps Seth Catlin, appointed and thereby maintain the political balance in the territory by installing a known Democratic quantity in Olympia.[12] But Miller had no interest in the office, perhaps because he had seen what grief it had brought Stevens. Instead, he let his friends in the Thurston County Democratic Convention enter his name for the territorial legislature. The Democrats wanted him partly because they knew he could be very persuasive in the post-Indian War deliberations in Olympia and partly because they thought his candidacy would aid other party candidates. Along with other Democrats in the county, including B. F. Shaw, Miller won election to the House of Representatives, where he served one session.

As rewarding as his election may have been to him, Miller's political ambitions lay in a different direction. He wanted to secure another appointed post. Considering that his Customs Service experience had ranged from aggravating to thoroughly frustrating, it may be surprising that he would have sought another job that exposed him to the crosswinds of national politics. But Miller saw benefits. He wanted to become the new superintendent of Indian affairs, where he could not only aid his friends with appointments to Indian agencies but also contract for services from territorial businessmen. In the territorial

West, control of Indian agencies and budgets constituted a treasure chest of patronage and economic rewards, a reality that Miller fully appreciated.

Getting this prize, however, tested Miller's patience and endurance. In March 1857, Stevens resigned his appointment as superintendent, an office he had held since becoming territorial governor. Congress took the opportunity, perhaps as a reflection of the continuing dispute over Indian War reimbursements, to combine the Indian superintendencies in Oregon and Washington. Joseph Lane, the Oregon territorial delegate and a rising Democratic politician, lobbied successfully for the appointment of James Nesmith, an Indian War veteran who had commanded a battalion of Oregon militia. Nesmith's selection, A. J. Cain told Miller in mid-March, had served Lane's political purposes and had nothing to do with what was best for the territory. Anderson had gone along with the choice of Nesmith rather than someone from Washington, according to Cain, because he hoped to gain something for his father-in-law, former Customs Collector John Adair. Although Cain believed firmly that Anderson had "sold out (I mean the interests of the Territory) for individual aggrandizement," it is unlikely that Anderson received any personal gain or that he knew of Miller's interest in the position.[13]

The major obstacle to Miller's appointment was the combined superintendency. Congress was unlikely to speedily reverse itself on the issue, partly because it was necessarily tangled in the territorial war debt labyrinth. This impediment helped delay Miller's appointment for nearly four years. Evidently, Nesmith put up little or no resistance to the idea. In June 1857, B. F. Shaw had felt Nesmith out on this and other questions and informed Miller that the superintendent was "a man of his own head which is all that you and I cared for." Stevens also wrote Nesmith when he turned over his records, suggesting that Miller and other loyal veterans of the Indian War should be rewarded with positions in the Indian Service. And Stevens carried the argument directly to Nesmith and Lane by meeting with them in Oregon before traveling east to Washington.[14]

Regardless of any strategy Stevens may have had in mind, Miller began gathering support for his appointment even before Stevens had arrived in the capital and established his office. Miller collected petitions from King, Island, Jefferson, Whatcom, Pierce, Thurston, and Clark counties, with more than two hundred signatures. Addressed to President Buchanan, the petitions asked that Miller be appointed superintendent in Washington because he had universal respect among citizens, had impeccable credentials as a loyal Democrat, and had substantial experience with Indian tribes. Many of the signatories were Indian War veterans, men who not incidentally relied on Miller to get compensation for scrip or vouchers they held. He also collected personal letters from Obediah McFadden, James Tilton, Charles Mason, and Governor McMullin. By February 1858, Miller had sent his stack of petitions to Stevens with an appended list of his qualifications. He also had secured additional letters from Washington Territory and Illinois and had prevailed on McFadden to write directly to the attorney general of the United States on his behalf.[15] Even six months after Miller's petitions began arriving in Washington, Stevens had made little headway in separating the superintendencies, despite his promises that the separation would be a reality by the end of the congressional session and his name would be on the president's desk. Undeterred and even optimistic, although he had been told that Stevens's "influence in Indian matters will be much weakened," Miller assumed his friend could get him the prize in 1858.[16]

Congress adjourned in 1858 with the superintendencies still combined. When the new congressional session opened in January 1859, Miller received word from an associate that he had competition; other politicians in Oregon and Washington had begun to lobby Lane, hoping to get the position. "I write you this that you may know your adversaries and be on your guard," Miller's friend wrote, cautioning him: "Leave no stone unturned. . . . "[17] Stevens assured Miller that he had been trying to get the separation approved, but Nesmith had suddenly changed his mind about the division of jurisdiction and had come around to a suggestion Stevens had made two years earlier—that the superintendencies be divided at the Cascades of the Columbia, making all of eastern Washington and Oregon into a single district. But by early 1859, Nesmith's political position had deteriorated. Whatever camaraderie Lane and Nesmith had enjoyed had died in a spate of internecine disputes among Oregon Democrats that were bound up in sectional issues, Oregon's application for statehood, and Lane's ambition to become the state's first senator. In consequence, Lane and Stevens easily dismissed Nesmith's new plan, while Congress paid little attention and continued to ignore the superintendency issue altogether. The split between Nesmith and Lane gapped larger in the spring of 1859 with Nesmith's removal from office and the appointment of Edward R. Geary—a Lane loyalist—as the new superintendent of Indian affairs. Congress adjourned in 1859 with the superintendencies still joined and Miller still waiting.[18]

While he avidly pursued federal appointment, Miller served his county and party in the territorial legislature, first in the House of Representatives and then in the Council. In the 1857–1858 session, the leadership in the House assigned Miller to the Ways and Means Committee, the Committee on Public Grounds and Buildings, and the Memorials Committee, which drew up petitions to Congress. Miller did not take the lead in legislative business and introduced only a few measures during the session: a bill to incorporate the Sons of Temperance in Olympia; a bill effecting Governor McMullin's divorce; a petition from friends wishing to incorporate a coal mine on Bainbridge Island; a bill to fund construction of public buildings in Olympia; and a bill to create a "Lunatic Asylum in Washington Territory."[19]

Miller's purpose in the legislature veered away from lawmaking and toward partisan politics. A prime example was his chief sponsorship of a resolution—framed in his Memorials Committee—that defended Stevens and the Indian War volunteers. In condemning General John Wool's military policies, the resolution labeled as "false and malicious" Wool's official report on Stevens and his actions during the war. Miller also helped friends and petitioners with favors when he could, but partisan interests came first. He floor-managed the elections of Stevens's friends and former volunteer officers to territorial posts, including his own to the position of quartermaster general. Miller drove the Democratic steamroller efficiently and successfully throughout the session, flattening any opposition with nearly unanimous votes in each tabulation. Only J. D. Hinckley, a Republican from Kitsap County, spoiled it by registering protest votes for the Duke of York on one ballot and Jenny Lind on another.[20]

Foremost among Miller's partisan achievements during the House session was the selection of Edward Furste as the territorial printer. Furste had been bargaining with J. W. Wiley for purchase of the *Pioneer and Democrat,* but he had little money to invest, save what he could borrow from Miller or cajole as investment. Butler Anderson, J. Patton Anderson's brother, had his or his brother's money to invest and contested Furste for ownership, even suggesting a partnership. Furste, and probably Miller, did not want to share control with Anderson, partly because his brother had reportedly played a cagey political game with the president in 1857 over his own candidacy for territorial governor and partly because Butler Anderson's loyalties were unknown. Miller wanted a hardrock Stevens newspaper. By securing the territory's public printing for Furste, he handed a means to finance the purchase to his friend and presented a loyalist newspaper to Stevens. Miller proudly wrote Stevens: "as long as Ed [Furste] has anything to do with the 'Pioneer' your enemies will exercize no control over it."[21]

Miller continued to play a role as a Democratic wheelhorse in the legislature during the following two years, but he did it from the higher chamber, having won election from Thurston and Sawamish counties. In the Council, he sat on nearly the same committees as he had in the House and served as chair of the Ways and Means Committee and the Committee on Public Buildings. The only issue of partisan importance he managed during his two sessions on the Council concerned the effort to move the territorial capital from Olympia to Vancouver. The House had passed the measure in December 1859, sending it on to Miller's Committee on Public Buildings for Council deliberations in January. Miller and his colleagues effectively blocked Council approval through a series of procedural and substantive votes, each one winning by the slimmest of margins.[22]

Although he used his business expertise and political skills to good advantage during three legislative sessions, Miller focused his sharpest vision on the larger political landscape. In that world, he functioned superbly as a political interlocutor between the parochially ambitious territorial politicians and Delegate Stevens. His handling of Fayette McMullin, the man who replaced Stevens as governor, is a case in point. A Virginian with strong ties to the Buchanan administration, McMullin came to the territory with his own agenda, one that would not go down well with the Stevens men.

Even before McMullin arrived, Miller had received warnings from colleagues. One of them called him "that wild Virginia Gov." and advised Miller: "He will not sute the people and the people will not sute him . . . [but] you might be able to use him for a time. . . ."[23] McMullin impressed another of Miller's correspondents as "very gentlemanly and affable, but not deep." More disturbing, however, was McMullin's perspective on his new office. "He avers his intention," Miller's informant offered, "of using his influence to secure all appointments to be made to residents of the Territory." He advised,

> I would respectfully suggest; would it not be better for you to have him play second fiddle to your crowd, than let him head that small cabal of would be's as he will be unable to head a crowd of his own.[24]

The new governor's intemperate actions would threaten to unbalance the party in the territory. Throughout the months-long disquiet McMullin created, Miller focused on maintaining stability and not fostering an overreaction, the best tack he could take for the benefit of Stevens and the party.

McMullin had not been in the territory long before he had reason to confer with Miller about the status of militia and quartermaster supplies. He gave Miller his due, addressing him in an official and measured way and confirming his responsibilities and prerogatives as the manager of territorial military supplies. Miller must have been apprehensive and may have "read him," as one of his friends predicted he would, but he also hoped that some harmony might prevail among Democrats in the territory, especially in matters of patronage. He took the initiative with McMullin by agreeing to introduce a private bill during the first week of the legislative session that would grant the governor a divorce from his wife. Still, Miller withheld his opinion of McMullin. As he explained to Stevens two months later, he "wanted to know how men stood" before reporting on political conditions.[25]

By March, Miller could see the landscape clearly. The new governor had shown no interest in becoming a member of the Stevens group, and he had stridently established his own position by interfering in three high-profile patronage decisions—the reappointments of Judges Chenoweth and Lander and Territorial Secretary Charles Mason. McMullin's surreptitious support for Chenoweth and Lander, men whom Stevens had determined to cashier, alerted everyone to the governor's capacity for intrigue.[26] McMullin openly obstructed Mason's reappointment by charging him with drunkenness, provoking a strong response among Mason's friends in the territory, who gathered letters and drafted petitions in his defense. McMullin did not press his charges, but the damage was done and the decision to reappoint Mason lingered for months. It is unclear what McMullin hoped to achieve.

Miller had been right in reading the governor as an opportunist, not a political spoiler, and he correctly predicted that he would leave office as soon as he could find a better position. McMullin's coy support for Lander and Chenoweth also fizzled and Stevens prevailed in blocking their renomination, in part because Chenoweth could not protect himself. "It will be no trouble," one of Miller's friends offered, "to put spiders in his dumplins, bell him and turn him out to graze." As it turned out, McMullin left office after less than a year in Olympia. Another eastern politician, Richard Gholson of Kentucky, replaced him in 1859.[27]

Throughout McMullin's brief tenure, Miller had to contend with the sometimes swirling political winds that blew through the party, bolstering Mason while he advised Stevens on conditions in the territory and tried to maintain cordial relations with the governor.[28] He worked hard for Stevens by feeding him names of men who should be rewarded with patronage jobs. Friendship and loyalty were the important factors, but neither Miller nor Stevens generally endorsed incompetents; they preferred loyal partisans who could carry out their assigned duties. The list of suggestions in 1858 read like a partial roll call of officers in the volunteer corps—Frank Matthias, Charles Weed, A. J. Cain, Seth Catlin, C. C. Phillips—men who had proved their worth and had stood by Stevens during the martial law crisis. Miller also suggested individuals whom he guaranteed were "already Stevens men" or "your most devoted friends." He gathered information by creating a network of correspondents in the territory, some who were his closest political allies and others who reportedly controlled political opinion in their counties. From the beginning of Stevens's term as delegate, Miller worried most about defections from the ranks. The "bolters" either pursued their own or resisted Stevens's agenda. "We have glorious democrats in this county," McFadden sarcastically informed Miller in mid-1858, "men who if things do not sut [sic] their whims are willing to unite with Black Rep[ublicans] or anybody else who will aid them."[29]

Threatening to join an opposition faction, however, was rarely a matter of whim. Office-seekers who controlled some political capital themselves knew full well that such threats gave them leverage, even if their opposition was not avowedly anti-Stevens. Miller often found himself in the middle, trying to referee political disputes, to serve Stevens's interests, and avoid compromising his own political relationships. In those situations, as Stevens once bluntly instructed him, Miller had to make peace. "I have thus written very freely to you in this matter [patronage]," Stevens wrote Miller in early 1858, "and hope that the conflicting claims of our friends can be harmonized." But finding harmony was often a difficult and thankless task. By June 1858, Miller had become so exasperated by the bickering over appointments in the northern portion of the territory and so tired of salving bruised egos among office-seekers on the Cowlitz that he announced to Stevens: "But enough of this, I am tired of recommendations for office and this is the last time I shall mention this matter at least until the Legislature meets next winter."[30]

One of the thorniest appointment squabbles for Miller during Stevens's first term erupted over the reappointment of Morris H. Frost as customs collector at Port Townsend. Frost had held the post since the tragic murder of Isaac Ebey at the hands of northern Indians in 1857. A loyal Democrat and Stevens supporter, Frost had not handled his duties competently and had drawn criticism, especially from Stevens's opponents.[31] Nevertheless, Stevens had determined to get Frost and his assistant, J. J. H. Van Bokkelin, reappointed. The issue steamed and boiled for months throughout 1858 and into 1859, as complaints against Frost increased and Stevens prepared for his reelection campaign. The tempest put Miller in a most uncomfortable position. He had befriended Frost, but he had little regard for Van Bokkelin, a man who had developed a haughty reputation as a commander of volunteers during the Indian War and had openly criticized Miller's management of the quartermaster department. Miller felt coolly enough toward him to be the only Democrat in the House not to vote for Van Bokkelin in an election for a territorial office.[32]

The situation in Port Townsend bedeviled Miller. All of the players, including the officeholders' allies and detractors, whined at him about patronage on the lower Sound. Frost and Van Bokkelin had cried to him in 1857 about appointments they thought J. Patton Anderson had made inappropriately. In 1858, they complained again when Stevens supported the appointments of E. C. Fitzhugh and William Strong to the territorial court as replacements for Chenoweth and Lander. Miller dutifully relayed their critique to Stevens, knowing that he would not change his decision. Stevens replied curtly that the Port Townsend men should stop their whimpering and second-guessing, noting that everyone contributes to the cause, that "we are not all alike and should agree to differ."[33] That was magnanimous advice—rarely followed by Stevens himself—but it did little to quiet the political turmoil or to ameliorate Miller's position.

In Port Townsend, Miller had to balance his personal friendships against the interests of the party. Enoch Fowler, an aggressive and grasping businessman, agitated for a federal appointment, suggesting it as payment for his support of Stevens during the 1859 campaign. Miller disliked the pressure, but he endured it until Fowler and others tried to hound Frost out of office. Miller knew that Frost had been guilty of favoritism and other indiscretions that had exposed the whole

Stevens cadre to political attack, but he also knew that Stevens wanted to retain him in office. Despite his dislike of Van Bokkelin, Miller allied himself with the deputy collector to fend off Fowler and protect Frost. In Jefferson County, where Stevens had been on the defensive, Miller also needed as much ground support as possible for Stevens's reelection campaign. Shaw had reported that everyone knew Fowler's ambitions, predicting "the pill will not go down well," but Miller continued to worry that the dispute would sabotage Stevens's chances in the county. Miller welcomed Van Bokkelin's promise to counterattack Fowler's politicking, but his swaggering must have grated. "I have worked secretly against Fowler for a long time," Van Bokkelin wrote Miller, "[and] I am satisfied that I can carry the county [Jefferson] for Stevens against him and his money."[34] Uncomfortable alliances, Miller discovered, were often necessary to hold the center and win elections.

In 1859, the specter of Democratic defections plagued Miller, especially in King, Pierce, and Jefferson counties, where anti-Stevens sentiment had incubated and flourished since the 1856 troubles. Stevens paid more attention to politics in Washington, D.C.—and his place in the ever-shifting alliances—than he did to the territorial political landscape. In Washington Territory, he relied on Miller. Stevens "has some mistrust of your adjuncts at the center," A. J. Cain informed Miller in early May, but he explicitly trusted him to keep affairs under control. Cain added:

> If he has any regard for his political future he [Stevens] must leave himself in the hands of those who can [and] will serve the party and him regardless of personal prejudices and interests.[35]

Stevens understood Cain's point, but he often jeopardized the party's future by disregarding its best interests, while he pursued his own. He wanted "to clean out the gophers"—anti-Stevens Democrats—as much as anyone, but only as a strategy for winning elections and promoting his own ambitions.[36]

Stevens had little to fear in the 1859 campaign. The Republicans had yet to congeal their strength; and Stevens's opponent, William H. Wallace, an erstwhile Whig and proto-Republican, actually ran as an Independent, serving more as a stalking horse for the Republicans than a credible candidate. Nonetheless, Wallace attracted support from the anti-Stevens forces. Crumline La Du, a Stevens loyalist from Monticello, predicted that Wallace would "catch all of the disaffected and unite them with the Black Republican Party in order to beat Stevens but I do not think he can do it." Miller heard like warnings from an informant on the Cowlitz: "The Niggers and their friends say Wallace with the 3rd Auditors letters will knock Stevens endwise." Wallace also reportedly received aid from Territorial Justice William Strong and other high-profile politicians. But the most worrisome of his collaborators was Selucius S. Garfielde, the flamboyant orator who had jumped off the Stevens bandwagon early in the campaign, in part because he had become a Douglas Democrat and thought Stevens would lose, thereby jeopardizing his appointment at the federal land office. "If Garfielde takes the stump," Stevens pleaded with Miller, "do try to make arrangements to have him followed and meet face to face on the stump." A squad of speakers countered Garfielde's anti-Stevens propaganda, but for Miller it was his effect on the party that mattered most. His hammering away at the Indian War payment issue, the petitions he surreptitiously circulated against Stevens, and his self-promoting oratory wedged open even wider the growing split among Democrats. All of it served to diminish party regularity.[37]

Stevens took nothing for granted and energetically canvassed the territory. In Vancouver, one of Miller's informants reported that he "floored his opponent on every point." He held sway in Walla Walla, with two of his volunteer officers working hard for him in the county, and his allies in Cowlitz, Pacific, Lewis, and Thurston counties attended rallies and wrote enthusiastic letters to the *Pioneer and Democrat*. To the charges that Stevens had done little for the territory, especially on the issue of the Indian War payments, Miller countered by circulating an open letter from Oregon Territorial Delegate Joseph Lane that lauded Stevens as the "most indefatigable of all the senators and representatives in Congress," the "best working man that I ever knew . . . all the time on duty, [and] seems never to tire or let up." On the stump,

Stevens avoided his record and challenged Wallace to take positions on national issues, while the *Pioneer and Democrat* criticized Wallace's politics and his "Independent" status.[38]

Stevens won all but four counties. Wallace took King, Pierce, Kitsap, and Jefferson, despite Van Bokkelin's promise to deliver that county. Stevens had overcome the Republicans and the "pizerinctum politicians" who had discharged their loyalties to the party and bet against his election. "We have met the enemy," B. F. Shaw reported from Whatcom, "and they are ours." It had been a grand victory and Miller had helped mightily in holding the center. But the glory truly belonged to Stevens, whose broad appeal, especially among those who honored his leadership during the Indian War, had guaranteed his success. Even those who had reason to withhold their support fell into line as the polling began. As one of Miller's men on the Cowlitz commented late in June, "I shall work for Stevens this time though he treated me like a d—d Indian three years ago."[39]

After the election, Miller continued his management of Stevens's political affairs in the territory. The political foot soldiers who had worked the hustings petitioned him for benefits and favors, and he obliged when he could by finding territorial jobs or recommending them for federal appointments.[40] For his own part, Miller continued to pursue the superintendency of Indian affairs. By the summer of 1859, he was collecting petitions for another round of politicking the federal administration. Cain had reported that politicians in Portland thought that the congressional investigator, Christopher Mott, would recommend splitting the superintendency into three districts: one covering everything east of the Cascades and one each for western Washington and western Oregon. Miller, it seemed, would be assured of getting the western Washington district. But Cain also warned Miller in August that he suspected "some unfair play with some of the Oregon politicians which the Gov. [Stevens] is not aware of . . . that Oregon may have both."[41]

Anteroom political maneuvering may have compromised Stevens's abilities to split the superintendency and get the appointment for Miller, but dramatic changes in national politics probably had as much or more effect. As early as 1858, when Miller had first made a pitch for the office, his friends in Illinois had cautioned him about his pro-Buchanan stance in the territory. They had helped Miller get Stephen A. Douglas's endorsement, but Douglas had split with the Buchanan administration over the slavery issue. Not only had Douglas's endorsement been diminished, but it was also difficult for him to continue his support for Miller.[42] Agitation over the slavery issue had, at least in part, prompted the defections of Selucius Garfielde and Butler Anderson from the Stevens Democrats. Garfielde and Anderson, who called the Stevens group a "sham democratic organization," were Douglas Democrats, politicos who criticized the Dred Scott Supreme Court decision of 1857, applauded Douglas's "Freeport Doctrine," and supported the doctrine of popular sovereignty in Kansas.[43]

Although many wished they could, politicians in Washington Territory could neither ignore nor avoid the divisive national issues that threatened the Democratic party and the Union in 1860. The slavery issue split Democrats in both Oregon and Washington, one faction pledged to Douglas and the principle of popular sovereignty, the other to Buchanan and a sympathetic hearing for southern complaints. Stevens moved away from the Douglas group and toward a national faction that had begun to tout Joe Lane for president. Miller followed, evidently both out of loyalty and a belief that political compromise, not the advocacy of abolition or slaveholding, should be the litmus test for the presidency in 1860. But Miller also held pro-slavery views. One of his Illinois friends had written in 1858, expressing surprise at his viewpoint. "By the way," he wrote, "it seems to me that you are in the wrong latitude to be ultra proslavery. I should think that it was dangerous ground for a public man to occupy, at least it is so with us."[44]

Miller perceived danger, but not because of the political position he or other Buchanan Democrats had taken on slavery. The danger was in the destruction of the Democratic party in the territory and Stevens losing his influence in Washington, D.C. In April, at the Democratic National Convention in Charleston, South Carolina, the destruction Miller had feared began. Southern delegations stormed out of the convention on the second day, leaving the northern and western delegates to patch together a platform and select a nominee. Stevens, who had gone to the convention with Joe Lane's personal proxy as a member of the Oregon delegation, stepped forward to champion Lane as a compromise candidate.[45] Despite Stevens's politicking, Lane drew few votes, but still enough to block Douglas's nomination. After more than fifty ballots and much rancor, the Douglas men realized they could not succeed, so they muscled through an adjournment and a re-convening of the convention several weeks later in Baltimore. The party had come apart at the seams. "We are in a mess," Lane wrote confidant Matthew Deady in Portland, "and I can hardly see how we can get out with whole bones, but we will see."[46]

At the Baltimore convention, Lane's fears were confirmed. The two sides had become more resolute, with even less chance for agreement. Stevens and the Oregon delegation continued to defend states' rights, thereby aligning themselves with the southern states. The Douglas delegations remained firmly against seating the original delegations, including those who had withdrawn from the Charleston convention. Rather than approve, Stevens came to the floor, telling the delegates that Oregon had "resolved to stand by [the states] and assert their rights . . . [and] have come to the conclusion to withdraw from the deliberations and take no further part in them."[47]

Joining with members of the Virginia, California, North Carolina, Tennessee, and Maryland delegations, the Oregonians met in a nearby hall and formed the National Democratic Convention. They nominated John C. Breckinridge of Kentucky for president and Joseph Lane for vice-president on a states' rights platform that emphasized non-intervention on the slavery question. Meanwhile, the regular Democrats had overwhelmingly nominated Douglas for president on a platform of popular sovereignty. Isaac Stevens accepted the chairmanship of the National Democratic Executive Committee, pledging to work tirelessly for Breckinridge and Lane. Within days, he had written to Olympia to enlist Miller's participation. "I hope our people," Stevens wrote, "will stand by Breckinridge and Lane."[48]

The 1860 campaign was like no other in American history. A sense of crisis permeated the political canvassing throughout the nation. Besides the two major candidates, Lincoln the Republican and Douglas the Democrat, voters could also choose Breckinridge representing the National Democrats or John Bell of the Constitutional Union Party, formed by former Whigs who could find no home in the fray over slavery. In Oregon and Washington, the political fracturing encouraged fusions between Republicans and Douglas Democrats, including Michael T. Simmons and Selucius Garfielde in Washington. Miller could do little, although he lent his influence in the territorial Council to moderate the Democratic split. Still, the leader of the territorial Democratic party had decided to stake his political future on the Breckinridge-Lane candidacy. "Some of our friends may doubt the policy and the course I have taken," Stevens confided in Miller, but he promised rewards.

> I shall have an influence in Congress the next session second to no man in either branch, if Breck & Lane be elected and hardly second to any man, if they be defeated. It is now recognized that I have power and ability. I showed it in the conventions, where I had a vote equally with the other delegates. . . . I was surprised to find how rapidly my influence increased from day to day.[49]

Isaac Stevens's political kite had flown high during the conventions, making him even more enamored of his political future. But for Miller and the Democrats in Washington Territory his success became a mixed blessing. They were the tail to his kite, and flight put them all in jeopardy of the whirlwinds spun by the 1860 campaign. The first problems came from Stevens men who complained to Miller that the delegate no longer kept in close touch with them, that he had in effect abandoned the territory in service of the Breckinridge campaign. O. B. McFadden, sarcastically commenting on Stevens's preoccupation with the National campaign, wrote to Miller: "Strange that there is no news from Washington. I never hear from Stevens anymore." To these complaints, Stevens protested. "If my friends complain that I do not write," he wrote Miller, "tell them I am not idle a moment."[50]

No one doubted that Stevens was busy; the issue was whose business he was tending. E. C. Fitzhugh, writing from Washington, D.C., informed Miller that Stevens had let several bills important to the territory "lie over amongst the unfinished business of the session," while he "was off attending a convention in Baltimore" instead of "keeping aloof from general politics."[51] Worse, though, was the old canard about his drinking habits. Miller had heard the charges before, but they had come from opponents, not from Stevens loyalists. In late 1859, A. J. Cain had informed Miller that Stevens had acquired a reputation as a drinker in Washington, D.C., but Cain discounted the rumors. Fitzhugh's account, however, came from a long-time Stevens ally. "As we feared," Fitzhugh wrote Miller,

> Stevens has been drinking ever since his return and chooses the most inopportune times to get drunk . . . [and] ought to be kept out of all conventions. He is too conceited (very much changed) that he does not think he can do anything wrong.

More chillingly, Fitzhugh wondered whether Stevens could do his work. "I really do not think, Miller," Fitzhugh commented, "that he will have another year—he looks wretchedly."[52]

Throughout 1860, Miller's position became more and more difficult. In the territory, he could not heal the widening split among Breckinridge and Douglas Democrats. The anti-Stevens men hammered away at the delegate's prominent role in the Breckinridge campaign, while Miller tried to give Stevens advice on patronage. During the campaign, Stevens loyalists demanded the removal of Michael T. Simmons as Indian agent and Selucius Garfielde as receiver at the federal land office. They charged Simmons with aiding Republicans in the previous election and Garfielde with being a traitor to democracy. Garfielde was castigated as a man "faithful to the disorganizing doctrines of Mr. Douglas," one in "whom innate hatred of everything within the pale of the democratic organization is instinctive."[53] Miller had urged Stevens to take swift action against Garfielde, which he did in January, but Garfielde's Kentucky Democrat friends had blocked the action, requesting that he be given a chance to respond. Stevens wrote Miller: "I want you quickly to get some evidence showing clearly the course that Garfielde took. It has been made an issue by the Kentucky delegation."[54]

On the other side of patronage, Miller sent Stevens a steady stream of names for federal appointments in the territory. Chief among them was Charley Phillips, one of Miller's business associates and debtors. Miller wanted to see Phillips installed as customs collector at Port Townsend, the position that had caused so much trouble during the 1859 campaign. Stressing his associate's loyalty, Miller advised Stevens: "Now Phillips is your friend over all other men in this Territory. He is a man that other men can't control or brow-beat and he always stands up for you."[55] Knowing the criticism that foes had hurled in Stevens's direction in 1860, Miller told him to take care of his friends. "Having an eye to your interest," Miller advised Stevens, he should take care of his friends promptly and well; he would need them at election time in 1861.

Stevens listened to Miller and appointed Phillips and several other Miller-approved men to posts in the territory.[56] But when it came to Miller's own pursuit of the Indian superintendency, Stevens stumbled. He had forwarded the petitions Miller had gathered to the secretary of the interior, but his influence with the bureaucracy seemed to fail him. During the spring of 1860, Stevens promised Miller again and again that his commission was imminent—"should be mailed today" (March 2); there will be no "trouble about your appointment" (March 18); the appointment "is on its way" (April 2)—but no documents arrived. Stevens blamed meddling politicians, the unresolved Indian War debt question, and unspecified distractions for his failure. Finally, on June 4, he admitted to Miller that the Indian Department would take no action on splitting the superintendency.[57]

Miller may have wondered if Cain's evaluation the previous August had been accurate, that Stevens overestimated his standing among politicians, especially in the bureaucracy. In this charged atmosphere, it is not surprising that Miller became suspicious, perhaps even wondering whether Stevens had also put him on the shelf in the heat of the Breckinridge effort. While Stevens had kept encouraging Miller to wave the Breckinridge-Lane banner, Fitzhugh had fed Miller news about Stevens's decisions on the superintendency and appointments, including information that Stevens had withdrawn Miller's name for another federal position.[58] This news so upset Miller that he fired off a letter to Stevens, charging him with at least insensitivity and perhaps capriciousness. "I am sorry you mentioned my name in conversation about Simmons' position," Miller heatedly wrote. "I do not want it. As my name went to the Senate for the position of Receiver and then was withdrawn I do not wish it to be used again in connection with any position." Then he added with foretold effect:

> I do not complain, I only think you will find yourself mistaken as to my popularity. I will leave the Council next summer more popular than when I entered it.[59]

As soon as Stevens received Miller's letter he responded, hurt by his friend's obvious lack of faith in him and baffled by the charges. He denied the story about submitting Miller's name and withdrawing it or that it had anything to do with his failure to secure the superintendency for Miller. In anger and confusion, Stevens wrote:

> I grieve . . . knowing as I do that the most perfect good face and the warmest friendship towards you has governed me, and I am entirely in the dark as to who has done me the foul injury. . . . Who is the maligner of character? Who dares come between two friends to sew discord and enmity?[60]

The maligner, no doubt, was Fitzhugh, who had openly suggested to friends that he wanted to secure the delegateship for himself in 1861. In fact, Miller had suggested to Stevens in October, as the national election neared, that Fitzhugh would be the best choice if Stevens decided not to run for reelection. Miller reminded Stevens that Fitzhugh "has stood by you like a man," calling him "a true friend and an upright man." But Fitzhugh turned out to be a dissembler and manipulator. Probably unknown to Miller, it had been Fitzhugh who had tried to block the appointment of Charley Phillips. Evidently, he also made up out of whole cloth the business about Miller's name being submitted for appointment and then withdrawn. Even without

Fitzhugh's machinations, however, Miller had good reason to be upset with Stevens. The Breckinridge campaign had put additional stress on Miller. He had single-handedly kept Edward Furste financially afloat at the *Pioneer and Democrat* because, as he explained to Stevens, Furste had given "unflinching support of you [Stevens]" and he had held firm in promoting the Breckinridge candidacy.[61] From Miller's viewpoint, Stevens had not appreciated Furste's efforts and actually criticized him for not doing enough personally to promote the Breckinridge campaign.[62]

In ill health and battered by the demands of the campaign, Furste had been forced to sell the paper to James Lodge, in association with James Tilton. The paper's new owners, who realized how unpredictable the 1860 election had become, declined to support Breckinridge or Douglas. Miller wrote to Stevens apologetically about this, but he made it clear "it has taken a load off my shoulders." He had done his service for Stevens but had yet to be compensated. Stevens finally succeeded in getting the superintendency bill passed on the last day of Congress, but by then there had been injured feelings, intemperate letters, and confusion in the minds of both politicians. For his own part, Miller had not been entirely forthcoming with Stevens about other issues of mutual interest. Although there is no evidence that Stevens knew, throughout the spring of 1860 Miller had been engaged in financial schemes with Stevens's old enemy, Francis Chenoweth. If Fitzhugh or someone else who might gain by splitting Miller and Stevens had told the delegate, it could explain some of Stevens's actions.[63]

Regardless of their mutual uneasiness, Miller and Stevens faced a new political landscape on November 5, 1860. The nation's voters chose Abraham Lincoln as president and ushered in a new and traumatic period in the nation's history. "The mail is in and nothing new from the states," Miller wrote O. B. McFadden.

"Honest Abe" Lincoln seems to have it all his way, and us locofocos had as well "hang our harps on a willow tree" and in case we can't find a willow tree quite convenient hang them on a fir tree'—anything to get them hung.

The advent of a Republican administration meant that patronage would be in the hands of the opposition, even if Washington Territory managed to send a Democrat to Congress in 1861. For the Stevens crowd, it meant the abrupt end of the political gravy line. "As far as our being routed horse, foot and dragoon, that is no more than I expected," B. F. Shaw wrote to Miller, adding,

> as for Isaac telling us to be of good cheer, I say with you Isaac be damned. . . . He has his head under water but his arse has drawn in full view ever since the canvass commenced. Isaac has damned himself and I fear that he has damned the rest of us with him, but I hope not.[64]

If Miller felt betrayed or disgusted with politics, he kept it to himself, but he agreed with at least part of Shaw's sentiment. He had extended himself for Isaac Stevens and followed him into the Breckinridge campaign, and it was unlikely he would do it again. And he may well have taken to heart Shaw's advice "to tend to our own business and be out of temptation's way."[65]

CHAPTER 7

In the Mazy Labyrinth

It soon becomes obvious that politics is the main pursuit of the population.

Francis Henry, "Notes Washington," 1862

Politics is a mazy labyrinth.

S. B. Curtis to Miller, February 18, 1860

In mid-November 1860, as election reports filtered in to Washington Territory, Miller and his Democratic allies squarely faced up to the capriciousness of politics. Eight years earlier, a change in national administrations had spun Miller's political world. Abraham Lincoln's victory threatened the same consequence. The patronage-fueled political ship Miller and other Stevens men in the territory commanded was suddenly imperiled. In 1853, Miller had responded to that earlier political sea change by abandoning a leaky Whig vessel. This time, he pledged to stay with the Democratic ship and help keep it afloat. Writing to Stevens, Miller put it succinctly:

It seems Lincoln will be elected beyond the possibility of a doubt, and us poor Locofocos will have to take the back seat for the next four years. But we must keep up the Organization of the Democratic Party and fight on and fight always.[1]

136

During the winter of 1860–1861, as Miller assured Stevens that "we shall do all we can to harmonize the party," the focus among the territory's Democrats was Isaac Stevens's candidacy for reelection as territorial delegate. Miller and his cohorts knew that maintaining some friendly representation in Washington, D.C., could limit the damage the new administration might wreak on their political fortunes. But no one could be certain that Stevens would run for reelection, and some even questioned whether he would be the best candidate. Residual complaints from the failed Breckinridge campaign still rankled some Stevens loyalists, and the Douglas men could hardly stand the thought of Stevens as the party's candidate. So the spring election season began with uncertainty. Nonetheless, while Miller admitted to Stevens that "a few faint-hearted Democrats" would probably join the opposition, he assured him that renomination was a near certainty.[2]

Not unlike a few of his closest political friends, however, Miller had become privately ambivalent about Stevens. Part of his ambivalence derived from the 1860 campaign and Stevens's near abandonment of the party's interests in the territory. But Miller also felt the sting of complaints from some of his political allies, who peppered him with questions about Stevens's apparent rejection of them. Miller's pledge to Stevens, then, to "fight on and fight always," was also a caveat. The delegate had better evince service to the party and its foot soldiers, Miller seemed to warn, or he could forget about renomination. It is unclear how much Stevens knew about Miller's "coolness" toward his candidacy, as one politico characterized it. He probably had heard rumors that Miller was preparing to support someone else, but apparently he ignored them. Rumors of that sort flew in flocks during election seasons. Stevens continued to rely on Miller's advice and to confide in him as the campaign season approached.[3]

In responding to Miller's queries about his political intentions, Stevens stated forthrightly that the sole question should be "who will best advance the interests of the Territory at Washington?" In a *mea culpa* of sorts, and perhaps anticipating Miller's support, he admitted his vulnerability on the war debt issue, a political debit that had plagued him for several years:

I know our people have a right to expect action this session. I cannot complain, should they ascribe non-action on the part of Congress to my want of efficiency.[4]

His "want of efficiency" had become an issue, not incidentally, with Miller himself. Stevens had not yet made good on his promise to separate the Indian superintendencies in Oregon and Washington and hand the Washington office to Miller.

With Congress in a "lame duck" session, Miller worried that the superintendency question would never make it to the floor for consideration. But Stevens faced additional political pressures in 1861. Like others in Congress, he fretted and shuddered at what seemed inevitable—the dissolution of the Union. Writing ominously to Miller about the impending crisis, Stevens labeled it "history," a reality, with the only hope vested in a general convention of the states. "The only chance now is reconstruction," he wrote Miller in late January, predicting "this will not be possible, if collision occurs."[5]

Miller was unsure what to think about Stevens's activities and his political interests. Miller's friends in Olympia suspected that Stevens had abandoned him on the superintendency issue, but he had Stevens's assurance that all was in order, that the post would be his. Edward Furste, former editor of the *Pioneer and Democrat,* informed Miller in late February that Stevens had rebuffed several petitioners and treated them shabbily. "I have always been loath to believe poorly of Gov. S.," Furste confided to Miller, "but I confess now that my opinion of him is materially changed." Furste added that other former Stevens men thought that perhaps he deserved to fall. But what most disturbed Miller was Furste's conclusion: "I am now satisfied that Stevens lied to you in his letters from beginning to end."[6]

What had Stevens done about the superintendency? How honest had he been with Miller? In mid-February 1861, Stevens had assured Miller that the bill splitting the superintendencies had been approved and he had submitted Miller's name to President Buchanan. Miller had heard such promises too often before, and he had received no official word on his appointment. Early the next month and after he had heard about Furste's charges, Stevens wrote again to reassure Miller:

> I know you will be entirely satisfied with my course towards you personally, when you learn the facts. . . . I shall satisfy you that there was no intend to do you wrong, but on the contrary that I acted the part of a friend. . . . You will receive your appointment as Supt. of Ind. Aff. by the time this letter reaches you.[7]

The breach between the two men, however large it might have become, narrowed when Miller received word of his appointment in mid-March. By early April, Miller had begun actively championing Stevens's candidacy, and Stevens was soon in the territory, ready to begin his canvass.[8] Early on, it became apparent that Stevens would face a challenge in most county conventions. Columbia Lancaster, the territory's first delegate, Judge William Strong, and Lloyd Brook had also thrown their hats in the ring, suggesting that at the least Stevens would have to offer them something to get them to withdraw. Although Miller had received some encouraging news from a couple of counties, he also had reports that some of Stevens's steadfast supporters had begun to distance themselves from his candidacy. Miller urged Stevens to visit each county and not to take anything for granted, and he agreed to go to up the Columbia River, delivering speeches at Vancouver, Skamania, and Walla Walla. "I noted your particular reference to the lukewarmness of friends," Stevens wrote Miller. "I know several of these are doing all they can to defeat my nomination . . . [but] they knowingly exaggerate the opposition to me."[9]

The opposition focused more and more on the national crisis and the perception that Stevens had honored the Union more in the breach than the reality by supporting Breckinridge. Before the outbreak of hostilities at Fort Sumter, the territorial Democrats had forthrightly proclaimed defense of the Union as their principal article of faith in January. By March, many leading Democrats, including Miller and Judge Obediah McFadden, had joined a nonpartisan group advocating resistance to secession and preservation of the Union. Stevens was no less dedicated to the Union, but his belief in a singular and united Democratic policy as the only solution to the national issue put him at odds with Douglas followers, who could not accept the legitimacy of the Dred Scott decision. "I am a Democrat of the Dred Scott school," Stevens told Miller, an opinion that put him on the other side of a political division among Democrats. The Republicans, sensing Stevens's weakness on the issue of Union, castigated him for suggesting that the Republicans should be held responsible for disunion, that no action was better than enforcement of Union prerogatives, and that fighting a war to defeat secession would be disastrous.[10]

More damaging within the Democratic fold, however, was Stevens's continued failure to mend political fences. It likely cost him the nomination. Benjamin Shaw howled at Miller that Stevens had treated him as if he were a "clodhopper," forgetting his earlier efforts on his behalf. It was Shaw, after all, who had enforced the governor's martial law ordinance and found himself clapped into jail by Judge Lander. What angered Shaw was not being told that Stevens had even entered the race for renomination. He had been entirely cut out of the process. Referring to his own offer to aid Stevens, Shaw commented:

> Proffered services sometimes stink—and to tell you the truth I was in the same fix you said you were when the fellow got his wife fucked, if he could stand it you could, so I thought if Stevens could stand it to have such advisors. . . . Why could he [Stevens] not write to me that he was a candidate and tell me what claims he had on the people for support so that I could have had something to work from?[11]

Miller could hardly answer Shaw's complaint or explain Stevens's actions. One week earlier he had received a letter from Stevens asking what was going on in Whatcom, where Shaw lived. "How is Shaw?" Stevens queried Miller, meaning "how does he stand? and what is he doing for me?" Miller stood in the middle. He realized that Shaw felt Stevens was ungrateful, but he also knew that Stevens honestly had been unable to maintain contact with all of his political allies in the territory. Miller again remained neutral, as he had in the disagreements over M. H. Frost's position at Port Townsend, pledging to aid Stevens in his bid for renomination while maintaining his ties with Shaw, a confidant and business partner.[12]

At the territorial convention in Vancouver, the Stevens opponents (mostly Douglas men) scored a major victory during the opening day when the chairman—the contentious J. J. Van Bokkelin—ruled against the admission of proxies, which crippled the Stevens effort. The convention soon devolved into a series of tactical battles between the two factions, with the anti-Stevens men holding the numerical edge, the chairmanship, and control of the rules. After losing two rounds, some Stevens men walked out of the proceedings, forcing Stevens to make the best choice available to him. He withdrew his name from nomination in the interests of party harmony. But harmony did not come, for the two factions continued on separate tracks, the regular Democrats nominating Selucius Garfielde and most of the Stevens men lining up behind Edward Lander.[13]

Stevens had decided to duck the political brickbats and chose the danger of the battlefield instead. Although he had been critical of the Lincoln administration's unyielding posture toward the secessionists, once shots had been fired at Fort Sumter he made his decision. In June, even before the Vancouver convention met, Stevens offered his services to the Union army. The campaign took on a different cast, and it played out differently without him. Garfielde and Lander seemed to contest each other as much as they battled against Republican nominee William H. Wallace. With Garfielde and Lander splitting the Democratic vote—Garfielde polling nearly twice as many as Lander—Wallace claimed the victory with only 43 percent of the vote.[14]

Miller and other Stevens men had been left with poor choices. Garfielde was anathema to most because of his opportunistic embrace of the Douglas supporters and his abandonment of Stevens in 1859. One Miller loyalist in Pierce County charged Garfielde with being "as treacherous as the devil [who] will stoop to anything to accomplish his ends." Lander had been one of Stevens's principal adversaries in the martial law flap in 1856 and had become an ally of James Tilton, an early critic of Stevens's performance as territorial delegate. By mid-

April, before Stevens withdrew from the race, he had become convinced that Tilton had made the *Pioneer and Democrat* "hostile root and branch" toward his candidacy. By late May, Stevens wrote Miller that the paper "must cease to be regarded as the organ of the Democracy. It has been and is simply the Tilton organ." Nonetheless, Lander's precise role in the political machinations in 1861, whether as a Tilton ally or an independent actor, is unclear. Staunch Republican Unionist Elwood Evans, for example, considered him one of the "avowed secessionists" among territorial politicians—a group that also included Butler P. Anderson, James Tilton, and C. H. Armstrong—but Tilton and Lander had mutually pledged their full support to the Union before the firing on Fort Sumter and staunchly maintained their support of the war effort throughout the campaign. It is more likely that Lander was the best known and ablest of available candidates, and he was opportunistic enough to accept the nomination from the Stevens men.[15]

Further complicating Miller's position was his personal relationship with Lander. He had been friends with Lander since 1852, when he first lent him money and socialized with him in the company of Isaac Ebey and others in Olympia. Both men had sat on the board of trustees of the Puget Sound Wesleyan Institute in 1856, and they had helped organize a local investor group for the Northern Pacific Railroad in 1857. By 1860, Lander had twice defaulted on loans to Miller, further complicating their relationship.[16] In the waning weeks of the campaign, Lander wrote to Miller, with the obvious knowledge of the uneasy positions they held:

> Of course, I do not expect you to vote for me, but there are many men who a word from you would have a great effect with and to whom that word or even a hint might be given.

Regardless of the complications, it would seem, Miller's endorsement was worth extra blandishments. Evidently, Lander's plea had little effect on Miller: there is no evidence that he obliged him, and in fact he may have voted for Garfielde.[17]

Despite the outcome of the election, Miller had a new job, one that for at least a time would make him the most important Democratic dispenser of patronage in the territory. As superintendent of Indian affairs, he had power to appoint agents, sub-agents, and clerks, plus enter into contracts for a range of services to the reservations. Miller knew his tenure would be brief. He had not sent in his official bond for the office until a month after Lincoln's administration had taken charge in Washington, and it was unlikely that the Republicans would reappoint him. "The hungry wolves," John Mullan warned Miller, "are after your place."[18] With the tenuousness of his position in mind, Miller acted swiftly to appoint friends to Indian Service positions. He rewarded former volunteer corps members Wesley B. Gosnell, B. F. Shaw, C. C. Paggett, and George Paige with agency positions at Nisqually, Tulalip, and Port Madison. Political confidant A. J. Cain served on the Nez Perce Reservation, and John Owen, who had been a strong Stevens man in the Bitterroot Valley, became agent to the Flatheads. Miller also rewarded political allies H. A. Goldsborough and L. D. Durgin with clerkships in Olympia and rented office space from another political associate, O. B. McFadden.[19]

As beneficial in patronage as his position might have first seemed, Miller's tenure as superintendent left him nearly as frustrated as he had been with Congress's dalliance over his appointment. Although he had received notice of his appointment in late February, as late as mid-May he still did not have the official records, account books, forms, and other paraphernalia of office. He complained to the commissioner of Indian affairs, but the former superintendent, Edward R. Geary, refused to release the records until all of Miller's paperwork had been approved in Washington. The governmental wheels ground slowly, while Simeon Francis, David Logan, and other Oregon Republicans tried to stall the transfer of office, assuming that Lincoln would soon replace Miller and leave the position open for local Republican patronage.[20] As late as August, Geary still had not transferred all of the funds, leaving Miller unable to pay some personnel and several contractors who supplied the reservations. When at last he received the appropriated funds, the commissioner notified him that President Lincoln had appointed Bion F. Kendall to his post.[21]

Miller had served less than six months as superintendent, most of it under duress and with little political or monetary return. By fall, Miller must have wondered about the supposed fortunes of officehold-ing. He was pestered by contractors and employees who could not get payment from the new superintendent and was pulled into a political stewpot because Kendall's policies created such an uproar among both Republicans and Democrats. Kendall refused to pay vouchers Miller had approved, charging that they were excessive, which put Miller and his associates on the defensive. Even the Republicans, as Shaw reported to Miller, "would rather see you keep it [the superintendency] and let them go. They will break the back of the elephant before long."[22] At least one Republican, Arthur Denny, lobbied the Lincoln administra-tion to retain Miller as superintendent, and Elwood Evans openly attacked Kendall as a "poltroon," a "man who has no soul, who is as sordid as self can make him." The Republican complaints fatally imperilled Kendall. His transgressions, including the sacking of James H. Wilbur, a popular and politically important Methodist minister who served as agent at the Yakima Indian Reservation, created an instant opposition that included nearly all the Methodists and Anson G. Henry, a close friend of President Lincoln and new surveyor general for Ore-gon. Kendall fought back, but he was forced out in early 1862, with the superintendency's accounts in some disarray. As one of his protectors, James Nesmith, informed him: "I made the best defence in my power, but had nothing positive to submit to contradict their statements."[23]

Regardless of Kendall's failures, Miller could not have expected the Republicans to put him back in office, and there is no evidence that he lobbied again for the job. By the fall of 1861, Miller looked ahead to a dim political future with few prospects. He had maintained his correspondence with the Civil War–bound Stevens, in contradiction to the rumors of a complete split between the two men, but he could see little for himself in Washington Territory. The Republicans had grabbed control of territorial patronage, and he had little or no influ-ence with William H. Wallace, Washington's territorial delegate.

Although he and a few other men had applied for a mail route on Puget Sound, he was not optimistic when he wrote Stevens in October, "I shall leave here for the states in the spring if nothing turns up to keep me here." In a hopeful tone, he added:

> I would like very well to be a paymaster or a Quartermaster in Uncle Abe's Army if he would have a place of that kind [for] a Democrat like me.[24]

Despite his business success in the territory, Miller wanted to acquire a government position, not only for its political and economic benefits but also as a contribution to the war effort. Like nearly every other politician after the war began, Miller measured politics and his political position against the question of disunion. Although some Democrats had found it impossible to join with Republicans in embracing the war and blocked passage of Union resolutions in the territorial legislature, Miller kept his distance from these opinions. He resisted the formation of a Democratic "peace party," which would agitate against pursuing the war against the Confederacy, and steadfastly argued, "That will never do. Patriotism and policy both forbid it. To go for a dishonorable peace is no better than to be an open secessionist."[25]

He remained a loyal Union man throughout the war. In the territory, he helped organize a chapter of the United States Sanitary Commission, a non-military support organization for the Union army, and he served as its permanent treasurer until 1865. By 1864, he had become a national associate member of the commission, in part a testament to the thousands of dollars he had collected in Washington and Oregon. He had also aided in the direct recruitment of a volunteer regiment to fight in the war, even though he found himself trying to organize a resistant population dominated by anti-war Democrats—his own political comrades.[26]

The most significant political change for Miller during the war years was the loss of his direct line to the territorial delegate. Although Stevens made an effort to remain involved in territorial politics during the early months of his service in the Union army, the two men's connection suffered from the twin casualties of distance and the war.

Stevens wrote Miller on a variety of political topics and answered his friend's questions, but the partnership had become crippled. At one point, Stevens responded favorably to Miller's suggestion that he help re-establish a reinvigorated *Pioneer and Democrat* to maintain a strong Democratic presence in the territory. But Stevens could not bring himself to back Edward Furste as editor. Furste had injured Stevens; and as long as Furste believed the stories told by men who Stevens dubbed his "pretended friends," Stevens would have nothing to do with the scheme. More significant to Miller's connection with Stevens, however, was the war itself. Most of Stevens's correspondence with Miller reflected his primary concerns—war plans, strategies, and battles.[27]

What might have developed between the two men became moot in September 1862 when a Confederate bullet ended Stevens's life on the battlefield at Chantilly. The Civil War had reached across the continent to inflict a personal and unexpected penalty on the territory. During the days of mourning that followed, Miller kept his personal reaction to Stevens's death to himself, but he immediately offered his services to Mrs. Stevens and her son Hazard, who had been severely wounded in the battle that had taken his father. During the decade following Stevens's death, Miller served as executor of the fallen governor's estate, counseled the family on financial matters, and advised Hazard Stevens on territorial political affairs.

Miller never developed another political partnership like the one he had enjoyed with Isaac Stevens. No doubt, that was due in part to the unique experiences the two men shared, but it was also unlikely that he would ever again bind himself so closely to any politician. He had vowed with B. F. Shaw to avoid making that mistake again. Regardless of his innermost and guileless feelings about Stevens, it was also true that Miller would probably not meet another quite like him, a politician his biographer calls a "young man in a hurry." The political aggressiveness that had practically defined Stevens was not to be found in his successors. Richard Gholson, Stevens's replacement as governor, had been a Buchanan favorite and was appointed in 1859 over the complaints of the Stevens crowd, who preferred Acting Governor Charles Mason. Miller had relatively little to do with Gholson, preferring to deal directly with Washington, D.C., through Stevens. Gholson remained on the outside of the Stevens coterie throughout his tenure.[28]

Abraham Lincoln's appointment was William Pickering, a steadfast party man in his mid-sixties who had been a politician in Illinois for forty years and had known Lincoln since 1836 when both voted Whig. Pickering would serve as Washington's governor throughout the war years. He did not arrive in Olympia until June 1862, months after newly appointed Territorial Secretary L. Jay S. Turney. Standing in as acting governor and introducing Olympians to the new Republican order, Turney got along surprisingly well with some Democrats. O. B. McFadden, for example, seemed pleased, writing to Miller that he had "all confidence in Secy Turney," even though he feared the "balance of the D____d crowd," referring to other Republican officeholders. McFadden predicted "there will be 'shenanigans,'" advising Miller to "keep your eyes open." It quickly became apparent to Miller and other Democrats, however, that the new governor was the man to keep under surveillance. Pickering expected to be more than a political caretaker; he planned to transform the territory into a Republican stronghold.[29]

After two months in Olympia, however, Pickering realized that the political conditions were less than ideal. Writing a confidant in July, he complained that Turney was only passing as a Republican. He was "as contrary as any Democrat can be" and far too cozy with the opposition. "I think his having been the Acting Governor from the time he came here until my arrival," Pickering suggested, "has spoiled him." Pickering reported to Lincoln that Turney had "wilfully and designedly quarrelled with every Republican office holder." Despite his warnings, as Pickering colorfully put it, Turney had "returned again like the Dog to his vomit," helping Democrats he favored. Pickering concluded that Turney was unfit for office and urged Lincoln to remove him. The new governor had been right about Turney, but Turney may have better understood that befriending well-placed Democrats, such as McFadden and Miller, was a faster road to individual political gain than extreme partisanship. He had helped elect McFadden to the Council in 1863, for example, and had also tried to acquire Miller's aid in his own pursuit of the delegate's spot, promising Miller: "If you do it, I shall not forget your course and you shall not regret it."[30]

In some ways, Turney and Pickering were no different than the Democrats who had preceded them. Turney seemed bent on pursuing his own interests regardless of partisan concerns, while Pickering focused on building a tightly managed political organization. And like the Democrats, the Republicans had their own difficulties administering patronage. As a result, cross-partisan coalitions developed in Washington Territory during the Civil War that reflected both the politically disruptive effects of the war and the common pursuit of gain that all territorial politicians seemed to chase.

Miller operated confidently and adroitly in Washington Territory's tenuously balanced wartime political arena, but he acted no differently than other politicians. What did make him different from the others was his political personality, not his politics. His briefly held interest in an army paymaster or quartermaster position in 1862, for example, reflected his continuing loyalties to Stevens as much as his own pursuit of gain and preference. With Stevens's death, Miller's interest and opportunities in the army evaporated. Within months, he had gravitated to another friend, one who had landed a federal appointment in the Republican administration. His long-time Olympia compatriot and sometimes business partner, H. A. Goldsborough, had become collector of internal revenue for the territory, a position he had received through family and personal connections with Secretary of the Treasury Salmon P. Chase. Goldsborough favored Miller by appointing him his deputy collector in January 1863. Under the new income tax law, which Congress had passed in 1861 and put into effect during the summer of 1862, citizens were liable for a two-step, graduated tax set at 3 percent on all incomes between $600 and $10,000 per year and a 5 percent on incomes above $10,000. The tax law, which was enacted during wartime as an emergency measure and was signed by a Republican president, had to be administered at the local level by individual revenue collectors. It is arguable how great a beneficence Goldsborough had given Miller, for as he understatedly warned him, the new law "may be somewhat unpopular at first with some fellow citizens."[31]

Miller admitted no discomfort from being a revenuer, but he may have squirmed some in his ironic position as a known Democratic wheelman serving in a Republican administration. It was an unusual appointment, but there are understandable reasons why the Republicans tapped him for the post and why he accepted. First, Miller's reputation as an honest financial manager made it easier for local Republicans to accept the choice. Second, his close friendship with Goldsborough helped allay national party men's fears. Since the early 1850s, Goldsborough and Miller had been business partners and shared a commitment to moderate politics, even though they had been on opposite sides during the martial law controversy. For Miller, accepting the job gave him little pause. In part it was the salary—$1,000 per year—but more important was the opportunity the position offered to keep him engaged in territorial government and prepared to aid his friends. More than anything else, Miller saw officeholding as a means to reciprocate political friendship, the governing principle of his political behavior.[32]

As Goldsborough had expected, Miller performed his job faithfully and with precision. But Miller often found himself in politically precarious positions, partly because he continued to entertain financial and political solicitations from his Democratic friends in opposition to his Republican employers and partly because he pragmatically used Republican aid to pursue his own interests. More important, his own dilemmas were embedded in the larger political pattern that characterized Pickering's tenure as territorial governor. The classic conflicts between a Democrat-controlled legislature and a Republican-controlled executive became convoluted and unpredictable when some Republican appointees seemed to favor Democrats as well as their own party members. A case in point centered on the selection of the public printer, a position with political ramifications because it guaranteed the recipient public printing business, often enough to finance a newspaper operation. In an effort to limit the Democrats' power, Pickering had declared in 1863 that the territorial secretary would appoint the public printer rather than leave it to the legislature. Miller and some of his friends in the legislature, O. B. McFadden and B. F. Shaw among them, had expected to influence the selection of the public printer, but the governor had interceded. The focus shifted to new Territorial Secretary Elwood Evans, who bent to the lobbying of Miller and others and tapped T. F. McElroy for the post.[33]

Miller and McElroy were long-time friends, and McElroy had joined Miller as a steadfast Union man, rejecting the "peace party" Democrats in the territory. McElroy had also been given a deputy collector of revenue position by Goldsborough. Because he had been a loyal Democrat during most of the 1850s, McElroy made Republicans suspicious. Likewise, because he had begun his political career in Thurston County as a Whig and had edited the Whig-controlled *Columbian*, he also made some Democrats uneasy. One Miller compatriot, for example, cautioned him that if McElroy edited a Democratic paper he would have to take unequivocal stands and "not be afraid of offending the Republicans," adding that "a dough-faced, wishy-washy, all-sided concern will not do."[34]

McElroy strode that middle political ground that had become familiar to Miller. He had sufficiently good ties to both major political parties and did not hesitate to use them to his advantage. His appointment as public printer came as a result of those bipartisan connections. Evans appointed McElroy, at least in part, because McElroy had strong connections with John G. Nicolay, Lincoln's private secretary. The two men had worked on a newspaper together in Pittsfield, Illinois, and Evans hoped that McElroy's connections with the administration would offset those of Governor Pickering and Territorial Secretary A. G. Henry, who had become even more exasperated with Evans. Another former Whig who had become Republican, Evans was a successful lawyer who had long-term ties to many of the territory's leading Democrats. Miller had been one of his early friends in Olympia, when they had both worked for Customs Collector Simpson Moses, and Miller had hired Evans as his counsel in numerous civil suits. But "Pud," as his friends called him, often found himself in poor financial straits, which put him on Miller's debtor account during most of the 1850s. Evans's connection with Miller deepened in 1863, when Evans had enlisted him as a bondsman to guarantee his character for the territorial secretary's position. Making the situation even cozier, McElroy had joined Miller as another of Evans's bondsmen. So Evans had compelling personal as well as political reasons to appoint McElroy public printer. For his Republican associates, however, it was just one more action that made him, at the least, a continuing nuisance. Pickering and Henry, another Lincoln confidant, thought Evans's conduct so egregious that they appealed directly to Lincoln for his removal. His crime, they claimed, was the dispersal of favors and monies to Democrats—men like McElroy, McFadden, and Miller. Pickering was especially outraged at Evans's befriending of McFadden, a man he had characterized to Lincoln as "an open mouthed reviler of yourself & a bitter opponent of every Act of your administration."[35]

Miller stood in the middle of an increasingly fractured political gridiron, acting sometimes as an unofficial referee, assisting, directing, or blocking the players. Although some Democrats watched the Republicans' grumbling with some glee, men like McElroy hoped Evans could protect himself and survive. Not long after receiving his appointment, for example, McElroy had written Miller urging him to "do all you can to keep him [Evans] in the saddle! You know how disastrous his removal will be to me." Another of Miller's interested petitioners, B. F. Shaw, acerbically advised that "old [A. G.] Henry is after Evans," but he could fend off the attacks with Miller's help "if Evans will keep still . . . but you [Miller] know him and can judge whether he will or not."[36]

The problems of Evans aside, the political situation for Miller had become even more unpredictable because of the 1863 elections. Although Democrats had taken advantage of Republican disorganization and triumphed in the territorial delegate polling, they sent a man to Washington who would likely do little to aid the entrenched politicians of Puget Sound. George E. "Ginger" Cole, the new territorial delegate, came from east of the mountains and represented a sectionalist political movement that was disdainful of the "clam-eaters," as eastsiders called the residents on the Sound. His mission to Congress would not include carrying water for the westside Democrats, Miller, or anyone else. When Goldsborough landed a patronage job in Washington, D.C., in August, Miller again found himself on the verge of losing his job, for it was all but certain that he would be replaced as deputy revenue collector.[37]

When Miller reflected on politics and his fortunes, he surely marveled at his place in Washington Territory's political environment. He had managed to chart his own course, even though the political environment had become a "mazy labyrinth," with like-minded Republicans and Democrats marching in tandem down the center corridors while hard-headed partisans frequently veered into left- or right-turning alleyways. In some ways, Miller had avoided the maze by standing at the political intersections and directing traffic, always aware of the speed and destination of the flow. He maintained his equivocal but pragmatic place by keeping his own counsel and making himself essential to men of diverse persuasions. Nonetheless, he could no more avoid the political consequences of the larger drama being played out on the nation's battlefields than his fellow frontier politicos. And with the rest of them, Miller looked carefully for a pathway out of the maze that would provide a fair shot at the main chance.

CHAPTER 8

Making Money and
Pursuing Family

*I think you have better come home and not just make
complaints as though you had just got there.*
                    Martha P. Miller to Miller, June 23, 1855

*It would be difficult at present to buy land in Missouri as
the country is full of Bushwackers who are not very
particular when they shoot.*
                    Frank Eames to Miller, July 26, 1864

In the last months of 1863, Miller stood at another
crossroad. At the intersection of several political and personal choices,
he could find no certain or compelling direction. Less held him to
Washington Territory than in previous years, and some business partners had suggested that he consider moving to San Francisco, where
the climate would benefit him and he could make lucrative investments. But his natural conservatism kept him from investigating the
possibilities. At the same time, his family in Illinois reiterated their
almost yearly requests that he come home, buy a farm, marry, and live
as they did. His family had exerted its power on Miller episodically
over the years, but he had resisted the pull. In the spring of 1861, Miller
had thought about visiting Illinois but had decided to remain in Washington to manage Stevens's campaign. Later that same year, when he

heard that his father's health was poor, he had again considered going home, but still he stayed in Olympia.[1]

Nonetheless, the familial core in Beardstown had gravitational mass. Six of Miller's siblings lived in or within fifty miles of Beardstown, each married with children. Two of his sisters, Mary and Elizabeth, had married prominent politicians, Judges Sylvester Emmons and John A. Arenz. His brothers, Robert and Edmund, operated large and prosperous farms. He and his brother Richard were the only two siblings who had not stayed within the family orbit in Illinois. By the mid-1860s and in their forties, they were also the only unmarried Miller siblings. Both had confessed to being homesick not long after emigrating to the West, but neither had wanted to return home until he had achieved some level of success. "I will not go home," Richard had written William in 1853, "without money, money, money." Miller corresponded with Richard more often than with his parents or other siblings, which created an even greater social distance that made Miller feel alternately guilty and frustrated. His family in Illinois did not make it any easier. As one of them pointedly wrote in 1855: "I think you have better come home and not just be gone to make complaints as though you had just got there."[2]

For Miller, going home had become inextricably tied to his original reasons for migrating and his expectations of a new life in the West. Although his poor health had improved considerably during the first years in Oregon, other items on his agenda had more moment. Both he and Richard had vowed to achieve economic success and get married before returning home. By mid-1855, Miller had acquired modest success—enough for Richard to encourage him to return to Illinois—but marriage still eluded him. This failure bothered him, and he complained to his family in Illinois. "You are the only one [of the brothers] that ever talks about it," one of the relatives pointedly reminded him in 1855. It was his sense of family—which was stronger than his actions indicated—that no doubt made marriage important, but his ambition to make money had driven him harder and had been a greater deterrent to returning home than his bachelor status.[3]

William Miller approached life in a pragmatic and reasoned way, evaluating risks and people using a similar calculus. In both personal and business affairs, he sought quotients that inherently included both the means and the ends. He fervently believed that the basis for civic and family life, whether in Washington Territory or Illinois, rested on a man's ability to build personal worth, which in Miller's mind meant economic wealth and social position. This was the kernel of his ambition. As ambitious as he was, however, he still acted with great prudence, and his inherent conservatism led him to confine his business relationships to immediate opportunities and men he trusted. He succeeded because he balanced his knowledge of local conditions with his evaluation of people, a talent that led him easily and almost confidently to lending money at interest. His success in moneylending, however, drew him incessantly toward the edge of financial danger. Lending money to nascent entrepreneurs on the South Sound paid in a somewhat predictable way, but that business just as surely tied Miller to his debtors' economic affairs, for good or ill. Its rewards also contained limitations, and Miller understood that to make more he had to risk more. By the mid-1850s, with enough confidence and capital, he sought larger opportunities.

Taking a cue from Josiah Lucas, his political adviser in Washington, D.C., Miller took advantage of government investments and business. When Lucas saw a series of claims pass through the office of the Treasury Department's 5th Auditor in Washington, he wrote Miller, chiding him: "You must not let a good chance escape." He advised Miller to invest in the claims by purchasing vouchers at a discount and then submitting them for payment. "Watch the points closely," Lucas counseled, but be sure "that the claims are genuine, authorized by the government and that the parties are honest." Once Miller surveyed the possibilities, he bubbled to Lucas that "something handsome may be made" on the purchase of government claims and suggested that he and Lucas strike up a partnership in the business.[4]

Once the Indian War erupted, opportunities for investments in government claims multiplied significantly, especially for Miller, who approved scrip for materiel purchases. Although the territorial government issued scrip, the pseudo-money functioned more like a bank or promissory note. Bearers of scrip could expect to receive only what the market would willingly pay, and that figure fluctuated during and especially after the war. Two factors affected the value of scrip after 1857. The discovery of gold along the Fraser River in British Columbia in 1858 injected a new source of specie into the regional economy, and Congress's hesitation in approving the Indian War claims of Oregon and Washington left much uncertainty about when and at what rate the scrip might be redeemed. Speculation in scrip joined the interests of those who had money to invest with those who had no cash but held scrip. Miller participated in the speculation, but not until after the war and his official duties as quartermaster had ended. By 1858, though, he had begun buying up scrip for friends, including Oliver Stevens, Isaac Stevens's brother in Massachusetts. Miller kept a close eye on the trading values both in Portland and in San Francisco and used what information he could get on the progress of congressional debate about the war claims from Lucas and his other contacts in the nation's capital to handicap his decisions on purchasing scrip.[5]

Although he bought scrip for others, sometimes in large blocks, it does not appear that he put much of his own money into the speculation. In part, that was because Miller already had a sizable amount of scrip from exchanges and purchases, but he had an even larger amount in war pay vouchers that volunteers had signed over to him as payment for minor debts. Accepting pay vouchers in lieu of debt was a form of speculation, but Miller made as much or more money working as a broker for investors and charging a modest commission. His aid to Oliver Stevens is a case in point. Stevens had asked Miller to select some good scrip, perhaps as much as $5,000, and purchase it in his name. Miller obliged and extended Stevens's investment an additional $1,200, explaining that he had bought verified scrip—"discharges of officers"—of the highest value but at a very low price. He advised Stevens in February 1859 to hold some additional money in ready because Miller believed scrip would drop to 25 or 20 cents on the dollar if Congress dallied much longer on the war claims issue. By September, however, Miller's prediction had proved to be wrong. Scrip had actually increased in value because, as Miller explained, it seemed to have gone into hands of men who are all and disposed to keep it and I do not know of a man in the vicinity who is a holder of scrip that will sell for less than 50 cents on the dollar.

Within months, however, Miller had extended his search and found some scrip for Stevens at 35 cents on the dollar. Miller charged Stevens $200 for his time and expertise.[6]

The hobgoblin of speculation is the uncertainty of the market, which usually cautioned Miller from risking too much of his or his friends' funds. The best hedge against uncertainty in speculative investments is accurate information, especially from inside sources. Miller assiduously pumped his friends and business associates for information. After he lost his customs service position, he had queried friends in Oregon and California about potential investments in real estate and livestock trading, but the prospects did not entice him.[7]

By the late 1850s, Miller had investigated investments in Seattle real estate, Hudson's Bay Company's properties in the territory, and land east of the Cascade Mountains along the Columbia River. These were genuine opportunities, but Miller stayed with what he knew and what had brought him success. He found the best returns and the least risk in the purchase and sale of commercial paper and loans. Following the example of regional financiers, such as William S. Ladd of Portland, Miller processed bank drafts on San Francisco and New York institutions. With no chartered banks in Oregon and Washington, handling commercial paper and bank notes posed a serious problem for businessmen. Bank notes had to be cashiered at either the issuing institution—often an eastern bank—or at a willing bank out of the region. These conditions were ready-made for men like Miller, who could afford to purchase drafts and were willing to pursue payment through their own channels. He did a modest business during the late 1850s by buying government drafts and commercial paper from men he knew and by charging direct commissions or acquiring the notes at a discount. In 1859, for example, he processed $4,000 through Ladd's New York connections and made a handsome profit.[8]

Regional economic conditions changed dramatically by the early

1860s. Gold from the Fraser River strikes in British Columbia had drawn great interest from Oregon and Washington residents; many deserted their work and went north to the goldfields, as they had a decade earlier during the California rush. The gold discoveries in Idaho and Montana during the early 1860s had an even more profound effect on the region's economy. The Columbia River became a gilded causeway to the mines on the Clearwater and Salmon rivers in Idaho, siphoning money to Portland and enriching the men who controlled transportation on the Columbia.[9] Walla Walla, a recently settled farming area in eastern Washington Territory, suddenly became the major "jumping off place" for coastal migrants rushing to the Rocky Mountain mining country. Steamboats carried thousands of hopeful prospectors and tons of supplies upriver from Portland, while it brought downriver millions of dollars in gold to Portland and hundreds of the inevitable losers in the goldfields. The infusion of gold revolutionized the Pacific Northwest economy by suddenly turning a cash-poor region into one that experienced inflation, a demand for services, and a surplus of capital.[10]

During the 1860s, most business exchanges in the region were conducted in gold and gold values. Merchants and informal lenders like Miller measured all forms of commercial paper against gold, so when U.S. government "greenbacks" first appeared in the local economy in late 1862 businessmen accepted them with some reluctance, knowing the paper money would suffer in any comparison with gold. Rejecting greenbacks, however, carried another kind of risk. Union patriots complained, charging that not using the new money was tantamount to supporting the Confederacy by diminishing the government's financial strength. Unionists staged rallies in the larger cities and towns in California, Oregon, and Washington to promote acceptance of the new currency, but greenbacks inevitably traded at a discount, sometimes as much as 70 percent. To create some stability, merchants tried to set standard discount rates by following those set in Portland by the Ladd & Tilton bank, which had based its rates on quotations from San Francisco. But there was no means of enforcement, save public pressure. A merchant who did not follow the rule and accepted green-

backs at face value, as one historian put it, was "promptly black-
listed . . . [and] became a commercial outcast." Creditors stood the
most to lose, not only from the possibilitiy that debtors would try to
repay gold debts with depreciated greenbacks but also from the inflationary effect that free trading of greenbacks would have on the general economy.[11]

For patriotic and financial reasons, Miller stood solidly with other
creditors on a gold standard. He had forthrightly attached himself to
the Union cause in 1861 and aided the war effort by soliciting for the
U.S. Sanitary Commission, but he also worried about his own accounts
and tried to avoid accepting greenbacks in payment for any outstanding
debts. Nonetheless, he could not avoid dealing in the new currency
and grudgingly agreed to accept it, but he required his debtors to pay
off their loans in full, including all accumulated interest and penalties. As he left for one extended trip in 1863, he instructed his agent:

> Confidential. From what I can learn I have no doubt but what several of those
> owing me will want to pay me in Green Backs as soon as I am gone if they
> can find who my Agent is. You must therefore keep dark and let no one know
> that you are my Agent.[12]

Miller also played the other side of the exchange by investing in
greenbacks, hoping to make up what he might lose if he had to accept
them in his own business dealings. The value of greenbacks fluctuated violently during the war years, reflecting public confidence in the
government, which nearly equated the Union army's success or failure on the battlefields. To find the best opportunities in the region,
Miller sent out queries to his associates. One counseled him to invest
only in the "by streets" where "banks and other capitalists" had not
penetrated and speculation could still pay. T. F. McElroy, his journal-
ist friend from Olympia, reported from Lewiston, Idaho, in the spring
of 1863 that greenbacks "can be bought off the soldiers for 50 cents on
the dollar," a good price considering that some Oregon merchants
accepted them at 80 cents. Urging Miller to act quickly, McElroy added:
"how long this will last is uncertain." But one year later, as greenbacks
in the Northwest rapidly depreciated, Miller was discouraged by

reports from San Francisco that greenbacks were selling for 39 cents; in Portland, they traded at 40 cents on the dollar.[13]

Currency exchange during the Civil War bedeviled everyone in the Pacific Northwest, but men with capital stood to profit most from such conditions. Miller's account books do not specify his investments in greenbacks, so there is no way to gauge if he won or lost on currency speculations. In the spring of 1864, though, he had evidently begun to veer away from sizable investments in paper money. Writing from New York to his brother in Illinois, Miller explained that on the advice "of some friends here" he had decided to let his greenbacks "slide" for a few days, hoping for additional rewards, but he would immediately put any gains "either in N York City bonds or into some staple articles such as whisky, tobacco, domestices, etc., etc., and ship them to our Coast." Speculations, as Miller well knew, invited trouble, especially with a volatile currency. It may well be that he agreed with one of his associates who railed about greenbacks: "Now may the curse of God rest on the man that thought about such a circulating medium."[14]

Perhaps because of the rapid economic changes that affected the Northwest during the 1860s or because he sought a broader opportunity for investment, Miller entered into two corporate ventures before the end of the decade. He had increased his wealth substantially after the Indian War, mostly through his lending business and some speculative investments. By the early 1860s, Miller had thousands of dollars tied up in loans, but he had kept close watch on his debtors and did not hesitate to haul them to court if they dallied in payments. Between 1859 and 1862, Miller secured ten sizable judgments. Times were hard, as one of his debtors pleaded: "I find that it has been dog eat dog and some have had better opportunities for swallowing than I have had."[15] But Miller foreclosed without much anguish, for he also needed money if he hoped to take advantage of investment opportunities. By 1862, Miller had cash reserves and investments totalling nearly $50,000, enough to advance in a corporate venture.[16]

Like other businessmen on the Sound, Miller had long complained about poor transportation. Moving freight, people, and even the mails took much too long, generally because of predictable maladies:

poor weather that shut down shipping, axle-deep mud on the road south to the Columbia River, and the failures of mail contractors. Nearly everyone clamored for relief, and each year during the 1850s the territorial delegate had introduced road-building bills to Congress and the territorial legislature had sent a steady stream of petitions to Washington. Miller himself had become entangled in the overland mail contract during the late 1850s, standing in as the guarantor and agent for the contractor.[17] But in 1862, he became embroiled in a much more important transportation venture, one that planned to operate on the Columbia River and promised significant economic and political rewards.

Two years before, a group of Portland investors had chartered the Oregon Steam Navigation Company to operate steamboats and portages on the Columbia River. Made up of former investors in several steamboat operations, the OSN soon dominated Columbia River transportation. The Idaho mining bonanza gave the OSN unprecedented opportunity, and the company took advantage of it. During the early 1860s, it averaged more than 23,000 passengers and 17,000 tons per year, charging what the traffic would bear. Soon merchants and the general public up and down the river complained and begged for competitors to challenge the combine.[18]

There were understandable reasons for complaint. The OSN had successfully fended off all independent steamboat operators and effectively tied up the three necessary portages on the river—at the Cascades on the Oregon and Washington sides and at The Dalles. The company was also making enormous profits. In its first six months, the company collected enough receipts to split its stock shares four for one; after one year, it marked up a 48 percent return on investment for its stockholders. These developments did not go without notice in Washington Territory, where the OSN had secured its corporate charter. Puget Sound businessmen like Miller howled in complaint at the OSN's high shipping rates and monopolistic practices. They pressured the territorial legislature to pass a series of laws that would restrict the company's control of portages on the Washington side of the river. The OSN dodged some of these statutes in 1862 by reincorporating in Oregon, but it still faced a genuine challenge when the People's Transportation Company began running boats between Portland and the Cascades.[19]

The PTC, a steamboat line on the Willamette River that was largely controlled by Stephen Coffin, attracted investment from many independent steamboatmen who wanted to break the OSN's stranglehold. A risk-taker, Coffin had come to Portland in 1847 and invested in real estate. By the late 1850s, he had consolidated his real estate wealth, which was valued at more than $130,000. He had become attracted to steamboating and incorporated the PTC in 1862, running his boats very profitably on the Willamette from Portland up to Eugene. But the real profits, as Coffin knew, were to be made on the Columbia. The next year he planned to challenge the OSN, promising to compete head-to-head all the way from Portland to Lewiston on the Snake River. Because the OSN controlled all of the portages, Coffin faced considerable odds, and it was this difficulty that gave Miller and his friends their opportunity.[20]

In late 1861, Miller entered into discussions with Port Townsend's leading lawyer, Paul K. Hubbs, and its leading merchant, Enoch S. Fowler, about investing in transportation on Puget Sound and perhaps the Columbia River. Whether the idea originated with Miller is unclear, although it is likely because of Miller's involvement in overland and Puget Sound mail contracts. His interest must have been keen, because he willingly joined with Fowler, who had challenged Miller's patronage decisions and created a small political crisis among Democrats in 1859. Furthermore, Fowler suggested including J. J. Van Bokkelin, the man who had nearly come to political blows with Miller just three years earlier. But that was politics, and this was business. As Fowler wrote to Miller: "I go in for the Sound [men] to stick together from this acct. and drop all past times."[21]

The Columbia River Transportation Company, which Miller and his cohorts organized in the spring of 1862, planned to develop a new portage on the river at the Cascades and perhaps join Coffin's challenge to the OSN. The core investors in the company—Miller, Hubbs, Fowler, B. F. Shaw, Alexander Abernethy, Charles Phillips, and Thomas

Fletcher—all had suggestions for investment strategies. Miller stood at the center, in part because the meetings were held in Olympia and in part because he held the proxies of a majority of the largest investors, the men who became directors of the company.[22] When the company's first organizational meeting took place in Olympia in mid-April 1862, Miller presided. The resulting articles of incorporation specified that the president and each director were

> hereby authorized to receive any and all propositions for running steamers, waggons or cars upon the line of travel of said Transportation Company . . . so soon as the line of travel can be fully opened by said arrangements, from Vancouver to Lewiston.[23]

The company received a charter from the Washington Territorial Legislature, which gave them authority to develop a portage road at the Cascades and to create a transportation service up the Columbia to Lewiston. Part of the appeal was a prospect of serving Walla Walla and breaking the OSN's high rates. For Miller, it was a great opportunity, but one that came with unknown risks and troubles.

Miller became the personal clearinghouse for the schemes that his fellow directors suggested during the two years that the company pursued its dream operation on the Columbia. Throughout the summer of 1862, Miller corresponded with his fellow stockholders, but the company made little progress until early 1863, when Benjamin Shaw, one of the directors and a close associate of Miller's during the Indian War, opened direct negotiations with Stephen Coffin in Portland.[24] Shaw and Thomas Fletcher of Vancouver hoped that the PTC group in Portland might purchase an access right for a portage on land at the Cascades that the Columbia River Transportation Company had secured on the basis of some early Donation Land Claims.[25]

While Shaw and Fletcher initiated tentative negotiations with PTC in Portland, Thomas Smith and Frank Clark, two other major stockholders, began to shop for purchasers in San Francisco, hoping to sell the company's charter. In early February, Fletcher frustratedly complained to Miller, pleading with him to take strong action before the company lost bargaining advantage. He suggested that Miller "come over" to Portland and negotiate the best deal he could with PTC, which Fletcher advised was the sale of the company's charter easement at the Cascades. "Either put them in possession of the road [at the Cascades]," Fletcher urged, "or go in with them and build a plank road, and Miller, there is money in it either way." Fletcher estimated they could pry $15,000 out of Coffin for the portage location. "Come over Miller as soon as possible," Fletcher hurriedly wrote in late February 1863,

> for I think the iron is hot. . . . come immediately, as it will afford you an oppor-
> tunity to assist your friends, which I know will be highly gratifying.[26]

Miller did not follow Fletcher's advice. He preferred to act only when there was a bonafide offer on the table, and Fletcher had so far failed to secure an official proposal from PTC's managers. The negotiations with PTC and Coffin stuttered along during March, with both Shaw and Fletcher trying to either make a sale of the charter or join with the Portland investors in developing a new portage at the Cascades. PTC "must have this portage," Shaw explained to Miller, because the alternative—a road on the Oregon side—would cost "four times over" what they would have to pay for the Columbia River Transportation Company charter. Nonetheless, Shaw could make no predictions. "Something new every day," he reported. "I can not tell [the chances] as I can not get into their secrets."[27] As Shaw continued the negotiations, it became clear that Coffin would purchase the company charter only with an exchange of PTC stock for Columbia River Transportation stock, a deal Miller disliked. By mid-April, Shaw pleaded with Miller to make a deal of some sort or the company's prospects would probably expire. Shaw laid out the situation explicitly:

> Now understand me, I do not pretend to say that you could positively do any-
> thing with the matter but you may be able to do more than any of us, as we
> all defer to you in business matters. So the people over here [Portland] have
> grown to think that you are a No. 1 businessman and the fact of such a man
> being in possession of a charter like this might have an influence in bringing

their company to terms especially if it was known that he was a man of means. This is what I think, but you do what you think best.[28]

Frustrated by the fractured negotiations with Coffin, a little skeptical, and knowing that PTC had decided to attempt building a new portage road on the Oregon side of the river and had created its own "Columbia Transportation Company," Miller chose not to follow Shaw's advice. The Columbia River Transportation Company, if it ever truly had a chance to sell its charter, failed to lure any purchasers. Coffin and his company saw the better side of their challenge to OSN and sold out to their rivals for a guarantee that OSN would stay off the Willamette in exchange for PTC vacating the Columbia. By July 1864, Paul Hubbs and other stockholders were trying to sell their shares in Columbia River Transportation stock for whatever they could get.[29]

Miller recorded no sales of the company's stock in his account books, so it is unclear how much he may have invested in the company and whether he suffered any losses. It is likely that no Columbia River Transportation Company stock certificates were ever made, and perhaps the whole business should be seen more as a manipulative stock offering. Yet, many of the men involved believed that with their charter in hand they could make a handsome profit, and it is clear that the twin frustrations of poor transportation and the OSN's usurious rates made their company's dream believable.[30]

Miller uttered no regrets about the Columbia River Transportation Company's foray. The failure of the negotiations, however, helped bring him to a crossroad in late 1863. By the mid-1860s, he had begun to rethink his place on the Sound and to consider relocation. In addition to his family's regular pleadings, his father's poor health no doubt encouraged him to consider moving back to Illinois. As early as 1860, Miller had known that his father's physical condition was declining. "Pa has been very feeble for some time back," Robert had written him in March 1860. "It would be worth ten years of your life just to see him. I think he would be perfectly happy if he could see you and Dick once more."[31] Two years later, Miller learned that his father was battling a debilitating disease. "I sometimes feel afraid his dissease [sic] is running in to consumpsion [*sic*]," Dorothy had informed him, adding "he has suffered a great deal at times." By September 1863, she reported that their father was depressed. Then, in December, she had to write the hardest truth:

> Our dear old Father is no more. He departed this life last Sabbath morning . . .
> I had hope that he might live for many years to come. But alas such are our
> hopes and I dont know why we should want him to live and suffer as he has
> done for the last ten years. Poor man we will never know what he has suffered
> in that time.[32]

Miller had worried about his father's declining condition in the fall and had planned a visit for late December or early January. He had taken his usual precautions by collecting his papers, making out an extensive will, and naming his three brothers and W. B. Gosnell as his executors, in case anything happened to him during his absence. Leaving Olympia, Miller traveled to San Francisco on his way to the Isthmus of Panama and continued steamship passage to New York and overland travel to Illinois. His sister's shocking news reached him in San Francisco, where he had paused for a few days to conduct some business. His reaction can only be imagined, but because of either grief or the wish to postpone a surely depressing visit home, Miller pursued his business in New York and Washington before traveling on to Beardstown in January.[33]

Miller had taken a bag full of requests, political chits, and calling cards when he left Olympia. His friends had thrust them on him, each urging him to wield any influence he might muster on their behalf in the nation's capital. He was mindful of his friends' petitions but he also packed along his own agenda, which was no less political and no less opportunistic than theirs. This time, rather than a political office, Miller wanted another kind of federal patronage benefit: the government contract to carry the mail on Puget Sound.

For more than a decade, residents had complained about the unreliability of mail service—both by sea from San Francisco and overland from the Columbia River. Miller had watched the situation for years and had joined in an ill-fated attempt with other investors to acquire the contract in 1861. This time, however, he stepped forward as the prime applicant with a chance at success. Philip Keach of Steilacoom, the mail contractor, had suffered financial reverses, owned an inadequate vessel, and had violated some of the contract provisions. Goldsborough, who was by then employed by the Department of the Navy in Washington, D.C., urged Miller to apply for the contract, promising all of his political aid. Bolstered by Goldsborough's support, Miller queried potential investors and decided to make application to the Post Office Department.[34]

When Miller arrived in the nation's capital on his hunt, his weapons were his business friends, congressional political allies, and a fistful of endorsements from political friends in Illinois and ranking Republicans in Washington Territory. Surveyor General Anson G. Henry, perhaps the most political of Republican officeholders in the territory, sent along a door-opening note that established Miller's political loyalties. "He [Miller] was at the last election for President a Breckinridge Democrat," Henry openly wrote, "he is now an unconditional Union Man, of the Andy Johnson stamp."[35]

Miller began his capital rounds in late January at the Office of Indian Affairs, where he asked the commissioner for long overdue reimbursement from his work as superintendent. He also delivered petitions and vouchers to the department for his territorial friends, including longtime business associate Isaac Lightner.[36] But Miller directed most of his attention to the Post Office Department. He had some small advantage because a friend, George W. McLellan, had recently been named 2nd Assistant Postmaster of the United States. Still, there was no guarantee. As Goldsborough had warned him, nothing could assure preference on government contracts. But then Miller received an even more impressive entrée. Through his Illinois friends and A. G. Henry's influence, Miller obtained a note of introduction to the postmaster general directly from Abraham Lincoln:

Post Master General please see the bearer Mr. Miller, now of Washington Territory, and son of an old friend of mine in Illinois, who originally went from Kentucky. He comes well recommended by neighbors on the Pacific.[37]

The work of getting the contract, however, involved more than skill-ful politics. Miller had to demonstrate that the current contractor, Philip Keach, had failed to complete the requirements and should be forced to give up the contract. Even if he succeeded in denying Keach, Miller still had to win the bid against other potential contractors in the territory. He had partially covered that problem by gathering com-mitments from some friends before he left Olympia. T. F. McElroy had enthusiastically joined the effort, hoping to get a return on what seemed a lucrative business proposition. "Count me in on the mail contract!" he wrote Miller in late 1863, "I aint timid on that." Miller hoped to dry up any capital that might be combined against him and also to gen-erally discourage other bidders. Even if Miller beat out any competi-tors, however, he still had to apply direct pressure at the Post Office Department. After Miller left the nation's capital in February 1864, Goldsborough attended to the legwork, using his contacts with George McLellan.[38]

By mid-summer, Goldsborough had reported to Miller that, although all seemed favorable, he still needed more evidence of Keach's failures. Miller acquired confirmation from the Olympia post-master that Keach did not have a suitable vessel to carry the mail and that he had failed to deliver mail or had risked delivery by contract-ing with untrustworthy captains. Penalties and extra expenses paid out to subcontractors had actually put Keach in debt and had made it nearly impossible for him to fulfill his contract. Miller's opportunity came in August, when the Post Office Department put Keach on pro-bation, responding to complaints from Puget Sound and the docu-mentation Miller had provided. By mid-month, the mail route contract had gone out on bid.[39]

The Post Office Department received no bids other than Miller's, so the fate of the contract devolved upon Goldsborough's continued lobbying efforts. By early September, Goldsborough could write Miller:

I have succeeded in getting you the contract for the mail on the Sound. . . . I
have very strongly given the appearance to them that you are loyal to the back-
bone, and will do your duty faithfully as a contractor.[40]

Goldsborough emphasized the loyalty issue partly because Keach was
a Republican and Miller's support of Breckinridge in 1860 may have
continued to paint him as a fair-weather Unionist, even though he had
taken a prominent position in Unionist gatherings and had worked
assiduously in the territory for the U.S. Sanitary Commission. Elwood
Evans had added a letter to Pennsylvania Senator William D. Kelley
to further assure the administration that Miller was, in fact, "our
wealthiest, promptest, best businessman . . . and a devoted Union
Man." The combination of his bid, confirmation of his loyalty, and
Goldsborough's diligent lobbying evidently satisfied, for McLellan
informed Miller in early September that he had won the contract. For
an annual compensation of $12,000, to run until June 30, 1866, Miller
agreed to make weekly mail runs between Olympia and Victoria.[41]

Miller's avid pursuit of the mail contract reflected both his pecu-
niary interest and a decision he had made after his trip in 1864. Once
back in Olympia, he had queried his family and others to ascertain
the best land bargains in Illinois. It is unclear whether he sought merely
an investment near his family or he seriously considered going back
home. There had been friction between Miller and his brothers prior
to their father's death and that may have deterred him from relocating from Olympia. The disputes were over money and promises of
financial support Miller had evidently made during the early 1860s.[42]
He had collected enough information, though, to determine that Missouri, not Illinois, provided the best opportunities. His cousin, P. T.
Miller, promised "no safer investment could be made." Other relatives,
however, thought the situation too unsettled and even dangerous. As
one of them offered: "It would be difficult at present to buy land in
Missouri as the country is full of Bushwackers who are not very particular when they shoot." Such conflicting advice, combined with the
prospect of returning to a disputatious family setting, turned Miller
away from investing in Midwest farmland or moving to Illinois.[43]

By the fall of 1864, with the Union army advancing on the Confederacy and Lincoln waging a battle against the Peace Democrats for the White House, Miller had cast his lot with the Unionist forces in the territory and decided to remain in the West. He continued to wage his own continuing contest with success, while episodically trying to establish a family of his own in Washington Territory. His surrogate families of the 1850s—the Ebeys on Whidby Island and the Stevens family in Olympia—had been nearly sundered by the wartime deaths of Isaac Ebey and Isaac Stevens. He was left alone with his brother Richard, the other familial dissenter who had pursued adventure rather than stay in the Illinois fold. Off and on during the years since their emigration west, the brothers had consoled each other in times of financial woe and personal trauma. They thought alike, yet so differently. "Your letter of the 18th [October]," Richard had written Miller in November 1857,

> take up the same topics and clothe them in almost the same language. It is a little singular that living five hundred miles apart we should without any concert whatever have written to each other letters almost precisely similar in thoughts and language.[44]

Yet, even as they exchanged letters and expressed a closeness that often set them apart from their Illinois kin, the two men pursued their goals in ways that could not have been more distinct. Richard never gave up on the gilded triumph. First in the placer camps of California and then in diggings in Nevada, he tried his hand at buying claims, at law, and at politics. Miller watched from Olympia, worried about his younger brother's heedless life but not knowing what to do. As Richard's fortunes declined and associates warned him against his drinking, Miller offered his brother money for the first time. It was nearly too much for Richard, who had failed again and lost another chance to return home a hero. His financial "embarrassment," as he put it, had become serious: "d___d near running me stark, staring mad. In fact I entertain serious doubts in regard to my sanity since September last." Richard proudly refused the support. Two years later, with

Richard still struggling, Miller again offered him money, and again Richard rejected it. "Your letters each of them," Richard replied, "are the essence of kindness and affection and to say that I am grateful would but poorly express my feelings," but "I need no assistance." In what had almost become a refrain, Richard found himself in dire straits two months later. He wrote Miller in desperation, asking for any kind of loan and admitting he had used up his last friend in Nevada. Explaining his condition, Richard reminded his brother that he knew "nothing about this place [Nevada] and how hard it is for me without a dollar, without credit and in debt." He hoped William would remain compassionate, but sensed he probably would not.[45]

Miller sent him money, but it was clear that their paths had parted, that they had gone directions too different from one another. In letter after letter, Miller had cautioned and criticized his brother, and Richard had responded defensively. In the last days of 1864, feeling chastised and inadequate, Richard saw the situation clearly:

> Your life has been spent among a quieter class of people than mine; you have been more of a philosopher than I and you have passed easily along almost without effort. If you were in my situation today you would be worse off than I am. . . . with me how different has it been. I have been the child of circumstance; the only wonder is that I should have lived to my present age.[46]

Richard had followed no set path or plan. When he had encountered crossroads, he had seemingly taken the one that glittered or provided escape. Miller had pondered his options and had cautiously chosen the stable road, the one that offered the promise of gain, substance, and stability. But contrary to Richard's envious assumption, he had not made his way "almost without effort." The powerful center of Miller's life spun around assiduously applied effort, an almost unremitting pursuit of achievement that had become, by the mid-1860s, at least partly an explanation for his migration west and continued separation from family. What Richard correctly perceived in his brother's life was Miller's commitment to an entrepreneurial life in Washington Territory.

CHAPTER 9

To Assist My Friends

No man can achieve any great success in political life,
who does not keep a complete and exact balance sheet of
Db. and Cr. between his enemies and his friends.
Editorial, *Washington Standard,* February 17, 1866

I have no ambitions or selfish ends to accomplish—I
only want the office in order to have active employment
and at the same time to be able to assist my friends. . . .
Miller to Hazard Stevens, November 22, 1866

Since the early 1850s, Miller had found his best opportunities through a network of political and business associates who
readily extended their services. He had always reciprocated, and such
relationships had proven to be business guideposts that were as sure
as he could have desired. More than perhaps any other factor that
explains Miller's success, his singular ability to craft partnerships
among other ambitious men consistently provided him with new
opportunities. He capitalized on those opportunities by focusing
more on larger economic and political goals than on smaller issues
that often divide men. A hallmark of his method was steadfast loyalty to friends and a readiness to overlook their blemishes, while he
joined with them in a common effort to enhance territorial economic

and political life. That approach had brought him his short-lived position as superintendent of Indian affairs for Washington Territory in 1861, and it landed him the contract for Mail Delivery on Route #15274 in 1864.

The contract won, however, Miller stumbled during the first months as he searched for a suitable ship. At the outset, he hoped that his friend David B. Finch, purser and captain of the *Eliza Anderson,* would be interested. But Finch's San Francisco partner, Captain John Wright, demurred because of the losses he had already suffered in his dealings with Keach. Miller then tried to secure the *Jenny Jones,* a steamer under skipper Jimmy Jones, but that ship had a troubled history and friends warned Miller to be cautious. The warnings were prudent, for several months later creditors seized the ship for debt at Victoria and had Jones clapped into jail. Miller finally invested his own money in the *Eliza Anderson,* buying a controlling interest in the ship in March 1865. He then subcontracted with Wright to operate the mail run for the full amount of the contract.[1]

While pursuing these negotiations, Miller purchased outstanding mail delivery certificates from Keach. Contractors had to present contract certificates and vouchers to the Post Office Department to get reimbursement. Miller had purchased unredeemed certificates from Keach, ones that covered several months of work but had not yet been presented to the department. The income Miller planned to collect by redeeming the certificates would help finance his operation on the Sound. He had need for cash, because in lieu of getting a firm subcontract with a substantial vessel, Miller had hired sailing vessels and other available craft plying the Sound to carry the mails. It was his hope that his resourcefulness and general competency would impress the Post Office Department sufficiently to get an extension of the contract in 1866. As he bragged to Goldsborough in April 1865, "My mail is being carried in the most regular and punctual style. It has not missed a trip. . . . I have had the mail carried with a regularity never known before" on the Sound.[2]

Miller had paid Keach nearly five thousand dollars for the certificates, which was only a portion of their redemption value. By mid-

1865, Keach's financial problems had worsened, prompting him to request the rest of his money, which he assumed Miller had received from the Post Office Department. "Unless I raise some money within a very short time," Keach pleaded to Miller in May 1865, "Hell won't save me!" Three months later he whined, "Can't you advance me 2000 in Greenbacks to go to Portland with to purchase grub?" Although Miller may have sympathized, he did little to help him. Keach's poor performance had made it more difficult for Miller, because Keach had not paid many of his subcontractors. More to the point, Keach's failure had hamstrung Miller's effort to redeem the certificates. The Post Office Department rejected the certificates, leaving Miller with no reimbursement at all.[3]

During the summer and fall of 1865, nine months into his mail contract, Miller set into a frustrating round of protracted negotiations to get his federal payments. In some ways, it repeated his experience with the Third Auditor over Indian War claims and the Indian Department with vouchers during his tenure as superintendent of Indian affairs. The Post Office Department would not release any of the money until Miller provided all of the vouchers for expenditures under the contract. But those documents were in the hands of Keach's subcontractors, who would not give them up until they were paid. Not only did Miller not have Keach's additional payments, but he also had no reimbursements for his own investment since September 1864. In a classic, almost humorous exchange of letters, Miller tried to explain the situation to auditor McLellan and anyone else in authority at the department. He received only bureaucratic doublespeak in response. Finally, in August 1865, Olympia Postmaster F. M. Sargent certified Miller's faithful work and explained his unusual predicament. Miller soon got some of the money owed him, but he still had Keach on his books for nearly five thousand dollars and he had expended between twenty and thirty thousand on the *Eliza Anderson*.[4]

By September, Miller was completely exasperated. Writing to new Territorial Delegate Arthur A. Denny of Seattle, he nearly pleaded for help to cut through the confusion at the Post Office. He also asked Goldsborough to apply what pressure he could through McLellan.

Finally, Miller received more of the money owed him, although none of the amount he had requested to compensate for the original certificates purchased from Keach. Miller worried that these difficulties with the department would prejudice his application for an extension of his contract. But Goldsborough assured him that all was well, adding,

> I must only remind you, my dear fellow, that you voluntarily told me that you would cheerfully give me one thousand dollars, if I succeeded in getting you the [original] contract which I did most effectually and that too under somewhat difficult circumstances. I shall leave that matter to your generous appreciation . . . as at present I am suffering from "impecuniosity."[5]

It was Miller's fate to get it from both sides. Keach nagged him for money he could not extract from the Post Office Department, while Goldsborough nudged him for a political commission. If Miller ever paid his lobbyist he probably did it under protest, because the contract was not extended in the spring of 1866. The Post Office Department opened it up to competitive bidding, an action a sheepish McLellan later admitted to Goldsborough was a miscalculation, and Miller lost out to another bidder by more than five hundred dollars. He quickly sold out his share of the *Anderson* and said goodbye to the mail delivery business.[6]

Although Miller's eighteen-month stint as the mail contractor on Puget Sound may not have netted him the income he had expected, it did demonstrate his increasing importance in territorial affairs. Men of both parties in the territory had affirmed their confidence in him, but opposition politicians increasingly sought his advice and attributed to him real and imagined powers. In late 1864, Joseph Cushman and A. A. Denny pressured Miller to lobby in Washington, D.C., for the territory because they were convinced that Pickering and Henry would do only the national administration's bidding and leave the territory defenseless. In the sometimes paradoxical world of Civil War politics in Washington Territory, Republicans were putting their faith in a Democratic wheelhorse in counterpoint to appointed Republican officials. Miller also found himself in the uncomfortable position of being chastised by a Democratic paper, the *Washington Democrat*, while the Republican *Washington Standard* defended him. That was partly explained by the *Democrat*'s Copperhead leanings and the *Standard*'s uncompromising Unionist platform, but the support some Republicans gave Miller had also gestated naturally from his careful nurturing of relationships in both parties. By mid-1865, even Thomas Prosch, the feisty Republican editor of the Steilacoom *Puget Sound Herald*—who in 1859 had called Miller "one of the thieves" of public monies in the territory—believed that Miller was "all powerful and can abrogate or establish a Post Office at will," even under a Republican administration. Miller had no such power, of course, but he did have well-placed Washington contacts in both parties, and he had no hesitancy in using them to his and the territory's best advantage.[7]

As a committed Unionist in 1864, Miller stood squarely in the middle of the territory's political spectrum, with committed Lincoln and abolitionist Republicans on one side and Copperhead Democrats on the other. His most nettlesome problem remained his relationship with Elwood Evans. Governor Pickering and Surveyor General Henry continued to grumble about Evans and his dispensing of federal monies, too often to Copperhead cronies. Pickering had called Evans's office the Copperhead's "Headquarters . . . where they meet *every night* till very late hours to concoct & mature all their plans." Even one of Evans's closest allies had objected to him that his "main supporters . . . [had] been the most rabid open mouthed secessionists." It worried Miller as well, although confidants had assured him in late 1864 that "Evans does not appear to be so thick with the Copperheads as he was last winter." Nonetheless, Pickering warned Miller that he had placed himself in genuine jeopardy by agreeing to be Evans's bondsman. With Evans dispersing money to Copperheads, Pickering advised Miller, "you will have to stand Godfather and Godmother for the faithful disbursement" of federal funds. Failure in that legal responsibility, Pickering reminded him, would expose him to liability for any malfeasance. Miller had tried earlier to get William H. Wallace to help remove him as Evans's bondsman without Miller having to go "to Evans himself, which I do not want to do," but Wallace evidently did little to help. When Miller had assured Pickering that Wallace had promised to intercede, the governor replied: "Bah, such nonsense." Wallace had actually been a strong defender of Evans's interests, Pickering informed Miller, and had stymied Pickering's own effort to have Evans removed as territorial secretary.[8]

The shifting political landscape gave Democrats and Republicans fits during the war years. Both parties were factionalized, leaving personal loyalties, business connections, and general opportunity the more predictable guides for political behavior. The Democrats had the worst of it, because they had practically no access to patronage and Republicans dominated the delegateship throughout the 1860s. The lone Democratic delegate, George E. "Ginger" Cole, hardly figured into the political equation at all. Elected in 1863 as something of a protest to the Puget Sound Democrats, Cole had Copperhead sympathies, which crippled him in Washington, where, according to Pickering in early 1865, he had no influence. Cole's Copperhead tendencies meant, as administration officials had told Pickering, that he "can never do any good for your territory, nor for any man in it."[9]

Miller and others outside the Republican circle in the territory felt relatively defenseless. With Lincoln's triumph over McClellan and the Peace Democrats in November 1864, it had become clear to Miller that only a strong Union man could be effective in Washington. By May 1865, the field of potential candidates for delegate had narrowed to representatives of two loose coalitions. The Republicans, calling themselves Unionists and attracting many erstwhile Democrats, including Miller, nominated Arthur A. Denny of Seattle. The Democrats, who had narrowed their appeal by adopting the Peace Democratic platform in 1864 and supporting McClellan, nominated James Tilton, the man who perhaps best symbolized the splintering of the Democratic party in the territory since the death of Stevens. Denny had solicited Miller's support as early as February, promising, "I shall be glad to hear from you and will never betray your confidence in anything you may suggest." Denny understood Miller's position well enough to know that he could not openly campaign for the Republicans, but even if he could persuade Miller to refrain from strongly supporting the Democratic nominee it would give his chances a boost.[10]

Miller, for his part, understood that Tilton had little chance to win, and if he did he would not favor Unionist Democrats. Tilton had won the nomination only because other candidates had withdrawn at the last moment and proxies went unvoted at the territorial convention. Miller, in fact, did not even attend the Democratic convention. Instead he quietly aided Denny's Union party effort. Although Democrats still outnumbered Republicans in the territory, not many voters favored Tilton's political position on the war and he lost badly. A poor speaker and reluctant campaigner, Denny enlisted Selucius Garfielde to go out on the stump, which he did with enthusiasm, as the *Washington Standard* put it, with "rolled up . . . sleeves and enlisted in the cause of the Union." Garfielde, no doubt, contributed to Denny's winning in all but four counties, some by huge majorities. In the larger counties, Denny trounced Tilton, winning by double or triple margins; in Jefferson, Denny won 245 votes to 8 for Tilton, and in Kitsap, Denny polled 258 to Tilton's 8.[11]

With Denny's election, a Republican would again represent the territory in Washington. But that did not mean a fairer day for Republicans or for Democratic Unionists like Miller. It turned out that Denny was not up to the job. In truth, he had not aggressively sought the office and had been pressured into running, which at least partially explains his timidity as territorial delegate. Within his first few weeks in Washington, he wrote Miller that the job was more than he could handle, confessing that all he wanted to do was go about his business and resume his life back home. It was patronage and the pestering of solicitous office-seekers that bedeviled him. Miller well understood those pressures and he may have had some sympathy for Denny, but he wisely demurred from helping the delegate with patronage decisions. Miller had no desire to get entangled in internecine struggles among Republicans. Yet, Miller was really little different from the pestering flock who pecked at Denny. He, too, wanted favors. Miller requested that Denny try to cut through the bureaucratic snags in the Post Office Department so he could finally get his full reimbursement for the mail contract. Denny responded with efficiency. By May 1866, Miller had his money.[12]

Miller's success with the Post Office Department and with Denny foretold nothing about his political future. No one's political future, in Washington Territory and throughout the nation, could be foretold with much confidence in 1866. The assassination of President Lincoln in 1865 and the ascendancy of Andrew Johnson to the presidency began one of the most trying periods of American history, one that was part and parcel of the crisis of Union and nearly its equal in political conflict. The reconstruction of the Union after the Confederate surrender focused congressional attention on the contentious political problems that had led to the Civil War. By 1870, Congress would pass three constitutional amendments, ending slavery and laying the basis for addressing inequalities in American society.

Throughout 1866, Miller and his cohorts in the territory felt the political reverberations from congressional conflicts over reconstruction. "Radical" Republicans insisted on punishing the South for its treason and laid down vindictive terms for reconstruction, including barring Confederate soldiers from political activity. Moderates of both parties feared more political divisiveness and favored more lenient reconstruction policies. "We are going through a great experiment in government," George Gibbs had written Miller from Washington, D.C., "a new one in history, for [compared to this] the pacification of England by Cromwell and by William the Silent was a simple matter." Unfortunately, the nation's political leader in 1866 had not the strength of Cromwell nor the fanaticism of William III, and he surely did not have the political skill of Lincoln. By mid-1866, President Andrew Johnson had become *the* political issue. An erstwhile Democrat from Tennessee who had joined Lincoln on the Union ticket in 1864 and had became president through tragedy, Johnson favored lenient policies toward the defeated states. Johnson's increasingly recalcitrant stance against Radical legislation aimed at the former Rebel states, his support of repressive "black codes" passed by southern state governments, and his intemperate political statements pushed more and more moderates into the Radical camp.[13]

The turmoil in the nation's capital affected politics in Washington Territory, where the Republicans split into warring camps. The officeholders who owed their jobs to Lincoln's men, as the *Olympia Transcript* put it, had to wave the Radical banner. Their opponents called them "bolters," because they would not support Johnson's policies, but by most definitions there probably were few "regular" party men left. The bolters included Governor Pickering, the newly appointed surveyor general, Selucius Garfielde, and R. H. Hewitt, publisher of the *Pacific Tribune*. The Johnson men in the Republican party actually proposed a new organization, the National Union Party. Elwood Evans represented the territory at the National Union Party convention in Philadelphia in August. Miller, along with a group of moderate politicians who included O. B. McFadden, T. F. McElroy, James Longmire, and George Blankenship, also championed Johnson. When the president took the fight against his congressional foes to the stump during the fall electoral campaign in 1866—a gamble that proved disastrous for him—Miller and his cohorts showed their support by holding a large public meeting. They met, pledged themselves to the defeat of Radicalism, and reeled out a broadside: "There are lepers South and lepers North that seek to destroy the Union. The one commands the radical, the other seeks to infest the conservative party." In the midst of these political fireworks, Miller and his fellows had taken their stand squarely at the conservative center.[14]

Regardless of their choices, all politicians became part of a national political gamble in 1866. If congressional Radicals defeated Johnson, then they would have the upper hand; if the president prevailed, then the Radicals would lose power. All patronage would be affected. William Pickering had felt sufficiently threatened to request aid from powerful Illinois Congressman Richard Yates, who wrote a personal letter to President Johnson urging Pickering's reappointment as territorial governor.[15] It was Miller's natural conservatism, not his political handicapping, that had inclined him toward Johnson's brand of reconstruction. It was, more or less, a reflection of his earlier support of Breckinridge in 1860. But there was also a full measure of opportunism in his joining the Johnson men in the territory. By staying in the political center and supporting the federal administration, Miller hoped to gain notice and perhaps some favors from Washington, D.C. His opportunity came in late 1866, when his allies in the territory suggested him for a second go at superintendent for Indian affairs. Facing another lobbying effort to obtain federal position, Miller knew that the key person in Congress representing the Northwest was Oregon Senator James Nesmith, himself a former superintendent of Indian affairs and an interested participant in Miller's earlier pursuit of the job. Miller had an entrée to Nesmith through Isaac Stevens's son, Hazard. He had served Hazard and his mother, Margaret Stevens, as executor of the estate and manager of their family affairs in Olympia. By 1866, he had become the family's most important adviser.[16]

In October, just after the Johnson men in the territory had organized, Miller wrote to Hazard and described the political situation:

> The scramble for offices has commenced here. The Johnson men here are determined that the Radical officials hereabouts shall walk the plank. In a full meeting of all the leading Johnson men of the Sound, held here not long since, it was determined to put my name forward for the Indian Superintendency. This they did without any solicitation of mine, but simply upon the ground as they thought that I was the strongest man.

His hat in the ring, Miller admitted to Stevens that "I don't want to be beaten." He needed the young Stevens's good relations with Isaac Stevens's friends, men who had a direct and powerful connection with federal appointments in the Northwest.

> The whole thing will depend on Nesmith and I want you to write to Nesmith and . . . [get] Gen. [Rufus] Ingalls to see Nesmith for me. My acquaintance with Ingalls is limited, but he knows of me well, and probably at your request he would put in for me. P.S. If you can pull any other strings for me, do it.[17]

Miller could have picked a better time to lunge for a federal appointment. The political divisiveness created by the conflict between Johnson and the Radicals made all political decisions mercurial, if not capricious. Miller wanted the office, as he protested to Hazard

Stevens, not because he had any "ambitions or selfish ends to accomplish" but only "in order to have active employment and at the same time to be able to assist my friends." Still, as he confessed, "I have never yet been defeated for any office I have tried for," and he intended to get it. "My friends in Illinois will do all they can with [Orville H.] Browning the Secretary of Interior who is an old friend of ours. Everybody here is for me." Despite his efforts, Miller fell short. The administration selected Thomas J. McKenny, a solid Johnson man from Iowa, as the new superintendent. Nesmith later wrote Miller that the decision had been made before he received any petitions supporting Miller's nomination, but it was almost certainly politics that nixed Miller's chances. Johnson's support in Congress had steadily eroded since the elections, and it is also likely that Miller had less than full support in the territory. Samuel D. Smith of Walla Walla, for example, had actively sought the post, and Miller suspected that Evans had secretly aided him while loudly proclaiming his endorsement of Miller. Later, Miller complained that he feared Evans had been "trying to 'play me.'"[18]

Politics in Washington Territory, reflecting the national tendencies, increasingly took on the paranoiac tenor Miller divulged in his worries about Evans. In late November, the president brought his own political problems to Olympia when he summarily dumped Governor Pickering in favor of former Democratic Delegate Ginger Cole, who had pledged unqualified support to Johnson. In a political atmosphere where a Democrat could serve a nominally Republican president, politicians in Washington Territory worried about who they could possibly find to represent them in Congress. They needed an adept centrist, someone who could connect with the broadest range of political interests. Likely it was those concerns that prompted several prominent men to urge Miller to run for territorial delegate in 1867. He might have stood a chance, but his loss of the superintendent position probably made him hesitate. Still, he must have been emboldened when a strong Democrat wrote him: "Old Wallace was bad enough but Denny! Ye Gods! In fact, since Stevens who have we had here so capable as W. W. [Miller]." Regardless of such demonstrations of support and a certain boost to his ego, Miller could write Hazard Stevens in early 1867:

> I have not the least earthly desire or ambition to run for Congress even were I sure of election. My ambition does not run that way and I shall content myself with carefully managing my private business so as to glide down the hill of life quietly, but I hope happily and free from anxiety about political ambition. I have seen so many disappointed politicians on this Coast who in their old age have been brought to want and grief. I dread being brought to a similar fate.[19]

Miller's focus on his private business was pushing politics into the background. His business interests had expanded; and in January 1867, when Democrats were suggesting that he run for delegate, he was in San Francisco tending to business affairs. He had first visited the city in 1861, but it was not until his short tenure as a mail contractor and contact with San Francisco investors that he began to think seriously about opportunities there. A. M. Poe, who had resettled in San Francisco in 1864, urged Miller to move down, promising he could make money and "at all events you could enjoy life better here than in Olympia." Miller surely understood Poe's reference to life's enjoyments, but the lures of a fast-paced life in San Francisco evidently were not enough in 1864 to convince him to abandon politics and the Sound. But when David Phillips, a business associate in Olympia who had moved to San Francisco in 1864, encouraged him to investigate possibilities in 1866, Miller seems to have been ready. Once there, he reacquainted himself with ship masters and owners he had known during his years in the customs service and made contacts with prominent real estate men.[20]

San Francisco shone brightly in Miller's eyes. The climate seemed to restore his health, and the city's allurements drew him more than he probably liked to admit. He may have been giving serious consideration to leaving Olympia by early 1867, but a disturbing episode in San Francisco likely stanched his interest. If there was a culprit in Miller's difficulties in the metropolis by the Bay, it was probably his awkwardness with women. From his days in Illinois, he had carried a reputation of being clumsy around women, even though he seemed to attract them. As his brother had put it, Miller was "afraid to look at anything that wears petticoats." Nevertheless, he had been intimately involved with a few women. A friend, writing him not long after he had arrived in Oregon, told him of the loss of one of his ardent girl-friends, a woman he had evidently known intimately. "Nancy Summer is married," his friend wrote, adding "poor fellow [the groom] he did not have first chance at Nancy's maidenhead."[21]

In Olympia and around Puget Sound during the 1850s, Miller had earned the reputation of attracting women but never pursuing relationships. Evidently, he knew enough women to field queries about who they were and where they could be found. Daniel Bigelow, an Olympia friend of Miller's, had written him in 1853 from Oregon City: "I want you to write me the names of the best girls in this vicinity and where they live."[22] He had written about marriage plans to his brother Robert on several occasions during the late 1850s, but it may be that one of his friends correctly identified his problem. "You know your failing on this subject," John Sewell had written Miller in 1859, "*you are too slow.*" Referring to a woman in Olympia, Sewell continued:

> She looks charming, I am in love with her myself but ruined my prospects by telling her that one of the richest men in the territory was in love with her. She is curious to meet you.[23]

There are suggestions that, along with his friends, Miller frequented bawdy houses. He appeared to have some manner of regular relationship with one woman referred to as "Becky" or "Fat Becky" and another named "Fanny." In 1865, Phillip Keach, one of Miller's business associates, made a jocular but lewd allusion to Miller's activities: "Dost ever think of Fanny? May she long live to wag her *tail.*"[24] Whether these affairs were numerous is impossible to tell, although as late as the spring of 1869, just months before he would marry, a friend wrote him that "your house of 'easy virtue' is about played out."[25]

During his several trips to San Francisco in the mid-1860s, Miller evidently established friendships with several women whom he met through business associates in the city. Mary Ann Palmer had recently been widowed and lived as a renter in the house of one of Miller's friends.[26] By 1865, he had established a romantic attachment to her, and for more than eighteen months Miller saw Mrs. Palmer during his visits to San Francisco. But then something went wrong. In late 1866, she filed a breach-of-contract complaint in San Francisco, specifying that Miller had promised to marry her but had reneged. Her suit charged that Miller had been "crafty and deceiving" in making her numerous promises, but finally had jilted her in October 1866. Palmer requested $30,000 in damages. Miller tried to dissuade her and then did his best to discourage attorneys from taking her case, but in the end he agreed to pay her $400.[27]

How culpable Miller was is impossible to tell, but there is some evidence that he may have been genuine in his promises to marry Mrs. Palmer. His erstwhile associate, T. F. McElroy, for one, was surprised when he learned that Palmer filed her complaint and he discovered that Miller had not already married her in San Francisco. Other friends found the whole affair amusing, and some, like S. D. Howe, wondered why Miller had tried to dodge the issue and duck his responsibility. "I heard you had all the lawyers engaged so that the sexy deluded gal could get no one to take her case," Howe wrote Miller. "Why the devil didn't you marry her and have done with it?" Miller never answered that question, but McElroy probably had it about right when he called the whole business a bit of bad judgment on Miller's part. "I see by the paper you sent me," McElroy commented, "that you and your 'pullet' have settled that little difficulty. You got off cheaper than I thought you would."[28]

Miller's interest in California, with or without Mrs. Palmer in his future, centered on his investments. Those investments, while not suficient to pull him away from Olympia, may have encouraged him to consider moving south, but territorial politics still pulled at him. By early February, McElroy had pestered him twice to come back to Olympia to aid the Democrats in the elections. Governor-designate Ginger Cole had come to Olympia to replace Pickering, but as McElroy reported to Miller: "'Pick' looked at his [Cole's] commission and pronounced it all right, but said he must have time to think about it." The legislature had no hesitation, though, and promptly welcomed Cole with a 100-gun salute. Pickering held out because he knew that a Congress that was becoming more Radical by the week might well question President Johnson's patronage choices, and they did. The Senate rejected Cole's nomination as governor, which again made Elwood Evans acting governor and created a small political whirlwind in the territory. A scramble ensued for the delegate nomination. McElroy wrote to Miller that "Cole is our choice for delegate. . . . he is the available man." In part, McElroy showed enthusiasm for Cole because Frank Clark of Steilacoom had thrown his hat in the ring, and McElroy— as well as many others—could not forget the anti-Stevens role Clark had played during the martial law controversy nine years earlier. "Come up as soon as you can," McElroy pleaded with Miller, "and help us nominate Cole."[29]

Miller must have felt under a political barrage in San Francisco. Politicos from Walla Walla, Olympia, and Port Townsend peppered him with requests to return home immediately. The Johnson men worried most, because they saw their centrist group softening. John T. Knox wrote Miller with a sense of urgency in mid-February, reporting that some Johnson backers had doubled back to their Democratic home bases because they feared the Radicals' increasing strength, nationally and in the territory. "So you see," Knox implored Miller,

> by you leaving the country our party [conservative Democrats] has been entirely ignored, and . . . [we] are again at sea without a pilot. Can't you come up and set us all strait [sic] again?[30]

Miller did not set his cohorts straight in 1867. In fact, he did not arrive back in the territory until after the convention, and then to face a most difficult political situation. Clark had won the Democratic nomination in April. In the June general election, Clark would face Union party nominee Alvan Flanders, a businessman from Wallula who had strong political ties to Oregon and California Republicans.[31] Once again, territorial voters had to choose between candidates who represented conflicting national and local political issues, making the choice especially unsatisfying. Frank Clark claimed to speak for residents along the Sound, but he carried the burden of connections with Copperheads and the legacy of his dispute with Isaac Stevens. Alvan Flanders stood squarely for Unionist principles, but represented eastside interests that reflected a growing impatience with the near stranglehold Puget Sound politicians wielded over public policy in the territory.[32]

The candidates addressed the most divisive political issue of the day, the fate of Andrew Johnson's Reconstruction program and his presidency, but the campaign spun around what the electorate saw as personal differences. Most newspapers backed Flanders, partly because of his Unionist platform and partly because he appeared more attractive than the "burly Democratic nominee," as the *Seattle Gazette* put it. Papers supporting Clark, including the *Washington Standard,* countered by charging that Flanders was really a tool of the milling and transportation corporations, especially the Oregon Steam Navigation Company. They also chided Flanders about his poor speaking ability and lampooned his reliance on Garfielde's oratorical talents. The Democrats printed up flyers depicting Flanders and Garfielde as Don Quioxte and Sancho Panza wandering about in search of voters, appended with this piece of doggerel:

> Alvan Flanders rode upon,
> A horse that wouldn't mind him,
> And so to act as fugleman
> Selucius rode behind him.
>
> Selucius was a proper man,
> And had so good a straddle
> That he could ride two horses with
> One office for a saddle. . . .
>
> And thus they rode from place to place,
> Where'er their poney bore them;
> When Flanders had to speak a piece,
> Selucius spoke it for him.[33]

While Flanders suffered witty barbs from the Democrats, the Republicans practically tore Clark apart. They pilloried him as the

"Orphan Boy of Pierce County" who offered as many opinions as he had audiences and chiefly pursued his own well-being. They charged him with being a stooge for Hudson's Bay Company, because he served as legal counsel for the Puget Sound Agricultural Company. But the most damaging criticism came from Garfielde on the stump, when he challenged Clark's opposition to the 14th Amendment to the U.S. Constitution. Garfielde told his audiences that Clark's Copperhead opinions proved that he and "the Democratic Party of Washington Territory [were] behind the times," that he was, as Garfielde put it, "like a pup nine days old." The Port Townsend *Weekly Message* asked the fundamental question: "Congress being Radical, would [it] be more apt to listen to a Republican delegate than one opposed to its interests?" The paper and other Flanders supporters answered in the affirmative.[34]

Miller's answer put him on the opposite side of the issue. Fearing the Radicals' domination of Congress, he supported Clark, even though he could hardly forget Clark's traducing of Isaac Stevens or his attempts to wrest the territorial capital from Olympia. After learning of Clark's nomination, Miller wrote Hazard Stevens from San Francisco and laid out his reasons for supporting Clark:

> Well I see the Democratic Conservative Convention has nominated Frank Clark for Delegate. I shall do all I can to secure Frank's election as I honestly believe that the salvation of the country depends on our ability to overthrow Radicalism.[35]

As much as he wished for Clark's election, Miller could do little to aid the Democrats' fledgling campaign. Clark canvassed the territory, but he drew small crowds and could not seem to escape his own political past. Flanders, on the other hand, attracted considerable attention and a number of Democratic defectors to his camp, including Hazard Stevens. One of Miller's informants explained Clark's failure in his county in starkly realistic terms:

Clark told his friends that he had plenty of money to spend and was going to spend it, [but] Flanders' friend bought all of the whiskey shops . . . and it elected him in this county.[36]

Flanders trounced Clark, winning all but one county. The election left Miller with a smaller political base than he had enjoyed since becoming a Democrat in 1853. Although he had fervently supported the Union cause during the war, his conservative political beliefs impelled him away from liberal Democrats and informed his opposition to Radical Republican policies. He decried congressional attacks on Johnson, referring to it as a reign of terror and the work of Jacobins. He felt most comfortable in the political center, which had coalesced for a time around Johnson's presidency, but that world had crumbled by the summer of 1868. Increasingly, Miller's political activities shifted from a focus on party organization to the desires and needs of his closest friends in the territory, friends who tended to agree with him that what mattered most was the furtherance of local enterprise and investments. His political opinions were still important to party members, especially to those who sought favors, patronage, or offices. Even when he sojourned to San Francisco—from January to April 1867 and from October 1867 to April 1868—he kept closely in touch with political events in Olympia, offering advice and responding to solicitations for his aid.[37] But it was his prominence as a territorial businessman that kept him involved in politics.

For more than a decade, Miller had ridden both horses, the political stallion and the economic mare, and he finally chose the surest finisher. By mid-1868, Miller had returned to his strength, his business acumen, and he pursued enterprise for all that it might bring. In that context, he measured his friends less by a political standard and more by a broader enterprise standard—those he could aid, those who could aid him, and those who owed him.[38]

CHAPTER 10

Pursuing the Main Chance

Miller, we have got Rail Road on the Brain over here.
Thomas Fletcher to Miller, December 25, 1868

A good many political adventurers are coming into
the territory, who they are or what they amount to we
shall see.
Miller to Selucius Garfielde, January 1, 1871

San Francisco lured Miller like a siren. At times, the city by the Bay drew his financial interest; at other times, its society, especially a community of businessmen, tempted him to consider relocating. But he consistently followed his conservative instincts, seemingly waiting for a compelling combination of economic and personal allurements to justify a move. Perhaps his affair with Mrs. Palmer in 1866 had expressed a desire to live in San Francisco. If so, its conclusion surely must have dampened his enthusiasm. Still, he initiated significant connections during extended visits in 1866 and 1867 that would keep him attached to San Francisco throughout the remainder of his life.

Miller's familiarity with San Francisco came through his friendship with steamboat Captains Duncan B. Finch and John Wright, who introduced him to the city's dynamic business environment. The city had first been established as the emporium and metropolis for the placer mining camps that sprouted along the gold-bearing streams that drained the Sierra, becoming an "instant city," as one historian called it. San Francisco capitalized on its harbor and a boisterous optimism that produced a boomer economy. By 1864, when Miller began spending some of each winter in the city, the rich Comstock mining district in Nevada was a dominant force in the city's life and continued to infuse gold and silver into the local economy. The concentration of capital in the hands of an aggressive entrepreneurial class made San Francisco the investment center of the Pacific Coast region.[1]

Miller's first investments that cycled through San Francisco and involved him with other entrepreneurs there came in 1866. One of Miller's acquaintances in the city, Captain George Plummer, sought capital to refurbish a declining Puget Sound mill property—the Freeport Mill—in which Plummer held a major share. Miller knew the other stockholders, Puget Sound residents C. C. Phillips and J. R. Williamson, and had extended both men credit in the past, but it was Plummer who proposed that Miller provide new capital for the mill. Miller delayed his response for several months, concerned that he might be burdened as he had been in Simmons's mill property in Olympia a decade earlier and wise enough to know that his dalliance might well improve the terms. The strategy paid off on at least one count, when he extracted assignment of deeds on the Freeport Mill and notes Plummer held on H. L. Yesler's Main Street Wharf in Seattle in exchange for $7,434 in cash, which Miller extended Plummer in early April 1867. But Miller's poor luck in mill-related business investments continued when a disastrous fire nearly leveled the property only weeks after his loan was given.[2]

The fire hastened Miller's return to the Sound from San Francisco in mid-April. Once in Seattle with the mill's stockholders, he played the key role in sorting out liabilities and financial obligations.[3] Those discussions resulted in a three-year involvement with Freeport Mill finances, but of more long-term consequence to Miller were the connections he made in San Francisco's financial community in 1866–1867.

His growing familiarity with businessmen and bankers led directly to an investment in city real estate. Just days after he had left for Seattle, J. B. Whitcomb wrote Miller about commercial lots in the city. Whitcomb was also an associate of David L. Phillips, one of Miller's Puget Sound merchant friends who had recently moved to San Francisco. He advised Miller that some prime lots could be obtained "with a little hush money" paid to certain parties who might facilitate a sale. The lead was promising enough for Miller to return to San Francisco during the fall of 1867 to look over Whitcomb's selections.[4]

An investigation led Miller to an expanding area of the city south of Market Street. During the early 1860s, the section had become a booming warehouse district, dotted with some small manufacturing businesses and many vacant lots. Miller wanted revenue-producing property, and lots without structures offered the widest possible use. Properties with buildings narrowed the lease market and thereby increased his risk. With these factors in mind, Miller paid $25,000 for several vacant lots on Folsom Street between Fourth and Fifth streets. It is likely that he settled on these specific lots because of suggestions from Henry L. Davis, whom Miller met through Phillips. Davis, who was president of the California Trust Company, owned a large parcel in the same block and evidently had encouraged other business associates to invest in the area. Whatever the sequence of events and his specific reasons, Miller ended his winter sojourn as a San Francisco property holder and taxpayer.[5]

Although he had made a sizable investment and had earlier written his brother in Idaho that he intended "to see if I can find a home down in California which will suit me better than Washington Territory," Miller decided against moving in 1868. He still had as much or more interest in real estate near Olympia, investments that might become very remunerative if the Northern Pacific Railroad selected the town as its western terminus.[6] And there were other investment opportunities on the Sound. Returning home in the spring of 1868, he left the management of his newly purchased properties in the hands of Young and Paxson, a San Francisco commercial house, which secured leases, collected rents, and advised Miller on taxes and other financial matters associated with the lots. By early summer, Young and Paxson had drawn up a fourteen-year lease with George Maxwell for the southside lots on Folsom Street with escalating rents that began at $100 per month for the first year and concluded with $600 per month charges. The lessee also was responsible for all taxes and assessments on the property. Miller must have felt quite satisfied with these arrangements. He had a secure lease with ample return on investment, plus the knowledge that property values in the city were on a sharp increase. As one associate commented:

> Your "head was right" when you determined to invest in lots in San Francisco without buildings on them, for the only chance of your property being injured in an earthquake will be by threats of a fissure and even then the hole would belong to you and could be filled up.[7]

Although Miller's "head was right" in his San Francisco investments, he had a more compelling interest in opportunities on the Sound. The most important one focused on the construction of the Northern Pacific Railroad and depended on decisions made in corporate board rooms far removed from the region. The selection of the railroad's western terminus was a prize coveted by nearly every sizable community on the Sound. It carried enormous economic rewards, for whichever community secured the prize would surely bolt to the forefront of Pacific Northwest cities. Along with several other Olympia businessmen, Miller hoped, gambled, and prayed that the NP would choose their town. Miller's second business opportunity, which was more modest in ambition and immediate in attainment, drew him into a political alliance of unusual dimensions. The business was coal, and the prospective political ally was Selucius Garfielde.

Garfielde had always hungered for the kind of success Miller enjoyed. A political gadfly whose instinct for the opportunistic chance knew no equal in Washington Territory, Garfielde had tasted some political success, but his financial desires had never been satisfied. In pursuit of the latter, he had joined Daniel and Clarence Bagley of Seattle in the development of a coalfield near Lake Washington. He had first become interested in the deposits while serving in the Washington Territory surveyor general's office, when he had established a few claims with the discoverers, Philip H. Lewis and Edwin Richardson. But Garfielde did not have enough funds to play a major role in the project, so he drew the Bagleys into the group. Pooling their claims and resources, the mine owners publicized their holdings as the richest in the region. Despite the quality of coal in the field, however, knowledgeable men predicted that the mines would be a "fizzle," because they could never compete with other, more developed mines, especially ones north on the Sound.[8]

The critics were right, even though the partners had managed to sell some coal to Seattle consumers. What the owners lacked was adequate transportation. The solution was a railroad around Lake Washington, but no one had enough capital, surely not Garfielde and his partners. Some wanted the recently chartered Northern Pacific Railroad to develop the mines, while others hoped San Francisco interests would become interested. Garfielde and Bagley attracted investors, but ended up offering all or part of the mining company stock for sale in 1868. Knowing his connections with San Francisco capitalists, Garfielde asked Miller to facilitate the sale of mining stock, and Miller obliged.[9]

Although Miller's political associations with Garfielde had been fractious and uneven, he had always admired his oratorical talents, especially when Garfielde had taken to the stump as a Stevens Democrat in the 1850s. But Miller despised the destructive political tactics Garfielde had used during the 1859 campaign, when he had switched allegiance and supported William H. Wallace against Stevens in the delegate race. It was easy to distrust Garfielde. His political path had been snakelike, which many judged to be the result of his singular and self-interested pursuit of offices and favors. He was just the kind of politician Miller detested, a man who cared little for party or personal loyalties. Despite his oily reputation, however, Garfielde had succeeded in aligning with winners and using his national political connections, especially among Democrats in Kentucky, to secure favors. By the late 1860s, he held the office of surveyor general and wielded considerable patronage power. Miller remained wary of him, although he did not object when Garfielde wrote an effusive letter to James Nesmith in support of Miller's application for superintendent of Indian affairs in 1866. By 1868, Miller had evidently put his political misgivings aside—or ignored them—and agreed to aid Garfielde and his Republican friends on the coal deal.[10]

Whether Miller's involvement in the sale of the mining company stock softened his attitude toward Garfielde or other factors convinced him to befriend the wily politician is unclear. Garfielde had always looked for the main chance, and by early 1869 he had deftly maneuvered himself into a strong political position. Two years earlier, he had joined with Territorial Governor Marshall Moore, a Unionist Democrat, to diminish the power of the more conservative Johnson forces in the territory and had succeeded in getting Elwood Evans removed as territorial secretary. The removal of Evans had altered the political balance of power in the territory, had deprived T. F. McElroy of the printing concession, and had thrown the selection of the public printer back into the spoils game. McElroy had sold his printing business to Republican interests—men who had established the *Olympia Transcript*—but he retained the mortgage. He hoped to become the public printer once again if the *Transcript*'s man, Alvan Flanders, won the delegate race. Flanders did beat his opponent, but by fewer than 200 votes of 5,000 cast. Standing on a wobbly and thin political base, Flanders dared not aid McElroy. But even if he had been inclined to, the new territorial secretary, Ezra Smith, took venality one step further by milking his own patronage opportunity and selling the public printer's office to Charles Prosch, publisher of the Republican *Pacific Tribune*. These internecine party disputes gave Garfielde his opportunity. By early 1869, he had taken over the middle ground and stood as a serious threat to Flanders's renomination.[11]

Garfielde had telegraphed his ambitions in the 1868 presidential contest when he had stumped Washington Territory and Oregon on behalf of U.S. Grant and Schuyler Colfax. His actions had drawn criticism from Elwood Evans, who correctly interpreted Garfielde's electioneering as the first round of his own candidacy for territorial delegate in 1869. The Democrats watched and warned the public that Garfielde could not be trusted and had likely already made a deal with the Grant men for a patronage job from the new administration. While Miller kept clear of any political activity in late 1868 and early 1869, one of his confidants advised him to get behind Garfielde for delegate. His chances were good, John Knox wrote to Miller: "I thought if he [Garfielde] would have a talk with you . . . there would be no doubt but you could understand each other."[12] The expected understanding between the men, Knox assumed, would be based on business and finance, not politics. But Miller hoped that O. B. McFadden might be persuaded to run for delegate. McFadden was a strong Johnson man and Unionist with conservative leanings, just the kind of Democratic candidate who could attract Republican votes, especially if Garfielde defeated Flanders for the Republican nomination.[13]

By March 1869, Miller had corresponded with Garfielde about the coming political season and his chances to secure election. He had stopped far short of endorsing Garfielde, but evidently had given the perennial candidate some advice. Responding to Miller's counsel, Garfielde pledged that he had read his suggestions "in detail" and that if elected he would take "every possible plan suggested by friends" and pursue them "with a pertinacity that will admit of no denial." He also promised Miller: "I will prove to you that your confidence has not been misplaced." Knowing that Miller had McFadden's ear, Garfielde openly entreated him to discourage the judge from running, boastfully adding that a contest between the two men "would greatly embarrass" McFadden. If Garfielde was nothing else, he was a gutsy politician, one who boasted easily and cobbled together deals whenever possible.[14]

Although Miller spent more than four months in California during the winter of 1868–1869, he regularly received reports on developments in territorial politics. He knew that the Republican press had chosen sides, the *Pacific Tribune* supporting Flanders and the *Territorial Republican* backing Garfielde. Republican divisiveness could have given the dispirited Democrats an unmerited opportunity in 1869, but President Grant stepped in and silenced the Republican squabble by appointing Alvan Flanders territorial governor. The Democrats lost their advantage and Garfielde got an unearned and open path to the Republican nomination. In their nominating convention, the Democrats countered by choosing Marshall Moore, the ousted territorial governor who had earlier angered Union party men by undermining President Johnson and reverting to his more partisan Democratic allegiances.[15]

The election of U.S. Grant in 1868 had signaled the end of wartime fusionist politics and a diminishing of the strident conflicts that had characterized the Johnson presidency. For the next decade, economic development and a particularly unbridled style in partisanship, much of it still centered on wartime political issues, would dominate national and regional politics. Both parties contended with internal divisions over important economic and social issues, but they had generally regrouped and coalesced around traditional political ideas, the Republicans emphasizing corporate economic growth and the Democrats resisting centralizing tendencies in the national government.

In Washington Territory, the 1869 delegate election demarcated a change as well—the return to two-party political competition. The contest between Garfielde and Moore suggested that the parties had about an even hold on the electorate; in fact, Garfielde prevailed by only 130 votes. But the closeness of the election was misleading. Garfielde, who had spent more than a decade on the stump or in appointed office, should have easily defeated Moore, who had been in the territory only two years. But Moore had paraded himself as a man of experience, a veteran of the war, and a confidant of important men, including General Sherman and President Grant, contrasting himself sharply with Garfielde, who carried a reputation as a draft dodger. Garfielde had "fled to British Columbia during the war," the *Washington Standard* charged, adding that he was a man "without principles of political honesty." But Moore's campaign failed to capitalize enough on the war issue and ended up sending a mixed message, primarily because the party platform undercut Moore's stridently patriotic posturing. The party had passed strongly worded resolutions in their convention critical of the Fourteenth and Fifteenth amendments. Worse yet, when O. B. McFadden took to the stump for Moore he seemed to contradict him by emphasizing a moderate and almost states' rights position on Reconstruction in the South, eschewing any waving of the "bloody shirt."[16]

More telling to the prime interests of both parties and the general direction of territorial politics was the exchange of charges that centered on Moore's connections with Portland economic interests. Miller got caught in the political volleys because it was well known that he and his cohorts had some financial connections with W. S. Ladd, Portland banker and heavy investor in Columbia River transportation, and that he had been a major stockholder in the Columbia Transportation Company, which had hoped to develop a river transportation business. The Republicans charged that McFadden had gone into the Vancouver convention with enough proxies to win, but Moore emerged the nominee after the Portland men had contributed heavily to the party, possibly through Miller's agency. Typical of such campaign charges, the "evidence" was scanty and unconvincing, but it underscored that economic issues, not national political battles, had become the most divisive.

The *Vancouver Register* charged that Moore was nothing more than a stalking horse for Portland capitalists who were afraid of Ben Holladay's meddlesome and powerful entrance into railroad politics in the Northwest. A flamboyant and aggressive financier, Holladay had used reckless methods in a head-on challenge to the Oregon Steam Navigation Company's control of Columbia River transportation and its potential connection with the Northern Pacific Railroad. "Are you cowards," the *Register* asked readers, "that you should so easily submit?" The *Weekly Message* stated the thesis more directly: "What was the inducement for this remarkable somersault of the Democratic Delegates? Oregon cash!" There were no credible documents to prove the Republicans' charges, but there is little doubt that McFadden would have been a more formidable candidate than Moore. For Miller, it must have been a difficult experience. There is every likelihood that he wanted McFadden to succeed, because he agreed with him politically and shared business interests. But even more saliently, the divisiveness that was centered on his friend coincided with his active pursuit of McFadden's twenty-nine-year-old daughter, Mary.[17]

Miller had probably met Mary McFadden during the late 1850s, when she was fifteen or sixteen. Then over thirty, Miller probably saw the difference in their ages as prohibiting any romantic interest, but it is just as likely that he had been attracted to her independent personality. Born in Pennsylvania in 1840, Mary had come to Washington Territory with her family—which then included six children—when she was thirteen years old. She was the second child and first girl born to Margaret and O. B. McFadden, who would have eleven children by 1858, including two sets of twins. Mary grew up in Washington and Pennsylvania, the daughter of one of the most prominent lawyers in the county, a member of the legislature, and a solid Jacksonian Democrat. Both parents inculcated a spirit of independence in their children. Rather than give them names at birth, for example, they let them choose their own, calling Mary "Sis" until her younger sister, Lucy, was born in 1845, then calling her "Big Sis." Taking the name Margaret, after her mother, she changed her name to Mary sometime before the move to Washington Territory.[18]

Mary could not have escaped politics nor missed the important consequences of political action. Her father sat on the territory's high court from 1853 until 1861 and then practiced law in Thurston, Lewis, and King counties. At the outbreak of the Civil War, McFadden had taken a strong Unionist stand, but he remained a Democrat and was very critical of Abraham Lincoln's policies, especially the Emancipation Proclamation. During the late 1860s, McFadden became one of the territory's strongest supporters of President Andrew Johnson, prompting some to charge that he had always been a southern sympathizer. Despite enduring some controversy, he emerged from the tempestuous 1860s as one of the territory's most popular and trusted politicians.

The conjunction of political interests between Miller and McFadden during the late 1850s brought Miller intimately into the justice's household. In 1860, one of Miller's Indian War buddies had assumed Miller would marry McFadden's daughter, referring to the judge as Miller's "father-in-law." When his brother Richard visited Olympia in 1860, he too thought Miller was on the verge of marrying, commenting that she was "a nice modest girl (a rare specimen in California) and would make a good wife." Richard added:

> I like her very much. Had I seen her about five or six or seven years ago, when prospects were good her name would probably have been Miller now.[19]

When McFadden returned to private law practice in 1861, he moved his family to a farmstead on Saunders Prairie, near present-day Chehalis in Lewis County. Miller's relations with the family diminished, but politics and an expanding law practice brought McFadden to Olympia often and the two men kept in close contact. In the late 1860s, McFadden built a substantial home in the capital city, where he spent much of his time, but he retained his farm and landholdings in Lewis County. It was then, during the years immediately after the Civil War, that Miller reacquainted himself with Mary, who had remained in Chehalis.[20]

What finally prompted Miller to pledge his love and ask for Mary's hand is left unmentioned in his correspondence and personal notes. Although he had finally written his family in Illinois in 1868 that Puget Sound would be his residence until death, he had seemed resigned to a bachelor's life. "A love sick man," he had written to a business associate in Lewis County in 1867, "wont attend to business." Nonetheless, he harbored a deep desire for a family of his own, and it is likely that his brother Richard's marriage in the spring of 1869 encouraged him to pursue Mary. It was also true that Mary had other suitors at her doorstep, including a Mr. Hillman, who may have proposed to her before Miller did.[21] Whatever the reasons for Miller's action, news that they would wed in November surprised both family and friends, who must have assigned Miller to permanent bachelorhood. The news flabbergasted Richard, who wrote:

> Who that knows you would have thought it? Were it not that you are a very matter of fact sort of person, not given to practical jokes, I might have some suspicion that I was being made the subject of a hoax. I confess I was much astonished as well as delighted at the intelligence . . . I met Miss McFadden . . . and was very much pleased and impressed with her.[22]

One of Miller's business associates was delighted at the wedding announcement and congratulated him on finally following the advice of himself and other friends who had been urging Miller to marry for years. "To think of living and dying an old bachelor," John T. Knox wrote Miller, "has always been something horrible to me, and I am glad to know that you finally came to that conclusion." Others saw the political side of the Miller-McFadden family concert. The union joined two of the most powerful Democrats in the territory, one with broad-gauged popularity and the other with a substantial fortune. "Speculation was rife," Selucius Garfielde wrote Miller, "whether McFadden will imbue Miller with his anti-coercion democracy or the latter convince the former of the value of moderate progressive ideas." Garfielde even worried out loud to Miller, "whether Garfielde gains or loses a friend by the new combination, let that result as it may."[23]

The Millers took an extended wedding trip to San Francisco, where they stayed the winter of 1869–1870. They remained there in part because of the salubrious climate, but also because they enjoyed visiting with Miller's business associates and mutual friends from Puget Sound who had moved to the city.[24] They returned to Olympia in the spring of 1870 and moved into a commodious house a few blocks from the downtown business district. Despite the potential implications of the joining of Miller and McFadden families, the marriage was not a political act nor was it part of Miller's business life. Once married, Miller appears to have kept his business and domestic lives separated. This is not to say, however, that his new relationship to O. B. McFadden had no political effect. McFadden had relied on Miller for loans more than once during the 1860s, and increasingly the two men used each other's access to people—for legal business and for political connections—to aid their careers. They were perceived by many as a political combination, even though they often disagreed. More important, the in-law relationship between the two men would prompt Miller to take an active role in McFadden's political career. In 1870, though, their political partnership was more potential than real.[25]

In 1870, Washington Territory altered its biennial election schedule to coincide with congressional elections, so Garfielde faced an electoral contest before he had served one year as delegate. He tried to ignore partisanship and to maintain a measure of independence, in part to avoid making any more enemies. Writing to Clarence Bagley in August, Garfielde warned against any alliances with T. F. McElroy or other partisans. McElroy had inherited ownership of the *Commercial Age*, which R. H. Hewitt had founded in 1868 as a Garfielde organ. "I hope our folks will have sense enough to avoid all 'entangling alliances,'" Garfielde wrote Bagley, "let everything be fair, square and honest and then we can defy the world." These were ironic words coming from Garfielde, the territory's most notorious political gamesman, but he well understood the tenuousness of his political hold and knew how important it was to have an effective public voice like the *Commercial Age*.[26]

His opponents barely let the congressional session begin when they began criticizing his policies. By December 1869, Garfielde's actions had fueled the still smoldering fires of division in the Republican party in the territory. The anti-Garfielde group, the "bolters," included Alvan Flanders, S. D. Howe, and A. A. Denny, men who had good reasons to oppose the delegate.[27] Charles Prosch tried to be a healer, using his *Pacific Tribune* to call for harmony among Republicans, but the conflict between Flanders and Garfielde continued hot. "I love peace," Garfielde wrote Miller in late December 1869, "but they [Flanders's administration] have actually driven me to the course I have taken and now they and I must abide the consequences." The two sides traded patronage blows by removing or forcing the removal of officeholders, thereby widening the split and forcing neutrals to choose between them. Garfielde fought to protect his friends, while Flanders took his complaints about Garfielde directly to Republicans in Washington, D.C.[28]

With only half of his party supporting him, his old Democratic friendships in Kentucky long gone, and Flanders spreading insidious stories about him in Washington—he called Flanders a "patent medicine" man—Garfielde eagerly welcomed advice from Miller. Miller offered his counsel, at least in part because he wanted the delegate's assistance on matters associated with railroad development in the territory. Garfielde appreciated the aid, writing Miller in January 1870:

"I thank you for all your suggestions, they are all wise and prudent, and will be complied with so far as I am concerned."[29]

As it had been the year before, the nexus between the two men connected them on the issue of economic development. In 1870, it was the transcontinental railroad that drew nearly all of their attention. In Oregon and Washington, the most important question was which city the Northern Pacific would choose for the terminus of its transcontinental line. Puget Sound communities hoped the road would either come down the north bank of the Columbia River and head north or that it would strike the river, cross the Cascades, and descend directly to the Sound. With this economic geography in mind, Miller had even suggested to a business associate in 1868 that they might combine in a bank at Walla Walla, a place Miller thought would boom when the railroad came. The most critical landscape was the river, and the most important player was the Oregon Steam Navigation Company, the Portland-based transportation behemoth. Where the NP routed its line near the Columbia became a much contested question. As one of Miller's confidants correctly surmised in 1868: "Any railroad that reaches the Columbia [from the East] kills Portland and makes a big town somewhere on the Sound."[30]

The OSN understood this, of course, and schemed to direct the railroad down the Columbia to a terminus in Portland. In the late 1860s, however, the company faced a stiff challenge from Ben Holladay, the "stagecoach king" from California, who planned to outflank the OSN by building a network of railroads serving California, Oregon, and Washington. Holladay had already secured a sizable land grant in Oregon, and he lusted for more. While the railroad and steamboat men schemed and locals like Miller boosted their towns as the best terminus, politicians and financiers in the East lobbied Congress for additional favors. In these circumstances, Garfielde became Miller's conduit to the NP's plans and political machinations. "General," Garfielde wrote Miller in December, "you may rely implicitly upon what I told you in regard to railroad matters. No movement within my knowledge shall transpire without your being posted, and that too at the earliest moment."[31]

Both men had a keen interest in a section of real estate on the Sound near Nisqually, the "Hog-em" homesteads, an ideal spot if the Northern Pacific chose Olympia for its terminus. Miller had spearheaded an investment in the land with several of his friends by buying up homestead and donation claims. J. M. Reed, the surveyor general for Washington Territory, had aided in the process, making sure that the lands were unencumbered by legal or financial claims. By mid-January 1870, Reed had assured Miller that all seemed clear, adding, "I thought it best to take a little time more [to file claims] for appearance sake." Nonetheless, not all of the homestead claims had been perfected, and Miller worried that the plan might become derailed. He enlisted Garfielde to pester the Interior Department to award patents to the original land claims, thereby making them saleable. He advised Garfielde on how to approach executive departments in Washington and how to maintain control of information, especially intelligences that might aid political and economic competitors.[32] On Garfielde's part, the delegate sent a steady stream of letters with news of railroad politics. In January, he optimistically informed Miller:

> I now consider the NPRR a fixture, and for the first time in thirteen years, think I see a speedy and important future for the territory. I regard it as safe and important to pick up loose pieces of land along the Sound. . . . Hog-em now looms up more important than ever, and . . . will prove of great interest to all the parties concerned.[33]

By February and March, Garfielde was directing a steady flow of intelligence to Miller about congressional discussions and corporate negotiations over the railroad's potential route in the Northwest, proposed financial agreements, and the machinations of Ben Holladay, a fellow Kentuckian. "There is brewing a big fight between Holladay and the NPRR Co.," Garfielde informed Miller in mid-February. "Both are after a land grant from the river to the Sound and it remains to be seen which has the largest pole." By early the next month, Garfielde could give Miller advance warning that Holladay's bold quest to get a congressional extension of his Oregon railroad land grant, which could have given him potential control of the terminus, had failed and that Northern Pacific financier Jay Cooke was on the verge of buying up the OSN's Columbia River route to secure a base in Portland.[34]

The ties that bound Miller and Garfielde were composed of intertwined economic and political strands. What served them best was a combination of business and political opportunity, which in Garfielde's mind meant victory in the June 1870 territorial delegate election *and* a piece of the action at Hog-em. For Miller, the relationship tilted predominantly toward business and the boosting of Olympia's economic development. Nonetheless, he willingly mingled the two goals and listened to Garfielde's solicitations. In March, with the election campaign looming, Garfielde suggested that the time had come for him to get a lead on real estate investment on the Sound. "Now it is already demonstrated that I cannot make a dollar here," Garfielde wrote Miller.

> Therefore I must take some chances in the way of legitimate speculation upon the rise of property in the territory. . . . I must have a finger in this pie at all hazards or I go to the wall financially whether re-elected or not.

He asked that Miller aid him with investment capital, promising that he would "steer clear of all 'jobs' and bribes," because of the "possible injury of my constituency." But Garfielde's avowal to use any legitimate "method of advancing my personal interest" must have made Miller pause.[35]

Responding cautiously to Garfielde's suggestion, Miller reminded his prospective partner:

> I have been doing this [speculating in land] on my own hook these ten years [and] my idea is that if you as Delegate could furnish any precise and definite information on the Sound I would like to go in with you and buy forty acres or a hundred and sixty at that point—farther than this I will not go.[36]

Garfielde responded enthusiastically with further promises of marketable information. "Don't fail to have that Nisqually reservation [Hog-em] fixed up and made water tight," he advised Miller.

> If it is not done soon there may be H_ll to pay. I am promised a peep into the inside just as soon as a terminus is determined upon. But I prefer to have some

lands along the Sound at the possible termini secured beforehand, and then when I get the "peep," we can strain a point to invest there also.[37]

Miller still remained circumspect and cautious, no doubt considering Garfielde a questionable political ally as well as a poor business partner. In fact, he had to bring suit against him in May for failure to pay interest on a $1,000 loan.[38] But the stronger deterrent was Miller's reluctance to bond too closely to the Republican delegate, considering that an election was looming in June. He also distrusted Garfielde's boasts. In a letter to Josiah Lucas in May, for example, Miller openly disputed Garfielde's intelligences on Holladay, calling the wily investor a "dark nag" who "has any amount of money, energy and impudence and . . . [could] carry off the prize in the end." And he confessed to W. S. Ladd that the political uncertainties made him very nervous. "I plan to go slow," he proclaimed to Ladd. "I have never made a cent by any one brilliant speculation." Nonetheless, the Hog-em investment had great promise, and Garfielde's help could make it less risky. With all of this in mind, Miller held back on political promises to Garfielde, but hinted that he might aid him in the campaign.[39]

Although Miller had reservations about aiding Garfielde, other politicians, including former Governor Fayette McMullin, thought Garfielde could do more for the territory in Congress than anyone else. He "has the ear of President Grant and his administration," McMullin wrote Miller in early March, "hence the importance to the territory of his reelection."[40] A further incentive for Miller was his own conservative inclinations that put him more in agreement with the economic plank in the Republican platform than the Democrats' proposals. He especially reacted to one of the Democrats' inflationary monetary plans, the promotion of George Pendleton's "Ohio idea," which called for the repayment of the national debt in greenbacks and the taxation of government bonds. With greenbacks worth about 70 cents on the gold dollar in 1870—and trading at a larger discount in the Pacific Northwest—Miller and his associates thought the "Ohio idea" a disastrous one that would "cause certain defeat of the party." He reported to Portland banker W. S. Ladd: "There is no place where the Pendleton financial policy is more unpopular than it is with the great mill owner[s] on Puget Sound."[41]

In some respects, Miller and other conservative Democrats on the Sound had few options in the 1870 election. The Democrats met in Walla Walla and selected an eastside candidate, J. D. Mix, a man who drew fire from westside politicians for advocating the separation of eastern Washington and its attachment to Idaho, with Walla Walla as the capital. Republican "bolters," who had spent much energy trying to derail Garfielde's renomination, met separately and put forth Marshall Blinn, a millowner from Seabeck on the Sound. Mix's southern origins, his caustic criticisms of Reconstruction, and his involvement in vigilante activity in 1864 made him even more unappealing to voters west of the Cascades. Blinn stood almost no chance because voters correctly perceived that the "bolters" wanted only Garfielde's defeat, even if that meant giving the election to Mix. In the June election, Garfielde won with a majority of more than six hundred votes, winning all but four counties.[42]

Returning from San Francisco in late April, Miller had contributed what he could to Garfielde's campaign. He had pledged to Fayette McMullin and the candidate that he would publicly endorse Garfielde and encourage his associates to give their support. It is doubtful that Miller's endorsement made any significant difference in the outcome; Garfielde had probably all but won the election when Mix and Blinn became his opponents. The candidate had effectively promoted himself as a Northern Pacific insider, suggesting that he could guarantee the swift arrival of the transcontinental railroad and its immense benefit to the territory. For Miller, having Garfielde in the nation's capital meant what it had in 1869. The measure of his expectation could be evaluated on two counts: Garfielde's promise of confidentiality to Miller and his commitment to the economic advancement of the territory.[43]

Developments on the Sound during the spring of 1870 at first encouraged Miller. Writing to fellow investor B. F. Shaw in June, Miller boasted: "I am inclined to think the time has come when the NPRR men must do something and very soon we may expect a solid move with plenty of cash." Nonetheless, he worried that the Hog-em speculation might stumble, so he maintained his surveillance on developments in Washington, D.C., and kept prodding Garfielde to protect the investment. In July, he chastened the territorial delegate for dawdling on the perfection of homestead patents:

> Would it not be well to hurry up the issuing of the patents for our Hog-em land, in order that there be no failure, after it has become immediately valuable in case lightning should strike it in the way of a "terminus"?[44]

As the rush for land near Olympia increased throughout 1870, however, Miller became more nervous and less optimistic that he and his friends would realize a bonanza. "It is no exaggeration to say," a contemporary later remembered, "that we were infatuated—we were crazed—we had become a population of speculators and gamblers, the madness increased as the Rail Road approached." Yet, that very infatuation made Miller wary. The more speculative activity he saw, the more his conservative warning bell rang. "We all intend to get rich," he wrote David Phillips in December, "but I am sadly afraid many of us will come out at the 'little end of the horn.'" One source of his worry was the NP and its lands department, which seemed determined to keep all locals from cashing in on the location of the terminus. "New Year's gift," he wrote to Garfielde on January 1, 1871.

> The rail road men are here in swarms [and] already owning one half of all of our lands they seem very much disposed to beg the other half out of our people. . . . For the love of mercy, try and have the [Hog-em] patents to all of our donation claims sent.[45]

Garfielde looked upon the prospects for development and gain with less trepidation and less concern for Puget Sound residents. There had always been something of the elitist in Garfielde, and he had made no secret of his unquestioning support of corporate development in the Northwest. During his campaigns, he had frequently boasted about his companionship with NP officials, a boast his opponents had either discounted or used against him. "You say the railroad men want all the land," he replied to Miller in March 1871. "That is quite natural," he explained, "indeed they differ but little from other human beings." More to the point, though, he asked Miller if Puget Sound people expected that the NP expended "a hundred millions simply for the purpose of benefiting the old settlers of the territory." It was in the natural course of development, he lectured Miller, that "the wise will grow rich in the melee—the unwise will remain poor."[46]

Neither Garfielde nor Miller desired to be among the unwise, and that kept the two men working in tandem. In addition to the railroad promotions, there were other economic and political issues that accrued mutual interest, from complicated land claims Miller pursued because of debt foreclosures to the always contestable patronage jobs that Garfielde tried to control.[47] Their partnership, though, had been tenuous from the beginning. Garfielde unabashedly stalked his own self-interest, while Miller maintained a justified caution in his political entanglements with the delegate. On only a very few occasions did he request Garfielde's aid in political matters. By late 1871, after one of his political friends had characterized Garfielde as "the great Pud-head" and others questioned his allegiance to the Republican delegate, Miller began to put political distance between them.[48]

His alliance with Garfielde, which cracked apart by 1872, had served two purposes. First, it had kept Miller in the midst of political activity in the territory, including important patronage issues and a direct line to congressional politics. Second, it had lubricated his pursuit of the main chance. He had become one of the acknowledged leaders in Olympia, the man with the most productive access to political power. He had positioned himself to gain handsomely if Northern Pacific managers selected his city as its terminus. In addition, he had married into a prominent family and had begun the fulfillment of one of his lifelong ambitions: to establish his own family. In the early months of 1872, Miller stood at the apex of his career.

CHAPTER 11

An Accomplished Life

*Now I do not want the land, as I have got all the wild
land I am able to pay taxes on!*
                    Miller to H. H. Pinto, July 22, 1872

*I am taking no active part in this railroad matter, in fact
the whole thing is an unmittigated* [sic] *bore to me.
However, I try and keep my tongue to myself and slide
along as smoothly as I can.*
                    Miller to O. B. McFadden, February 10, 1874

Miller had become a town father in Olympia. His business abilities had made him the town's richest citizen by 1872, and
Democrats and Republicans alike acknowledged his political sagac-
ity. He had done what others had not. By successfully working with
politicians on opposite sides of disputatious issues, from the Martial
Law controversy in the 1850s to the chameleon politics of Selucius
Garfielde in the 1860s, Miller had become a virtuoso political match-
maker. During an era of fractious and unsettled politics, he had steadily
championed territorial economic development. By the early 1870s, his
focus and that of his fellow Olympians pinpointed the coming of the
Northern Pacific Railroad as both economic salvation and harbinger

of a boundless future. In part because he stood hip-deep in railroad politics in the territory and in part because he was Olympia's most accomplished businessman, Miller stood for election as city mayor in the spring of 1872.

Politicians had urged Miller to run for elective office many times, but aside from serving in the territory's legislative chambers during the mid-1850s he had shunned electoral politics. He had always preferred playing an organizational role or serving in appointed office where he could work the patronage game.[1] But in 1872, realizing that this was Olympia's most important hour and that the city needed aggressive leadership, he agreed to run for mayor. The electorate gave him an overwhelming victory, hoping that his extensive political connections could solve the city's looming financial problems and guarantee its selection as the terminus city. The city had become mired in debt, paying out more than 18 percent in interest while plans for municipal projects in anticipation of the rail connections gathered dust.[2]

"Upon taking charge of my office," Miller wrote Garfielde in early April, "I find the city treasury and the city credit (if it has any at all) in a very bad condition indeed." Few solutions were available. Miller knew that any prudent lender would require some assurance that the city would not default, but the territorial Organic Act prohibited the legislature from guaranteeing municipal bond issues. With that in mind, Miller quickly drafted a proposed congressional statute allowing the city to float low-interest municipal bonds that could amortize the debt and provide capital for new projects. He sent the draft on to Garfielde, requesting that "it get through Congress before the end of the present session if possible."[3]

Garfielde's response must have both angered and surprised Miller. In a condescending tone, Garfielde labeled most bills of the kind Miller had sent "buncombe," the kind most members of Congress did not take seriously. While he offered to help out, he seemed not to take the situation seriously, questioning the character of the city debt, how it had been accrued, and what debt reduction had been attempted. "It is idle to attempt to do anything," he informed Miller, "until armed at all points." Garfielde's response left Miller little recourse but to attack the budget deficit head-on and to reconsider his relationship with Garfielde. By mid-June, he had compelled the city council to adopt new measures that would commit a portion of all city revenues to reducing the debt, and he had talked O. B. McFadden into running against Garfielde in the 1872 election.[4]

In May 1872, the *Washington Standard* reported that Thurston County Democrats were cajoling McFadden to run for territorial delegate. "In this instance," the paper editorialized, "it may be truly said, the office sought the man." That overstated the case, but as late as January Miller had informed an associate that McFadden had no interest in the office and that Garfielde "will be re-elected without doubt." Three developments probably made the difference in Miller's attitude between January and June. First, although he had openly predicted that Olympia would be chosen as the NP terminus, Miller had increasing misgivings about Garfielde's ability to influence the railroad's managers. The more information Miller received about the NP's local machinations, the more he distrusted Garfielde's boasts. Second, his failure to bail Olympia out of its debt had likely demarcated the limits of his political partnership with the wily Garfielde. Finally, new problems had developed in his promotion of the Hog-em real estate speculation, and he believed a friendlier representative in Congress might be to his group's advantage.[5]

Miller queried politicians about McFadden's chances in the general election, expecting that he could help engineer his father-in-law's selection as the party's nominee. The new fall date for the territorial delegate election, which had previously been held in the spring, posed additional unknowns that Miller could not evaluate in Olympia. The Democrats had been in disarray for more than three years, in part because of the disastrous campaigns of Marshall Moore and J. D. Mix in 1869 and 1870. The east-west split in the territory—expressed in the nearly perennial movements in Walla Walla to attach that section to Oregon or even Idaho—also threatened to give the election to Garfielde unless the "Democrats and liberals" settled on a single candidate. Garfielde had made few friends around the Sound, as Miller found out, a consequence of two decades of venal-appearing politics, but he still had strength east of the Cascades. Miller's informants in Walla Walla thought McFadden could win there; but McFadden was not a compelling speaker, and they worried that the longer campaign season might work in favor of Garfielde's oratorical abilities.[6]

McFadden had nearly captured the territorial delegate nomination in 1869, so his candidacy in 1872 garnered widespread support among Democrats. Although he stood perhaps a little right of the political center of the party, more progressive voters saw him in contrast to the conservative Garfielde, who had played heavily on his closeness to corporate NP managers and the Grant administration. But Garfielde's identification with Grant also injured him. As the notorious scandals rocked the White House and demeaned Republicans generally, Garfielde shared the label of venality along with Grant and his cronies. Nonetheless, McFadden took nothing for granted. The aging lawyer and former jurist carried his canvass throughout the territory, including trips to Walla Walla, Pacific County, and Whatcom. Miller worked his contacts on the Sound, up the Columbia, and in the eastside districts, making appointments for McFadden and ensuring that his candidate got local support. J. D. Mix, James Tilton, J. E. Wyche, and other party wheelhorses also stumped the territory for McFadden, acting as a counterbalance to the oratorically proficient Garfielde.[7]

The campaign stretched from late August to election day in November. It was the territory's first modern-style campaign in which candidates had to stay on the trail for several months and keep their newspaper allies firing salvos at the opposition. By the last days of September, Miller's informants gave McFadden a solid lead, with only the eastside prospects counted on the soft side. A cadre of conservatives on the Sound, led by Frank Clark of Steilacoom, had agitated briefly for a second Democratic convention to review McFadden's nomination, but Miller and others quickly squelched the idea and convinced them to fall in line for the judge. Momentum for McFadden built steadily throughout September. Even in Walla Walla, where Dorsey Baker and other Republicans could usually be counted in Garfielde's column, there were anti-incumbent rumblings. Baker, who had launched his own railroad project in 1871, had reportedly criticized

Garfielde's support of legislation favorable to the NP, making the believable charge that he had sold out the territory for his own self-interest. Others wrote Miller that the people "are getting tired of G[arfielde] and are just in the mood to throw him overboard" and that "the NPRR people . . . are not friendly to Garfielde."[8]

By early October, Garfielde's character had become the Democrats' chief target. His political biography practically guaranteed such attacks, and scurrility was not uncommon in most campaigns. Still, the broiling national critique of venal political behavior added strength and inevitability to assaults on Garfielde's character. Writing Miller from The Dalles on his way up the Columbia, McFadden fed his son-in-law material for distribution to friendly newspapers. "I incline to think I will succeed," he wrote.

> My conversations with some of them [NPRR men] has been free and full. [J. C.] Ainsworth is very decided. None of them went to hear G[arfielde] at Kalama. Tell Murphy [editor of *Standard*] to pitch into G[arfielde] for claiming that Garfield of Ohio is his cousin. . . . One spells his name with an "E" they are a different breed of pups. G. of Ohio has a sobering contempt for him [Garfielde].[9]

The *Standard* took Miller's cue and severely criticized Garfielde's prostrations for the NP. The Democrats hit Garfielde's connection to the NP from both sides by doubting his claims of influence and then chastising him for being too cozy with the corporation. This approach sold well in Olympia, because most, including Miller, held few illusions that the railroad managers would select their city as terminus. Miller had written one of his co-investors, W. S. Ladd of Portland, that the NP's feigned interest in Olympia was likely "a rumor or a smokescreen for other NPRR moves." The idea that Budd Inlet would become the terminus was "a perfect bilk or as Andy Johnson would say 'a dead dog'. . . . the whole thing is dead, dead, dead."[10]

The railroad issue plagued Garfielde, even in places like Walla Walla, where he had counted on solid support. "The Garfieldites . . . were not very harmonious . . . [their] friends are terribly discouraged, disheartened, and demoralized," one of Miller's friends reported in mid-October.[11] Garfielde could not fend off the criticisms in Walla Walla and suffered from the "lukewarms" among the Dorsey Baker contingent. Reversing his field, Garfielde suddenly abandoned the NP and began critiquing them from the stump. His about-face met with a gleeful response from the *Washington Standard,* which lampooned one of Garfielde's oft-mentioned claims that he had worked out the NP route with financier Jay Cooke:

> He [Garfielde] now advises those east of the mountains who have settled on odd sections, to abandon their claims without delay. This is quite a different tune from what he played through the last canvass [in 1871], when he was crawling about that big map on all fours with Jay Cooke and holding a fiddle-bow between his teeth. Whatever may be the condition of his unmentionables at that time, it cannot be denied that there is now a trifling exhibition of person—sufficient to greatly facilitate his sporting friends in what, we are informed, they contemplate doing.[12]

As the campaign proceeded, the railroad issue and the general decline of Republican strength boosted McFadden's chances. He benefited from the defection of previously pro-Garfielde newspapers, especially the *Vancouver Register,* which had been one of Garfielde's prime organs in 1870 and 1871. In some places, including Olympia, temperance advocates had gained control of the Republican county organizations, which pushed many voters toward McFadden.[13] As the election drew nearer, Miller worried most about election fraud, especially the wholesale enlistment of Indians to vote in the elections in remote districts on the Sound. In a series of letters sent out in late October, he warned Democrats living near Indian reservations to watch the polls carefully. Miller and other Democrats feared that the Republican-appointed Indian agents would use Indian votes to protect their patronage jobs. "Watch and don't let them [Republicans] vote Indians," he wrote M. H. Frost at Port Townsend, "a reservation Indian has no more right to vote than a hog or a dog."[14]

McFadden triumphed at the polls in November. "The Ring is broken," the *Washington Standard* proclaimed, and the territory would send an "honest man" to Washington. For Miller, it was a sweet victory, as he gloatingly wrote to Samuel Smith in Walla Walla:

> The battle is over and we can now count the dead, wounded and missing. Enough is known to show us that Selucius the Silver-tongued is routed horse, foot, and dragoon [by] 800 to 1000 votes in the Territory.

To his brother-in-law John Simms, an Indian agent east of the mountains and a Republican who worried for his position, Miller crowed: "a perfect revolution [but] it cannot be claimed as a democratic victory for men of all shades of political opinion voted for the Judge." That had been the short reason to the victory: McFadden had enormous popularity, stood politically in the center, and could not be blamed for anyone's economic or political problems. Garfielde had carried the burden of being nearly everyone's favorite target, save those who feared for their jobs with a change in congressional representation.[15]

Miller had worked hard for his father-in-law's victory, and it surely advanced his own and the Democratic party's interests. The campaign also signaled a return for Miller to party politics, even though he continued to spend much more time pursuing his investments in the territory and in San Francisco. But in some measure, his participation in McFadden's campaign was a family enterprise, an extension of his growing involvement with his relations. That involvement included financially aiding his wife's siblings and other in-laws, such as John Simms. Nonetheless, Miller's primary family focus centered on Mary and establishing a family. By mid-1872, Mary had given birth to two sons, Winlock William in 1871 and Edmund Pendleton in 1872.[16]

What kind of family life Miller had conceived for himself is difficult to discern. He had decided to marry just as he reached the zenith of his civic and business success, and it is clear that he had a difficult time pulling himself away from his work. He spent fully a quarter of his time away from home, mostly in San Francisco tending to business. Even when he was home in Olympia, he seemed to spare little time from his business pursuits. The few letters to Mary that have survived disclose a loving husband, but also a man who attended to business first. "I am so anxious to hear from you and Lock & Pen," he wrote from San Francisco in 1873, "it seems like an age since I saw you."[17] That sentiment expressed, though, he added that "business has not gone just to suit me," so he would stay an additional three weeks. There is no doubt that he felt a strong attachment to Mary. On another trip to San Francisco in 1872, he wrote with emotion:

> My dear Mary I could but think of you and a tear came to my eyes when I opened my trunk, everything was so nicely put in its place. I am sure no one could have done it so well, as she whom I love above all earthly things.

But there are also hints that the differences in their ages informed their relationship. He often referred to her as "my dear child" and instructed her more like a father than a husband.[18]

Mary often expressed feelings of loss and distance when her husband spent long periods away from home. "I cannot help crying just a little bit," she wrote Miller in San Francisco in 1871. "Oh, Willie dear do come back as soon as you can for we all miss you so much." Miller reciprocated those feelings, often expressing a sense of longing. "Oh! what a hard thing it is for me to be . . . away from my dear sweet little wife who is always so good to me."[19] Yet, Miller could also protest a bit too much about how lonely he felt in San Francisco and how boring his social life in the city was without her presence. "Everything about this city [San Francisco] is hateful to me," he wrote in 1872, "because I want to get home so bad." Sometimes, as during a particularly long absence, he could lay it on too thickly:

> I live a very regular life [in SF]. I have been to no place of amusement since I came down. Now I would go if I had any *desire* to do so . . . but my dear sweet pet I have no wish to go any place of enjoyment without you are along with me.

And in another instance, he complained about being "forced" to go to the theater with sea captain David Finch and his wife:

I am writing to my dear wife, and thinking of my dear, dear wife and sweet little boys. The play was a French sentimental affair set through with quite a variety of dancing girls—once I would have enjoyed the play very much, but now such things have no charms for me. My mind turns to our dear home and family.[20]

Miller was like other entrepreneurial men of his era who embraced their roles as achievers and assigned to their wives the responsibility for "making a home" and generally providing support for their business lives. But there were other dimensions to Victorian family life in America, ones that emphasized the nurturing of children and inculcation of social responsibility. Miller probably invested as much or more heavily in those family values as he did in his relationship with Mary. Seemingly transgressing his own self-professed avoidance of gaming establishments, he wrote pointedly from San Francisco about the importance of "training up" their boys to abstain from the gambling he had witnessed. After observing that it "brings misery (often suicide) upon 999 out of 1000 of its votaries," he offered her a pledge:

> Oh! My dear sweet wife let us be careful to teach our boys to avoid *all* species of gambling. Not only the card table and faro-bank but "trying to make a fortune in one day." Which is nothing more than gambling.[21]

This was good advice perhaps, but it flew in the face of some of Miller's own behaviors. While he was a conservative investor and shunned all shaky schemes, he also purchased state warrants, wartime pay vouchers, and scrip, which verged on gambling. More to the point of his own past, he had spent plenty of time in Olympia with Alonzo Poe, Edward Furste, Isaac Ebey, and others in the early 1850s, crowded around a card table learning penalties of foolish gaming. His admonition to himself and his wife was as much a confirmation of what he believed to be virtuous and what he had learned as guideposts for raising their children. Miller had made his fortune by limiting his risks and avoiding most gilded opportunities, from the time he turned north on the Oregon Trail, away from the California goldfields. The basis of a good part of his wealth was vested in the most conservative of valuations—land.

Much of his acquisition of land, however, was not purposeful but devolved directly from his money lending. Throughout the 1860s and 1870s, Miller acquired increasing amounts of land through foreclosures and partnerships. The majority of it was what he called "wildlands"— tracts of thickly timbered land in the South Sound region—but he also owned town lots in Olympia, Seattle, and Chehalis and numerous farms in Thurston, Pierce, and Lewis counties.[22] After the conclusion of the Indian War, Miller had continued to advance money to borrowers, which increasingly made him into a property manager as well as a financier. In many cases, his debtors had to offer landholdings as security that were worth much more than the loan value, and in some instances the properties had complex histories, which engaged Miller in long and drawn-out legal processes. He acquired a few significant tracts that had a variety of previous liens placed on them or were part of original Donation Act grants, Homestead Act claims after 1862, or lands gained through military bounty certificates. By the mid-1870s, Miller had acquired undivided interests in eight major Donation Act claims and partial interest in nine others.[23]

A case in point is the "Daufina Claim" in Lewis County, a full section of land on Grand Prairie. Miller acquired a part interest in the claim in 1866, but his effort to perfect his interest and to make it not only profitable but also sensible took nearly a full decade to accomplish. Oliver Dauphine (or Daufina) made the original claim with his wife Catherine, but he died intestate, leaving the south portion to his wife and north portion to his heirs. Miller received eighty acres of Catherine Dauphine's claim through a foreclosure on a debt owed him by Fred Clarke, an erstwhile partner of Miller's in a cattle-buying business. Catherine Dauphine had remarried twice since her husband's death, first to Xavier Cathman and later to Henry Barker. While married to Cathman, she had conveyed the property to Clarke as payment of an outstanding debt. When Miller entered the picture, the land had come under Henry Barker's control, in part because Clarke had never perfected his title but also because of Barker's resistance.[24]

In pursuit of his legitimate ownership of the property, Miller began legal proceedings in 1867, first to convince Barker to relinquish his claim without resort to the courts and then to force the whole business into court where the entire history of the parcel could be reviewed and adjudicated.[25] In 1871, Miller prevailed in court, but his success presented a further conundrum. With only a portion of the original claim, which had been platted in an unusual shape to maximize the prairie lands in Cathman's ownership, Miller could not expect to realize much gain. He needed more of the claim to maximize its value. His best opportunity was to acquire some of the lands held by Oliver Dauphine's heirs.

Miller had begun tracking down Dauphine's heirs after he foreclosed on Clarke. By 1871, he had acquired enough of the claim to significantly enhance his ownership of the southern half of the original donation claim. Nonetheless, he could not quite avoid the problems posed by the irregular-shaped parcels. When Harold Pinto, another Dauphine heir, proposed selling Miller the remainder of the claim, he agreed, even though he truly wanted no more land. Writing to Pinto in 1872, Miller explained:

> No I do not want the land, as I have got all the wild land I am able to pay taxes on! . . . But as I own the other two thirds of the husband's half and also a portion of the wife's half, I will give you for your interest what I gave . . . Mrs. Barker for her's, i.e. $300 gold coin. I repeat, I do not want your land but I make this offer in order to avoid the trouble of partition.[26]

Miller also acquired a majority interest in the Donation Land claim of Antoine Gobar, one of the oldest settlers in the territory. Gobar had been one of the Hudson's Bay Company farmers who had come to the Cowlitz River country in the 1840s, and he had staked a claim to his farmland near Grand Prairie in Lewis County in 1851. Miller's involvement began with a debt extension he had offered to Gabriel Jones in 1866, which included as security land owned by Gobar. By 1868, Jones had given up his interest in Gobar's property by transferring it to Joseph Broshears, another Lewis County resident and sometime debtor to Miller. Meanwhile, Miller himself purchased the majority of the claim directly from Gobar.[27]

Exchanging property in lieu of debt payment and the fixing of liens to secure debt payments had become standard practice among territorial landowners. It was the most efficient and trustworthy means of securing loans and facilitating the advancing of capital in an often cash-poor economy. But in this case the creditors and debtors struck a snag. Gobar had assumed that he held claim to 640 acres, as prescribed under the Donation Land Law for heads of household, but Miller discovered to his dismay that Gobar could claim only 320 acres because he was not married until 1854, several years after he had filed his original claim. Miller pursued the matter through an old friend in the General Land Office in Washington, D.C., hoping to find a quick solution to the problem, which practically invalidated the security for several loans between three individuals, including himself. Miller's friend, J. Thomas Turner, advised him to have Gobar file a revised or second claim as a married man. But that required a search for Gobar's naturalization papers, which took months.[28]

With perfected patents and deeds in hand, Miller pursued his own money interest. In this case, it was his financial dealings with Joseph Broshears. By spring 1872, the patent to the original Gobar claim had cleared, whereupon Broshears used it as security for a $100 loan at 2 percent per month from Miller. The following year Broshears quadrupled his loan to purchase the rest of the Gobar claim, which Miller still held. Unfortunately for Miller, Broshears was either an incompetent farmer or a poor money manager. By February 1874, he had defaulted on his loan—now at more than $600—and Miller got the entire Gobar property through foreclosure. But Miller had never intended to acquire the land, preferring to loan money and collect interest.[29]

Miller's other real estate investments, in Seattle and Olympia town lots and in San Francisco, involved fewer legal wranglings, but they were not trouble-free, especially those in San Francisco. During the several years he had owned his Folsom Street lots, Miller's lessee, George Maxwell, had built a three-story wooden building in 1868 and rented part of it to a carriage manufacturing company. He had also rented spaces on the second lot—the so-called Miller Place—to other tenants. Miller's property agents in the city, Young and Paxson, paid little attention to Maxwell and the improvements, letting tax and assessment fees go unpaid and rents uncollected. When Miller learned about these failings in the spring of 1870, he cancelled his agreement and negotiated a new contract with the California Trust Company, where his friend Henry L. Davis was president.[30]

A few months after Miller had changed agents and increased the property rent to $300 per month, Maxwell sent him a list of renters and suggested that the $1.50/square foot rental charge, established in 1868, should be decreased. The city's rental market had suffered one of its volatile swings, and this was an especially difficult time. Miller demurred on the rent hike, in lieu of the missing income that Young and Paxson's management had caused him. Meanwhile, Maxwell's fortunes declined, forcing him to offer Miller a half-interest in the building and other improvements. Claiming that he had maintained the property, put down four-inch planking, and built a solid redwood sewer, Maxwell thought half interest to be a bargain at $7,000. Miller rejected the proposal. He wanted to avoid managing a building, and he also sensed that Maxwell might be in some financial trouble. On further investigation, Miller discovered that Maxwell had also failed to pay taxes, thereby exposing the property to liens. After angrily writing Henry Davis and requesting additional vigilance, Miller put Maxwell on notice that he would be held fully liable for all rents and that a foreclosure would necessarily make all buildings and other improvements Miller's property.[31]

Miller's uneasy relationship with Maxwell continued throughout 1871, as Miller tried to accommodate his lessee's financial woes and his failure to collect full rents. When Maxwell suggested that California Trust Company collect rents, Miller strenuously objected and warned Davis to reject all such payments. Maxwell's renters were his concern, Miller reminded Davis, and he wanted none of their money in his bank account. Miller was fearful that he would end up pursuing Maxwell's renters while Maxwell dodged the taxes and city assessments. Finally, in late 1871, Miller voided the lease agreement. Maxwell had taken him one step too far and shown himself to be untrustworthy,

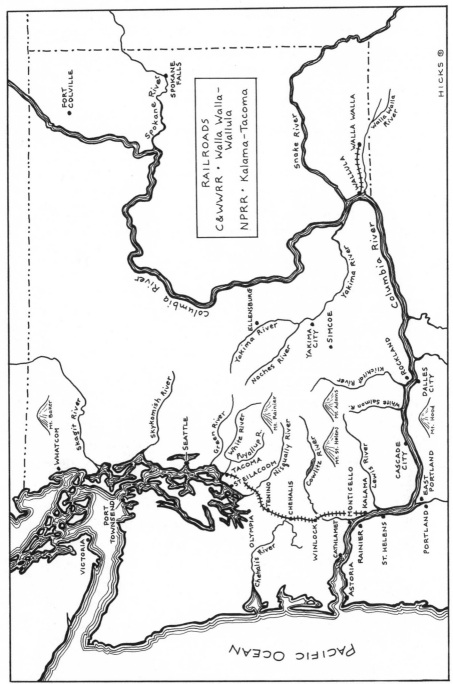

Map 3. Washington Territory, 1876

a deathknell in business relationships with Miller. Within weeks, Davis had found a new lessee, N. P. Perrine, and fashioned a new agreement. But six months later Perrine also pleaded poverty. This time, Miller agreed to lower the rents, evidently his only hope that Perrine might collect enough to meet the tax and insurance requirements. "Maxwell had got the lowest kind of people there—a poor dissapated [sic] crowd," Perrine informed Miller, and he was having trouble holding more than a few reliable tenants.[32] Miller's correspondence with Perrine during the next three years followed the same pattern, while he queried Davis every few months about his lessee's business habits, whether he was doing anything "sub-rosa," and especially if he paid the taxes. "My own opinion," Miller wrote Davis in the spring of 1874,

> is that Perrine is making a good thing out of his leases but he is mean enough to try to work upon my feelings and thereby get me to give him something more But this I am not willing to do and I shall hold him to the terms of the lease in all particulars.[33]

These experiences might well have discouraged Miller on San Francisco, but there was more to his economic interest in the city in 1874 than his lots on Folsom Street. First, his associates had convinced him that there were great opportunities in capital investments in the city, especially in mining stocks. Second, in mid-1873, the Northern Pacific Railroad had selected Tacoma, not Olympia, as its terminus. "Olympia hangs her underlip low," Miller had written a businessman in Seattle, "terminus gone to hell, everybody cursing the railroad men generally." Finally, he and Mary had once again begun considering a move to San Francisco. Miller's periodic illness had become more frequent, and the California climate seemed to have a therapeutic effect.[34]

His decision to invest in speculative mining stocks, however, is probably the best measurement of his serious interest in San Francisco. Mining investments, as he had explained in letters to Mary, were no different than gambling. He had also lectured his brother Richard numerous times that the pursuit of glitter in gold or quick-return investments was bogus, that it was not "legitimate business." Yet, in 1875, Miller took the "foolish risk" himself.[35]

The mining stocks he purchased, however, seemed more reliable. He had assurances from knowledgeable men that they were stable, even though investors had driven up some mining issues as much as 400 percent in a matter of months. He bought shares in National Gold Bank and Trust Company, which had boomed in 1874 when new strikes were discovered in Nevada's Comstock district. Nonetheless, Miller knew how volatile these investments were, and his nearly endemic fear of speculation kept him on edge.[36]

Within months of purchasing the stock, Miller's worst fears materialized. After a disastrous fire in the new mines on the Comstock in August 1875, gold shipments to San Francisco declined precipitously, sending shock waves through the city's financial district. Some mining stocks dropped to one-tenth of their previous value, and the Bank of California and the National Gold Trust Bank closed their doors to prevent a run on their deposits. Although the banks soon reopened and Miller retained his shares, the experience shook Miller's confidence in his investments. Still, he stayed with National Gold Trust, probably because Henry Davis had become the bank's president in 1874 and the possibility of moving his family to the city remained real.[37]

More and more after 1873, Miller's financial ambitions pulled him toward San Francisco. But the counterbalancing attraction of family and civic responsibility bound him to Olympia and the South Sound. His sense of family had expanded to include Mary and his two boys, his siblings in Illinois, his brother Richard and his family, and the extensive McFadden clan. For all of them, Miller provided a kind of ultimate financial insurance against which they all drew at times. The tragic death of his brother Richard in early 1873 and the temporary aid he offered Richard's widow further heightened his concern for family. By that time, his commitment to community, especially through political activities, revolved around his father-in-law's career.[38]

McFadden's victory in the territorial delegate election in November 1872 thrust Miller back into the center of Democratic politics in the territory. For several years, Miller had concentrated more on his business affairs than on politics, especially with the prospect of Olympia's choice as the NP terminus, but with McFadden's election he had returned to political organizing. His father-in-law's tenure in Washington also bound the Miller and McFadden families closer, for Miller helped support McFadden's wife and children, who remained behind in the territory while the judge was in the nation's capital. In politics, Miller played the same role for McFadden that he had for Stevens, although with Stevens he had been an aide to a political dynamo and with McFadden he served more as a guide and protector.

McFadden had beaten Garfielde by practically stealing the eastside vote from the wily Republican. His election also had gone against the standard wisdom that a territorial delegate of the same party as the holders of the White House would bring the greatest rewards to the territory. Miller knew this well and understood that to be reelected McFadden would have to serve both sides of the territory—the Sound and the Upper Columbia River regions—and that transportation issues were paramount. On the west side, the NP's official selection of Tacoma as its terminus in June 1873 had killed land speculation in the Olympia area, even though Miller and others with advance warning had already felt a deflation of their hoped for boom. Meanwhile, construction crews laid ties and rail north from Kalama on the Columbia River to the new railroad town at Commencement Bay. During the fall, J. C. Ainsworth's track-layers worked rapidly and under duress, trying to stretch the available monies far enough to complete the Kalama-Tacoma section. The collapse in September of the railroad's chief bond seller and financial house, Jay Cooke and Company, threatened the entire railroad enterprise in the territory, including the completion of the road north from the Columbia to the Sound. In fact, Cooke's failure helped trigger a four-year national economic depression, which stalled the completion of the Northern Pacific a full decade. But by December 1873, the westernmost segment of the railroad had reached Tacoma and a town plat had been completed under the NP's Tacoma Land Company.[39]

These developments left Miller and other Olympia businessmen with little hope of acquiring direct rail connections for Olympia; the

NP came no closer than Tenino. Nonetheless, a group headed by Hazard Stevens lost little time in organizing its own railroad company, with plans to connect the city to the NP line at Tenino. It was in general service of that effort that Miller engaged in a lengthy instruction of McFadden during the winter and spring of 1874, an instruction in which he underscored for the delegate just how crucial attending to transportation issues would be to his political success. The national depression had begun to affect economics on the Sound, and what capital was available seemed to be flowing to Tacoma, where the NP put its first lots up for sale in the spring of 1874. Seattle and Olympia both wanted rail connections, and several companies floated schemes in both communities. In Olympia, the Stevens group hoped to get authority to issue construction bonds that would attract additional capital to their project.[40]

The Olympia men took two avenues to advance their railroad plans. They drafted a congressional statute that would allow Thurston County to issue railroad bonds, and they prompted the territorial legislature to memorialize Congress on behalf of settlers whose lands had been condemned by the Northern Pacific per the terms of its land grant. Miller held himself aloof from the Olympia-Tenino railroad group, in part because he had little interest in investing his own money in the project and also because he feared that competing companies might make the railroad issue a political disaster. "I am taking no active part in this rail road matter," he wrote McFadden, "in fact the whole thing is an unmittigated bore to me. However, I try and keep my tongue to myself and slide along as smoothly as I can." He probably protested a bit too much, but it is clear that Miller's interest in the railroad promotion related much more to McFadden's political interests than Miller's own economic concerns. In part, Miller also suspected that Stevens's company really planned to involve California railroad interests in the project. Discovering that the bill introduced into Congress in early January had actually been written by "California railroad men," Miller's political antennae sensed danger. "It seems to me," he instructed the judge, "it would be well for you to quietly add a proviso to the bill before it leaves committee" that would require a plebescite on any railroad bond agreements. "There can be no harm in this," he assured McFadden, "because the people here want the road and any contract made by the commissioners that is fair and reasonable will be approved by the people." Miller predicted that the whole railroad effort could be damaged if the public became disenchanted, adding that some piece of legislation had to be approved and "you will be blamed if it is not done."[41]

The schemes authored by Seattle promoters also worried Miller, but more because of territorial politics than the fate of the Olympia-Tenino road. Seattle businessmen, like their counterparts in Olympia, had felt the same loss when the NP chose Tacoma. Several plans emerged to salvage their interests, including a direct link across the Cascades from Walla Walla to Seattle. Miller called such plans "a mere myth," a function of an almost traditional Olympia-Seattle rivalry, which made "everybody that is not for them [Seattle] open mouthed they think is against them." Although he cautioned the judge to mend fences with the Seattle men, especially A. A. Denny and Hilory Butler, he pushed him hardest to get Olympia's railroad bond bill approved. By early February, with some of McFadden's opponents already taking aim on the railroad issue, Miller sharpened his warnings:

> For God's sake get your bill giving Thurston County authority to issue bonds in aid of said road passed into law as soon as possible. If you fail to get the bill passed your enemies here will try to make it out that you were induced to kill the bill by the NPRR Co.[42]

McFadden's response begged understanding on Miller's part. "The RR bills can't be passed any faster," he explained. "You must bear in mind, it takes time to get legislation [passed] that is even favorably regarded." Miller understood, but any delay, he reminded McFadden, courted serious political problems. He had kept himself out of the squabbles, as he wrote, "when people here ask me about you [McFadden] I tell them I have not had a word from you since the 27th of November," but he made sure that McFadden knew the size and location of political pitfalls. "One thing is certain," Miller cautioned him in March,

the war between the different factions of the Republican party in the Territory is going to be hot and either one side or the other will want to ally with
the Democratic party, . . . and each [faction] will try to get you to take sides
with them. Be careful what you write to these men about the quarrels in their
party. Remember . . . "that it was better to go a hundred miles to tell a thing
rather than to write it."[43]

By the end of March, McFadden had succeeded in refashioning the
legislation and Miller freely circulated it in Olympia, gaining approval
from Stevens and other railroad promoters. McFadden's opponents
began waging a political counterattack in opposition newspapers, especially the *Puget Sound Courier,* while he struggled to get the final bill
approved. As the 1874 campaign season loomed near in late spring,
Miller worried that McFadden's failure might spell his doom.[44]

Throughout May, June, and July, Miller received reports from the
Sound, along the Columbia, and districts east of the Cascades.
Although the Republicans were in disarray, most voters seemed to be
either lukewarm toward McFadden or angry that more internal
improvements had not taken place during his term. Democrats in Walla
Walla complained because there had been little activity in pursuing a
canal and locks at The Dalles, although McFadden had successfully
introduced bills providing for a full survey of Columbia River navigation, which later led to the first engineering studies of a canal and
locks at the Cascades. His problems in Vancouver and Seattle were more
specific to complaints by officeholders and men who thought he had
not pushed hard enough for the Seattle-Walla Walla railroad bill. By
August, A. J. Cain reported to Miller that the judge had come in for
"much injustice" and it was "unfortunate he is not upon the ground
to counteract all misrepresentations."[45]

Aside from the unsettled condition of territorial politics and the
mixed reviews on McFadden's effectiveness, other factors were at play
in the summer of 1874 that combined to take McFadden out of the
delegate race. "I will write you very fully when I get out and get some
rest," McFadden wrote Miller as he left Washington, D.C., for Pennsylvania in July. "The Delegateship certainly is not a bed of roses and

my experience is that it is not a position to be coveted much less to be worked and paid for," referring to the money he would have to raise to wage a territory-wide campaign. McFadden never made it back to the territory that summer. A stroke in September left him partially paralyzed; he needed a cane for walking and had lost the use of one hand. In December, a public meeting in Olympia suggested that a lawyer be sent to Washington to take over the delegate's duties. He rallied in early 1875, as Congress resumed its session, working hard through the end of February on pending legislation. The session ended, however, with the railroad issues still unresolved and McFadden only marginally improved. By May, he had returned home to Olympia but in a much weakened condition, which worsened by late June. In early July, with his family in attendance, O. B. McFadden died at age sixty-one. It was tragic death for family and friends, especially considering the months of criticism that had been leveled at the judge. Defending him as a politician and man, Miller wrote to a mutual friend an explanation of their friend's death:

> He literally killed himself, trying to faithfully discharge his duty as Delegate in Congress; and while he did all he could to serve his constituents and friends, he did not do a malicious or unkind act towards any human being.[46]

McFadden's death seemed to close out Miller's life in politics. He had limited his political activities during the preceding years and focused more attention on business and family. His father-in-law's death cut off perhaps the last compelling personal link between himself and active party politics in the territory. He still maintained his political contacts and did not hesitate to apply pressure to officeholders if he thought he could affect policy, but that measurement of personal loyalty and shared commitment for the economic betterment of the territory no longer drove him. Perhaps the failure of Olympia's bid for the NP terminus had been too great a letdown, one that could make railroad affairs "boring" to him. McFadden's death also added to his family burdens, for he soon found himself advising his mother-in-law and his wife's siblings in business affairs, from property management to cattle trading.[47]

His business success continued apace, despite the national economic depression. Miller had collected so much money on loans in May 1875, for example, that he worried his money might remain idle too long. Within a month, as he informed an associate, he had made "large loans for a small man like myself to the large mill owners down the Sound." Increasingly during the year, however, he had shifted his attention more and more to California. "Olympia is dull, very dull," he had complained to David Phillips in San Francisco.[48] It was in May that he purchased stock in the National Gold Trust Company, and all indications from his business activities in Olympia and Seattle suggested that he was prepared to transfer even more of his wealth to San Francisco investments. The speculative investment in National Gold Trust, of course, nearly evaporated in the fall of 1875, when the bank had to stop payments. The bank's quick rebound in October turned into another disaster by early November, when it was forced to close once again. After an exchange of letters with Phillips, Miller decided to make an extended trip to California and make sure his money had been secured.[49]

Miller planned to leave Olympia in November, spend two or more months in San Francisco, and then proceed on to Washington, D.C., Philadelphia, and New York. "Much of my business is now in California," he had written his old friend H. A. Goldsborough in late November, "and I spend a large portion of my time there." He expected to steam to San Francisco within days of writing the note to Goldsborough, but a virulent respiratory infection laid him low throughout most of December. Limiting his activity to some family matters and gaining his strength, Miller felt ready by the New Year to leave on his trip. But suddenly the malady returned, forcing him back to his bed. Again he rallied, this time with more strength, and he set off on his journey in mid-January, only to catch cold yet again in Victoria. He returned to Olympia and more convalescence.[50]

In the late afternoon of January 24, 1876, William Winlock Miller struggled to leave his bed. He called to his wife and physician for assistance. "He expressed the desire to walk," as Mary later described the scene for her children.

> We helped him up and he walked a few steps and he then got upon the bed, reclining against some pillows (for he had not been able to lie down for four days and nights) I ran to the back of the bed to arrange the pillows when the Doctor discovered that he was dying. I caught him in my arms. He breathed a few moments and made an effort to answer me as I spoke to him and it was all over and Mamma and her two dear boys were left without Papa.[51]

CHAPTER 12

A Life's Legacy

What Papa's loss has been to me your young hearts
cannot know and I feel that I could not have lived under
my burden of sorrow had not God given me strength to
live for my two dear boys who I hope to bring up to be
an honor to their Father.

Mary Miller to Winlock and Pendleton Miller,
May 2, 1876

As quickly as William Winlock Miller had whispered his last words, Mary Miller was left alone with two young children and burdens she could only imagine. Within days, as the shock of his unexpected death waned, she walked into a new and complex world dominated by business affairs, a world that had existed mostly as a backdrop. She had only the sketchiest knowledge of her husband's business affairs, his investments, extensive landholdings, and plans. She knew even less about his methods and what he expected from his investments. During their six years of marriage, Miller had kept his business life at arm's length from his wife, so in death he left her a legacy of unarticulated burdens.

With the aid of Arthur A. Denny and Franklin Matthias, two of her husband's trusted business friends, Mary carried out the execution of his will and assumed responsibility for the family estate. Miller had bequeathed substantial landholdings in Washington Territory, prime commercial lots in San Francisco, Seattle, and Olympia, hundreds of commercial paper issues and government bonds and warrants, sizable business investments, and thousands of dollars owed by debtors.[1] Denny and Matthias helped her through the first few months, advising her on the value of her landholdings and investments and suggesting which properties she should retain or sell. She listened carefully, but as the legal guardian of her children and their interests in the estate, Mary determined early on to manage the estate to its greatest advantage. She set her course to transform a burden into economic opportunities.[2]

Why Mary Miller decided to pursue an active management of the Miller estate is unclear. Although she clearly had great concern about the welfare of her children and she felt some obligation to the memory of her husband, she easily could have dodged the responsibility, sold off some of the properties, and rested content and comfortable with proceeds from her husband's investments in land and business ventures. But she chose the harder path. Her parents had instilled in her a strong sense of independence, but her father's example in financial affairs could hardly have provided much instruction. O. B. McFadden had relied heavily on William Miller for advice and cash during most of the 1870s. Nonetheless, Mary Miller bucked what might have been conventional wisdom and plunged directly into managing the estate. Within eighteen months of her husband's death, she had reviewed her investments in the territory, had met with her husband's business associates in San Francisco, and had surveyed her properties there. She proceeded cautiously at first, preferring to maintain the San Francisco properties and local investments, including Miller's earlier commitment to the Thurston County Railroad Company, which greatly pleased local promoters in Olympia.[3]

By the early 1880s, however, Mary Miller felt confident enough to make investment decisions, sometimes against the advice of others. Arthur Denny advised that she take a conservative line in the use of her investment capital in 1883, advice she considered but then rejected for a more aggressive strategy. Following her husband's successful tactics, she put her money out at interest, using the Denny and Horton bank in Seattle. During the expansive 1880s, when Washington Territory's population and economic activity boomed, she increased the Millers' loan portfolio substantially. By the early 1890s, her assets included additional investments in commercial properties in Seattle, a brick-making plant owned by Denny, and the Seattle, Lake Shore & Eastern Railway Company.[4]

As she mastered the financial dimensions of the family estate and began to chart her own course, Mary also began the time-consuming process of overseeing her landholdings. Miller had accumulated most of his land through foreclosures, which included large and small blocks of agricultural and timber lands in seven counties. Each property carried a burden, including management of resources, taxes, oversight of tenants or lessees, and general liability. It was tedious business, especially keeping track of tax payments and the condition of the properties. She assigned oversight of most of the properties in Lewis and Cowlitz counties to her husband's old friend, Wesley B. Gosnell. Gosnell kept watch on the large and profitable farms in the Cowlitz Valley, including the Warbass, Gobar, and Dauphine Donation claims.[5]

Although she concentrated on business affairs during the 1880s, Mary worried nearly as much about her sons, Winlock and Pendleton. Her first concern, as it would have been with her husband, was education. Mary was determined that they would attend first-class schools. She began by sending them to the exclusive Belmont School in Palo Alto, California, near the soon-to-be-completed Leland Stanford, Jr., University. The school specialized in training students for matriculation at Ivy League colleges. To be nearer to them and at the ready to provide assistance, she spent most of each winter in Oakland, where she could also take care of business in San Francisco.[6]

The two boys scored adequately enough at Belmont, but the school's teachers gave them less than the highest marks. They discouraged Winlock, for example, from trying to gain entrance to Harvard, suggesting that he try Yale, where Belmont evidently had more influence. He went to Yale with the fall 1889 incoming class. Pendleton followed one year later. In New Haven, the academic rigor battered the Miller boys, forcing both of them to rely on tutors to pass qualifying exams. Winlock stumbled more than Pendleton and had to re-take at least two classes and stand out for a semester before graduating in 1894. Judging from letters between Lock and his mother and letters from professors at Yale to Mary, he spent too much time away from studies and seemed to concentrate more on sports and enjoying college life than on academics. Mary intervened by hiring a tough-minded tutor, who corralled Winlock and kept him tied to a strict study schedule. She also spent several months in New Haven during one season, when Lock suffered from a brief but acute illness.[7]

Mary lavished affection on both boys, even though it is clear from their correspondence that she felt some guilt about sending them away for school and pursuing her own interests. By the time the boys went to school in California, she had already moved away from Olympia, choosing to reside in Seattle at Stacy House. She still had friends and family in Olympia and Chehalis, but her world revolved more and more around Seattle and her business interests there. She participated little in civic affairs during the 1880s and 1890s, partly because she spent a good portion of her time on extended business in San Francisco and also because her inclinations attracted her to business and her own pleasures. In 1892, when the return on her investments was probably at its height, she dropped everything for three months and took an extended trip to Japan. It might be harsh to characterize her as selfish, but there is no doubt that Mary Miller did as she pleased, sometimes without regard to the effect on her family.[8]

By the early 1890s, it was clear that Mary Miller had established herself as a businesswoman. As careful and sagacious as she was in her investments, however, she could not escape the bludgeoning meted out by the economic depression of the 1890s. The drop came after nearly a decade of booming growth, which had dramatically increased population and business activity around Puget Sound. Like others in business, Mary had to adjust quickly to the contraction that came with the depression. But unlike some, she had seen early signs of economic problems and had been wary, even conservative in her decisions. Feeling uneasy at the onset of an inflationary trend in the early 1890s, for example, she had directed her banker in Seattle not to accept silver currency from her debtors: "I fear a change in gold values." By early summer 1893, the crash had come to financial markets, shaking and then toppling banks and businesses in cities and towns throughout the nation. In Seattle and Portland, business failures and soaring unemployment created a near crisis, motivating workers to organize protests and politicians to advocate extreme reform measures.[9]

It was a time of turmoil and unpredictability unknown in the Pacific Northwest. The value of most natural resource properties declined precipitously, including timberlands, which the Millers held in abundance. Creditors found it more attractive to renegotiate property-secured loans than to foreclose on debtors, so the Millers, who felt property-poor already, preferred extending more credit to buying more land. Winlock and Pendleton, who had joined their mother in managing the family properties in 1894, kept a close watch on their tax liabilities and informed Mary when payments were due. By mid-decade, declining rental income had compromised their cash reserves and forced them to borrow $3,000 from Dexter Horton to pay their taxes. They were under enough pressure that Winlock had to say no to a relative who requested a low-interest loan. Their real estate, as Winlock explained, produced no income but "requires constant outlay for the very heavy taxes and necessary improvements." By the end of the decade, however, the Millers had retained all of their property holdings and their income increased as the economy improved.[10]

During the financial contraction, Mary created a family corporation, Mary Miller and Sons. She had divided stock evenly between herself and her two sons, with the intent that Winlock and Pendleton would take an increasingly more active role in managing the family's properties and investments. The untimely death of Pendleton in 1904 changed the corporate structure, vesting two-thirds of the stock with Mary and one-third with Winlock. During the prosperous first decade of the new century, Mary and Winlock continued to manage their investments and property cautiously, but that did not keep them from investing in attractive business propositions, such as a milling com-

pany in Seattle and a steamship transportation company set up to ferry
Klondike-bound miners to Alaska.[11]

Mary had evidently tired of the business world by 1917, when she
dissolved the corporation and divided the family estate equally between
herself and Winlock. During the remaining ten years of her life, she
devoted more time to civic affairs, but the fortunes of the family properties more and more depended on Winlock's oversight and management. After his graduation from Yale in 1894, he had read law with
Judge Thomas Burke in Seattle and joined the Seattle bar, but increasingly he devoted more time to managing family properties. By the late
1890s, he had abandoned the practice of law and devoted his time to
business.[12]

When Mary Miller died in 1927, Winlock became the sole proprietor of the Miller family holdings. Included in the execution of her
will was a remarkable letter she had written to her sons in 1876, just
months after the death of their father. She had written it, as she
explained, to be read at her death because she wished them to "know
about" their father. She feared that "as time passes your recollection
of him may gradually fade away." Because she wrote it so soon after
her husband's death and her children could hardly have had deep
knowledge of their father, it is as likely that she also feared her own
memories would "gradually fade away." But her salient reason was to
impress upon her children their father's clarion legacy.[13]

In the letter, Mary Miller emphasized that her husband's legacy
rested principally in how he conducted his life. In a word, his legacy
was his character. Miller ordered his life on principles that personi-
fied the importance and rectitude of loyalty, honesty, and friendship.
Adherence to these values, she informed her sons, made their father
a success, not his achievements in business and politics. In a powerful prescriptive, she implored her children:

> Always remember what you owe to the memory of your Father. . . . Never do
> a dishonorable deed or any base action. . . . Do not be too free to make friends,
> but when you find a true friend cherish him as such. Keep your own counsel

in business matters and when you need advice go to those whom your Father trusted.[14]

She had highlighted the highest object of William Miller's life and perhaps his principal talent—his ability to work and succeed in a community of equals. He had held friendship and mutual service in the highest esteem and made it a test of his relationships, but more important to the course of his life he had made it the principal method in his business and personal activities. From his first days in Oregon, Miller had pursued his own best interests through the agency of others. While he had benefited from the associations he had nurtured, he had worked assiduously to pursue his goals with honesty and perseverance. What is also clear is that he owed his success to those associations.

His sons and grandsons followed Mary Miller's prescriptive advice. Building upon the security inherent in the family's significant fortunes, Winlock Miller pursued civic interests, serving as the state of Washington's Federal Fuel Administrator during World War I and as a member of the Board of Regents for the University of Washington for thirty-seven years, dying in 1963. He had married in 1904, the year of his brother's death, and his two sons—Winlock W. Miller, Jr., and Pendleton Miller—continued the family tradition of service. Winlock Jr., an accomplished lawyer in Seattle, accumulated a nationally significant collection of Northwest historical manuscripts and books. An important cultural leader in Seattle, he died prematurely in 1939. His collection, which he bequeathed to his Alma Mater, Yale University, became a major component of the Beinecke Library collections in Western Americana. Winlock's brother, Pendleton, also pursued a career as a lawyer in Seattle and contributed significantly to University of Washington projects.[15]

William Miller's legacy to his family, apart from the financial wealth he left them, is part of his larger legacy to his community. He was one of a dozen or more men who found places in the political and economic world that became Washington Territory. His purposes had been selfish, not unlike those of thousands of others who had come overland and by sea to the Oregon Country at mid-century. But his

methods were as much communitarian as they were singular. He spoke
and acted as a civic leader, not as a brash "Robber Baron" who would
cheat his fellows to line his own chests. Yet, he kept his own counsel
and rarely sacrificed any of his wealth as a contribution to a greater
cause. Miller was not philanthropic. Instead, he acted in full belief that
his gain was the community's larger gain, that economic energy could
be shared as community property when men set about to build a territory beyond the comforts of the metropolis.

That sense of a shared goal and a common effort puts a civic sheen
on his steady pursuit of gain and accomplishment. He had expressed
it perfectly for himself not long after he had settled in Puget Sound,
when he confessed that he was not content "to be a 'nothing' in the
world."[16] But being something other than a "nothing" soon came to
mean being part of a larger universe than among the wealthy. It was
his need to be important to others and his sincere belief in the sanctity of comradeship and loyalty to cause and friends that merged so
easily with his pursuit of gain. Success came at least partially from har-
nessing these two ambitions, but the more salient factor in William
Miller's rise to importance in Washington Territory came from his use
of politics and the enormous resources he gleaned from federal investments and expenditures in the region. He acted out the self-made man
myth, but the plot line of his story owed its dynamic and strength to
government and its beneficences. William Miller helped make Washington Territory, but it is also as true that the territory made William
Miller.

Notes

Abbreviations and short forms used in the Notes can be found on pp. 291–95 of the Bibliography.

Chapter 1. Young Man to the Frontier

1. *Illinois Daily Journal* (Springfield), March 25, 1850; Richard T. Miller to WWM, March 27, 1853, Box 1, Winlock W. Miller (cousin) to Winlock W. Miller, June 4, 1915, Miller-UW; John D. Unruh Jr., *The Plains Across* (Urbana: University of Illinois Press, 1979), 119–20; Merrill J. Mattes, *Platte River Road Narratives* (Urbana: University of Illinois Press, 1988), 2–3.

2. Alfred Elder to J. C. Planck, March 5, 1850, as printed in *Illinois Daily Journal,* May 18, 1850.

3. For examples of letters recounting the trip west by Illinois parties, see B. R. Biddle letters printed in *Illinois State Journal,* June 6, 1849, to December 20, 1849; Benjamin A. Watson letters printed in *Illinois Daily Journal,* May 29, August 9, 1849; Waters Curtis letter printed in *Illinois Daily Journal,* August 8, 1849.

4. George Goudy to mother, September 30, 1849, as printed in *Illinois Daily Journal,* January 24, 1850; Rice Dunbar to "Friends" as printed in *Beardstown Gazette,* September 10, 1847; "From Oregon," *Illinois Daily Journal,* February 4, 1847. Goudy had printed a paper in Beardstown, *The Tattler,* circulated for the benefit of bachelors. After emigrating, he worked as a printer at the *Oregon Spectator,* the territory's first newspaper at Oregon City in 1849. He later worked for the *Oregonian* in 1852 and the *Pioneer and Democrat* in 1853. See George H. Himes, "History of the Press of Oregon," *OHQ* 3 (December 1902): 353–54. For discussion of booster literature and decisions of overland migrants and their routes, see Dorothy O. Johansen, "A Working Hypothesis for the Study of Migrations," *PHR* 36 (February 1967): 1–12; Unruh, *Plains Across,* 92–97; Mattes, *Platte River Narratives,* 14–15.

5. Judith E. Hager, "Mile Eighty-Eight: The History of Frontier Beardstown, 1818–1860" (M.A. thesis, Northern Illinois University, Dekalb, 1965), 10; Robert P.

Howard, *Illinois: A History of the Prairie State* (Grand Rapids, Mich.: Wm. B. Erdmans Publishing, 1972), 156, 161; Alexander Davidson and Bernard Stuve, *A Complete History of Illinois* (Springfield: Illinois Journal Co., 1874), 451; Judson F. Lee, "Transportation: A Factor in the Development of Northern Illinois Previous to 1860," *Journal of the Illinois State Historical Society* 10 (April 1917): 76; J. M. Peck, *Gazetteer of Illinois in Three Parts* (Jacksonville: R. Goudy, 1834), 181; William Oliver, *Eight Months in Illinois* (London, 1843), 67. Hogs were trailed for fifty or more miles to Beardstown, where they were shipped down to the Ohio and Mississippi rivers. See J. N. Gridley, "The County Seat Battles of Cass County, Illinois," *Journal of Illinois State Historical Society* 7 (October 1914): 182. On the general development of agricultural settlements on the prairies of Illinois and Iowa, see Allen G. Bogue, *From Prairie to Corn Belt: Farming on the Illinois and Iowa Prairies in the Nineteenth Century* (Chicago: University of Chicago Press, 1963); Robert P. Sweirenga, *Pioneers and Profits: Land Speculation on the Iowa Frontier* (Ames: University of Iowa Press, 1968).

6. The comment on muddy road conditions is in *Illinois Daily Journal,* May 3, 1850. For articles and editorials about transportation problems, see *Illinois Daily Journal,* December 22, 1848, June 29, 1850; *Beardstown Gazette,* January 31, 1849.

7. *Beardstown Gazette,* May 1, 1850.

8. Genealogical record, Miller–UW; Robert W. Miller to WWM, May 14, 1859, S. F. Elam to WWM, December 17, 1852, Miller1-Yale; William Henry Perrin, *History of Cass County, Illinois* (Chicago: O. L. Baskin & Co., 1882), 252–53.

9. Perrin, *History of Cass County,* 252–53; Genealogical record, Miller-UW. The Millers' children were Mary Louisa (b. 1815), Dorothy Ann (b. 1817), Edmund Pendleton (b. 1819), Elizabeth Winlock (b. 1820), William Winlock (b. 1822), Sarah Magdalene (b. 1823), Richard Thomas (b. 1828), Robert Walker (b. 1830). All but Richard and Robert were born in Greensburg, Kentucky. For a perceptive analysis of the attitudes of early Virginia-born settlers in Kentucky, see Stephen Aron, "Pioneers and Profiteers: Land Speculation and the Homestead Ethic in Frontier Kentucky," *WHQ* 23 (May 1992): 179–98.

10. William Thomas, *History of Morgan County* (Chicago: Donnelly, Lloyd & Co., 1878), 270, 285; Peck, *Gazetteer of Illinois,* 147–48; Morgan County Poll Books, 1832, Poll-IHS; Illinois State Census Enumeration, 1835, Census-ISA, p. 56; Morgan County Census, 1840, Census-ISA, p. 428; Jacksonville Poll Book, 1832, Poll-IHS; Jacksonville Poll Book, No. 1, Special Election, November 25, 1839, Poll-IHS, p. 2; Election Returns, 1842, Morgan County, Elect-ISA.

11. Alexis de Tocqueville, *Democracy in America,* 2 vols. (1835; reprint, New York: Vintage Books, 1959), 2:256, 1:305.

12. Ellen M. Whitney, *The Black Hawk War, 1831–1832,* 3 vols. (Springfield: ISHL, 1973), 1:64–69; *Sangamo Journal* (Jacksonville, Ill.), September 1, 1832; Frank E. Stevens, "A Forgotten Hero: General James Dougherty Henry," *Illinois State Historical Society Transactions, 1934* (Springfield: ISHL, 1934), 108; Benjamin Thomas, *Abraham Lincoln* (New York: Alfred A. Knopf, 1952), 30–34. Miller family legend suggested that William Miller had lived in New Salem before moving to Springfield and had first met Lincoln there, but Miller had already moved to Springfield the year before Lincoln settled in New Salem. By the time Lincoln had moved to Springfield in 1837, the Millers had moved to Jacksonville. There is no doubt, however, that William Miller and Lincoln became friends during and as a result of the Black Hawk War.

13. *Sangamo Journal,* September 1, 1832; Stevens, "Forgotten Hero," 108.

14. Isabel Jamison, "Independent Military Companies of Sangamon County in the 30's," *Journal of the Illinois State Historical Society* 3 (January 1911): 29–30.

15. Richard Yates, who was born in Kentucky and moved to Illinois in 1831, had a long and continuous connection with the Miller family. In the late 1830s, when Yates had just established his legal practice in Jacksonville, he represented Miller in four civil cases. "Richard Yates," in Federal Writers Project Files, Box 148, WPA–IHS; Morgan County, Circuit Court Orders, August 1831–April 1842, Illinois State Historical Society, Springfield [IHS]; Population Schedules of the Seventh Census of the United States, 1850, Morgan County, Illinois, Illinois State Archives, Springfield [ISA]. Some in the family felt Yates owed a significant debt of gratitude to their father. See Richard Miller to WWM, November 19, 1865, Miller–UW.

16. Robert W. Miller to WWM, June 3, 1858, Box 2; D. W. Forsythe to WWM, September 8, 1854 Box 1, Miller-UW. Forsythe fondly remembered their schoolboy days in Jacksonville and commented on Miller's popularity and nickname of "Buni." Goudy biographies, unidentified newspaper clipping, 1839, Goudy-IHS; John Moses, *Illinois: Historical and Statistical,* 2 vols. (Chicago: Fergus Printing, 1892), 994, 998; Thomas, *History of Morgan County,* 330–33; Joseph P. Garlick to Jessie Palmer Weber, May 20, 1913, Garlick Family Papers, IHS. The first statewide education association held its first convention in Jacksonville in 1845.

17. Gridley, "County Seat Battles," 173; Oliver, *Eight Months in Illinois,* 67; Arthur Crumin, ed., *1840 Atlas of Cass County, Illinois* (Virginia, Ill.: Cass County Historical Society, 1984), 2; Cyrus Epler, "History of the Morgan County Bar," *Journal of the Illinois State Historical Society* 19 (October 1926–January 1927), 162; Cass County Teaching Certificate, May 15, 1845, Morgan County Teaching Certificate, November 14, 1846, Cass County Teaching Certificate, April 14, 1849, Miller1-Yale. On Illinois College, see Don Harrison Doyle, *The Social Order of a Frontier Community: Jacksonville, Illinois, 1825–70* (Urbana: University of Illinois Press, 1978), 23–36.

18. John F. Nolte to WWM, February 14, 1869, Joseph P. Garlick to WWM, February 14, 1865, Miller–UW; WWM to Joseph P. Garlick, March 4, 1865, Miller1-Yale.

19. Miller family lore suggests that he may have suffered from some form of kidney disease, but other evidence indicates that he may have suffered from a blood disorder as a consequence of either fever or disease. His wife's contention after his death that he had been an "invalid" since childhood is demonstrably untrue. See WWM Research File, Box 11, Mary Miller to Winlock and Pendleton Miller, May 2, 1876, Richard Miller to WWM, November 27, 1853, Miller-UW.

20. *Beardstown Gazette,* December 27, 1848; Robert M. Miller to WWM, August 13, 1862, Box 2, Miller-UW; Merrill J. Mattes, *The Great Platte River Road* (Lincoln: University of Nebraska Press, 1969), 15–21, 501–7; Aubrey D. Haines, *Historic Sites Along the Oregon Trail* (Gerald, Missouri: The Patrice Press, 1981), 121, 222, 234; Unruh, *Plains Across,* 342–50.

21. Robert W. Miller to WWM, May 14, 1859, Miller-UW. There has long been confusion about when Miller made the overland journey and where he went. In research notes compiled by Winlock W. Miller, Miller's grandson, in the 1930s, Miller's overland trek was described: "Crossed plains in 1849 after travelling down Rogue River Valley stayed at Jefferson, Oregon to teach school (Jefferson Institute for one term)." Winlock Miller did not know about the earlier journey to California, and he misiden-

tified the school at Jefferson. The Jefferson Institute was not organized until 1857, six years after Miller left the community. WWM, Research Notes, Box 15, Miller1-Yale; Joe Benninghoff, "The Early History of Jefferson," *Marion County History* 4 (June 1958), 6–8. On population in the Willamette Valley in 1850, see Jesse S. Douglas, "Origins of the Population of Oregon in 1850," 41 *OHQ* (April 1950): 95–108; William Bowen, "The Oregon Frontiersman: A Demographic View," in *The Western Shore: Essays Honoring the American Revolution,* ed. Thomas Vaughan (Portland: Oregon Historical Society, 1976), 181–97.

22. Jefferson File, 1938, WPA-UO; Hubert Howe Bancroft, *History of Oregon,* 2 vols., 1848–1888 (San Francisco: H. H. Bancroft, 1888), 2:716–17; Manuscript Seventh United States Census, Oregon [January 1850], Marion County, Census-OSA; Sherrill Hochspeier and Ann Hochspeier, *Jefferson Cemetery, Jefferson, Marion County, Oregon, 1861–1990* (Salem: Willamette Valley Genealogical Society, 1990), 7.; Frederick Steiwer to WWM, October 12, 1854, Miller1-Yale. Jefferson was originally called Conser's Ferry after Jacob Conser's ferry across the Santiam River. The town grew rapidly after a flood in 1851 wiped out the downriver town of Syracuse. Jefferson, a derivative of Jefferson Institute, was not applied to the place until the late 1850s.

23. Benninghoff, "Early History of Jefferson," 6; Agreement to Send Scholars to W. W. Miller for Instruction, August 27, 1850, Miller1-Yale.

24. Bates memoir and Julia A. Vaughn memoir, quoted in Benninghoff, "Early History of Jefferson," 3–4; Jesse Steiwer Douglas, "Syracuse and Santiam City, 1845–61," *Oregon Historical Society* 32 (September 1931): 195–212; C. H. Stewart, "The Old Emigrant Trail," *Democrat* (Albany, Ore.), November 14, 1920.

25. Douglas, "Santiam City," 197–201; MSS Census for Oregon, Marion County, 1850, Census–OSA; United States Mail Route Agreement, "Looney Station," 1867, Marion-OHS; "Marion County History," 1938, WPA-UO; Gilbert Looney Scrapbook, in private hands, Jefferson, Oregon. Jesse Looney was a cousin of Andrew Johnson and an active opponent of slavery, reportedly the reason for his emigration from Tennessee to Oregon. A stalwart Democrat, Looney served several terms in the state legislature.

26. John B. Looney to WWM, December 14, 1852, Miller1-Yale; Susan Steiwer to WWM, 1868, Miller-UW; Agreement to Send Scholars, August 27, 1850, Miller1-Yale; Dorothy O. Johansen and Charles M. Gates, *Empire on the Columbia,* 2d ed. (New York: Harper & Row, 1967), 274; newspaper clipping, *Jefferson Review,* 1949, in Gilbert Looney Scrapbook.

27. Jacob Conser to WWM, July 31, 1852, Box 1, Miller1-Yale; *Oregon Spectator,* December 13, 1849, December 19, 1850; Benninghoff, "Early History of Jefferson," 5–6; Hochspeier and Hochspeier, "Jefferson Cemetery," 2–3; Douglas, "Santiam City," 203–4. Jacob Conser was born in Pennsylvania in 1818, left home at an early age, settled in central Illinois, married in 1839, and went to Oregon in 1848. In 1850, when Miller first met him, Conser listed $6,000 in personal property wealth on the 1850 census. He was a Methodist and a Democrat and was elected to the territorial legislature in 1849 from Linn County and again in 1850 from Marion County. He was one of the principal organizers of the Jefferson Institute in the mid-1850s and donated the land and endowment for the school in 1856. He served on Willamette University's Board of Trustees and was an incorporator of the Oregon Central Railroad.

28. WWM to Robert B. Biddle, November 12, 1854, Miller1-Yale. Biddle was later

Indian Agent at Siletz Agency, Oregon, at the same time that Miller was Superintendent of Indian Affairs for Washington Territory.

29. WWM to Robert B. Biddle, November 14, 1854, Miller1-Yale. When Miller left Jefferson, he left his copy of the original partnership agreement with Frederick Steiwer, instructing him to pursue the matter.

30. B. R. Biddle to WWM, July 7, 1856, Militia–WSA; Biddle to WWM, October 24, 1854, January 23, 1855, August 19, 1856, Miller1-Yale.

31. WWM to Robert B. [B.R.] Biddle, November 12, 1854, Miller1-Yale.

32. WWM to Robert B. [B.R.] Biddle, November 14, 1854, Miller1-Yale.

33. B. R. Biddle to WWM, December 14, 1854, James C. Looney to WWM, April 21, 1853, John B. Looney to WWM, December 14, 1852, Miller1-Yale. Biddle confessed to Miller that Campbell had completely duped him, making him believe that he "was very rich" and that he "could command his thousands at any time."

34. Frederick Steiwer to WWM, January 23, 1854, Miller1-Yale.

35. Jacksonville Poll Book, Special Election, 1843, Poll–IHS.

36. On the relative position of the Whig and Democrat parties nationally in 1850–1852, see David M. Potter, *The Impending Crisis, 1848–1861* (New York: Harper Collins, 1976), 224–28. For the relative strength of Whigs and Democrats in Oregon, see David A. Johnson, *Founding the Far West: California, Oregon, and Nevada, 1840–1890* (Berkeley: University of California Press, 1992), 162–71; Robert W. Johannsen, *Frontier Politics on the Eve of the Civil War* (Seattle: University of Washington Press, 1955), 10–14.

37. Harry E. Pratt, ed., "22 Letter of David Logan, Pioneer Oregon Lawyer," *OHQ* 44 (September 1943): 260. David Logan—the son of Stephen Logan, Lincoln's law partner in Illinois—had come to Oregon in 1849 with Miller's former mentor, George B. Goudy. The Logans were family friends of the Millers in Illinois. Richard Miller to WWM, November 19, 1865, Miller-UW.

38. Appointment Paper, William M. [W.] Miller, Surveyor and Inspector of Customs, Port of Nisqually, Oregon Territory, March 11, 1851, Department of Treasury, Washington, D.C., Miller1-Yale. The first document incorrectly listed Miller's middle initial as "M". A second document signed by the acting secretary of the Treasury, March 11, 1851, rectified the mistake.

39. "Richard Yates," WPA-IHS; Frank William Scott, *Newspapers and Periodicals of Illinois, 1814–1879* (Springfield, 1910), 18; Hager, "Mile Eighty-Eight," 40–1.

40. For discussions of the Nauvoo events and the *Nauvoo Expositor,* see Leonard J. Arrington and Davis Bitton, *The Mormon Experience: A History of the Latter-Day Saints* (New York: Alfred A. Knopf, 1979), 76–82; Leonard J. Arrington, *Brigham Young: American Moses* (New York: Alfred A. Knopf, 1985), 98–112.

41. For Sylvester Emmons's biography, see Hager, "Mile Eighty-Eight," 41–2; Perrin, *History of Cass County,* 239. On Miller's relatives, see *Beardstown Gazette,* July 26, 1848.

42. John McDonald to WWM, April 24, 1851, Box 1, Miller–UW; WWM to Thomas Corwin, Secretary of the Treasury, July 25, 1851, Surveyor of Customs Letterbook, p. 14, Customs-WA. Miller had suggested to Corwin that he contact Lucas and Yates in Washington to verify his character. He also mentioned Illinois Senator Stephen A. Douglas, a Democrat and one of his father's friends.

43. Samuel Thurston to Shannon, March 1, 1850, Thurston-WSL; Thurston diary

entries, January 11, 29, 1850, in George Himes, ed., "Diary of Samuel Royal Thurston," *OHQ* 15 (September 1914): 177–78, 183. As early as April 1851, rumors in Oregon suggested that H. A. Goldsborough had been appointed collector, and Goldsborough seems to have taken the rumor seriously. See Peter Skene Ogden to W. F. Tolmie, April 10, 1851, H. A. Goldsborough to Tolmie, May 18, 1851, Box 1, Tolmie-UW.

44. Bond for W. W. Miller, Surveyor of Customs, March 17, 1851, Box 10, Miller1-Yale. It is unclear when the bond was actually executed. The date is the official date of engrossment at the Department of Treasury. When Miller actually received it is unclear, but he had already secured the agreements of Simmons, Goldsborough, and Sylvester.

45. WWM to Thomas Corwin, July 25, 1851, Customs-WA. On the creation of the Port of Nisqually, see Harvey Steele, "The United States Customs Service in Washington," to be published by the U.S. Customs Service.

Chapter 2. In the Government's Service

1. WWM to Letitia Work, February 22, 1854, Box 9, Miller1-Yale.

2. Mary Jane Brown, "Memoir" (unpublished, 1929), Washington State Library, Olympia [WSL]; Notes on Edmund Sylvester's Narrative, 1878, MS PB-22, Hubert H. Bancroft Collection, University of California, Berkeley [Bancroft]. See also "Edmund Sylvester's Narrative," *PNQ* 36 (October 1945): 331–39.

3. Hubert H. Bancroft, *History of Washington, Idaho, and Montana* (San Francisco, 1890), 8–9; Mrs. George E. Blankenship, *Tillicum Tales: Early History of Thurston County, Washington* (Olympia, 1914), 8; Ann Saling, "George Washington Bush," *Columbia* 6 (Winter 1992–93): 16–21.

4. John S. Galbraith, *Hudson's Bay Company as an Imperial Factor, 1821–1869* (Berkeley: University of California Press, 1957), 263; Gloira Griffin Cline, *Peter Skene Ogden and the Hudson's Bay Company* (Norman: University of Oklahoma Press, 1974), 198; Jesse S. Douglas, "Origins of the Population of Oregon in 1850," *PNQ* 41 (April 1950): 95–108.

5. Katharine Simmons, "The Cultural Beginnings of Olympia, Washington, 1850–1865" (M.A. thesis, State College of Washington, Pullman, 1948), 6; Darrell Millner, "George Bush of Tumwater: Founder of the First American Colony on Puget Sound," *Columbia* (Winter 1994–95): 14–16. Although it is certain that Olympia is named for the Olympic Mountains, there is confusion about who suggested the name. In Edmund Sylvester's Narrative, Charles Smith is given the credit (see also "Edmund Sylvester's Narrative"), but Bancroft used information from Elwood Evans and assigned Isaac N. Ebey the credit. Later Evans thought better of it and gave credit to H. A. Goldsborough. See James R. Tanis, "The Journal of Levi Lathrop Smith," *PNQ* 43 (October 1952): 282. Sylvester purchased the *Orbit* for $2,500, presumably with money he brought from Maine and perhaps with money he earned in the goldfields. For a description of the *Orbit*'s trip north, see Isaac N. Ebey to Family, February 20, 1850, Box 1, Ebey–UW.

6. Lewis A. MacArthur, "Early Washington Post Offices," *WA Quart.* 20 (April 1929): 129. Oregon Territorial Delegate Samuel Thurston had pressured the administration to designate Portland and Nisqually as new post offices and then got the Whig ad-

ministration to appoint Democrat Simmons to the post. See Thurston diary entries, December 28, 31, 1849, in Himes, "Diary of Samuel Royal Thurston," 168.

7. Murray Morgan, *Puget's Sound: A Narrative of Early Tacoma and the Southern Sound* (Seattle: University of Washington Press, 1979), 76–9; Gordon R. Newell, *So Fair a Dwelling Place* (Olympia, 1950), 7; Simmons, "Cultural Beginnings of Olympia," 7–9. A meeting had been called at Cowlitz Landing in August 1851, which forwarded a petition to Oregon Delegate Joseph Lane urging territorial status for land north of the Columbia. See Edmund S. Meany, "The Cowlitz Convention: Inception of Washington Territory," *WA Quart.* 13 (January 1922): 3–19. In 1852, the Oregon Territorial legislature created a county for Olympia, Thurston County, named in honor of Samuel Thurston, Oregon's first territorial delegate.

8. For descriptions of Portland's early growth and connection to Columbia River steamboat transportation in 1850–1851, see E. Kimbark MacColl, *Merchants, Money, and Power: The Portland Establishment, 1843–1913* (Portland: The Georgian Press, 1988), 27–55.

9. On the "Cowlitz Corridor" route, see John M. McClelland Jr., *Cowlitz Corridor: Historical River Highway of the Pacific Northwest* (Longview, Washington: Longview Publishing Co., 1953); Kent D. Richards, "A Good Servicable Road: The Cowlitz Columbia River to Puget Sound Connection," *Columbia* 6 (Winter 1992–93): 6–11. On the Cowlitz Portage, see James R. Gibson, *Farming the Frontier: The Agricultural Opening of the Oregon Country, 1786–1846* (Seattle: University of Washington Press, 1985), 86–90. For specific descriptions of Cowlitz Landing and the travel route, see C. B. Bagley to T. C. Elliott, March 22, 1912, and Edward Huggins, "Something about Fording Rivers in Pierce and Thurston Counties in Washington Territory between 1850 and 1890," in Elliott-OHS; Herman A. Leader, ed., "Douglas Expeditions, 1840–1841," *OHQ* 32 (March 1931): 10–12; "Ancotty (Long Ago)," Caroline Cook Dunlap Reminiscence, MSS 657, p. 64, Oregon Historical Society [OHS]; Joseph Schafer, ed., "Documents Relative to Warre and Vavsour's Military Reconnaissance in Oregon, 1845–6," *OHQ* 10 (March 1909): 56.

10. Abbé Jean Bolduc quoted in Gibson, *Farming the Frontier,* 60. The original Fort Nisqually, which lay close to the tidewater, had been abandoned in 1842 as inadequate to meet the new demands of the PSAC. A new fort was built about a mile back from the Sound. For agricultural statistics of PSAC at Cowlitz and Nisqually and shipment figures, see ibid., 100–4, esp. tables 18, 19.

11. Galbraith, *Hudson's Bay Company,* 264; Cline, *Ogden and the Hudson's Bay Company,* 197–200.

12. Galbraith, *Hudson's Bay Company,* 452, n. 50; Galbraith, "The British and Americans at Fort Nisqually, 1846–1859," *PNQ* 41 (April 1950): 112–14. On Simmons's and other Americans' business relations with Tolmie, see Victor Farrar, ed., "The Nisqually Journal," *WA Quart.* (April, July, October 1921): 137–48, 219–28, 300–1. On the history of smuggling and customs surveillance in Puget Sound, see Roland L. DeLorme, "The United States Customs Bureau and Smuggling on Puget Sound, 1851–1913," *Prologue: The Journal of the National Archives* 5 (Summer 1973): 77–88. Galbraith, *Hudson's Bay Company,* 452, n. 50; idem, "The British and Americans at Fort Nisqually," 112–14.

13. "John Adair," Meany Pioneer Files, Special Collections, University of Washington Library, Seattle [UWL]; Galbraith, *Hudson's Bay Company,* 263–5; Cline, *Ogden and the Hudson's Bau Company,* 199. Reportedly, Adair had been urged when he

stopped at San Francisco on his way north to Astoria to stay there and recommend that the new customs office be established in San Francisco. Adair rejected the advice and went on to his appointed destination. Fred Lockley, *History of the Columbia River Valley: From The Dalles to the Sea* (Chicago: S. J. Clarke & Co., 1928), 3 vols., 1:9. It took years to adjudicate Washington citizens' claims against HBC and PSAC. It ended in 1869, when HBC paid $650,000 for claims and lands. See Mary A. Gray, "Settlement of the Claims in Washington of the Hudson's Bay Company and the Puget's Sound Agricultural Company," *WA Quart.* 21 (April 1930): 95–102.

14. Tolmie journal entry, April 20, 1850, in Farrar, "Nisqually Journal," 220. See also Harvey Steele, *Hyas Tyee: The United States Customs Service in Oregon, 1848–1989* (Washington: U.S. Treasury Department, 1990), 16; Galbraith, *Hudson's Bay Company,* 265; Cline, *Ogden and the Hudson's Bay Company,* 200–1. The violations in the *Albion* case revolved around HBC's policy of paying Indian labor with furs, which customs officials interpreted as constituting a prohibited trade in furs. The *Cadboro* had items in its hold not included on the manifest and was held for more than two months before Adair released it.

15. John Adair to Thomas Corwin, Secretary of Treasury, January [?] 1851, Customs-WA. Adair had hired Thomas W. Glasgow, an American who had squatted on HBC land in 1847, to serve as customs inspector at Nisqually.

16. Thurston diary entries, December 28, 31, 1849, "Diary of Samuel Royal Thurston," 170–2. Thurston pestered the Secretary of Treasury regularly, inquiring about customs surveillance of sea commerce in Northern Oregon.

17. Governor John Gaines had many discussions with Delegate Thurston about conflicts over HBC land titles, so it is likely he had inside knowledge of political discussions in Washington and may have passed them on to Miller. See "Diary of Samuel Royal Thurston," 153–205. On the relationship between Gaines and Thurston, see Johnson, *Founding the Far West,* 52–53.

18. Carl E. Prince and Mollie Keller, *The U.S. Customs Service: A Bicentennial History* (Washington, D.C.: U.S. Department of Treasury, 1989), 60, 117, 120–1; George Richard Reynolds, "The United States Coast Guard in the Northwest, 1854–1900" (M.A. thesis, University of Washington, Seattle, 1968), 3.

19. H. A. Goldsborough to William F. Tolmie, May 18, 1851, Tolmie-UW. Goldsborough's brother, Louis M. Goldsborough, was captain of the American cutter *Massachusetts,* which had been sent to Fort Steilacoom in 1849. H. H. Bancroft and John S. Galbraith labeled the Puget Sound settlers as "extreme patriots," but the men engaged in commerce with HBC at Olympia were probably more moderate or in some conflict in their views, considering that resolution of the difficulties was in their best interest. Galbraith, *Hudson's Bay Company,* 265; Bancroft, *History of Washington,* 48.

20. WWM to Thomas Corwin, July 31, 1851, Customs-WA; Richard T. Miller to WWM, September 27, 1851, Box 1, Miller-UW.

21. James Douglas to WWM, September 9, 1851, Box 2, Miller1-Yale; WWM to Douglas, September 10, 1851, Customs-WA. For a full discussion of HBC's investment on Vancouver Island and its impact on company policies, see Richard Mackie, "The Colonization of Vancouver Island, 1849–1858," *B.C. Studies* 96 (Winter 1992–93): 3–40.

22. WWM to John Adair, September 12, 1851, Adair to WWM, September 15, 1851, Customs-WA.

23. John Adair to James Douglas, September 15, 1851, Box 13, William F. Tolmie to

WWM, September 22, 1851, Box 7, Miller1-Yale; Peter C. Newman, *Caesars of the Wilderness* (New York: Viking, 1987), 301–2.

24. WWM to Thomas Corwin, Secretary of Treasury, September 27, 1851, Customs-WA; Elisha Whittlesey (Comptroller) to Thomas Corwin, September 23, 1851 (copy), Box 13, Miller1-Yale.

25. WWM to Thomas Corwin, July 12, 1852, Customs-WA; Account Ledger for Receipts from November 1851, Organization of Port of Nisqually for Simpson Moses, Collector, Box 9, Miller1-Yale. Edward Huggins at Nisqually reported that Miller inspected the loading of the *Cadboro* in late September. See Farrar, "Nisqually Journal," 294.

26. Josiah M. Lucas to WWM, November 4, 1852, Box 4, Miller1-Yale. For interpretations of Moses's actions, see Bancroft, *History of Washington,* 54; Galbraith, *Hudson's Bay Company.* George B. Roberts, "Recollections of George B. Roberts," MS P-A 83, Bancroft Library, University of California, Berkeley [Bancroft]. Some historians have suggested that Moses especially pandered to Simmons, but there is much evidence that Simmons had a serious falling out with Moses. See I. N. Ebey to James Guthrie, Secretary of Treasury, August 1, 1853, Collector's Letterbook, Customs-SF.

27. Moses informed Treasury Secretary Thomas Corwin of the conflict between HBC and American settlers and explained his plan to "make a strict and thorough examination" of smuggling on the Sound. S. P. Moses to Thomas Corwin, November 20, 1851, Customs-SF.

28. WWM to Simpson P. Moses, November 26, 1851, Customs-WA; Account Ledger for Expedition to Commencement Bay, November 21, 1851, Box 9, Miller1 Yale.

29. Nisqually Journal, November 27, 1851, Fort Nisqually Papers, Nisqually-OHS; H. A. Goldsborough, Affadavit of Events, November 19, 1852 (copy), Box 5, Bagley-UW. On the passengers aboard the *Beaver,* see Edward Huggins to Eva E. Dye, May 27, 1904, Dye-OHS.

30. Moses told his inspectors—in a directive labeled "Keep Secret"—to "immediately seize" any suspected violator of revenue laws and send the vessels "and persons to the port of entry to report to the Collector. It may be necessary to put a force of citizens on board of vessels seized to ensure their arrival at this place, in which you will not hesitate to act." S. P. Moses to Henry Wilson (Inspector, Port Townsend), February 18, 1852, Collector's Letterbook, Customs-SF.

31. Elwood Evans to Simpson P. Moses, November 28, 1851, Collector's Letterbook, Customs-SF; Goldsborough, Affadavit of Events, Bagley-UW; Bancroft, *History of Washington,* 54–55. While on board the *Beaver,* Goldsborough reported, he had received a letter from Moses asking him to take charge of the vessel, but he "declined to have anything to do with the seizure." Goldsborough had made strong friendships with HBC personnel, including Peter Skene Ogden, W. F. Tolmie, and James Douglas. See Peter Skene Ogden to W. F. Tolmie, April 10, 1851, Tolmie–UW.

32. Simpson P. Moses to Charles Edward Stuart, Master of Schooner "Beaver," December 2, 1851, and Proceedings of District Court, District of Oregon for Puget's Sound, January 21, 1852, Collector's Letterbook, Customs-SF; Goldsborough, Affidavit of Events, Bagley-UW; Bancroft, *History of Washington,* 54–55.

33. Nisqually Journal, December 1, 5, 7, 9, 1851, Nisqually-OHS.

34. Simpson P. Moses to Judge William Strong, December 12, 1851, Collector's Letterbook, Customs-SF.

35. James Douglas to W. F. Tolmie, December 17, 27, 1851, Box 1, Tolmie-UW.

36. WWM to Brigantine *Mary Dare,* December 11, 1851, Surveyor's Letterbook, Customs-Seattle; WWM to A. Monat, Master of *Mary Dare,* January 7, 1852, Box 9, Miller1-Yale; Edward Huggins to Eva E. Dye, May 27, 1904, Dye-OHS; WWM to David Logan, December 24, 1851, Box 8, Miller1-Yale.

37. Nisqually Journal, January 21, 25, 1852, Nisqually-OHS.

38. WWM to *Beaver* in port, January 25, 1851, WWM to S. P. Moses, January 29, 1852, Surveyor's Letterbook, Customs-WA; Nisqually Journal, January 29, 1852, Nisqually-OHS.

39. S. P. Moses to WWM, February 6, 1852, Moses to W. F. Tolmie, February 6, 1852, Moses to Tolmie, December 8, 1851, Collector's Letterbook, Customs-SF.

40. Nisqually Journal, February 6, 1852, Nisqually-OHS; Bancroft, *History of Oregon,* 2:107. HBC had appealed to the Department of the Treasury, which dropped the fines against the *Mary Dare* and the charge against Captain Stuart.

41. Simpson P. Moses to W. F. Tolmie, February 21, 1852, Tolmie-UW.

42. Nisqually Journal, February 23, March 8, 1852, Nisqually-OHS. For a description of the HBC storehouse and Tolmie's regulations, see Edward Huggins to Eva E. Dye, April 1, 1904, Dye-OHS.

43. WWM to Thomas Corwin, July 16, July 20, 1852, Surveyor's Letterbook, Customs-WA.

44. W. F. Tolmie to WWM, July 15, 1852 [two letters], Box 7, Miller1-Yale; WWM to Thomas Corwin, July 20, 1852; WWM to Tolmie, July 15, 1852, Surveyor's Letterbook, Customs-WA.

45. WWM to S. P. Moses, July 20, 1852, Surveyor's Letterbook, Customs-WA.

46. W. F. Tolmie to WWM, September 15, 1852, Box 7, Miller1-Yale. HBC workers completed Miller's house on October 9, 1852, after twelve weeks of steady work. See entries in Nisqually Journal, July 29, August, 23, 26, 30, September 20, 21, 22, October 1, 5, 9, 1852, Nisqually-OHS.

47. HBC Governor George Simpson had put direct pressure on the Secretary of the Treasury to exempt Puget's Sound Agricultural Company shipments from Nisqually. Moses refused to alter the rules but told Tolmie he had already allowed the ships an exemption. But the intent was clear. Moses had made it an unofficial action so he might revoke it whenever it pleased him. S. P. Moses to W. F. Tolmie, July 16, 1852, Customs-SF.

48. On the controversy over the *John Davis,* see S. P. Moses to WWM, August 7, 1852, WWM to S. P. Moses, August 9, 1852, S. P. Moses to WWM, August 10, 1852, in Surveyor's Letterbook, Customs-WA; WWM to S. P. Moses, August 9, 1852, Box 9, Miller1-Yale.

49. WWM to Thomas Corwin, November 3, 1852, Surveyor's Letterbook, Customs-WA. See also WWM to S. P. Moses, September 8, October 20, 1852, Customs-WA.

50. WWM to Thomas Corwin, October 28, 1852, Surveyor's Letterbook, Customs-WA; S. P. Moses to Corwin, November 6, 1852, Customs-SF. Moses was responding to legislation in Congress that proposed eliminating the Port of Entry from Puget Sound. When moving the Port of Entry had come up in August, Moses had written President Fillmore, urging him to retain Port Nisqually.

51. James Douglas to W. F. Tolmie, January 26, 1863, Box 1, Tolmie-UW.

52. WWM to Simpson P. Moses, July 28, 1852, Box 9, Josiah M. Lucas to WWM, November 10, 1852, Box 4, Miller1-Yale.

53. WWM to C. W. Rockwell, Commissioner of Customs, February 1, 3, 1853, Customs-WA. Miller had already been severely frustrated in getting a $1,000 draft Moses had sent to Treasury in late 1852. He finally succeeded in getting payment, but only after he enlisted help from his Illinois political friends, Representative Richard Yates and Josiah M. Lucas. WWM to Yates, December 18, 1852, Box 9, Thomas Corwin to Yates, February 13, 1853, Box 14, Lucas to WWM, January 14, 1853, Box 4, Miller1-Yale.

54. Report of WWM to Simpson P. Moses, February 8, 1853, Box 9, Miller1-Yale.

55. WWM to C. W. Rockwell, Commissioner of Customs, March 31, 1853, Customs-WA; Josiah M. Lucas to WWM, January 14, 1853, Box 4, Miller1-Yale.

56. John D. Barclay, Acting Commissioner of Customs, to WWM, October 31, 1852, WWM to S. P. Moses, January 13, 1853, Surveyor's Letterbook, Customs-WA; Moses to WWM, January 29, February 12, 1853, Collector's Letterbook, Customs-SF. Miller's brother-in-law wrote in early 1853: "I suppose you expect to get your walking papers from Genl. F. Pierce." John McDonald to WWM, February 23, 1853, Miller-UW.

57. WWM to Thomas Corwin, May 5, 1853, Customs-WA; WWM to Isaac N. Ebey, July 18, 1853, Box 9, Miller1-Yale. Ebey wanted the collector's job, as he wrote his brother in 1853, because he estimated the collectorship to be worth $2,500 per year plus another $1,000 in fees and he intended to bankroll his farming operation on Whidby Island. Isaac N. Ebey to W. S. Ebey, May 20, 1853, Box 1, Ebey-UW.

58. Isaac N. Ebey to James Guthrie, Secretary of Treasury, August 1, 1853, Collector's Letterbook, Customs-SF.

59. Josiah Lucas had reported to Miller that Moses had tried to extract $1,900 from Customs to pay for rent, even though he had already been advanced $1,000 for rent just after he arrived in Olympia. The commissioner ordered Moses to pay the rent out of Customs receipts. The transaction between Moses and Simmons had been witnessed and confirmed by affidavit by H. A. Goldsborough. See Isaac N. Ebey to Commissioner of Customs, November 1, 1853, Collector's Letterbook, Customs-SF. Moses had garnered a poor reputation among Olympia businessmen as well. Years later, Edward Furste described Moses as a "busy-body" who walked around "full of business papers, all pockets full, stopping and talking a moment to someone in a most earnest manner and continuing this all day." Edward Furste to WWM, April 21, 1862, Box 2, Miller1-Yale.

60. A. M. Poe to WWM, February 17, 1853, Box 5, Miller1-Yale. Even William F. Tolmie contributed information to the indictment of Moses at the Treasury Department. See Tolmie to WWM, November 18, 1853, Box 7, Miller1-Yale.

61. Deputy Collector, Letter of Appointment, August 13, 1853, signatory Isaac N. Ebey, Box 10, Miller1-Yale.

62. WWM to H. J. Anderson, Commissioner of Customs, April 10, 1854, Customs-SF.

63. Isaac N. Ebey to H. J. Anderson, Commissioner of Customs, November 20, 1853, Collector's Letterbook, Customs-SF; A. M. Poe to WWM, August 8, 1853, Box 5, Josiah M. Lucas to WWM, June 14, 1854, Box 4, Miller1-Yale. For Miller's rate of pay, see WWM to W. S. Ebey, August 28, 1858, Box 1, Ebey-UW. Miller retained the office of Deputy Collector through the fall of 1854, but the Treasury Department objected to Ebey's presumptuous naming of Miller, even though it eventually paid Miller's salary.

Chapter 3. Making a Life

1. Richard T. Miller to WWM, March 27, 1853, Box 1, Miller-UW; Thurston County Tax List, 1852, Doc. 14182, Microfilm 24, Reel 80, OreRec-OSA. Only four men—Edmund Sylvester, M. T. Simmons, George Bush, and George Barnes—had more personal and real property in November 1852 than Miller.

2. Simmons and Smith Account Book, 1850–1852, in W. W. Miller Accounts, Miller2-Yale.

3. William W. Miller, Account Book, Loans, 1852–54, Miller2-Yale.

4. On Beardstown and Illinois socio-economic conditions at mid-century, see William Cronon, *Nature's Metropolis: Chicago and the Great West* (New York: W. W. Norton, 1991), 57–8, 81–81; Don Harrison Doyle, *The Social Order of a Frontier Community: Jacksonville, Illinois, 1825–70* (Urbana: University of Illinois Press, 1978); A. W. French, "Early Reminiscences," *Transactions of the Illinois State Historical Society for the Year 1901* (Springfield, Ill, 1901), 61; Gridley, "County Seat Battles," 182; Hager, "Mile Eighty-Eight," 74–5; Lee "Transportation in Northern Illinois," 76.

5. [A.M.] Poe to WWM, July 19, 1853, Box 2, Miller-UW.

6. Isaac N. Ebey to Family, February 24, 1850, Box 1, Ebey-UW.

7. William Strong to M. T. Simmons, D. R. Bigelow, J. W. Swan, C. Crosby, et al., March 27, 1852, Box 14, Memorandum of Agreement, April 15, 1853, Box 10, Miller1-Yale.

8. Quitclaim, February 14, 1852, Lewis County, Oregon Territory, Lot 7, Block 11, Olympia, J. Henry Murray to W. W. Miller and Michael T. Simmons, Box 10, Lease Agreement, March 26, 1852, Henry Murray House, Edmund Sylvester to W. W. Miller, Box 10, Miller1-Yale. Miller had some ready cash by late spring 1852—he lent at least $100 to Quincy Brooks—but it is likely that he had little more to gamble than the $600 he invested in this property in February. Evidently, J. Henry Murray had defaulted on his purchase of the property from Sylvester and was living as a squatter on HBC lands at Nisqually Bottom. The lease term was set at three months, suggesting that Sylvester may have rented the house to give Miller time to find another renter.

9. W. W. Miller Account Book, Loans, 1852, Miller2-Yale.

10. William Strong to M. T. Simmons, D. R. Bigelow, T. W. Swan, C. Crosby, et al., March 27, 1852, Box 14, Miller1-Yale; John Swan, *Olympia, the Pioneer Town of Washington, Its Socialization, Origin and Early History from a Pioneer's Retrospection* (Olympia, n.d.), 15. Ruling from his residence in Cathlamet on the Columbia, Judge Strong approved Miller's plan to aid his friends, giving the whole scheme legal standing in court.

11. Memorandum of Agreement, H. A. Goldsborough, M. T. Simmons, W. B. Gosnell, W. W. Miller, April 15, 1853, Box 10, Quincy A. Brooks to WWM, July 18, 1853, Box 1, Miller1-Yale. Miller required $450 as the first payment, on September 1, 1853, and slated two payments of $225 on December 1, 1853, and February 1, 1854.

12. During construction, the mill incurred additional costs due to several accidents, including the destruction of the mill dam. As a result, the operation was hamstrung from the beginning. Wesley Gosnell to WWM, November 29, 1853, Box 1, Miller-UW.

13. The promissory note carried a 10 percent per annum charge. Miller helped Gosnell out of the debt bind by selling his land to David Forbes, who in turn purchased an interest in the mill from Simmons. Miller Account Book, Miller2-Yale; Memoran-

dum of Agreement, W. W. Miller, H. A. Goldsborough, M. T. Simmons, Wesley B. Gosnell, September 21, 1855, Box 4, Miller-UW.

14. James G. Strong to WWM, October 4, 1853, Box 7, D. R. Bigelow to WWM, March 5, 1853, Box 1, Miller-UW. In some instances, Miller agreed to aid others in their financial problems by pursuing debtors or servicing debt, when the transaction had nothing to do with him and he stood to receive no gain. See, for example, Peterson Cherry to WWM, May 8, 1854, Box 1, Miller-UW.

15. Miller did not hesitate, however, to pursue his own interests in court, something he had to do increasingly during the mid-1850s. In most cases, he used the threat of legal action to recover debts. See W. W. Miller *vs.* N. Delen and W. T. Simmons, March 29, 1855, Case #68, and W. W. Miller *vs.* John Swan, May 1859, Territorial Court Cases, Washington State Archives, Olympia [WSA].

16. James G. Strong to WWM, July 11, 1853, Box 2, Miller-UW; Isaac N. Ebey to WMM, August 31, 1853, Box 2, T. J. Dryer to WWM, August 2, 1852, Box 2, Josiah M. Lucas to WWM, November 27, 1855, Box 4, Miller1-Yale.

17. W. W. Miller Account Book, 1853–1854, W. W. Miller Account Book, Loans, 1855, WWM-UW; William J. Wills to WWM, July 3, 1855, Box 8, Miller1-Yale; Thurston County Tax Lists, 1852, MF Film 24, Reel 80, Doc. #14182, Oregon State Archives, Salem [OSA].

18. Winlock W. Miller [son of Robert Miller] to Winlock W. Miller [son of WWM], June 4, 1915, Box 37, Miller-UW. The brothers had left San Francisco by ship for the Isthmus of Panama, then traveled to New Orleans, and up the Mississippi to St. Louis and Illinois. Cousin Winlock Miller told his cousin that William W. Miller was the eldest of the four brothers who traveled west in 1850; but he was in error, for Edmund Miller was three years older than William. What this might disclose is the relationship the brothers had or perhaps the reputation in the family of William's later success in Washington Territory.

19. Richard T. Miller [RTM] to WWM, September 27, 1851, Box 1, John McDonald to WWM, April 24, 1851, Box 1, Anna Rew to WWM, December 4, 1852, Box 2, Miller-UW.

20. Martha W. Miller, September 24, 1852, Box 1, Miller-UW.

21. John Arenz to WWM, August 25, 1853, Box 1, Sylvester Emmons to WWM, December 6, 1852, Box 1, John McDonald to WWM, February 23, 1853, Box 1, Miller-UW. Arenz, for example, detailed the business successes of his brother Edmund and brother-in-law Emmons, emphasizing their investments in land. McDonald wrote that his business was so successful he was tempted to sell it for a large profit.

22. John Arenz to WWM, October 19, 1855, Box 1, Miller-UW. Miller had assiduously kept the details of his financial dealings and wealth from his family. Even years later, when an associate visited the family in Illinois, Miller had asked him to "pass over as quietly as possible" details of his finances. Edward Furste to WWM, December 24, 1861, Box 2, Miller1-Yale.

23. RTM to WWM, October 1, 1853, WWM to RTM, September 1853, Box 1, Miller-UW.

24. Martha Pentecost Miller to WWM, June 23, 1855, July 11, 1852, Box 1, Miller-UW. Martha "Pentecost" Miller had been with the family for at least ten years, but references to her "growing full up" suggest that she had lived with the family as a youth and teenager before becoming the family's maid.

25. George A. Ropp to WWM, July 18, 1851, Box 2, Miller-UW.

26. George A. Ropp to WWM, January 30, 1853, Box 2, Miller-UW.

27. RTM to WWM, June 7, 1854, Box 1, Miller-UW.

28. T. F. McElroy to Sally Bates, August 10, 1852, Box 1, McElroy-UW; John Johnston to WWM, March 20, 1853, Box 4, Miller1-Yale.

29. Isaac Burpee, "The Story of John Work," December 1943, Work-OHS; MSS Pierce County Census, 1857, WSA; Sylvia Van Kirk, *Many Tender Ties: Women in Fur Trade Society, 1670–1870* (Norman: University of Oklahoma Press, 1980), 134–36. For a recent and compelling consideration of Metis women in the fur trade, see Juliet Pollard, "The Making of the Metis in the Pacific Northwest. Fur Trade Children: Race, Class, and Gender" (Ph.D. diss., University of British Columbia, Vancouver, 1990).

30. *The British Colonist*, December 23, 1861; E. E. Rich, *History of the Hudson's Bay Company*, 3 vols. (Toronto: McClelland & Stewart, 1960): 3:763; Glyndwr Williams, ed., *Hudson's Bay Miscellany, 1670–1870* (Winnipeg: Hudon's Bay Record Society, 1975), 199; Burpee, "John Work," 98; John Work to Edward Ematinger, December 10, 1849, Work-UW; Mackie, "The Colonization of Vancouver Island," 13, 21–3; W. Kaye Lamb, "The Census of Vancouver Island, 1855," *British Columbia Historical Quarterly* 4 (January 1940): 51–8.

31. On Letitia's childhood, see Edward Huggins to Eva E. Dye, February 8, 1904, Dye-OHS. Letitia Work's first recorded visit at Fort Nisqually was in June 1851. Nisqually Journal, June 8, 1851, Nisqually-OHS. See also Theodore Winthrop, *The Canoe and the Saddle, or Klalam and Klickitat* (Tacoma: John H. Williams, 1913), 25. Winthrop described being paddled from Victoria to Port Townsend in a canoe with a group of Indians that included Letitia Work.

32. Henry C. Wilson to WWM, March 5, 1853, Box 8, Miller1-Yale; Edward Huggins to Eva E. Dye, February 8, 1904, Dye-OHS.

33. WWM to Letitia Work, July 22, 1853, Box 9, Miller1-Yale.

34. WWM to Letitia Work [draft], July 22, 1853, Box 9, Miller1-Yale.

35. WWM to W. F. Tolmie, July 22, 1853, Box 9, Miller1-Yale. Miller had spent time at the Ebeys' home on Whidbey Island and had helped promote emigration to the island. See Mrs. Isaac Ebey's diary entry, February 21, 1853, in Victor J. Farrar, ed., "The Ebey Diary," *WA Quart.* 8 (April 1917): 133.

36. WWM to W. F. Tolmie, July 22, 1853, WWM to Letitia Work, July 22, 1852, Box 9, Miller1-Yale.

37. WWM to W. F. Tolmie, July 22, 1853, Box 9, Miller1-Yale.

38. On Indian women in the fur trade in Oregon, see Van Kirk, *Many Tender Ties*, esp. chapters 5–7. For women's lives at Oregon fur posts and changing attitudes toward Indian wives, see John Hussey, "The Women of Fort Vancouver," *OHQ* 92 (Fall 1991): 265–308.

39. WWM to W. F. Tolmie, September 8, 1853; July 22, 1853, Box 9, Miller1-Yale.

40. W. F. Tolmie to WWM, August 19, 1854, Box 7, Miller1-Yale.

41. Ibid.; Manuscript Pierce County Census, 1857, WSA. There is some evidence that John Work clearly preferred that his daughter marry an HBC man. That arrangement melded more easily with the larger web of family relationships, and Work had a low opinion of Americans, fearing they all wanted to absorb Canada into the "Yankee Union." See Mackie, "Colonization of Vancouver Island," 34.

Chapter 4. In Washington Territory

1. For a superb discussion of Oregon Democratic perspectives during the 1850s, see Johnson, *Founding the Far West*, 56–64. For background on the role of the Whig party in western territories before mid-century, see Michael A. Morrison, "'New Territory* versus *No Territory*': The Whig Party and the Politics of Western Expansion, 1846–1848," WHQ 23 (Winter 1992): 25–51.

2. Josiah M. Lucas to WWM, November 4, 1852, Box 4, Miller1-Yale.

3. Bancroft, *History of Washington*, 29; "Isaac N. Ebey," Meany-UW.

4. Isaac N. Ebey to Winfield S. Ebey, March 22, 1853, Ebey-UW.

5. October 3, 4, 1851, diary entries, in Farrar, "Ebey Diary," 46.

6. February 21, 1853, diary entry, in ibid, 133; WWM to W. F. Tolmie, July 22, 1853, Box 9, I. N. Ebey to WWM, August 31, 1853, Box 2, Miller1-Yale. Rebecca Ebey may have been the more important catalyst in Miller's desire to move to the island. Mrs. Ebey wrote often about the need to create a God-fearing community and how idyllic it could be. Further, Miller may have been considering a move from the Sound once he knew he would lose his office. In March 1853, he wrote friends in Oregon querying them on available land, prices, and conditions. John Johnston to WWM, March 20, 1853, Box 4, Miller1-Yale.

7. For a description of the first call for a convention, see a descriptive article in *Washington Standard* (Olympia), May 2, 1868. Travel between Puget Sound and Oregon City on the Willamette River took most of three days, whether by the water and overland route or by sea and seamboat up the Columbia and Willamette rivers. The first petition to Congress for Northern Oregon independence included this passage: "No Wagon Roads have yet been made from the Columbia or else where, to the interior of the Territory and hence wholly inaccessable except by water: and all the commerce of the North being monopolized by the Hudson Bay Co. . . . " For descriptions of the route, see Oscar Osborn Winther, "Inland Transportation and Communication in Washington, 1844–1859," PNQ 30 (October 1939): 371–86. For discussion of the Cowlitz Convention and its importance, which is often overlooked even in modern discussions of Washington political history, see Edmund S. Meany, "The Cowlitz Convention: Inception of Washington Territory," WA Quart. 13 (January 1922): 13–19.

8. Miller supported and aided efforts to get a post office at Nisqually in April 1852, and in July of the same year he was a leader in petitioning Oregon Territory to establish Olympia as the Thurston County seat. William Packwood to WWM, April 25, 1852, Box 2, Miller1-Yale; Petition of Citizens of Thurston County to Legislative Assembly of Oregon, July 22, 1852, MF 24, Reel 51, Doc. No. 4518, OreRec-OSA.

9. Appointment as Deputy Marshal, Oregon Territory, July 23, 1852, Box 10, William Strong to WWM, March 27, 1852, Box 7, Miller1-Yale. Strong may have been warning Miller about getting too close to Ebey, who he considered to be an aggressive politician. William Strong, "History of Oregon," p. 38, Bancroft-UCB.

10. WWM to Stephen A. Douglas, March 15, 1852, Box 8, Jacob Conser to WWM, July 31, 1852, Box 2, Miller1-Yale.

11. David Logan to WWM, August 10, 1852, Box 4, Miller1-Yale. Logan's devotion to the Whig party, as David Johnson has suggested, remained strong "long after it was practical to do so." But Logan's viewpoint on politics may have been too crass for Miller's blood. Logan offered that the immigration to Oregon seemed to be strong in

1852; "consequently we all expect to have a fine time fleecing them this winter." For Logan's relationship to Illinois and Oregon political interests, see Johnson, *Founding the Far West*, 166–72. Whigs continued to attempt to enlist Miller's help as late as 1854, when Francis Henry tried to convince him to invest in a Whig newspaper in Steilacoom. Francis Henry to WWM, August 31, 1854, Box 3, Miller1-Yale.

12. Edmund S. Meany, "Newspapers of Washington Territory," *WA Quart.* (July 1922): 256–57. It is instructive that Miller had written Stephen Douglas about the certainty of a petition for separation from Oregon months before Daniel Bigelow's July Fourth oration in 1852, which many historians have credited for beginning the separation movement. WWM to Stephen Douglas, March 15, 1852, Box 8, Miller1-Yale; Meany, "Cowlitz Convention," 4–5. For a cogent explanation of Oregon's enthusiasm for separation, see Kent Richards, *Isaac I. Stevens: Young Man in a Hurry* (1979; reprint, Pullman: Washington State University Press, 1993), 154–55.

13. Richards, *Isaac I. Stevens*, 155–57, 162–65; Galbraith, *Hudson's Bay Company*, 266–74; Mary A. Gray, "Settlement of the Claims in Washington of the Hudson's Bay Company and the Puget's Sound Agricultural Company," *WA Quart.* 21 (April 1930): 95–102.

14. Letter of Appointment, Deputy Collector of Customs, August 13, 1853, Box 10, Miller1-Yale; Isaac N. Ebey to Simpson P. Moses, June 4, 1853, Ebey to James Guthrie, Customs-SF.

15. Ebey's arguments seemed to make some impression, because one month later he sent on a confirmation of Miller's appointment to Treasury. Isaac N. Ebey to James Guthrie, August 10, 1854, September 11, 1854, Customs-SF.

16. John C. Ainsworth to T. F. McElroy, September 26, 1853, Box 1, McElroy-UW. Thomas J. Dryer had sent the Ramage printing press (which he had bought from the *Alta California* paper and used to publish the *Oregonian*) on to Olympia to print the *Columbian* as part of his investment in the Whig paper. It is suggestive, then, that Dryer was Miller's only debtor in Oregon in 1852 and is a link between the *Columbian* and its Democratic successor. Johnson, *Founding the Far West*, 162–63; Statement of Accounts, 1852, W. W. Miller Account Book, Miller2-Yale.

17. On the creation of the new Democratic paper, see Richards, *Isaac I. Stevens*, 168–69. The paper's interim name was *Washington Pioneer*, and it published its first issue on December 3, 1853. It adoped *Pioneer and Democrat* by February 1854. On the slow start of the partisan press in the Oregon Country, see Warren J. Brier, "Political Censorship in the *Oregon Spectator*," *PHR* 31 (August 1962): 235–40.

18. *Pioneer and Democrat*, October 15, 1854.

19. David Johnson called the party "a system that projected local desires (and men) from secluded precincts into the state (or territorial) and national political arenas." Johnson, *Founding the Far West*, 58.

20. Josiah Lucas to WWM, September 23, 1853, Box 4, Miller1-Yale; Johnson, *Founding the Far West*, 154–56; James E. Hendrickson, *Joe Lane of Oregon: Machine Politics and the Sectional Crisis, 1849–1861* (New Haven: Yale University Press, 1967), 68–70, 80–85; Malcolm Clark Jr., *Eden Seekers: The Settlement of Oregon, 1818–1862* (Boston: Houghton Mifflin, 1981), 266–69, 275–76.

22. Isaac Stevens to WWM, April 18, 1853, Box 6, Miller1-Yale; Stevens to J. Paton Anderson, April 18, 1853, Box 2, Stevens-UW; *Columbia*, April 30, 1853; Richards, *Isaac I. Stevens*, 159–60. Stevens was careful during his railroad survey expedition to write

Douglas regularly, informing him about the progress of examining and expanding western travel routes. See Allan Nevins, *Ordeal of the Union: A House Dividing, 1852–1857* (New York: Scribners, 1947), 85–87.

23. For the best account of Stevens's political strategies and the quickly formed cadre of loyalists he attracted, see Richards, *Isaac I. Stevens,* 153–80, 313–17.

24. For examples of Miller's use of money to connect politicians, see James G. Strong to WWM, October 4, 1853, Box 7, R. H. Lansdale to WWM, August 28, 1855, Box 4, William J. Wills to WWM, July 5, 1855, Box 8, Declaration of Uses, May 13, 1855, William Rutledge to WWM, Box 5, Miller1-Yale; W. W. Miller Personal Accounts, 1856, Indenture between Edward Furste and W. W. Miller, July 16, 1858, Box 5, WWM-UW.

25. Isaac Stevens, "Address," Railroad Convention, Vancouver, Washington, May 20, 1860. For discussion of Isaac Stevens's development as a military officer and practical bureaucratic politician, see Richards, *Isaac Stevens,* chaps. 4, 5.

26. Richards, *Isaac Stevens,* 164–77; Isaac I. Stevens to WWM, June 15, 1854, Box 6, Miller1-Yale; *Pioneer and Democrat,* December 3, 1853. Stevens wrote Miller in a formal manner, suggesting that at this juncture their political relationship had just begun and that perhaps Stevens felt it necessary to "confide" in Miller to gain his confidence.

27. For a discussion of Stevens and the history of Indian treaty negotiations in the Pacific Northwest, see Richards, *Isaac Stevens,* chaps. 8, 9; Robert Ignatius Burns, S.J., *The Jesuits and the Indian Wars of the Northwest* (New Haven: Yale University Press, 1966), chaps. 3, 4; C. F. Coan, "The Adoption of the Reservation Policy in the Pacific Northwest," *OHQ* 23 (January 1922): 2–15.

28. Richards, *Isaac Stevens,* 313; Burns, *Jesuits and Indian Wars,* 67–76.

29. Richards, *Isaac Stevens,* 169–72; Bancroft, *History of Washington,* 83–90.

30. WWM to Isaac Stevens, January 26, 1855, Box 12, Miller1-Yale.

31. *Pioneer and Democrat,* February 6, 1855.

32. Isaac Ebey to WWM, March 11, 12, 26, 1855, Box 2, Miller1-Yale; Isaac Ebey to W. S. Ebey, April 29, 1855, Box 1, Ebey-UW.

33. Isaac Ebey to WWM, December 30, 1854, Box 2, Edward Lander to WWM, July 28, 1854, Box 4, Ebey to A. M. Poe, April 25, 1853, Box 13, Miller1-Yale; Ebey to James Guthrie, August 10, June 30, September 11, 1854, Ebey to F. Bigger, September 11, 1854, Custom-SF. Ebey replaced Poe at Bellingham Bay with E. C. Fitzhugh, a solid Stevens supporter who later served as Indian agent at Bellingham during the Indian War years.

34. Mrs. Patton Anderson to Edmund S. Meany, July 23, 1902, Meany-UW; Margaret Anderson Uhler, ed., "Well and Strong and Fearless: Etta Anderson in Washington Territory, 1853–1856," *Montana, the Magazine of Western History* 32 (Summer 1982): 32–39. Anderson and his wife, Henrietta Adair, were first cousins; and their uncle, John Adair, served as collector of customs at Astoria during the early 1850s.

35. J. Patton Anderson to WWM, October 10, 1855, WWM-UW; Anderson to WWM, February 3, 1856, Miller1-Yale. Anderson left his Olympia town lots in the care of his brother, Butler Anderson, who reportedly lost control of them when the Civil War began and his brother had accepted command of a Confederate regiment. Uhler, "Etta Anderson," 39.

36. J. Patton Anderson to WWM, November 16, 1855, Box 1, Anderson to Edward Lander, January 29, 1856, Box 1, Miller1-Yale.

37. J. Patton Anderson to WWM, November 19, 1855, Box 1, Miller1-Yale.

38. *Pioneer and Democrat,* June 8, 1855; Robert W. Johannsen, *Frontier Politics on the Eve of the Civil War* (Seattle: University of Washington Press, 1955), 28–29, 83–85. The American Party, or Know-Nothings, had their strongest following in larger cities where mid-century immigration made its xenophobic politics popular; but in the Oregon Country, the party also played into the anti-Catholic prejudice of HBC opponents and Methodist politicians. Terrence O'Donnell, *Arrow in the Earth: General Joel Palmer and the Indians of Oregon* (Portland: Oregon Historical Society Press, 1991), 185–90; Richards, *Isaac Stevens,* 169, 273; Nevins, *Ordeal of the Union,* 323–28.

39. Memorandum of Notes and Monies, August 1, 1855, Box 3, Miller1-Yale; *Pioneer and Democrat,* May 26, 1855.

Chapter 5. Friends in War

1. The principal members of Stevens's party at Medicine Creek included Benjamin F. Shaw, interpreter; James Doty, secretary; Michael Simmons, Indian agent for the tribes west of the Cascades; George Gibbs, surveyor; and Hugh A. Goldsborough, who handled supplies. Charles E. Garretson, "A History of the Washington Superintendency of Indian Affairs, 1853–1865," (M.A. thesis, University of Washington, Seattle, 1962), 18; Richards, *Isaac Stevens,* 197.

2. Many commentators have remarked on the Chinook Jargon's limited vocabulary, the impossibility of translating some treaty provisions faithfully, and Stevens's refusal to have translations made directly in each tribe's language. See Richards, *Isaac Stevens,* 197–98; Robert Ruby and John Brown, *Indians of the Pacific Northwest* (Norman: University of Oklahoma Press, 1981), 131; Colonel B. F. Shaw, "Medicine Creek Treaty," *Proceedings of the Oregon Historical Society, 1901* (Portland, 1901), 27–29; James B. Wickersham, "The Indian's Side of the Puget Sound Indian War" (Washington State Historical Society, October 1893), 6; Carole Seeman, "The Treaties of Puget Sound," in *Indians, Superintendents, and Councils: Northwestern Indian Policy, 1850–1855,* ed. Clifford Trafzer (Lanham, Md.: University Press of America, 1986), 24; Barbara Lane, "Political and Economic Aspects of Indian-White Culture Contact in Western Washington in the Mid-19th Century," May 10, 1973, 28–29, OHS.

3. For the text of the Medicine Creek Treaty, see Charles J. Kappler, ed., *Indian Affairs, Laws, and Treaties,* 4 vols. (Washington, 1904), 1:661–64.

4. The treaties concluded at Point Elliott and Point-No-Point councils are in Kappler, *Laws and Treaties,* 1:669–77, 682–85; those negotiated at the Walla Walla council are found in ibid., 698–706.

5. R. H. Lansdale to WWM, June 12, 1855, Box 4, Miller1-Yale; Eldridge Morse, "Notes on History," pp. 120–1, Bancroft-UCB.

6. Major Gabriel Rains to Major E. D. Townsend, January 29, 1854, Sen. Ex. Doc. 16, 33d Cong., 2d sess., 16–17; Clifford E. Trafzer and Richard D. Scheuerman, *Renegade Tribe: The Palouse Indians and the Invasion of the Inland Pacific Northwest* (Pullman: Washington State University Press, 1986), 33–35; Richards, *Isaac Stevens,* 212; A. J. Splawn, *Ka-mi-akin: Last Hero of the Yakima* (Portland: Kilham Stationery, 1917), 38; William N. Bischoff, S. J., "The Yakima Campaign of 1856," *Mid-America* 31 (1949): 164–65.

7. R. H. Lansdale to WWM, June 29, 1855, Box 4, Miller1-Yale. For discussions of

the Walla Walla Council, see Lawrence Kip, "The Indian Council at Walla Walla, May and June, 1855," *Sources of the History of Oregon* 1:pt.2 (Eugene: Contributions to the Department of Economics and History, University of Oregon, 1897), 13–15; Richards, *Isaac Stevens*, 215–26; Trafzer and Scheuerman, *Renegade Tribe*, 46–59; Alvin Josephy, *The Nez Perce Indians and the Opening of the Pacific Northwest* (New Haven: Yale University Press, 1965), 314–17. The text of the treaties can be found in Kappler, *Laws and Treaties*, 2:694–705.

8. R. H. Landsdale, in a letter to Miller written from the Council Grounds at Walla Walla in June, mentioned Palmer's warning to Indians about the gold discoveries and the likelihood that miners would "steal" the Indians' lands. Lansdale to WWM, June 7, 1855, Box 4, Miller1-Yale. The *Puget Sound Courier*, July 12, 1855, published reports of gold discoveries and a public statement attributed to Isaac Stevens and Joel Palmer that the lands east of the Cascades were open for settlement, thus prompting more trespassing by whites during the summer months. The subject of interim settlement by whites, before the treaties were ratified in Washington, was not discussed at the Walla Walla Council. See discussions in Richards, *Isaac Stevens*, 223–24; Josephy, *Nez Perce*, 338; Click Relander, *Strangers on the Land* (Yakima: n.p., 1962), 45.

9. The best accounts of Bolon's death and the immediate consequences are in Lucullus V. McWhorter, *Tragedy of Wahk-Shum: Prelude to the Yakima Indian War, 1855–56; the Killing of Major Andrew J. Bolon* (Yakima: n.p., 1937); Splawn, *Ka-mi-akin*, 41–43. There is dispute among historians whether Bolon had antagonized Yakama leaders, especially Kamiakin. For another view, see Trafzer and Scheuerman, *Renegade Tribe*, 62–63.

10. The first volunteer force organized in Washington Territory was established by Isaac N. Ebey on Whidbey Island in June 1854 (*Pioneer and Democrat*, June 10, 1854). Stevens asked for authority to call up volunteers in his first message to the territorial legislature, *Journal of the House of Representatives of the Territory of Washington*, 1st. sess. (Olympia, 1855), 21–2. George Webb, comp., *Chronological List of Engagements . . . Regular Army . . .* (St. Joseph, Missouri, 1939), 12–15. R. H. Lansdale, who accompanied Stevens on the treaty tour, wrote Miller that the Stevens party had "few and lorrid [*sic*] details by letters, etc. of the Indian atrocities in the Yakima and adjacent counties. . . . We can only hope the regular and volunteer troops have ere this given the treacherous savages a severe chastising—such a one as they shall remember for years to come." Lansdale to WWM, June 7, 1855, Box 4, Miller1-Yale.

11. *Pioneer and Democrat*, October 12, 1855; Ezra Meeker, *The Tragedy of Leschi* (Seattle, 1905), 76–84; Richards, *Isaac Stevens*, 237, 255.

12. Blankenship, *Tillicum Tales*, 29.

13. The Connell's Prairie area had long been an Indian camping and meeting place, especially for Nisqually and Puyallup Indians who had family connections with tribes from east of the Cascades. Marian W. Smith, *The Puyallup-Nisqually* (New York: Columbia University Press, 1940), 22. For two near eyewitness accounts of the attacks at Connell's Prairie, see *Pioneer and Democrat*, October 30, November 9, 1855; U. E. Hicks, *Personal Recollections of Scenes, Incidents, Dangers and Hardships Endured During the Yakima and Clickitat Indian War, 1855 and 1856* (Portland: George Himes, 1885), 1–5. Hicks lived at Chamber's Prairie, about five miles east of Olympia, and was one of the first settlers to learn of the conflicts on the White and Puyallup rivers.

14. James Tilton to George Gibbs, November 25, 1855, Tilton-Yale; Eldridge Morse,

"Notes on History and Resources of Washington Territory," pp. 19–21, 76–82, Morse-UCB; "General Orders, Adjutant General's Office, Olympia, W.T." November 13, 1855, Box 2, Army-OHS; John Cain to Col. B. F. Shaw, October 25, 1855, Cain-Yale; Andrew Jackson Chambers, "Recollections," 25–29, Special Collections, UW; Hicks, *Personal Recollections*, 3; Arthur A. Denny, *Pioneer Days on Puget Sound* (Seattle: A. Harrison Co., 1908), 77–8; *Messages of the Governor of Washington Territory . . .* (Olympia: Edward Furste, 1857) [*Messages of the Governor*], 274–75; Richards, *Isaac Stevens*, 256–57.

15. James Doty, "Journal of Operations," December 31, 1855; Richards, *Isaac Stevens*, 258–62. For details of Stevens's disputes with General Wool and their relevance to the conduct of the war, see *Messages of the Governor*, which includes the governor's correspondence during the war. Stevens's general orders in late December 1855 identified Col. B. F. Shaw as commander of volunteer forces in eastern Washington and assigned Lt. Col. James Doty responsibility for command of one major battalion to protect the governor's party in its westward march. "General Orders, A" and "General Orders, B," *Messages of the Governor*, 36–37. See also W. S. Lewis, "The First Militia Companies in Eastern Washington Territory," *WA Quart.* 11 (October 1920): 243–49. Eldridge Morse expressed views held by others when he wrote in 1880 about Stevens's just anger at Wool: "Is it any wonder, when Stevens saw such golden opportunities wasted [Wool's reluctance to attack Indians] that he should yield somewhat to a just resentment against such triflers with the lives and interests of the people of the Northwest?" Morse, "Notes On History. . . , " vol. 35, Book 6 Indian War, 1855–56, p. 68, Morse-UCB.

16. *Messages of the Governor*, 27; Isaac I. Stevens to "Mother," August 28, 1856, Stevens 2-Yale; Morse, "Notes on History . . . ," vol. 34, Book 5, Indian War (1855–56), 69–70, Morse-UCB. See also Isaac I. Stevens to George A. Manypenny, January 26, 1856, in *Report of the Secretary of the Interior*, Sen. Ex. Doc. 46, 34th Cong. 1st. sess. (Serial 821).

17. "General Orders No. 3," February 1, 1856, "General Orders, No. 4," February 25, 1856, *Messages of the Governor*, 38–39. One of the most thorough contemporary considerations of Stevens's viewpoint on military discipline and a defense of the governor's actions can be found in Morse, "Notes on History . . . ," vol. 36, Book 7, Indian War, (1855–56), 6–30, Morse-UCB.

18. There is evidence that in the fall of 1855 James Tilton, at least, wanted H. A. Goldsborough to take on the quartermaster general's position, but he evidently declined. As Tilton put it, "he has made a happy escape." James Tilton to George Gibbs, November 25, 1855, Tilton-Yale. But there is also evidence that Stevens had selected Miller from the beginning to be his quartermaster, that it was C. H. Mason who had tried to enlist Goldsborough, and that Tilton was Mason's man, not Stevens's. In fact, A. J. Cain reported to Miller that Stevens had told him that Miller was "the man" to assure the entire volunteer organizational effort. A. J. Cain to WWM, January 21, 1856, Miller1-Yale. When Miller was appointed, the February 8, 1856, *Pioneer and Democrat* praised the appointment, claiming he could make supplies "move as by magic."

19. The first elected brigadier general of the Washington Territorial Militia was George Gibbs; but when Mason called for volunteers in the aftermath of Bolon's murder, he appointed Major Gabriel Rains as brigadier general. James Tilton was appointed adjutant general of the force when the Second Regiment was organized. *Statutes of the Territory of Washington*, 1854, 1st sess. (Olympia, 1855), 20–22; Roy N. Lokken, "Frontier Defense of Washington Territory, 1853–1861" (M.A. thesis, University of Washington, Seattle, 1951), 42–4.

20. *Pioneer and Democrat,* January 25, 1856; Isaac Stevens to Jefferson Davis, March 9, 1856, Sen. Ex. Doc. No. 66, 34th Cong., 1st. sess., 28–29; Isaac Stevens to George Manypenny, January 26, 1856, *Report of the Secretary of the Interior,* Sen. Ex. Doc. No. 46, 34th Cong., 1st sess. (Serial 821); Lokken, "Frontier Defense," 83; Richards, *Isaac Stevens,* 259–60.

21. Stevens's Third Annual Message, January 21, 1856, as quoted in Richards, *Isaac Stevens,* 260.

22. James Douglas to James Tilton, November 6, 1855; Tilton to Douglas, November 1, 1855; Invoice, *Traveller,* November 5, 1855. Tilton had first requested arms from Fort Nisqually, but Tolmie had none and urged Tilton to request them from Victoria. W. F. Tolmie to James Tilton, October 30, 1855, Tilton-Yale. See also Tolmie to Douglas, March 3, 1856, and Tolmie to Dugal Mackintosh, March 15, 1856, in Clarence B. Bagley, ed., "Attitude of the Hudson's Bay Company During the Indian War of 1855–56," *WA Quart.* 8 (October 1917): 302–3. Douglas had developed a poor opinion of Americans during his years on the Columbia River and often chafed at their attitudes toward HBC. See Keith A. Murray, "The Role of the Hudson's Bay Company in Pacific Northwest History," in *Experiences in a Promised Land,* ed. G. Thomas Edwards and Carlos A. Schwantes (Seattle: University of Washington Press, 1986), 28–39.

23. Report of Captain of Engineers, December 1856, *Messages of the Governor,* 54–56; R. S. Robinson to WWM, February 14, 1856, Box 11, Militia-WSA; WWM to R. S. Robinson, February 22, 1856, Letterbook of William Winlock Miller, U.S. Army, Washington (Volunteers), Army-UW.

24. "General Orders No. 4," *Messages of the Governor,* 38–39; "Governor's Appointments," Elwood Evans, Writings on the Indian War, Box 58, Miller-UW; Quartermaster Operations, 1856, Box 9, Miller1-Yale; Memorandum Letter, February 25, 1856, Volunteer Letterbook, Army-UW. Miller's adviser in Washington, D.C., later warned him about the issuance of scrip, pointing out that it was the operation that was most often manipulated for fraud during wartime. Josiah M. Lucas to WWM, April 1, 1856, Box 4, Miller1-Yale.

25. Bagley "Hudson's Bay Company," 306.

26. In 1851, John Montgomery, a former HBC employee at Fort Nisqually, established a farm and way station on his donation land claim on the emigrant road across the Cascades. The barn he built in 1853 served as a storehouse for military supplies in 1855. His was the easternmost farm on the road and a perfect staging place for the volunteer troops charged with patrolling the Nisqually and Puyallup rivers. W. P. Bonney, "Marker for Camp Montgomery," *WA Quart.* 22 (October 1931): 293–95.

27. "General Orders No. 4," *Messages of the Governor,* 38; WWM to [W.B.D.] Newman, Wagonmaster [February 1856], WWM to R. S. Robinson, February 26, 1856, Volunteer Letterbook, Army-UW; WWM to Charles Weed, February 14, 18, 1856, Box 12, Militia-WSA.

28. Isaac Stevens to WWM, February 18, 1856, WWM to Stevens, February 18, 1856, Stevens to WWM, February 20, 1856, *Messages of the Governor,* 222–24.

29. WWM to Isaac Stevens, February 28, 1856, *Messages of the Governor,* 227–28. Miller reported that everything had been accomplished, save the construction of all the ferry boats.

30. WWM to Isaac Stevens, March 2, 1856, Stevens to WWM, March 3, 1856, *Messages of the Governor,* 228–29.

31. A few citizens raised questions about the pursuit of Leschi and Quiemuth in the fall of 1855. More pointed criticisms began to appear by late January 1856, especially in the Whig *Puget Sound Courier,* which wondered if the entire war effort were not an attempt by Stevens to concentrate his political power. *Puget Sound Courier,* January 25, 1856.

32. W. P. Wells to WWM, March 11, 1856, Box 12, Militia-WSA; WWM to R. S. Robinson, March 6, 1856, Volunteer Letterbook, Miller-Army. Miller cautioned Robinson: "exercise your judgment in furnishing those *only* who really and necessarily require it."

33. The Central Battalion took 60 men from Shaw's newly organized company, leaving him with 80 men. "War Notice," March 1, 1856, p. 49, B. F. Shaw to Isaac Stevens, March 9, 1856, Stevens to Shaw, March 12, April 16, 1856, *Messages of the Governor,* 239–41; Lokken, "Frontier Defense," 87–89; Richards, *Isaac Stevens,* 258–59, 270–71.

34. For descriptions of the fight at the Cascades, see Nathaniel Coe to Joel M. Collum, [April] 6, 1856, Coe Family Papers, OHS; L. W. Coe to Putnam Bradford, April 6, 1856, Coe-Yale; Bischoff, *Yakima War,* 168; Carl P. Schlicke, *General George Wright: Guardian of the Pacific* (Norman: University of Oklahoma Press, 1988), 122–23; Paul Andrew Hutton, *Phil Sheridan and His Army* (Lincoln: University of Nebraska Press, 1985), 8–10; Richards, *Isaac Stevens,* 291–92.

35. Fred Lockley, *A History of the Columbia River Valley,* 3 vols. (Chicago: S.J. Clarke, 1928), 1:98–99; H. R. Crosbie to Isaac Stevens, April 5, 1856, Box 4, Stevens-UW; WWM to M. R. Hathaway, April 4, 1856, Volunteer Letterbook, Army-UW; Hathaway to WWM, April 13; 19, 1856, Box 11, Militia-WSA; Edward Furste to WWM, April 26, 28, 1856, Box 2, Miller Collection-Yale.

36. James Tilton to W. F. Tolmie, March 2, 1856, Tolmie to Tilton, March 9, 1856, Tilton-Yale; Roy N. Lokken, "The Martial Law Controversy in Washington Territory, 1856," *PNQ* 43 (April 1952): 91–93; Charles E. Garreston, "A History of the Washington Superintendency of Indian Affairs, 1853–1865" (M.A. thesis, University of Washington, Seattle, 1962), 58–61.

37. James Tilton to Jared S. Hurd, March 2, 1856, Box 5, Bagley-UW.

38. H. J. G. Maxon to James Tilton, March 24, 1856, *Messages of the Governor,* 299–300; Isaac Stevens to Maxon, March 18, 1856, *Council Journal of Washington Territory, 1856–1857* (Olympia, 1857), 193; Stevens to Gilmore Hays, March 17, 1856, Box 4, Gilmore Hays Papers, UW; W. B. Gosnell, "Indian War in Washington Territory," *WA Quart.* 17 (April 1930), 295.

39. Richards, *Isaac Stevens,* 275–7.

40. Isaac Stevens to B. F. Shaw, May 1, 4, 1856, Box 4, Militia-WSA; Morse, "Notes on History . . . ," vol. 37, Book 8, Indian War, 1855–56, p. 50, Morse-UCB. For the governor's position on the controversy, see *Vindication of Governor Stevens, for Proclaiming and Enforcing Martial Law in Pierce County, W.T.* (Olympia, May 10, 1856). For the opposing viewpoint, see *A Brief Notice of the Recent Outrages Committed by Isaac I. Stevens, Governor of Washington Territory* (Steilacoom, 1856), a pamphlet written by George Gibbs and H. A. Goldsborough. For extensive discussion of the whole martial law controversy, see Richards, *Isaac Stevens,* chap. 11; Lokken, "The Martial Law Controversy."

41. Isaac Stevens to WWM, March 19, 1856, Box 6, Miller1-Yale.

42. Isaac Stevens to Silas Casey, April 3, 1856, Casey to Stevens, April 3, 1856, B. F.

Shaw to Stevens, May 10, 1856, *Council Journal of Washington Territory, 1856–57*, 81–82, 85–86, 200–1; Morse, "Notes on History . . . ," vol. 37, Book 8, Indian War, 1855–56, pp. 53–55, Morse-UCB.

43. George Gibbs and H. A. Goldsborough to William Marcy, May 11, 1856, Box 12, Miller1-Yale; *Papers Relating to the Proclamation of Martial Law in Washington Territory*, Sen. Ex. Doc. 98, 34th Cong., 1st sess. (Serial 823), 3–7. For a succinct discussion of the rationale behind the Gibbs and Goldsborough letter to Marcy, see Richards, *Isaac Stevens*, 280–82.

44. John D. Biles to Michael Albright, May 30, 1856, Box 1, Malick-Yale.

45. Isaac Stevens to B. F. Shaw, April 29, 1856, Box 4, Militia-WSA.

46. Charles E. Weed to WWM, May 23, 1856, Box 11, Militia-WSA. Stevens had received similar advice from Warren Gove, quartermaster at Steilacoom. Isaac Stevens to B. F. Shaw, May 21, 1856, Box 4, Militia-WSA.

47. Isaac Stevens to B. F. Shaw, May 21, 1856, Box 4, Militia-WSA. Victor Monroe "Old Kentuck," to WWM, May 27, 1856, Box 11, Militia-WSA. Miller had signed the governor's Thurston County Martial Law proclamation. *Pioneer and Democrat*, May 9, 1856. Monroe had been one of the original territorial justices, but his drinking had forced his removal in 1854. Nonetheless, he was widely honored for his professional abilities.

48. Isaac Stevens to B. F. Shaw, May 28, 1856, Box 5, Militia-WSA; Lokken, "Martial Law," 112–15. Stevens's letter to Chenoweth argued that Shaw was desperately needed in prosecuting the war effort east of the Cascades and asked that he be fined rather than incarcerated for his offense.

49. *Pioneer and Democrat*, April 10, 1856.

50. [T. F. McElroy] to George C. Blankenship, July 26, 1856, Blankenship-UW; J. Patton Anderson to WWM, July 3, 1856, Box 1, Miller1-Yale. Cass had criticized Stevens's use of martial law on the floor of the Senate on July 2. Stevens had been called to accounts in a trial held in the territory, with Judges Strong and Monroe presiding.

51. Richards, *Isaac Stevens*, 286–88.

52. WWM to B. F. Shaw, marked "private," August 20, 1856, Militia-WSA.

53. WWM to B. F. Shaw, marked "private," September 2, 1856, Box 11, Militia-WSA; Isaac Stevens to WWM, August 31, Box 15, Miller1-Yale. During September, Shaw was with Stevens at Walla Walla.

54. Dorothy M. Rew to WWM, May 5, 1856, Box 2, Miller-UW.

55. WWM to Benjamin F. Shaw, June 29, 1856, Box 12, Militia-WSA.

56. Dorothy M. Rew to WWM, May 5, 1856, Box 2, Magdalene McDonald to WWM, June 2, 1856, Box 1, Miller-UW.

57. Isaac Stevens to B. F. Shaw, May 18, 31, 1856, Shaw to Stevens, May 22, 1856, *Messages of the Governor*, 244–46; *Pioneer and Democrat*, March 14, 1856. For typical criticism of Wool and Wright, see [A.L.] Coffey and [William] Sharp to J. Patton Anderson, June 7, 1856, Coffey-Yale; John D. Biles to Michael Albright, May 30, 1856, Box 1, Malick-Yale.

58. George C. Blankenship Diary, Blankenship-UW; B. F. Shaw to James Tilton, June 22, July 1, 1856, *Messages of the Governor*, 257–9; *Pioneer and Democrat*, August 8, 1856; Richards, *Isaac Stevens*, 294–98; Schlicke, *George Wright*, 127–29.

59. The best description of Stevens's failed council meeting and the firefight is in Richards, *Isaac Stevens*, 298–306. See also *Pioneer and Democrat*, October 10, 1856; Schlicke, *George Wright*, 131–35.

60. Isaac Stevens to WWM, August 2, 1856, *Messages of the Governor,* 223.

61. WWM to Frank Matthias, July 17, 1856, WWM to R. S. Robinson, July 22, 1856, WWM to Whitfield Kirtley, July 28, 1856, WWM to Warren Gove, July 28, 1856, WWM to Charles E. Weed, July 29, 1856, WWM to M. B. Millard, August 6, 1856, Army–UW. Millard had remonstrated against the plan to purchase supplies with cash rather than vouchers, explaining to Miller that such an action would immediately depreciate the value of scrip in Portland. Miller acknowledged the risk but went ahead with the purchase.

62. R. S. Robinson to WWM, April 24, 1857, Army-UW. Robinson had employed 80 Indians and 13 of their canoes to transport the goods to Fort Tilton for auction. *Pioneer and Democrat,* August 29, 1856.

63. Miller to Charles E. Weed, July 29, 1856, Weed to WWM, August 3, 1856, Army-UW; E. C. Fitzhugh to WWM, August 28, 1856, Box 11, Militia-WSA. The friction at Port Townsend involved one of Miller's personal enemies, J. J. Van Bokkelin, who refused to disband until he had received 500 rations for his men and assorted materiel.

64. WWM to M. R. Hathaway, February 25, 1856, Militia-WSA; M. B. Millard to WWM, April 20, June 16, July 7, 11, 1856; Edward Furste to WWM, April 26, 28, 1856, Box 2, Miller1-Yale.

65. Scrip was issued as a promissory note, which was signed by Miller as quartermaster general and Governor Stevens as authorizing officials. Each scrip denomination carried a sequential serial number, handwritten in the corner in Arabic numerals, and was filled in check-style. Vouchers were issued for all payments of services and included a "power of attorney" section to assign the payment to another individual. At the end of the war, another series of scrip was issued for materiel used but not purchased by the government during the course of the war. Horses, for example, were usually appraised at between $200 and $400; the rental of a pasture was set at $100. Those who accepted scrip on the open market took the risk that it would not be redeemed, so they heavily discounted its face value. The purchase or acceptance of vouchers was even riskier, because scrip had not yet been assigned to them. Nonetheless, there was a brisk business in purchasing and accepting vouchers that had been assigned with a power of attorney.

66. *Pioneer and Democrat,* March 21, 1856; WWM to T. M. Patton, April 4, 1856, WWM to James K. Hurd, May 26, 1856, Volunteer Letterbook, Army-UW; Josiah Lucas to WWM, April 1, 1856, Box 4, Miller1-Yale; W. S. Ebey to WWM, August 25, 1856, Box 11, Militia-WSA. The Oregon scrip evidently traded a bit higher, because there was the general belief that Oregon's politicians could more easily get congressional repayment than Washington's.

67. *Pioneer and Democrat,* August 1, 1856.

68. WWM to M. B. Millard, August 20, 1856, Army-UW.

69. WWM to James K. Hurd, September 28, 1856, WWM to Isaac Stevens, September 14, 1856, Volunteer Letterbook, Army-UW; *Pioneer and Democrat,* August 29, 1856.

70. *Report of J. Ross Browne,* 35th Cong., 1st sess., 1858, H. Ex. Doc. 45 (Serial 955); *Expenses of the Indian Wars in Washington and Oregon Territories,* 35th Cong., 1st sess., 1858, H. Ex. Doc. 114 (Serial 955), 2.

71. *Expenses of the Indian Wars,* 6–8.

72. R. J. Atkinson to Secretary of Treasury, *Claims Growing Out of Indian Hostilities in Oregon and Washington,* 35th Cong., 2nd sess., 1858, H. Ex. Doc. 51 (Serial 1006), 38–40.

73. Fayette McMullin to WWM, September 25, October 10, 1857, Box 2, McMullin-WSL; *Claims Growing out of Indian Hostilities,* 55–58. For discussion of the specific records Miller had to send to the Third Auditor, see J. R. Daniel to WWM, June 18, 1857, Box 5, Lafayette Grover to WMM, August 6, 1857, Box 3, Miller1-Yale.

74. Richards, *Isaac Stevens,* 335–42.

Chapter 6. Political Advantages

1. By 1856, Miller had more than ten leading political men on his books as debtors, most of them owing $500 to $1,000. W. W. Miller Account Book, Loans, 1856, Miller2-Yale.

2. Washington Territory did not follow the political paradigm among western territories. Partisanship mattered from the beginning, but there was more accommodation than in the States. For an analysis of party organization and political behavior in western territories, see Kenneth N. Owens, "Pattern and Structure in Western Territorial Politics," *WHQ* 1 (October 1970): 373–92.

3. *Pioneer and Democrat,* February 6, May 26, 1855. Edmund Sylvester and Butler Anderson, brother of J. Patton Anderson, were other principals in the Democratic Club. Within months, Miller also added another political job to his portfolio when he was appointed district clerk of the 2nd Judicial District in Washington by Chief Justice Edward Lander.

4. Ebey wrote Miller often in 1854 and 1855, asking advice on how he should mount a campaign for territorial delegate. There is no evidence that Miller ever encouraged Ebey's candidacy. Isaac N. Ebey to WWM, December 30, 1854, March 11, 12, 26, 1855, Box 2, Miller1-Yale.

5. *Pioneer and Democrat,* July 4, October 17, 31, 1856.

6. John Cain to WWM, August 13, 1856, A. J. Cain to WWM, August 24, 1856, Box 1, Miller1-Yale.

7. Josiah M. Lucas to WWM, April 1, 1856, Box 4, Miller1-Yale. On the reports of Stevens's drinking and its role in the governor's declining popularity in Washington, D.C., see Richards, *Isaac Stevens,* 316.

8. *Pioneer and Democrat,* April 10, 24, 1857.

9. Franklin Matthias to WWM, April 14, 1857, Box 5, Silas B. Curtis to WWM, February 28, 1857, Box 2, Miller1-Yale. Both Curtis and Matthias had worked for Miller in the Quartermaster Corps during the Indian War.

10. Josiah M. Lucas to WWM, February [n.d.] 1857, Box 4, Isaac Stevens to WWM, June 28, 1858, Box 6, Miller1-Yale; Stevens to B. F. Yantis, June 28, 1858, Stevens-UW; Richards, *Isaac Stevens,* 314–15.

11. Morris H. Frost to WWM, June 16, 1857, Box 2, Isaac Stevens to WWM, June 7, 11, 1857, Box 6, John Catlin to WWM, July 1, 1857, Box 1, Franklin Matthias to WWM, July 15, 1857, Box 5, Miller1-Yale; *Pioneer and Democrat,* June 5, 6, July 24, 1857.

12. J. Patton Anderson to WWM, January 17, March 17, 1857, Box 1, Miller1-Yale; Anderson to J. W. Wiley, May 12, 1857, as printed in *Pioneer and Democrat,* July 17, 1857. Miller had written Anderson in January 1857, urging him to "set [his] pegs for the Governorship," but Anderson replied that he had rejected the possibility months earlier only to find his name submitted to President Buchanan. If he had accepted when it

was first offered by President Pierce, Anderson believed Stevens would have been removed immediately. Anderson clearly thought that information would quiet Miller's suggestion that he accept the governor's spot in January, since Pierce would not leave office until the first week of March.

13. A. J. Cain to WWM, March 18, 1857, Box 1, Miller1-Yale. The combination of superintendencies effectively made the Oregon superintendent responsible for both territories. Absalom F. Hedges, who had been selected to replace Joel Palmer in 1856, resigned in 1857 because of ill health. Lane tried to get Nesmith appointed during the Pierce administration, but failed, in part because Indiana politicians wanted Palmer reinstated. When the Buchanan administration took office, Lane got Nesmith's appointment with help from J. Patton Anderson. Stevens had proposed dividing the region into three superintendencies, with one covering eastern Washington and Oregon, but Congress thought otherwise. James E. Hendrickson, *Joe Lane of Oregon: Machine Politics and the Sectional Crisis, 1849–1861* (New Haven: Yale University Press, 1967), 132, 143–4; Richards, *Isaac Stevens*, 310–11.

14. B. F. Shaw to WWM, June 10, 1857, Box 2, Miller-UW; Isaac Stevens to James Nesmith, July 25, 1857, Box 4, Stevens-UW; Richards, *Isaac Stevens*, 317–18.

15. Martin H. Capell to WWM, February 15, 1858, Box 1, Miller-UW; Political Petitions, November-December 1857, Box 13, WWM to Isaac Stevens, December 26, 1857, Box 12, James H. Goudy to Stephen A. Douglas, December 8, 1857, Box 13, WWM to O. B. McFadden, January 16, 1858, Box 8, McFadden to Judge Black, February 6, 1858, Box 13, Miller1-Yale.

16. C. C. Pagett to WWM, May 5, 27, 1858, Box 5, James Tilton to Isaac Stevens, May 14, 1858, Box 12, O. B. McFadden to WWM, June 12, 1858, Box 4, Stevens to WWM, April 18, May 3, 1858, Box 6, A. J. Cain to WWM, July 4, 1858, Box 1, Miller1-Yale.

17. A. H. Robie to WWM, January 18, 1859, Box 6, W. B. Rankin to President James Buchanan, January 3, 1859, Box 13, Miller1-Yale.

18. Isaac Stevens to WWM, January 18, 1859, Box 7, Miller1-Yale; Hendrickson, *Joe Lane*, 198–99, 207–8; Richards, *Isaac Stevens*, 346–47; Johannsen, *Frontier Politics*, 73.

19. Journal of the House of Representatives (December 1857), 1, 4–5, 25, 40, Journal of the House of Representatives (January 1858), 87, 146, 239, Journal of the Legislative Assembly of Washington Territory, Legis-WSA.

20. House Journal (January 23, 1858), 214, (January 27, 1858), 236–37, Legis-WSA.

21. House Journal (January 27, 1858), 233–34, Legis-WSA; WWM to Isaac Stevens, June 4, 1858, Box 12, Miller1-Yale. Miller may have had reason to worry about Anderson as even co-proprietor of the *Pioneer and Democrat,* considering the information John Cain had passed on to him that characterized Anderson as self-serving. Butler Anderson stayed in Washington Territory for a time, with power of attorney over his brother's property interests and serving as prosectuing attorney for Washington Territory. But when the Civil War erupted and his brother joined the Confederate side, reportedly Butler was hounded out of the territory. John Cain to WWM, August 9, 1857, Box 1, Miller1-Yale; Uhler, "Well Strong and Fearless," 38–9; "Two Documents About Chief Leschi," *WA Quart.* 1 (January 1907): 59.

22. Council Journal (December 14, 1859), 276, (January 6, 1860), 339–42, Legis-WSA.

23. John Cain to WWM, August 9, September 7, 1857, Box 1, Miller1-Yale.

24. A. J. Cain to WWM, September 6, 1857, Box 1, Miller1-Yale.

25. Fayette McMullin to WWM, October 10, 1857, Box 1, Miller-UW; Receipt of Pub-

lic Property, McMullin to WWM, September 25, 1857, McMullin-WSL; WWM to Isaac Stevens, February 12, 1858, Box 12, Miller1-Yale.

26. McMullin evidently had requested a full description of Chenoweth's side of the Martial Law controversy to use as ammunition in his attempt to contest Stevens's action. See F. A. Chenoweth to Fayette McMullin, March 6, 1858, Box 2, McMullin-WSL.

27. WWM to C. H. Mason, April 24, 1858, Box 8, John Cain to WWM, July 27, 1858, Box 1, Miller1-Yale; Richards, *Isaac Stevens*, 322–23.

28. McMullin, however, left something of a mess behind him concerning a fund that had been collected for construction of the capitol. Miller privately grumbled about it with O. B. McFadden, who worried that the idle money might provide political enemies with an issue. Miller made a public statement criticizing McMullin's handling of the money and his extra-territorial interests. Fayette McMullin to WWM, April 29, June 24, December 17, 1858, Box 5, O. B. McFadden to WWM, August 4, 1858, Box 4, "Goes a Begging," draft of newspaper article, [1859], Box 10, Miller1-Yale.

29. WWM to Isaac Stevens, February 12, 1858, Box 12, O. B. McFadden to WWM, July 18, 1858, Box 4, Miller1-Yale.

30. Isaac Stevens to WWM, April 4, 1858, Box 6, WWM to Stevens, June 4, 1858, Box 12, Miller1-Yale.

31. Travers Daniel, a well-connected Democrat who himself had been charged with incompetence as an Indian agent, pushed hard to get the post and used his political influence to put pressure on Stevens. During the early 1850s, Daniel had tried to interest Miller in some investments and had tried to get Miller to use his influence to aid Daniel in getting a government contract. Travers Daniel to WWM, September 18, 1855, Box 2, Miller1-Yale; Travers Daniel to WWM, July 21, 1856, Box 11, Militia-WSA. For background on the political issue, see Richards, *Isaac Stevens*, 322–23.

32. J. Patton Anderson to WWM, March 12, 1857, Box 1, Miller1-Yale; WWM to [J. K. Hurd], September 12, 1856, Volunteer Letterbook, Army-UW; Charles Weed to WWM, August 3, 1856, Box 11, Militia-WSA; House Journal (January 27, 1858), 237, Legis-WSA.

33. Morris H. Frost and J. J. H. Van Bokkelin to WWM, June 5, 1857, Box 2, Isaac Stevens to WWM, July 18, 1858, Box 6, Miller1-Yale. Van Bokkelin and Fitzhugh had been at odds during the Indian War. Fitzhugh remarked on one occasion that Bokkelin typically was "making a beast of himself" among other commanders. E. C. Fitzhugh to WWM, August 28, 1856, Box 11, Militia-WSA.

34. E. S. Fowler to WWM, May 16, 1858, Box 2, J. J. H. Van Bokkelin to WWM, May 16, 1858, May 5, 1859, Box 8, Morris H. Frost, September 30, 1858, February 2, March 4, 1859, Box 2, B. F. Shaw to WWM, February 24, 1859, Box 6, Miller1-Yale. Frost had been charged with falsifying reports, favoring one or two shippers, and wrongfully discharging one of his employees. Fowler, who desired a federal appointment above all else, probably had a legitimate complaint that Frost had routed business to Fowler's competitors.

35. A. J. Cain to WWM, May 2, 1859, Box 1, Miller1-Yale.

36. WWM to A. J. Cain, March 6, 1859, Box 8, Cain to WWM, April 24, June 25, 1859, Box 1, Isaac Stevens to WWM, June 6, 15, 20, 22, 1859, Box 7, J. S. Jaquith to WWM, April 17, 1859, Box 3, Miller1-Yale. Miller headed up a territorial Democratic campaign committee that included J. W. Wiley, G. H. Williams, Crumlin LaDu, H. J. G. Maxon, B. L. Heness, Edmund Sylvester, Warren Gove, L. D. Durgin, and John Catlin.

37. Isaac Stevens to WWM, June 15, 1859, Box 7, Crumline La Du to WWM, May

7, 1859, Box 4, Henry Miles to WWM, June 25, 1859, Box 5, W. F. O'Harven to WWM, May 8, 1859, Box 5, Miller1-Yale.

38. Joseph Lane to WWM, February 15, 1859, Box 1, WWM–UW; L. D. Durgin to WWM, May 8, 1859, Box 2, O. B. McFadden to WWM, May 11, June 20, 1859, Box 4, A. H. Robie to WWM, April 17, 1859, Box 6, Miller1-Yale; *Pioneer and Democrat,* June 10, 1859.

39. S. B. Curtis to WWM, April 25, 1859, Box 2, Henry Miles to WWM, June 25, 1859, Box 5, B. F. Shaw to WWM, July 12, 1859, Box 6, Miller1-Yale.

40. James G. Swan to WWM, September 26, 1859, Box 7, James B. La Du to WWM, September 21, 1859, Box 4, Miller1-Yale.

41. A. J. Cain to WWM, August 19, 1859, Box 1, Miller1-Yale.

42. Martin H. Capell to WWM, February 15, 1858, Box 1, Miller-UW. For a concise description of Douglas's break with the Buchanan administration in 1857–1858, see Allan Nevins, *The Emergence of Lincoln: Douglas, Buchanan, and the Party of Chaos, 1857–1859* (New York: Scribners, 1950), 256–59.

43. Butler P. Anderson to Asahel Bush, March 8, 1859, as quoted in Johannsen, *Frontier Politics,* 86.

44. Martin H. Capell to WWM, February 15, 1858, Box 1, Miller-UW; Richards, *Isaac Stevens,* 346–48; Hendrickson, *Joe Lane,* 216–19; Johannsen, *Frontier Politics,* 101–2.

45. Stevens could not represent a territory but had Lane's personal proxy because so many of the Oregon delegation could not attend.

46. Isaac Stevens to WWM, April 19, 1860, Box 7, Miller1-Yale; Joseph Lane to Matthew Deady, May 13, 1860, Box 7, Deady-OHS; Hendrickson, *Joe Lane,* 225–27; Richards, *Isaac Stevens,* 348–49.

47. Stevens's speech recorded in Murat Halstead, *Caucuses of 1860,* as quoted in Johannsen, *Frontier Politics,* 107.

48. Isaac Stevens to WWM, July 10, 1860, Box 7, WWM to O. B. McFadden, June 16, 1860, Box 8, Miller1-Yale.

49. Isaac Stevens to WWM, August 8, 1860, Box 6, Miller1-Yale.

50. O. B. McFadden to WWM, August 15, 1860, Box 7, Isaac Stevens to WWM, April 3, 1860, Box 7, Miller1-Yale. After the election, Stevens maintained that he had done his duty for his constituents by working hard for the Breckinridge ticket: "I believed that, in my humble sphere, I was striking a blow for the honor and renown of my country, and for the perpetuity of its institutions." Stevens in *Congressional Globe,* 36th Cong. 2d sess., p. 207, as quoted in Johannsen, *Frontier Politics,* 129.

51. Edmund C. Fitzhugh to WWM, July 22, 1860, Miller1-Yale. A. J. Cain had earlier reported to Miller that Stevens had been reported doing some heavy drinking in Washington, but he brushed it off: "I have heard it rumored the Gov. was drinking hard, but suppose his enemies are magnifying the matter." A. J. Cain to WWM, August 19, 1859, Box 1, Miller1-Yale.

52. E. C. Fitzhugh to WWM, July 22, 1860, Box 2, Miller1-Yale. On the numerous charges about Stevens's drinking, see Richards, *Isaac Stevens,* 316, 359–60.

53. O. B. McFadden to Isaac Stevens, April 11, 1860, Box 12, Petition to Stevens, March 15, 1860, Box 12, WWM to [Isaac Stevens], August 22, 1860, Box 9, Miller1-Yale. Prominent signers of the petition against Garfielde included James Tilton, O. B. McFadden, Edward Furste, and Miller. Perhaps even more angering to the Stevens men was Garfielde's participation in the Oregon campaign, where he joined with the fusion

forces of Republicans and Douglas Democrats to fight the Breckinridge-Lane ticket. *Oregon Statesman,* June 3, 1860; Johanssen, *Frontier Politics,* 133.

54. Isaac Stevens to WWM, January 16, 1860, Box 7, Miller1-Yale. Stevens told Miller that Garfielde had rendered some important service to the Kentucky Democrats in 1856 and they were beholden to him: "there is strong feeling towards him on the part of his friends [in Kentucky]."

55. WWM to Isaac Stevens, July 1, 1860, Box 12, Miller1-Yale. Miller had earlier recommended Phillips to Stevens as Indian agent to replace R. H. Lansdale in 1855. But more importantly Phillips had been one of Miller's co-investors in business since the late 1850s, including investment in land on the Tulalip Indian Reservation and in sawmills. Proceedings of Board of Appraisers at Tulalip Indian Reservation, Island County, September 4, 1860, Tulalip-WSU; Statement of Estate and Detail Notes, November 1, 1863, Box 3, Miller-UW; WWM to Isaac Stevens, January 26, 1855, Box 12, Miller1-Yale.

56. Stevens appointed Isaac W. Smith, register of the Land Office; Michael T. Simmons, Indian agent; Charles E. Weed, U.S. marshal; Butler P. Anderson, district attorney; Warren Gove, surveyor of Nisqually.

57. Isaac Stevens to Jacob Thompson, Secretary of the Interior, February 27, 1860, March 28, 1860, Superintendent of Indian Affairs, Appointment File, Department of the Interior, RG 48, National Archives, Washington, D.C. [WASH–NA]; B. F. Shaw to WWM, April 27, 1860, Box 6, Isaac Stevens to WWM, March 2, 3, 18, April 2, May 20, June 4, 1860, Box 7, A. J. Cain to WWM, July 8, 1860, Box 1, Miller1-Yale. A. J. Cain reported to Miller in July that the reports that A. P. Dennison (an Oregon politician who had helped Stevens carry Lane's name at the Charleston convention) would get the spot were ridiculous, even though Stevens had offered this as an excuse to Miller.

58. E. C. Fitzhugh to WWM, July 22, 1860, Box 2, Isaac Stevens to WWM, August 10, Box 7, Miller1-Yale.

59. WWM to Isaac Stevens, October 6, 1860, Box 12, Miller1-Yale. Miller's name had been mentioned in relationship to the Indian agent's position held by Michael Simmons, who had angered all of the Democrats by aiding Republicans during the 1859 campaign. Miller thought it a "petty government position," considering that he hoped to be given the superintendent's job.

60. Isaac Stevens to WWM, November 13, 1860, Box 7, Miller1-Yale.

61. WWM to Isaac Stevens, October 6, 1860, Box 12, WWM to Edward R. Geary, August 20, 1860, Box 8, Miller1-Yale. Miller had written to Edward R. Geary: "Over here we are going to stand by Breckinridge and Lane to the last."

62. Isaac Stevens to WWM, October 17, 1860, Box 7, Miller1-Yale. Stevens criticized Miller for just sending "agents" out with the Breckinridge campaign materials. "But I wish you would come on yourself. Your influence and exertions would do more than those of a hundred agents."

63. F. A. Chenoweth to WWM, February 13, March 21, April 30, May 3, 1860, Box 1, Miller-UW.

64. B. F. Shaw to WWM, November 6, 1860, Box 6, Miller1-Yale.

65. Ibid., November 30, 1860.

Chapter 7. In the Mazy Labyrinth

1. WWM to Isaac Stevens, November 18, 1860, Box 4 Stevens-UW.

2. WWM to Isaac Stevens, November 20, 29, 1860, Box 4, Stevens-UW; Stevens to WWM, February 11, 1861, Box 7, Miller1-Yale; Richards, *Isaac Stevens,* 353–54.

3. Edward Furste to WWM, February 24, 1861, Box 2, Miller1-Yale; *Pioneer and Democrat,* January 25, 1861; Johannsen, *Frontier Politics,* 212.

4. Isaac Stevens to WWM, January 4, 1861, Box 7, Miller1-Yale.

5. Isaac Stevens to WWM, January 21, 1861, Box 7, Miller1-Yale.

6. Edward Furste to WWM, February 25, 1861, Box 2, Miller1-Yale; James Tilton to WWM, September 8, 1866 WWM-UW. Furste told Miller that William Randall, one of James Tilton's political allies and business partners, had requested aid from Stevens in early 1861 only to be rejected and deceived. Randall told Furste that Stevens was "a God d____n shitass and an ungrateful wretch."

7. Isaac Stevens to WWM, February 11, March 8, 1861, Box 7, Miller1-Yale. Stevens complained to Miller that he had not talked with Furste for months and had not seen him when he had been visiting the East. It is likely that the politics of confrontation in Washington had distracted Stevens and he had lost contact with territorial politics. See Richards, *Isaac Stevens,* 352–53.

8. A. B. Greenwood, Commissioner of Indian Affairs, to WWM, March 2, 1861, WSIA2-NA; Certificate of Appointment, Superintendent of Indian Affairs for Washington Territory, February 23, 1861, Box 10, [Christopher Higgins] to WWM, February 15, 1861, Box 12, Miller1-Yale.

9. Silas B. Curtis to WWM, April 14, 1861, Box 2, Seth Catlin to WWM, April 13, 1861, Box 1, George A. Paige to WWM, April 22, 1861, Box 5, P. Ahern to WWM, April 24, 1861, Box 1, Edward R. Geary to WWM, April 20, 1861, Box 2, John Mullan to WWM, April 19, 1861, Box 5, Isaac Stevens to WWM, April 11, 14, 1861, Box 7, Miller1-Yale.

10. *Pioneer and Democrat,* January 25, 1861; *Washington Standard,* March 16, 1861; Isaac Stevens to WWM, December 5, 1861, Box 7, Miller1-Yale; Johannsen, *Frontier Politics,* 212–13.

11. Benjamin F. Shaw to WWM, April 23, 1861, Box 6, Miller1-Yale.

12. Isaac Stevens to WWM, April 15, 1861, Box 7, Miller1-Yale. Both Furste and Shaw had extended themselves for Stevens during the caustic martial law controversy, so it is possible that they both expected extraordinary treatment by him—something they did not receive.

13. *Pioneer and Democrat,* May 24, 1861; *Washington Standard,* May 25, 1861.

14. Isaac Stevens to James Nesmith, May 22, 1861, Stevens-UW; Richards, *Isaac Stevens,* 356–58; Johannsen, *Frontier Politics,* 213–15. There is no indication that Stevens told Miller before the convention met that he intended to quit the race or join the army. In letters he wrote on the eve of the convention, Stevens was tallying committed votes and predicting victory. See Isaac Stevens to WWM, May 6, 9, 11, 1861, Box 7, Miller1-Yale. Some Republicans had even hoped that Garfielde would run on their ticket. Alexander Abernethy had written Elwood Evans that Garfielde would "be the man for us" if they could get him to run. Alexander Abernethy to Elwood Evans, March 7, 1861, Evans-Yale.

15. Isaac Stevens to WWM, April 15, May 27, 1861, Box 7, J. S. Jaquith to WWM, December 6, 1860, Box 3, Miller1-Yale; Elwood Evans to W. H. Wallace, September 1, 1861

Wallace-UW; James Tilton to Edmund Lander, March 10, 1861, Tilton–Yale. Robert Johannsen classified Lander and Tilton as "Copperheads," a term that is loose enough to include Miller, O. B. McFadden, and even Garfielde along with many other Democrats in Washington and Oregon who preferred peace to war but stood solidly for union over disunion. See Johannsen, *Frontier Politics*, 215–16.

16. W. W. Miller Account Book, 1852, Miller3-Yale; *Pioneer and Democrat,* December 26, 1856, February 6, 1857; Edward Lander to B. F. Kendall, January 15, 1858, Kendall-OHS; Edward Lander to WWM, March 2, 1860, Box 4, Miller1-Yale.

17. Edward Lander to WWM, June 23, 1861, Box 4, Miller1-Yale. There is some evidence that even ardent Stevens men, disgusted with Lander and Wallace, eventually voted for Garfielde. See Caleb Miller to Isaac Stevens, Box 12, Miller1-Yale; Isaac N. Ebey Diary, May 31, 1861, Ebey-UW.

18. WWM to Charles E. Mix, Acting Commissioner of Indian Affairs, April 14, 1861, Mix to WWM, June 5, 1861, WSIA2-NA; Edward R. Geary to WWM, April 20, 1861, Box 2, John Mullan to WWM, April 19, 1861, Box 5, Miller1-Yale.

19. *Pioneer and Democrat,* April 26, 1861; W. B. Gosnell to WWM, June 4, 1861, Box 3, Miller1-Yale.

20. Simeon Francis to G. W. Dole, Commissioner of Indian Affairs, May 18, 1861, Francis to Senator E. C. Baker, May 18, 1861, Francis to Senator Lyman Trumbull, May 18, 1861, Edward R. Geary to G. W. Dole, May 18, 1861, Geary to WWM, May 17, 1861, WWM Geary, May 27, 1861, WSIA2-NA.

21. Statement of Public Funds Transfer, August 8, 1861, Box 10, Charles E. Mix to WWM, August 19, 1861, Box 10, Voucher for Superintendent of Indian Affairs Salary, September 19, 1861, Box 10, Voucher for Repayment, L. D. Durgin, September 19, 1861, Box 10, Voucher for Repayment, H. A. Goldsborough, September 19, 1861, Box 10, Voucher for Office Expenses, September 19, 1861, Box 10, Account Ledger, Office Expenses, September 19, 1861, Box 10, Miller1-Yale.

22. Statement of Funds Transfer, Superintendent of Indian Affairs, September 19, 1861, Box 10, B. F. Shaw to WWM, August 24, September 14, 1861, Smith and Davis to WWM, November 12, 1861, Box 6, Benjamin Harned to WWM, [September 1861], Box 3, Miller1-Yale. Republican wheelhorse Alexander Abernethy had written Elwood Evans that Kendall should be "condemned both by the people and by the administration." Abernethy to Evans, November 1, 1861, Evans-Yale.

23. Elwood Evans to W. H. Wallace, September 1, 1861, Charles Hutchins to Wallace, October 4, 1861, Box 1, Wallace-UW; G. W. Dole to B. F. Kendall, November 7, 1861, WSIA2-NA; Alexander Abernethy to Kendall, October 24, November 21, 1861, Kendall to Abernethy, November 30, 1861, James W. Nesmith to Kendall, December 30, 1861, March 1, 1862, Kendall to David Logan, December 7, 1861, Box 1, Kendall-UW; Ladd & Tilton to WWM, May 22, 1862, Box 1, WWM-UW. Edward Furste had told Miller that he thought Kendall wanted to use the office to gain the delegateship. Furste to WWM, February 25, 1861, Box 2, Miller1-Yale. Kendall was removed from office and replaced by C. H. Hale, one of Miller's quartermasters during the Indian War. Kendall's life ended tragically in early 1863, when a political opponent quarreled with him and shot him dead in an Olympia office. *Washington Standard,* January 10, 1863.

24. WWM to Isaac Stevens, October 11, 1861, Box 4, Stevens-UW; S. B. Curtis to WWM, August 12, 1861, Box 14, Stevens to WWM, October 20, 23, 1861, Box 7, Miller1-Yale. Miller continued to play to Stevens's political ambitions by suggesting that when

Washington became a state—"in a year or two," as he predicted—"that you will for many a long year represent us in the U.S. Senate."

25. Johannsen, *Frontier Politics,* 217–19; WWM to Isaac Stevens, October 11, 1861, Box 4, Stevens-UW.

26. Sanitary Commission of Washington Territory, Statement of Purpose and Principles, October 6, 1862, Box 10, Account Ledger for Sanitary Commission, April 16, 1863, Box 10, H. W. Bellows to WWM, June 15, 1863, Box 1, Francis Fowler to WWM, August 30, 1864, Box 8, Miller1-Yale. Miller served as permanent treasurer of the Washington Territory Sanitary Commission from 1862 to 1865. See also Alvin M. Josephy, *The Civil War in the American West* (New York: Alfred A. Knopf, 1992), 265–66.

27. Isaac Stevens to WWM, December 1, 1861, April 7, 8, July 31, 1862, Box 7, Edward Furste to WWM, April 21, September 13, 1862, Box 2, Miller1-Yale. Furste could praise Stevens in death, but he could not quite let go of his enmity: "His death proves his devotion to his country . . . if he was not a true man to his friends he has proved himself a brave man and a true one to his country."

28. R. D. Gholson to WWM, January 8, 12, 1860, Folder 1, Gholson-WSL; Victor J. Farrar to Edmond S. Meany, October 1, 1915, Box 73, Meany-UW. Richard Gholson did not endear himself to the Olympia men, because he was part Cherokee and he brought a "foppish" personal secretary with him whom the locals derided and called "Sweetbriar."

29. O. B. McFadden to WWM, August 7, 1862, Box 4, Miller1-Yale; Frank A. Kittredge, "Washington Territory in the War Between the States," *WA Quart.* 2(October 1907): 33–39.

30. William Pickering to J. W. Stephenson, July 26, 1862, William Pickering to Abraham Lincoln, August 10, 1862, Pickering-Yale; B. O. Flower, "William Pickering: War Governor of Washington Territory," Box 75, Meany-UW. Pickering had strongly advised that Lincoln appoint Elwood Evans to the post of territorial secretary, which Lincoln did in 1863.

31. H. A. Goldsborough to WWM, January 1, February 20, 1863, Box 3, W. N. Walton to WWM, January 21, 1863, Box 8, Miller1-Yale; *Washington Standard,* January 3, 1863; Nevins, *The War for the Union,* 169, 214; Phil Roberts, "Taxing the Few: The First Federal Income Tax in Washington Territory," *PNQ* 79 (April 1988): 58–59. Miller was assigned the counties of Thurston, Lewis, Sawamish, Chehalis, Pierce, King, Snohomish, Whatcom, Kitsap, Jefferson, Island, and Clallam.

32. Receipt of Accounts, Deputy Collector of Internal Revenue, W. W. Miller, March 21, April 18, May 14, August 15, 1863, Box 11, Miller1-Yale; *Puget Sound Herald,* March 12, 1863; Roberts, "Taxing the Few," 59–60; Thomas W. Prosch, "Washington Territory Fifty Years Ago," *WA Quart.* 4 (April 1913): 96–104.

33. Alonzo Poe, an old friend of Miller's and a former Whig, had been the public printer for a time, as had George A. Barnes, another old friend of Miller's. Poe had also established the *Overland Press* in 1861 as a "War News" newspaper, but he sold it to B. F. Kendall in 1862. It was when Kendall was proprietor of the paper in early 1863 that he was shot and killed in the office. The paper was then purchased by L. G. Abbott and R. H. Hewitt and renamed the *Pacific Tribune.* Meany, "Newspapers of Washington Territory," *WA Quart.* 8 (October 1926): 284–92. For a discussion of the politics of the public printer's position, see W. A. Katz, "Public Printers of Washington Territory, 1853–1863," *PNQ* 51 (July 1960): 103–14; (October 1960): 171–81.

34. Blankenship, *Tillicum Tales,* 13–14; I. S. M. Van Cleave to WWM, January 13, 1863, Box 8, B. F. Shaw to WWM, December 18, 1863, Box 6, T. F. McElroy to WWM, April 27, 1863, Box 4, T. W. Glasgow to WWM, April 12, 1863, Box 3, Miller1-Yale. McElroy served as deputy collector for Internal Revenue in the eastern counties of Washington in 1863, but the granting of territorial status for Idaho was certain to limit McElroy's revenue job and may have inclined him to pursue the position even though he had written Miller that he had no interest in returning to journalism. Miller might have suggested that Edward Furste become public printer, but Furste had died at his family home in Indiana in the spring of 1863. Miller served as executor of his estate in Washington Territory.

35. W. W. Miller Account Book, 1855, Box 3, WWM to W. G. Gosnell, November 9, 1863, Box 3, Miller-UW; William Pickering to Abraham Lincoln, August 10, 1862, Pick–Yale. McElroy and Nicolay had worked together on the *Pike County Free Press* during the 1840s. Alexander Abernethy had criticized Evans for appointing McElroy, writing him, "I am afraid your [sic] allowing your feeling to get the better of your judgment." Abernethy to Elwood Evans, January 15, 1864, Evans-Yale.

36. T. F. McElroy to WWM, November 16, 1863, Box 4, B. F. Shaw to WWM, December 18, 1863, Box 6, Miller1-Yale; Elizabeth Allison and W. A. Katz, "Thornton Fleming McElroy—Printer, Politician, Businessman," *PNQ* 54 (April 1963): 54–65.

37. Edward Lander to WWM, April 12, May 5, 1863, Box 4, A. J. Cain to WWM, May 24, 1863, Box 1, Miller1-Yale; Johannsen, *Frontier Politics,* 218. Cain wrote Miller to be wary of Cole, that none of the men east of the mountains thought he was a true Democrat and that he was really a sectionalist and anti-Sound man. Miller and his friends had hoped Edward Lander would make a decent showing in the conventions, but Cole prevailed.

Chapter 8. Making Money and Pursuing Family

1. James Tilton to Edward Lander, March 10, 1861, Tilton-Yale; Edward Furste to WWM, December 24, 1861, Box 2, Miller1-Yale; Alice Emmons to WWM, December 6, 1861, Box 1, Miller-UW.

2. Miller Family Genealogical Record, Box 1, Martha P. Miller to WWM, February 26, 1852, June 23, 1855, Box 1, Richard Miller to WWM, September 27, 1851, September 15, 1853, Box 1, Miller-UW.

3. Richard Miller to WWM, October 1, 1853, May 7, 1855, Martha P. Miller to WWM, June 23, 1855, Box 1, Miller-UW.

4. Josiah M. Lucas to WWM, November 25, 27, 1855, January 9, 1856, WWM to Lucas, December 15, 1855, Box 4, Miller1-Yale.

5. Josiah M. Lucas to WWM, January 19, 1857, Box 4, David Logan to WWM, February 18, 1857, Box 4, E. A. Turpin to WWM, June 28, July 27, 1857, June 3, 1858, Box 7, William P. Wills to WWM, May 15, 1858, Box 8, Oliver Stevens to WWM, August 3, 1858, Box 7, Miller1-Yale; W. S. Ebey to WWM, August 25, 1856, Box 11, Militia-WSA. On the general financial and banking conditions in Oregon just prior to the Civil War, see James H. Gilbert, *Trade and Currency in Early Oregon: A Study in the Commercial and Monetary History of the Pacific Northwest* (New York: Columbia University, 1907); Arthur Throckmorton, *Oregon Argonauts: Merchant Adventurers on the Western Fron-*

tier (Portland: Oregon Historical Society, 1961), 215–17. Miller purchased more than $11,000 in scrip for Oliver Stevens in 1858 and 1859, buying it when the discount fell below 40 cents on the dollar.

6. WWM to Oliver Stevens, February 24, September 5, 1859, Box 9, Stevens to WWM, April 18, 1859, Box 7, Miller1-Yale. Stevens had left the commission fee up to Miller's discretion. Charging $200 for the purchase of approximately $2,000 of scrip was probably fair and average for that kind of financial service.

7. D. I. Liste to WWM, March 1854, Box 1, Miller-UW; Norris Humphrey to WWM, May 1, 1856, Box 1, WWM-UW. Humphrey had assured Miller that the two of them could make a significant amount of money by investing in Willamette Valley real estate and small businesses.

8. Parrott and Company (San Francisco) to WWM, October 15, 1860, Box 3, Miller-UW; C. E. Tilton to W. S. Ladd, June 14, 1859, Ladd-OHS; Ladd to WWM, August 12, 1861, May 21, June 1, 1862, Miller1-Yale. On the manipulations of commercial paper just prior to the Idaho gold strikes, see Gilbert, *Trade and Currency in Early Oregon*, 96–98; N. R. Knight, "The Background of Early Washington Banking," *WA Quart.* (October 1935), 243–63. Ladd advised Miller that he could expect a ¾% charge for running bank drafts through any of the larger San Francisco banks, so he ought to charge accordingly for the service.

9. For discussion of the effect of the gold rush in Idaho on Portland business and the development of transportation on the Columbia, see Donald W. Meinig, *The Great Columbia Plain: A Historical Geography, 1805–1910* (Seattle: University of Washington Press, 1968), esp. chap. 8; Alton B. Oviatt, "Pacific Coast Competition for the Gold Camp Trade of Montana," *PNQ* 56 (October 1965): 168–76.

10. For discussion of steamboat competition on the Columbia and its effects on the regional economy and Portland, see MacColl, *Merchants, Money, and Power*, 121–34; Throckmorton, *Oregon Argonauts*, 260–63; Randall Mills, *Sternwheelers Up the Columbia* (1947; reprint, Lincoln: University of Nebraska Press, 1974), 80–88; Johansen, "Oregon Steam Navigation Company," 179–88. On Walla Walla's rise as a regional entrepôt, see G. Thomas Edwards, "Walla Walla: Gateway to the Pacific Northwest Interior," *Montana, the Magazine of Western History* 40 (Summer 1990): 29–43.

11. *Oregonian*, December 5, 1862, February 14, 1863; Throckmorton, *Oregon Argonauts*, 188–9; Gilbert, *Trade and Currency in Oregon*, 98–103. The value of greenbacks in Portland fluctuated from a high of 80 cents in August 1863 to a low of 40 cents in May 1865. By the end of the war their value rose, only to decline again by 1866. Despite the public clamor for patriotic acceptance of the legal tender bills, Oregon and Washington counties rejected payment of taxes in greenbacks in 1863 and 1864.

12. WWM to Wesley Gosnell, November 9, 1863, Box 3, A. Frankel to WWM, April 2, 1863, Miller-UW.

13. T. F. McElroy to WWM, April 27, 1863, Box 4, Miller1-Yale; A. M. Poe to WWM, July 17, 1864, Box 1, WWM-UW; Gilbert, *Trade and Currency in Oregon*, 106.

14. WWM to Robert W. Miller, April 10, 1864, Box 3, Miller-UW; William R. Melville to WWM, April 11, 1863, Box 1, WWM-UW.

15. Thomas Glasgow to WWM, January 12, 1863, WWM-UW. Glasgow had been one of Miller's steady debtors. Miller had advanced him more than $2,000 during the preceding five years, but he felt he could carry him no longer. Receipt, April 7, 1860, Box 11, Miller1-Yale.

16. Court Judgment against Fred Clarke, April 16, 1860, Box 11, Court Judgment against H. Jackson, September 22, 1860, Box 11, Court Judgment against L. M. Collins and H. M. Chambers, October 19, 1860, Box 9, Miller1-Yale; Court Judgment against John M. Swan, September 6, 1859, Box 4, Court Judgment against Moses Hurd, March 2, 1860, Box 4, Court Judgment against Hillory Butler, H. L. Yesler, Gilmore Hays, August 4, 1860, Box 4, Court Judgment against Thomas Glasgow, July 28, 1862, Box 4, Court Judgment against J. J. Westbrook, July 29, 1862, Box 4, Court Judgment against John Remley, July 29, 1862, Box 4, Court Judgment against William Rutledge, August 8, 1862, Box 5, W. W. Miller, Statement of Business and [Cash] Estate Value, October 1, 1861, WWM to Wesley B. Gosnell, November 1863, Box 3, Miller-UW. In 1863, Miller estimated his total investments in real and personal property to be worth $75,000.

17. Mail Contract #12755 Correspondence, 1858–1860, Power of Attorney between William Littlejohn, March 3, 1862, Box 5, Miller-UW.

18. Johansen, "Oregon Steam Navigation Company," 180–82; Throckmorton, *Oregon Argonauts,* 253.

19. Throckmorton, *Oregon Argonauts,* 201–2.

20. On Coffin's career, see MacColl, *Merchants, Money, and Power,* 13–17, 49–61, 125.

21. B. F. Shaw to WWM, February 24, 1859, Box 6, Miller1-Yale; E[noch] S. Fowler to WWM, January 3, 1862, Box 1, WWM-UW. Miller aided both men politically in 1862 on other issues. He wrote a strong letter to Territorial Governor Pickering to secure a governmental position for Hubbs's son. WWM to William Pickering, September 8, 1862, Folder 11, Backus-UW.

22. Paul K. Hubbs to WWM, March 7, 21, 1862, A. R. Burbank to WWM, March 17, 1862, Box 4, Miller-UW; B. F. Shaw to WWM March 8, 1862, Box 6, Miller1-Yale. Named and silent investors in the company also included A. A. Denny, Frank Matthias, and Dexter Horton of Seattle; Frank Clarke of Steilacoom; P. D. Moore of Port Townsend; and Dorsey Baker of Walla Walla.

23. By-Laws of Columbia River Transportation Company, May 1862, Box 4, Miller-UW. A limit of $350,000 was placed on the initial issuance of stock. Any increase would require a majority vote of the directors.

24. Paul K. Hubbs to WWM, April 12, 22, 1862, Alexander S. Abernethy to WWM, May 26, 1862, WWM to B. F. Shaw, May 6, 1862, Box 4, Miller-UW; Edward Lander to WWM, May 22, 1862, Franklin Matthias to WWM, June 21, 1862, O. B. McFadden to WWM, July 20, 1862, Box 4, Miller1-Yale. Hubbs hoped that a combination of arrangements could be made that would link Abernethy's sawmill and shipping interests at Oak Point on the lower river with the overland mail route to the Sound. Matthias hoped it would all develop in a new townsite at the Cascades. Lander emphasized the importance of securing a place at Wallula at the mouth of the Snake River.

25. One of those claims was held by George Washington Bush but was contested by Daniel Bradford, the owner of several lots and the store at the Cascades and also an OSN stockholder. The issue was resolved in Bradford's favor in April 1863. Another claim was held by Thomas Smith, one of the Columbia River Transportation Company major investors. Smith resigned from the company in April 1863 and attempted to make a separate deal with Coffin and the PTC. B. F. Shaw to WWM, April 2, 1863, Box 2, Miller-UW.

26. Thomas J. Fletcher to WWM, February 2, 16, 1863, Box 2, Miller1-Yale.

27. B. F. Shaw to WWM, March 17, 1863, Box 6, Miller1-Yale.

28. B. F. Shaw to WWM, April 2, 1863, Box 2, Miller-UW; Shaw to WWM, April 19, 1863, Box 6, Miller1-Yale.

29. Paul K. Hubbs to WWM, June 23, July 4, 1864, Box 4, Miller-UW. None of the Columbia River Transportation Company stock certificates remain in Miller's papers, so it is probable that he either never made any out for himself or destroyed them.

30. At one point in the negotiations with PTC, Shaw wrote Miller explaining that something had to be done quickly with the company's books and stocks if they expected to sell anything to Coffin: "What Coffin wants is for us to give him legal possession of a majority of the stock. In a word I do not think that they would buy unless they could see the books and proper certificates of stock and the only way that we can do anything is to have the books made out right and certificates of stock issued." B. F. Shaw to WWM, March 23, 1863, Box 2, Miller-UW.

31. Robert W. Miller to WWM, March 17, 1860, Dorothy Rew to WWM, April 8, 1859, Box 2, Miller-UW.

32. Dorothy Rew to WWM, May 13, 1862, September 6, December 8, 1863, Box 2, Miller-UW.

33. Anna Rew to WWM, October 27, 1861, Box 2, Robert Miller to WWM, November 30, 1861, Box 2, Sylvester Emmons to WWM, December 8, 1863, Box 1, WWM to Edmund P. Miller, December 23, 1863, Box 3, Miller-UW; WWM to B. F. Shaw, June 29, 1856, Box 12, Militia-WSA. Miller informed his brother Edmund in 1863 that he would be leaving $31,216 in Gosnell's care and would carry $146 in "pocket money," just so Edmund would know what an assailant might get if he were mugged or killed enroute to Illinois.

34. A. A. Denny to Daniel Bagley, December 8, 1863, Box 1, Bagley-UW; Philip Keach to W. H. Wallace, October 15, 1861, Box 1, Wallace-UW; Isaac Lightner to WWM, November 24, 1861, Box 4, T. F. McElroy to WWM, November 16, 1863, Joseph Cushman to WWM, December 6, 1863, Box 2, Lightner to WWM, December 25, 1863, Box 4, Miller1-Yale. Acquiring postal and military supply contracts depended on the applicant's political and personal friendships and sometimes involved reciprocation for favors. When Keach applied for the main contract in 1861, he promised Territorial Delegate Wallace: "if you succeed in getting it for me I will give you five hundred dollars, to be paid whenever you think proper to draw on me."

35. Anson G. Henry to Senator B. F. Harding, November 18, 1863, Box 13, Miller1-Yale.

36. Isaac Lightner to WWM, November 9, 23, 1863, Louis W. Neustadter to WWM, January 28, 1864, WWM to W. P. Dole, Commissioner of Indian Affairs, February 29, 1864, Box 3, Miller-UW.

37. Abraham Lincoln to Postmaster General, February 23, 1864, Lincoln-Yale. The Postmaster General was Montgomery Blair of Missouri, son of Francis P. Blair, an old Jacksonian who had been one of the founders of the Republican party. Montgomery Blair was Lincoln's cabinet officer who best represented the Border States on war issues.

38. H. A. Goldsborough to WWM, March 9, 1864, Box 3, T. F. McElroy to WWM, November 16, 1863, Box 4, Miller1-Yale. Keach had acquired the contract by default, being the principal bondsman for the contractor, George Parkinson, who had skipped out on the business in 1863. Thomas W. Prosch, "Washington Mail Routes in 1857," *WA Quart.* 6 (April 1915): 107–8.

39. H. A. Goldsborough to WWM, July 25, 1864, Box 3, Miller1-Yale; H. A. Golds-borough to WWM, August 2, 8, Box 6, Miller-UW.

40. H. A. Goldsborough to WWM, August 23, 1864, Box 3, Miller1-Yale; Golds-borough to WWM, September 3, 1864, F. M. Sargent [Olympia Postmaster] to George W. McLellan, October 9, 1864, Box 6, Miller-UW. One of Keach's subcontractors, Captain John Wright, had gone to Washington to lobby for a continuance, but Goldsborough evidently convinced the Post Office Department to abrogate Keach's contract and award it to Miller.

41. H. A. Goldsborough to WWM, November 1, 22, 28, 1864; Contract for Mail Delivery on Route #15274, September 1, 1864, Box 6, Miller-UW; Elwood Evans to William D. Kelley, July 11, 1864, Box 13, Miller1-Yale. Evans claimed that the current inadequate mail contract was William H. Wallace's way of "punishing" the territorial voters for not returning him to office. The contract specified that the mail would leave Olympia on Monday morning, arrive in Victoria on Tuesday, and return to Olympia on Thursday. The route included stops at Steilacoom, Seattle, Port Madison, Port Gamble, Port Ludlow, Port Townsend, Port Angeles, Victoria.

42. Isaac Lightner to WWM, December 25, 1863, Box 4, Miller1-Yale; Sylvester Emmons to WWM, July 25, 1864, Edmund Miller to WWM, August 21, 1864, Box 1, Miller-UW. Emmons had privately groused about having to pay for food for the elder Miller during his last days, but he had written apologetically to Miller to explain that his refusal to take any money from him as compensation for taking care of his father was not meant as an insult. He hoped it all could be forgotten, but clearly it was still an issue. Once back in Washington Territory, Miller gathered information on land prices in Illinois and Missouri, but he failed to follow up the leads.

43. Frank Eames to WWM, July 26, 1864, Box 7, WWM to Robert W. Miller, April 10, 1864, Box 3, WWM to Postmaster, St. Joseph, Missouri, June 1, 1864, P. T. Miller [Jefferson City, Missouri] to WWM, August 18, 1864, Sylvester Emmons to WWM, November 14, 1864, Box 3, Janet "Nettie" McDonald to WWM, July 26, 1864, Box 1, WWM to Wesley Gosnell, November 9, 1863, Box 3, Miller-UW. For discussion of the effect of the Civil War on Chicago and Illinois, see Cronon, *Nature's Metropolis,* 210, 229–30, 301.

44. RTM to WWM, November 25, 1857, Box 1, Miller-UW.

45. RTM to WWM, August 1, 1862, January 8, 1863, Box 1, Miller-UW.

46. RTM to WWM, December 14, 1864, Box 1, Miller-UW.

Chapter 9.   To Assist My Friends

1. Allen Francis to WWM, September 28, October 14, November 8, 1864, February 22, 1865, Box 1, D. B. Finch to WWM, December 2, 1864, F. M. Sargent to WWM, December 19, 1864, February 19, 1865, Agreement Between W. W. Miller and D. B. Finch, October 1, 1864, Box 6, Memorandum of Agreement Between W. W. Miller and John T. Wright, March 10, 1865, Box 2, Miller-UW. Francis had warned Miller that Jones was a "poor manager" and had "no friends here [Victoria] or on the other shore to relieve him." Goldsborough had cautioned Miller not to let Wright have any part of the contract, but Miller had little option if he wanted a worthy vessel. Wright agreed to carry the mail on the *Anderson* for the full contract price awarded Miller. Signifi-

cantly, he also agreed to pay all fines and penalty fees that might be levied for failure to perform and also to provide Miller with free passenger and freight passage, an additional benefit of securing the contract. That was how Finch had made a sizeable fortune as the *Anderson*'s purser and captain. Charles Prosch, *Reminiscences of Washington Territory* (Seattle, 1904), 57.

2. WWM to H. A. Goldsborough, April 6, 1865, Box 3, Miller-UW.

3. Philip Keach to WWM, May 15, July 14, August 13, 1865, Box 6, Miller-UW. Keach had compounded his problems by giving at least one of his subcontractors property in Steilacoom as collateral on his debt.

4. WWM to Postmaster General, February 8, 1865, WWM to George McLellan, June 1, August 20, 24, 25, 1864, McLellan to WWM, July 23, 1865, I. N. Arnold [Auditor] to WWM, July 19, 1865, F. M. Sargent to George W. McLellan, August 3, 1865, Miller-UW.

5. H. A. Goldsborough to WMM, September 25, 1865, Box 6, Miller-UW. Miller had enlisted Governor William Pickering's aid in getting his contract approved for an early extension in 1865. William Pickering to WWM, March 11, 1865, Box 5, Miller1-Yale.

6. D. B. Finch to WWM, May 21, 1866, Box 6, Miller-UW.

7. Joseph Cushman to WWM, December 17, 1864, Box 2, A. G. Henry to WWM, October 22, 1864, J. S. Jaquith to WWM, May 20, 1859, Box 3, Miller1-Yale; Philip Keach to WWM, July 14, 1865, Box 6, Miller-UW. The *Washington Democrat* was a Copperhead Democratic paper that began publication in 1864 specifically to promote the candidacy of George McClellan and to support the Crittenden Compromise. The paper was edited by Urban E. Hicks.

8. Joseph Cushman to WWM, December 17, 1864, Box 2, William Pickering to WWM, December 22, 1864, Box 5, Miller1-Yale; Pickering to Abraham Lincoln, January 4, 1864, Pick-Yale; WWM to William H. Wallace, September 28, 1864, Box 1, WWM-UW; Alexander Abernethy to Elwood Evans, February 2, 1864, Evans-Yale. Pickering had tried to shame Miller by telling him that the Democrats taking money from Evans "laugh at him in their sleeves and think him both a rogue and a fool." But Miller had aided Evans because of financial reasons, not political ones, and his fear in late 1864 was Evans's potential to expose Miller to a hefty financial liability.

9. William Pickering to WWM, March 11, 1865, Box 5, Miller1-Yale.

10. *Pacific Tribune*, January 14, February 18, 1865; A. A. Denny to WWM, February 12, 1865, Box 2, Miller1-Yale.

11. *Washington Standard*, May 13, 1865; Joseph Cushman to WWM, April 13, May 6, 1865, Box 2, Miller1-Yale; Washington Territory Election Returns, 1865, Elect-UW.

12. William Pickering to WWM, June 30, 1865, Box 5, A. A. Denny to WWM, December 9, 1865, January 27, February 14, May 9, 1866, Box 2, Miller1-Yale.

13. George Gibbs to WWM, July 24, 1865, Box 3, Miller1-Yale.

14. *Washington Standard*, October 6, 1866.

15. Richard Yates to President Andrew Johnson, May 5, 1866, Pick-Yale. Evans had hoped to convince the administration to remove Pickering, with the clear intention of securing the office for himself or, at the least, retaining his secretaryship. John T. Knox to WWM, August 28, 1866, Box 4, Miller1-Yale.

16. For the relationship between Miller and the Stevens family, see Margaret Stevens to WWM, March 13, 1863, August 28, 1864, January 18, September 12, 1865, Box 7, Hazard Stevens to WWM, July 13, 1866, Box 6, Miller1-Yale; WWM to Margaret Stevens, November 2, 1865, WWM to Hazard Stevens, February 20, March 20, 1866,

Stevens-UO. Miller had negotiated the lease of the family home in Olympia to Governor Pickering, although he put himself in the uncomfortable position of being a nagging rental agent to get Pickering to pay the rent.

17. WWM to Hazard Stevens, October 14, 1866, Stevens-UO.

18. WWM to Hazard Stevens, November 22, 25, 1866, Stevens-UO; James W. Nesmith to WWM, December 2, 1866, Box 5, C. H. Armstrong to WWM, November 15, 1866, Box 1, T. F. McElroy to WWM, January 13, 1867, Box 4, Miller1-Yale. Nesmith had not been consulted in the appointment of McKenny but went and asked Secretary of the Interior Orville H. Browning if he was as solidly behind the president as Miller. Browning assured Nesmith that McKenny was "a good conservative and supporter of the President's policy."

19. WWM to Hazard Stevens, January 6, 1867, Stevens-UO.

20. Isaac Lightner to WWM, November 24, 1861, Box 4, J. B. Whitcomb to WWM, April 26, 1867, Box 8, Miller1-Yale; A. M. Poe to WWM, July 17, 1864, Box 1, WWM-UW; David L. Phillips to WWM, May 1, 1867, Miller-UW; Obit., David Phillips, *Puget Sound Courier,* March 9, 1872. Miller investigated business properties near the waterfront in an area dominated by warehouses and small manufacturing businesses.

21. WWM to William F. Tolmie, July 23, 1853, George A. Ropp to WWM, July 18, 1851, Box 2, Miller1-Yale; Richard Miller to WWM, June 7, 1854, Box 1, Miller-UW.

22. Daniel Bigelow to WWM, March 5, 1853, Box 1, Miller1-Yale.

23. John Sewell to WWM, January 21, 1859, Box 6, Miller1-Yale.

24. Phillip Keach to WWM, July 14, 1865, Box 6, Miller-UW; Fred A. Clarke to WWM, December 19, 1864, Box 1, S. D. Howe to WWM, March 3, 1868, Box 3, Miller1-Yale.

25. T. F. McElroy to WWM, March 24, 1869, Box 4, Miller1-Yale. In a similar vein, Leonard Durgin wrote Miller (March 3, 1867, Box 1, Miller1-Yale) about a friend's foray at one of the men's favorite bawdy houses: "Rutledge . . . paid tribute to her by taking one night's lodging there and pronounced it *good!*"

26. *The San Francisco Business Directory for the Year Commencing in 1865* (San Francisco: Towne & Bacon, 1865), 350; *The San Francisco Business Directory for the Year Commencing in 1869* (San Francisco: Towne & Bacon, 1869). No record of Mary Ann Palmer shows up in subsequent San Francisco business directories.

27. Complaint, Summons, Judgment—Mary Ann Palmer *vs.* William W. Miller, January 21, 1867, Box 4, Miller-UW.

28. T. F. McElroy to WWM, February 10, 1867, Box 4, Miller1-Yale.

29. T. F. McElroy to WWM, January 13, February 10, 17, 1867, Box 4, Miller1-Yale.

30. John T. Knox to WWM, February 12, 1867, Box 4, Samuel D. Smith to WWM, January 23, 1867, Box 6, W. A. Ball to WWM, May 2, 1867, C. H. Armstrong to WWM, May 2, 1867, Box 1, Miller1-Yale; WWM to Hazard Stevens, April 18, 1867, Stevens-UO. Miller returned to Washington Territory in late April, but business interests in Seattle dominated his time until the first week in May, leaving him little opportunity to become involved in politics.

31. *Seattle Gazette,* April 29, 1867. Flanders had wrested the nomination from Selucius Garfielde, who had arrived at the convention with pledges from Denny's supporters but soon realized that he could not win. Throwing his support to Flanders, Garfielde assured his nomination. Flanders had come west in 1851 to San Francisco, where he had worked with men like E. D. Baker in creating the state's first Republican party organization. He had helped establish the *San Francisco Times* newspaper

and received two patronage jobs from the Lincoln administration before coming to Washington Territory in 1863, where he opened a business at Wallula to take advantage of the Idaho gold rush. Flanders arrived at Wallula about the time the first attempts were made to separate Walla Walla from Washington and join Oregon, a group one of Miller's friends called the "vigilante Oregon annexation crowd." Samuel D. Smith to WMM, May 9, 1867, Box 6, Miller1-Yale. On the separation issue in the 1860s, see C. S. Kingston, "The Walla Walla Separation Movement," *WA Quart.* 24 (April 1933): 95–97.

32. *Weekly Message* (Port Townsend), May 20, 1867; *Washington Standard,* April 20, 1867.

33. *Seattle Gazette,* May 13, 1867; Political flyer, 1867, Stevens-UO.

34. *Weekly Message,* May 20, 27, 1867; *Seattle Gazette,* May 6, 20, 1867.

35. WWM to Hazard Stevens, April 18, 1867, Stevens-UO.

36. Hazard Stevens to WWM, May 18, 1867, Box 6, Frank Clark to WWM, April 27, May 14, 1867, W. A. Ball to WWM, June 1, 1867, Box 1, Miller1-Yale.

37. Washington Territorial Election Returns, 1867, Elect-UW; WWM to John T. Knox, November 19, December 2, 1867, WWM to Wesley B. Gosnell, November 26, 1867, WWM to O. B. McFadden, November 30, 1867, Letterbook A, WWM to G. O. Haller, October 7, 1867, Box 5, Miller-UW; John T. Knox to WWM, October 20, December 31, 1867, Box 4, C. H. Armstrong to WWM, October 19, 1867, Box 1, WWM to George Gibbs, September 2, 1867, Box 8, Miller1-Yale.

38. WWM to Leonard Durgin, December 8, 1867, WWM to Joseph Cushman, December 28, 1867, Letterbook A, Miller-UW. Joseph Cushman to WWM, January 29, 1868, Box 2, T. F. McElroy to WWM, March 5, 1868, Box 4, Miller1-Yale.

Chapter 10. Pursuing the Main Chance

1. On San Francisco's development in the 1860s, see Gunther Barth, *Instant Cities: Urbanization and the Rise of San Francisco and Denver* (New York: Oxford University Press, 1975), 210–13; William M. Camp, *San Francisco Port of Gold* (Garden City, N. Y.: Doubleday, 1948), 115–20; Earl Pomeroy, *The Pacific Slope: A History of California, Oregon, Washington, Idaho, Utah and Nevada* (1965; reprint, Lincoln: University of Nebraska Press, 1991), 122–25. The *Alta California,* May 23, July 3, 1874, for example, reported economic conditions worsening in early 1864, but predicted an upturn, advising readers to "hold on and take your chances."

2. George Plummer to WWM, March 31, December 3, 1866, April 5, 20, 1867, Memorandum of Loan Agreement between W. W. Miller and George Plummer, San Francisco, April 9, 1867, Box 5, Miller-UW; D. R. Lord to WWM, May 1, 1867, Box 4, Miller1-Yale. Lord reported to Miller that the mill's boilers "is sunk in about 3 fathoms of salt water and the machinery is under the ground floor."

3. WWM to Hazard Stevens, April 18, 1867, Stevens-UO; Memorandum of Agreement between George Plummer and J. R. Williamson, April 22, 1867, Warranty Deed for Freeport Mill, George Plummer to John R. Williamson, May 10, 1867, Complaint Motion by Elizabeth Phillips in Case of Granville O. Haller and Elizabeth Phillips vs. John R. Williamson, William W. Miller and William Rowland, [December 15, 1868], Box 5, Miller-UW.

4. J. B. Whitcomb to WWM, April 26, 1867, Box 8, Miller1-Yale; D[avid] L. Phillips to WWM, May 1, 1867, Box 2, Miller-UW

5. San Francisco Block Book, 1868, SF Block-UCB. Miller probably purchased lots previously owned by C. O. O'Connor.

6. WWM to Edward P. Miller, October 29, 1867, Box 3, D. L. Phillips to WWM, November 16, 1868, Box 2, Miller-UW. Phillips asked Miller to reserve him choice lots in "Milleropolis," his nickname for Miller's townsite investments near Olympia.

7. Isaac W. Smith to WWM, November 1, 1868, Box 6, D. L. Phillips to WWM, January 10, February 8, 1869, Box 5, Miller1-Yale; John Paxson to WWM, July 23, 1868, Box 6, WWM to Young and Paxson, August 11, 1868, Box 6, Miller-UW. Even Phillips was impressed with Miller's investment, writing him: "You are all right on your Folsom Street property. I only wish I had made some investment at the same time you did."

8. Joseph Cushman to WWM, April 26, 1866, July 26, 1868, Box 2, Miller1-Yale; Selucius Garfielde to Clarence Bagley, November 24, December 1, 1867, Box 1, Bagley-UW.

9. WWM to Selucius Garfielde, April 12, 1868, Box 1, Selucius Garfielde to WWM, April 27, 1868, Box 1, WWM-UW. Daniel Bagley, Clarence Bagley's father, had joined Philip H. Lewis, Josiah Settle, George Whitworth, and Garfielde to form the Lake Washington Coal Company. The Bagleys became powerful components of the Republican party in the territory and consistently supported Garfielde. F. E. Melder, "History of Discoveries and Physical Development of the Coal Industry in the State of Washington," *PNQ* 29 (April 1938): 154–55.

10. Although Garfielde wrote a letter to Nesmith, there is no indication that Miller had solicited the letter. Further, the letter may have actually injured Miller's candidacy, for Nesmith also distrusted Garfielde, calling his political treachery "peculiarly odious." James Nesmith to T. F. McElroy, August 25, 1867, McElroy-UW

11. T. F. McElroy to WWM, February 12, 1868, Box 4, Miller1-Yale; *Territorial Republican,* September 28, October 5, 12, 1868. The Republican press factionalized during the late 1860s, as politicians vied for influence and spoils. R. H. Hewitt sold the *Pacific Tribune* to Charles Prosch in 1868 and then got control of the *Territorial Republican,* which he renamed the *Commercial Age.* Allison and Katz, "Thornton Fleming McElroy," 60–62. Blankenship, *Pioneer Life on Puget Sound,* 43.

12. *Territorial Republican,* October 19, 1868; John T. Knox to WWM, November 15, 1868, Box 1, Miller-UW. The *Republican* defended Garfielde, pointing out that Garfielde had gone out on the stump in 1864 and 1866 with no promise of any money or offices.

13. T. F. McElroy to WWM, March 5, 1868; *Pacific Tribune,* February 20, 1869.

14. Selucius Garfielde to WWM, March 12, 1869, Box 2, Miller1-Yale. Garfielde predicted that McFadden might do well on the Sound, "but he will lose on the [Columbia] River." Besides, Garfielde wrote, McFadden could not financially afford the campaign.

15. *Pacific Tribune,* March 13, May 29, 1869; *Territorial Republican,* March 1, 15, 29, May 3, 1869. Marshall Moore was a life-long Democrat who had fought in the Civil War under Generals McClellan and Sherman. Born in 1829 in Binghamton, New York, Moore had studied law at Yale and had practiced in Iowa and Ohio before becoming territorial governor in 1867. He died in Olympia in 1870.

16. *Territorial Republican,* May 10, 24, 1869; Port Townsend *Weekly Message,* May 12, 1869; *Olympia Transcript,* May 22, 1869; *Washington Standard,* May 8, 1869.

17. *Vancouver Register,* May 12, 1869; *Weekly Message,* June 2, 1869. The *Weekly Mes-*

sage claimed it had an affidavit from a Snohomish County delegate who described the whole contrivance and added that votes were selling for $500 a piece. On Ben Holladay and transportation politics in Portland and the lower Columbia, see E. Kimbark MacColl, *Merchants, Money, and Power: The Portland Establishment, 1843–1913* (Portland: Georgian Press, 1988), 135–37. Miller had been interested in Columbia River transportation since the mid-1860s, when he invested in the Columbia River Transportation Company with O. B. McFadden, Benjamin F. Shaw, Paul K. Hubbs, J. J. H. Van Bokkelin, and several other Indian War veteran friends. See also Thomas J. Fletcher to WWM, December 25, 1868, Box 2, David L. Phillips to WWM, January 10, 1869, Box 5, Miller1-Yale, for discussions of control of the Columbia River passage by railroad interests and effects on the Puget Sound region.

18. McFadden Genealogy, 1934, Eulogy, O. B. McFadden, 1875, Box 24, Miller-UW; Charles Prosch, *Reminiscences of Washington Territory*, 63.

19. RTM to WWM, January 8, 1863, Box 2, Miller-UW; Edmund Fitzhugh to WWM, May 23, 1860, Box 2, Miller1-Yale.

20. N. B. Coffman, "The Jackson Prairie Courthouse, Washington's Oldest Judicial and Administrative Building and the O. B. McFadden Home in Chehalis, Commemorating the Seventy-Fifth Anniversary of Its Construction," Annual Meeting of the Washington State Historical Society, Tacoma, February 3, 1934 (Tacoma: Washington State Historical Society, 1934); *Pacific Tribune*, October 12, 1867. McFadden's eldest son William had taken up a claim adjoining the original McFadden homestead and ran a livestock operation. In 1867, Mary McFadden served as postmistress at Saundersville, the large block of land owned by McFadden south of Chehalis.

21. WWM to Wesley B. Gosnell, November 30, 1867, Letterbook A, 1867–1868, Anna Rew to WWM, February 14, 1869, Box 2, Miller-UW; O. B. McFadden to John A. Simms, January 2, 1870, Box 1, Simms-WSU. An added incentive for Mary might have been her younger sister's earlier marriage to John A. Simms, a merchant from The Dalles.

22. Richard Miller to WWM, November 30, 1869, Miller-UW.

23. John T. Knox to WWM, January 19, 1870, Box 4, Selucius Garfielde to WWM, December 13, 1869, Box 2, Miller1-Yale; *Pacific Tribune*, October 12, 1867, November 24, 1869; WWM to R. G. Stuart, December 10, 1869, Box 3, Miller-UW.

24. Margaret Stevens to WWM, November 18, 1869, Box 2, Miller1-Yale.

25. Loan Payment Receipt, May 7, 1860, WWM and O. B. McFadden, Box 11, WWM to McFadden, June 16, 1860, Box 8, McFadden to WWM, October 5, 1860, February 3, 1862, May 31, 1863, Box 4, Miller1-Yale McFadden to John A. Simms, January 2, 1870, Box 1, Simms-WSU.

26. Selucius Garfielde to Clarence Bagley, August 26, 1869, Box 1, Bagley-UW; *Commercial Age*, December 25, 1869.

27. *Territorial Republican*, November 27, December 25, 1869; *Pacific Tribune*, December 11, 1869.

28. *Pacific Tribune*, December 11, 1869; Selucius Garfielde to WWM, December 30, 1869, Box 2, Miller1-Yale. Garfielde complained to Miller that Flanders "has become as much a nuisance on the streets [in Washington, D.C.] as the distributors of patent medicine advertisements."

29. Selucius Garfielde to WWM, January 10, 1870, Box 2, Miller1-Yale.

30. WWM to David Phillips, January 7, 1868, Letterbook A, 1867–1868, Miller-UW; Joseph Cushman to WWM, March 1, 1868, Box 2, Miller1-Yale.

31. Selucius Garfielde to WWM, December 14, 1869, Box 2, Miller1-Yale. On the OSN and NPRR competition against Ben Holladay in Oregon and on the Columbia, see MacColl, *Merchants, Money, and Power*, 135–38, 154–55, 205–12; Carlos Schwantes, *Railroad Signatures Across the Pacific Northwest* (Seattle: University of Washington Press, 1993), 53–56.

32. J. M. Reed to WWM, January 14, 1870, Box 6, Samuel Coulter to WWM, January 23, 1870, Box 2, Miller1-Yale; List of Contributors to Purchase Map of Hogem, [1870], Miller2-Yale. Included in the list of investors at Hog-em were U. B. Hicks, T. F. McElroy, Hazard Stevens, C. G. Bagley, and David Finch.

33. Selucius Garfielde to WWM, January 12, 1870, Box 2, Miller1-Yale.

34. Selucius Garfielde to WWM, January 24, February 13, March 7, 21, 1870, Box 2, Miller1-Yale; Charles E. Tilton to W. S. Ladd, March 30, 1868, Tilton-UCB. On Holladay's ploys, see David M. Ellis, "The Oregon and California Railroad Land Grant, 1866–1945," *PNQ* 39 (October 1948): 254–57. Holladay was also a potential competitor for prime lands in Olympia and had purchased several homestead claims in the area as early as mid-1869. Hazard Stevens to WWM, December 18, 1869, Box 6, Miller1-Yale.

35. Selucius Garfielde to WWM, March 7, 1870, Box 2, Miller1-Yale.

36. WWM to Selucius Garfielde, March 15, 1870, Box 8, Miller1-Yale.

37. Selucius Garfielde to WWM, March 21, 1870, Box 2, Miller1-Yale.

38. Ibid.; Complaint against Selucius Garfielde, Samuel Coulter, M. R. Tilley, by W. W. Miller, May 30, 1870, Box 4, Miller-UW. The loan was made to the men as co-proprietors of the *Commercial Age*, Garfielde's political newspaper in Olympia.

39. WWM to Josiah Lucas, May 10, 1870, WWM to W. S. Ladd, May 8, 9, 1870, WWM to Samuel Linkton, May 10, 1870, Letterbook B, 1867–1872, Miller-UW. Miller wrote Linkton that Holladay would surely win the economic battle over the railroads, but Garfielde would probably win the delegate race, so he needed to ride both possibilities.

40. Fayette McMullin to WWM, March 5, 1870, Box 1, WWM-UW; Hazard Stevens to WWM, January 17, 1870, Box 6, O. B. McFadden to WWM, April 2, 1870, Box 4, Miller1-Yale.

41. WWM to W. S. Ladd, May 10, 1870, Letterbook B, Miller-UW.

42. *Commercial Age*, May 14, June 11, 1870; *Olympia Transcript*, June 11, 1870; *Weekly Message*, May 23, 1870. Marshall Blinn held controlling interest in the *Olympia Transcript*, a paper the *Message* labeled "a fictitious sausage, an intestine stuffed with red flannel."

43. WWM to W. S. Ladd, April 29, May 9, 1870, WWM to Selucius Garfielde, May 13, 1870, WWM to Isaac Lightner, May 13, 1870, Letterbook B, Miller-UW. Miller even reported to Garfielde that Elwood Evans, his erstwhile nemesis, had left the "bolters" and come out in favor his candidacy.

44. WWM to Selucius Garfielde, July 29, 1870, WWM to B. F. Shaw, June 14, 1870, Letterbook B, 1867–1872, Miller-UW.

45. Francis Henry, "Notes on the Railroad," n.d., Box 15, Miller1-Yale; WWM to David Phillips, December 1, 1870, WWM to Selucius Garfielde, January 1, 1871, Letterbook B, 1867–1872, Miller-UW. On the NP lands department and its methods in the Northwest, see Ross R. Cotroneo, "Western Land Marketing by the Northern Pacific Railway," *PHR* 37 (October 1968): 299–320; Schwantes, *Railroad Signatures*, 83–86.

46. Selucius Garfielde to WWM, March 21, 1871, Box 2, Miller1-Yale. For generalized fears of land speculation and its effects, see *Seattle Intelligencer*, May 22, 1871.

47. WWM to Selucius Garfielde, July 8, 1871, Letterbook B, 1867–1872, Miller-UW; S. Garfielde to WWM, August 4, 1871, Box 1, Miller-UW; S. Garfielde to Hamilton Fish, August 5, 1871, Garfielde-UW.

48. WWM to Selucius Garfielde, July 7, 1871, Letterbook B, 1867–1872, Miller-UW; G. S. Smith to WWM, December 28, 1871, Box 6, Miller1-Yale.

Chapter 11. An Accomplished Life

1. B. F. Shaw, E. C. Fitzhugh, and others had encouraged Miller to run for everything from mayor to territorial delegate. Mary had alerted him while he was in San Francisco in February 1872 that his name had been mentioned for the office. Mary Miller to WWM, February 9, 1872, Box 1, Miller-UW.

2. Mayor of Olympia, Letter of Appointment, April 2, 1872, Box 10, Miller1-Yale; WWM to Selucius Garfielde, April 4, 1872, Letterbook B, 1867–1872, Miller-UW; Olympia City Council Minutes, April 3, 1872, Olympia-WSA. Miller had been in San Francisco from mid-January to early March, tending to his business interests and had no inkling that he would run for Mayor in early April.

3. *Washington Standard,* February 5, 1870; Olympia City Council Minutes, April 10, 1872, Olympia-WSA; WWM to Selucius Garfielde, April 4, 1872, Letterbook B, 1867–1872, Miller-UW.

4. Selucius Garfielde to WWM, April 22, 1872, Box 2, Miller1-Yale; Ordinance #96, May 13, 1872, Olympia2-WSA. Miller also got the council to increase local user taxes and fines as a means of increasing city revenues. See Ordinance #99, June 28, 1872, ibid.

5. *Washington Standard,* May 11, 1872; O. B. McFadden to WWM, February 11, 1872, Box 4, Miller1-Yale; WWM to G. S. Smith, December 27, 1871, January 4, 1872, WWM to Isaac Smith, April 2, 10, 12, 1872, Letterbook B, 1867–1872, Miller-UW. New investors had acquired portions of original donation claims and had, as Miller put it to Smith, "bought into our 'ring' without our consent." More investors might have meant additional political problems.

6. Kingston, "The Walla Walla Separation Movement," 100–4; WWM to Samuel Smith, June 16, 1872, Letterbook B, 1867–1872, Miller-UW; Samuel D. Smith to WWM, June 28, 1872, Box 6, Miller1-Yale.

7. Samuel D. Smith to WWM, September 9, 1872, Box 6, George O. Calhoun, to WWM, September 24, 1872, Miller1-Yale; WWM to J. E. Wiche, September 16, 1872, Letterbook B, 1867–1872, Miller-UW. James Tilton was employed by the NP as a general agent in the Office of the Assistant Treasurer.

8. J. H. Lasater to O. B. McFadden, September 29, 1872, Box 13, J. E. Wyche to WWM, September 11, 1872, Box 8, John A. Simms to WWM, October 5, 1872, Box 2, Miller1-Yale; WWM to Samuel D. Smith, September 18, 1872, Letterbook B, 1867–1872, Miller-UW. Miller disputed the often voiced opinion that most new migrants to the territory were Republican in politics. Miller believed that there were as many Democrats and that locals should canvass their own newcomers.

9. O. B. McFadden to WWM, October 7, 1872, Box 4, Miller1-Yale.

10. WWM to W. S. Ladd, July 18, 1872, Letterbook B, 1867–1872, Miller-UW. Ladd and Miller had grown nervous because NP-sponsored investors had begun to buy up donation claims at a site well outside of Olympia on Budd Inlet, suggesting that they

might attempt to build a town apart from Olympia with port and rail facilities. Miller reported that no one in Olympia had bitten on the potential sales of town lots at the proposed location.

11. J. N. Cole to WWM, October 10, 1872, Box 2, Miller1-Yale. "Among the democrats and the liberal republicans," Cole told Miller, "there is one cry and that is make everything bow to the great object of 'Old Mac's success.'"

12. *Washington Standard*, October 26, 1872. The *Standard* also claimed that Garfielde had accepted a $4,000 bribe from Ben Holladay to promote his line from California through Portland to the Sound, but then gave it back to Holladay when the NP offered him $5,000 to drop his support of Holladay's plan.

13. WWM to Frank Clark, October 12, 1872, WWM to O. B. McFadden, October 10, 1872, Letterbook B, 1867–1872, WWM to B. F. Shaw, October 13, 1872, Letterbook 2, 1872–1875, Miller-UW.

14. WWM to M. H. Frost, October 25, 1872, WWM to James Tilton, October 31, 1872, Letterbook 2, 1872–1875, WWM to John P. Judson, October 11, 1872, Letterbook B, 1867–1872, Miller-UW; Fred A. Clark to WWM, October 30, 1872, Box 1, Miller1-Yale. In much the same tenor, Miller wrote to Henry Roeder in Whatcom (October 25, 1872): "A reservation Indian has no more right to vote than a hor or a horse. Therefore watch your Indian Agents and don't suffer them to vote Indians."

15. WWM to Samuel D. Smith, November 7, 1872, WWM to J. A. Simms, November 10, 1872, Letterbook 2, Miller-UW. Miller tried to quell Simms's anxieties by assuring him that Garfielde was not a vindictive man and he might well survive the change in administration, because he could be sure his father-in-law, McFadden, would protect him in Washington. Garfielde himself landed on his feet, getting the Collector of Customs office from an appreciative Grant administration.

16. Mcfadden family materials; genealogy, Miller-UW.

17. WWM to Mary M. Miller, Mary M. Miller, September 10, 20, 1873, Box 2, Miller-UW.

18. WWM to Mary M. Miller, September 9, 1873, October 28, 1873, Box 2, Miller-UW.

19. Mary Miller to WWM, February 11, 1871, Box 1, WWM to Mary Miller, February 20, 1871, Box 2, Miller-UW.

20. WWM to Mary Miller, February 1, 9, 1872, Box 2, Miller-UW.

21. WWM to Mary Miller, February 3, 1872, Box 2, Miller-UW.

22. Miller had more than 100 parcels of land in six counties at the time of his death in 1876. The undeveloped lands alone were worth more than $16,000. W. W. Miller, Probate Summary, 1876, Thurston County, Probate, Washington State Archives, Olympia.

23. Statement of Executors of the Amount of Real Property of W. W. Miller, undivided, July 23, 1877, Probate Court Decrees, Court-WSA; Lewis County Abstract Company, Tax Roll Assignment for Daufina Donation Claim, December 21, 1926, Chehalis, Washington, Box 37, Miller-UW.

24. Deed of Land, Catherine Cathman to Obidiah Small, February 11, 1857, Cathman to Frederick A. Clarke, July 2, 1858, Box 4, Miller-UW; William W. Miller vs. Henry Barker and Catherine Barker, 2d Judicial District, Washington Territory, July 23, 1870, Court-WSA.

25. J. W. Anderson to WWM, March 27, 1866, Javan Hall to WWM, December 20, 1868, Box 1, WWM-UW; WWM to O. B. McFadden, January 15, 1869, Box 8, McFad-

den to Harry Barker, February 8, 1869, WWM to Harry and Catherine Barker, May 25, 1870, Box 4, Miller-UW.

26. WWM to H. H. Pinto, July 22, 1872, Letterbook B, 1867–1872, Miller-UW.

27. Quit Claim, Miller to Gabriel Jones, December 31, 1866, Deed, Antoine and Angelique Gobar to W. W. Miller, June 14, 1867, James Wilson, Territorial Land Commissioner, to Register and Receiver, Territorial Land Office, February 16, 1867, Quit Claim, Gabriel Jones to Joseph Broshears, August 17, 1868, Box 5, J. Thomas Turner, General Land Office, to WWM, February 9, 1867, Box 2, Miller-UW.

28. J. Thomas Turner to WWM, July 5, 1867, Box 2, WWM to Edwin Marsh, November 30, 1867, James Wilson to WWM, December 11, 1868, Box 5, Miller-UW.

29. Deed, W. W. Miller to Joseph Broshears, May 22, 1871, Deed, W. W. and Mary Miller to Joseph Broshears, October 11, 1871, Mortgage, Joseph Broshears to W. W. Miller, April 15, 1872, Mortgage, Joseph Broshears to W. W. Miller, September 1, 1873, Deed, Joseph Broshears to W. W. Miller, February 10, 1854, Box 5, WWM to Joseph Broshears, May 16, 31, June 23, 1871, Letterbook B, 1867–1872, Miller-UW; Joseph Broshears to WWM, April 22, 1872, Box 1, WWM-UW. Joseph Broshears and his wife ended up renting the Daufina Claim land from Miller in 1873–1875, but he had additional difficulties with Broshears, forcing him to severely reprimand him in 1875 and end his arrangements with him. WWM to Joseph Broshears, April 27, 1875, Letterbook 2, 1872–1875, Miller-UW.

30. Revocation of Agreement with Young and Paxson, February 28, 1870, WWM to California Trust Company, February 28, 1870, Power of Attorney, William W. Miller to California Trust Company, March 1, 1870, Henry L. Davis to George Maxwell, March 1, 1870, Box 6, Miller-UW.

31. WWM to California Trust Company, July 13, 1870, WWM to Henry L. Davis, November 30, December 1, 1870, WWM to George Maxwell, November 30, 1870, Letterbook B, 1867–1872, Memo, Maxwell to WWM, [July 1870], Maxwell to WWM, October 21, 1870, W. W. Miller Rental Accountbook, 1868–1872, Box 6, Miller-UW. Maxwell reported that he had spent nearly $3,500 in taxes, stump pulling, tilling, planking, sewers, and insurance. As a hedge on the renters, he also suggested securing their insurance policies, so any fires or other calamities would benefit Maxwell and Miller.

32. N. P. Perrine to WWM, January 8, 1872, February 20, July 22, 1873, January 16, 1874, Box 6, Miller-UW.

33. WWM to Henry L. Davis, March 4, 1874, Letterbook 2, 1873–1874, Miller-UW. Miller had agreed to lower the rents on the Folsom Street lots from $300 to $225 per month in February 1873.

34. Morgan, *Puget's Sound,* 162–5; WWM to Frank R. Matthias, June 23, 1873, Letterbook 2, 1872–1875, Miller-UW.

35. WWM to Mary Miller, February 3, 1872, Box 2, WWM to RTN February 26, 1865, Box 3, Miller-UW; "Mining Speculations," news clipping, January 12, 1875, Ogden-UCB.

36. David L. Phillips to WWM, April 15, 1875, Box 2, Miller1-Yale; WWM to Henry L. Davis, May 4, 1875, Letterbook 3, 1875–1876, W. W. Miller Accounts at First National Gold Bank, September 1875, WWM-UW. Charles L. Tilden, "William C. Ralston and His Times" (1938), Bancroft; Neil C. Wilson, *400 California Street: A Century Plus Five, the Story of the Oldest Incorporated Commercial Bank in the West and Its First 105 Years in the Financial Development of the Pacific Coast* (San Francisco: Bank of California, 1969), 40–7; news clipping, September 7, 1875, Ogden-UCB.

37. Samuel Emlen to Sister, November 14, 1875, Samuel Emlen Correspondence, Bancroft; D. L. Phillips to WWM, November 10, 1875, Box 2, Miller-UW; Wilson, *400 California Street*, 47–9.

38. J. L. Hall to WWM, April 23, 1873, Mary Wortley Miller to WWM, May 20, 1873, April 5, September 6, 1874, Box 1, Miller-UW. There is evidence that Richard died from alcoholism, although Miller did not learn of an official cause of death. Mary Wortley Miller had two children from a previous marriage when she married Richard in Silver City, Idaho, in the spring of 1869.

39. Morgan, *Puget's Sound*, 164–70; Sol H. Lewis, "A History of Railroads in Washington," *WA Quart.* 3 (July 1912): 186–97. The *Seattle Intelligencer*, July 19, 1873, wailed that landholdings north of Tacoma would suddenly decrease in value, thus creating a recession in the Sound region.

40. Morgan, *Puget's Sound*, 171–74. The NP had hired Frederick Law Olmsted to design the town plan, but his aesthetically sensitive contoured street plan looked too risky to Frederick Billings and other NP officials. They rejected his plan in January, just weeks after they had commissioned him. Laura Wood Roper, *FLO: A Biography of Frederick Law Olmsted* (Baltimore: The Johns Hopkins University Press, 1973), 347–48, 520.

41. WWM to O. B. McFadden, January 6, February 10, 1874, Letterbook 2, 1872–1875, Miller-UW; *Washington Standard*, January 10, 1874; *Pacific Tribune*, January 11, 1874.

42. WWM to O. B. McFadden, January 12, February 4, 1874, Letterbook 2, 1872–1875, Miller-UW; *Washington Standard*, January 10, 1874.

43. *Washington Standard*, February 14, 1874; O. B. McFadden to WWM, February 27, 1874, Box 4, Miller1-Yale; WWM to McFadden, February 10, March 3, 1874, Letterbook 2, 1872–1875, Miller-UW.

44. WWM to O. B. McFadden, March 24, April 22, 1874, Letterbook 2, 1872–1875, Miller-UW; James Tilton to WWM, March 14, 1874, Box 7, McFadden to WWM, April 17, 29, 1874, Box 4, Miller1-Yale; *Puget Sound Courier*, April 21, 1874. In his April 29 letter, McFadden exclaimed at his failure to get the bill passed: "My God it is tedious business."

45. James Tilton to John P. Judson, June 8, 1874, Box 13, A. J. Cain to WWM, August 22, 1874, Box 1, C. H. Armstrong to WWM, May 3, 15, 1874, Box 1, Miller1-Yale; WWM to Armstrong, July 22, 1874, Letterbook 2, 1872–1875, Miller-UW.

46. McFadden Obit., *Washington Standard*, July 3, 1875; John P. Judson to WWM, December 5, 1874, O. B. McFadden to WWM, September 18, December 15, 1874, February 1, 13, 27, March 24, 1875, Box 4, A. A. Denny to WWM, February 27, 1875, Box 2, Miller1-Yale; WWM to McFadden May 13, 1875, WWM to C. H. Armstrong, July 5, 1875, Letterbook 3, 1875–1876, McFadden "Eulogy," Box 24, Miller-UW.

47. WWM to Margaret McFadden, November 30, December 2, 6, 1875, WWM to Frank P. McFadden, December 3, 1875, Letterbook 3, 1875–1876, Miller-UW.

48. WWM to David L. Phillips, May 19, 1875, WWM to Philip Ritz, June 4, 1875, Letterbook 3, 1875–1876, Miller-UW.

49. WWM to D. L. Phillips, November 3, 1875, Letterbook 3, 1875–1876, Miller-UW; David L. Phillips to WWM, November 10, Box 2, Miller1-Yale.

50. WWM to H. A. Goldsborough, November 30, 1875, Letterbook 3, 1875–1876, Miller-UW.

51. Mary Miller to Winlock and Pendleton Miller, May 2, 1876, Box 1, Miller-UW.

Chapter 12.   A Life's Legacy

1. Final Account, Probate of William Winlock Miller Estate, Thurston County, February 15, 1876; Surety Bond, Mary Miller Guardianship, Thurston County, September 14, 1882; Probate, William Winlock Miller Estate, Thurston County, January 24, 1894, Washington State Archives, Olympia. Miller's probated estate left $132,989.32 cash on hand, $16,343.75 in undeveloped real estate, and $74,740.09 in other investments.

2. A. A. Denny to Mary Miller, April 27, 1876, Box 13; Guardianship Appointment, Probate Court, Thurston County, July 25, 1877, Box 16, Miller-UW. The guardianship for the estate required a $157,332 bond with names of surety bondholders. Miller's will had divided his estate in three portions, with the two children's portions held in trust by their mother as guardian.

3. John P. Judson to Mary Miller, January 10, June 25, July 15, 1878, Box 14, Miller-UW. Judson had been O. B. McFadden's former law partner and stepped in after Miller's death to provide Mary with legal advice on political and financial matters in Olympia and Thurston County.

4. A. A. Denny to Mary Miller, December 5, 22, 1891; Dexter Horton to Mary Miller, January 11, 1885, Box 13; Mary Miller to Seattle & Eastern Construction Company, February 15, 1888, Mary Miller Letterbook, 1887–1888; George Van Tine, May 7, 1893, Box 16, Miller-UW.

5. Mary Miller to R. L. Calvin, February 8, 1882, Mary Miller to W.B. Gosnell, March 1, 1882, Mary Miller to Assessor of Mason County, March 24, 1882, Mary Miller Letterbook, 1881–1883; W.B. Gosnell to Mary Miller, August 31, October 1, November 28, 1889, Box 13, Miller-UW.

6. Winlock Miller to Mary Miller, September 19, 1887, January 19, May 20, 1888, Pendleton Miller to Mary Miller, August 19, October 10, 1888, February 6, April 22, 1889, Box 11, Miller-UW. Most of the letters, like those from most children to parents during school, included requests for money. Mary rarely withheld presents or money from her children. When they were at Yale, she provided them with $100 each per semester in addition to all room and board costs and tuition. Nonetheless, both still managed to run up sizable bills that she covered. Pendleton's given name was Edmund Pendleton Miller, after William Miller's older brother.

7. Henry P. Wright [Yale University] to Mary Miller, January 14, 1892, Box 22, Pendleton Miller to Mary Miller, October 4, 26, 1890, February 15, 1891, September 29, October 9, 1892, January 15, 1894, Winlock Miller to Mary Miller October 29, 1893, January 11, April 15, 1894, Box 11, Miller-UW. Lock wrote his mother long letters detailing football games and rallies and describing activities with his Yale chums, but with very little about academics.

8. Pendleton Miller to Mary Miller, October 20, 1892, January 11, 1893, Winlock Miller to Mary Miller, October 29, 1893, Box 11; Mary Miller to Winlock Miller, Box 22, Mary Miller to U.S. Consul General [Kanagwa, Japan], September 10, 1893, Mary Miller Letterbook, 1893–1894, Miller-UW.

9. Mary Miller to Dexter Horton, July 21, 1891, Mary Miller Letterbook, 1890–1891. On the effects of the 1890s depression on Washington, see Carlos Schwantes, *Coxey's Army: An American Odyssey* (Lincoln: University of Nebraska Press, 1985).

10. Corporate By Laws, Mary Miller & Sons, October 22, 1894, Box 26, N.H. Latimer [Dexter Horton Bank] to Mary Miller, July 1, October 26, 1895, Box 25, Winlock

Miller to Mary Miller, May 20, 1897, Box 11, Winlock Miller to Lucy A. Sims, September 11, 1894, Mary Miller Letterbook, 1893–1896, Miller-UW. Lucy Sims was Mary Miller's sister, who along with two brothers, had come to rely on Mary's aid. At one point, Mary became so exasperated with her relatives that she replied, "I do not propose to consider myself as a bank lender to be called upon for supplies of funds whenever any other members of the family feel in need of money." Mary Miller to Cal McFadden, March 10, 1892, Mary Miller Letterbook, 1892–1901.

11. Internal Revenue Service Protest, Winlock W. Miller, April 12, 1940, Box 37, Mary Miller & Sons, Articles of Incorporation and Minutes, 1894–1917, Box 26, Miller-UW.

12. *Seattle Times*, November 10, 1950.

13. Mary Miller to Winlock and Pendleton Miller, May 2, 1876, Box 1, Miller-UW.

14. Ibid.

15. *Seattle Times*, November 10, 1950; *Seattle Post-Intelligencer*, January 15, 1958.

16. Miller to Letitia Work, February 22, 1854, Box 9, Miller1-Yale.

Bibliography

Although all of the major sources consulted in the writing of this biography are listed below, other materials are included in the endnotes. Consult specific citations for those references. The manuscript collections are arranged by depository, with catalog or other classification numbers if they exist. The shortened titles, e.g., Miller-UW, are used in endnote citations. Other shortened titles that are frequently used in the endnotes are listed below.

OHQ	*Oregon Historical Quarterly*
PHR	*Pacific Historical Review*
PNQ	*Pacific Northwest Quarterly*
WA Quart.	*Washington Historical Quarterly*
WHQ	*Western Historical Quarterly*

Manuscripts

UNIVERSITY OF WASHINGTON LIBRARIES, MANUSCRIPTS DIVISION, SEATTLE

Army–UW	William Winlock Miller, U.S. Army Letterbook, VF 822
Backus–UW	Manson F. Backus Collection, VF 42
Bagley–UW	Clarence Booth Bagley Papers
Bagley2–UW	Daniel Bagley Papers, TO186F
Blankenship–UW	George Blankenship Papers
Ebey–UW	Ebey Family Papers, VO244C
Garfielde–UW	Selucius Garfielde Papers, VF 261

Garfielde2–UW   Selucius Garfielde, VF 29
Goldsborough–UW Hugh A. Goldsborough Papers, VF 33
Kendall–UW   Bion F. Kendall Collection, TO753E
McElroy–UW   McElroy Family Papers, TO183D
McMicken–UW   McMicken Family Papers, Acc. No. 40
Miller–UW   Miller Family Papers, MS 3912
Plummer–UW   George Plummer Papers, VF 282
Stevens–UW   Isaac Stevens Papers
Tolmie–UW   William Fraser Tolmie Papers, MS 1919
Wallace–UW   William H. Wallace Papers, VO1870
Work–UW   John Work Papers, VO249C
WWM–UW   William W. Miller Papers, VO239C

UNIVERSITY OF WASHINGTON LIBRARIES, SPECIAL
COLLECTIONS, SEATTLE

Meany–UW   Edmund S. Meany Collection, MMS 106-07-12
Prosch–UW   Thomas Prosch Collection
Elect–UW   Washington Territory Election Returns, MF A2014

YALE UNIVERSITY, BEINECKE RARE BOOKS AND
MANUSCRIPT LIBRARY, NEW HAVEN, CONNECTICUT

Biles–Yale   John D. Biles Papers, MS S-276
Cain–Yale   John Cain Papers, MSS 59
Coe–Yale   L .W. Coe Narrative
Coffey–Yale   [A. L.] Coffey and [W.] Sharp Papers, MSS 95
Davis–Yale   A. I. Davis Papers, MSS S-52
Evans–Yale   Elwood Evans Papers
Lincoln–Yale   Abraham Lincoln Papers, MS S-1155
Malick–Yale   Malick Family Papers, MSS S-1296
Miller1–Yale   William Winlock Miller Papers, MSS S-1172
Miller2–Yale   William W. Miller Papers, MSS 343
Miller3–Yale   W. W. Miller Papers, MSS S-119
Mooney–Yale   P. S. Mooney Papers, MSS S-722
Pick–Yale   William Pickering Correspondence, MS S-184
Stevens1–Yale   Isaac I. Stevens Letters, MSS S-192
Stevens2–Yale   Isaac I. Stevens Papers, WA MSS-443
Tilton–Yale   James Tilton Correspondence, MSS 475
War–Yale   Indian War Reports, MS-66

OREGON HISTORICAL SOCIETY, MANUSCRIPT
ARCHIVES, PORTLAND

Army–OHS   Military Miscellany, MSS 1514

Astoria–OHS	U.S. Customs, Astoria Customs House Papers, MSS 878 (Micro)
Deady–OHS	Matthew P. Deady Papers, MSS 48
Dye–OHS	Eva Emery Dye Papers, MS 1089
Elliott–OHS	Thompson Coit Elliott Papers, MS 231
Garrison–OHS	Abraham H. Garrison Letters, MSS 874
Himes–OHS	Judson Himes Diary, MS 753B
Kendall–OHS	Bion Freeman Kendall Papers, MSS 1038
King–OHS	William W. King Papers, MSS 1142
Ladd–OHS	William S. Ladd Family Papers, MSS 579
Looney–OHS	Jesse Looney Papers, MSS 2263
Marion–OHS	Marion County Records, MSS 1273
Nisqually–OHS	Fort Nisqually Papers, Micro 60
Parrish–OHS	E. E. Parrish Diaries, MSS 648
Shaw–OHS	Benjamin Franklin Shaw Papers, MSS 412
Thurston–OHS	Samuel R. Thurston Papers, MSS 379
Work–OHS	John Work Correspondence, MS 319

OREGON STATE ARCHIVES, SALEM

Census–OSA	Manuscript Census, Oregon 1850
OreRec–OSA	Oregon Provisional and Territorial Records
Ore Govt–OSA	Oregon Territorial Government Records

UNIVERSITY OF OREGON LIBRARIES, SPECIAL COLLECTIONS, EUGENE

Stevens–UO	Hazard Stevens Papers, Ax 42
WPA–UO	Historical Records Survey, Bx66

WASHINGTON STATE ARCHIVES, OLYMPIA

Court–WSA	Frontier Justice Collection
Lands–WSA	Thurston County Taxable Land Plats
Legis–WA	Journal of Territorial Legislative Assembly
Militia–WSA	Territorial Volunteer Papers
Olympia–WSA	Olympia City Council Minutes
Olympia2–WSA	Ordinances, Town of Olympia
Tax–WSA	Municipal Tax List, Olympia 1873

WASHINGTON STATE LIBRARY, OLYMPIA

Blinn–WSL	Marshall Blinn Papers, MSS 023
Gholson–WSL	Richard H. Gholson Papers, MSS 009
Hale–WSL	Calvin H. Hale Papers, MSS 020

McMullin–WSL   Fayette McMullin Papers, MSS 008
Mason–WSL   Charles H. Mason Papers, MS 010
Pierce–WSL   Census of Pierce County 1857, MSS 028
Thurston–WSL   Samuel Thurston Papers, MSS 137

WASHINGTON STATE UNIVERSITY ARCHIVES, PULLMAN

Simms–WSU   John A. Simms Papers, Cage 213
Tulalip–WSU   Tulalip Indian Agency Records, Cage 256

ILLINOIS STATE HISTORICAL SOCIETY, SPRINGFIELD

Arenz–IHS   Francis and John A. Arenz Papers, SC 36
Goudy–IHS   Calvin Goudy Papers, SC 576
Poll–IHS   Poll Books, Morgan County, Illinois
WPA–IHS   Federal Writers Project, Illinois
Yates–IHS   Yates Family Papers

ILLINOIS STATE ARCHIVES, SPRINGFIELD

Census–ISA   Illinois State Census, Micro. 1
Court–ISA   Circuit Court Records, Morgan County
Elect–ISA   Election Returns, Micro. 30–864

HUBERT H. BANCROFT LIBRARY, UNIVERSITY OF CALIFORNIA, BERKELEY

Bancroft–UCB   Hubert H. Bancroft Collection
Cooper–UCB   James Graham Cooper Letters
Morse–UCB   Eldridge Morse, "Notes on the History and Resources of Washington Territory, 1880"
Ogden–UCB   Richard Ogden, San Francisco Scrapbook
SF Block–UCB   San Francisco Block Book, C-I 22, Vol. 1
Tilton–UCB   Alfred E. Tilton, Charles E. Tilton, William S. Ladd Financial Papers

UNITED STATES CUSTOMS SERVICE, SEATTLE, WASHINGTON; SAN FRANCISCO, CALIFORNIA

Customs–SF   Collectors Letterbook, Puget Sound District, 1851–1857
Customs–WA   Surveyor's Letterbook, Port Nisqually, 1851–1854

NATIONAL ARCHIVES FEDERAL RECORDS CENTER, SEATTLE, WASHINGTON

Survey–NA   Registers and Letters Received from Surveyor General of Wash-
                ington Territory, 1854–1883, RG 49
WSIA1–NA   Letters from Agents, Washington Superintendent of Indian
                Affairs, 1853–1874, Microfilm #9, RG 48
WSIA2–NA   Letters Received, Washington Superintendent of Indian Affairs,
                Microfilm #8, RG 48

NATIONAL ARCHIVES, SUITLAND, MARYLAND

Appt–NA   Appointment File, Superintendent of Indian Affairs, Depart-
                ment of the Interior RG 48
Wash–NA   Letters Received by the Office of Indian Affairs, Washington
                Superintendency, 1861–1862 RG 48
Wars–NA   Letters Sent Relating to Oregon and Washington Indian Wars,
                1861–1871 RG 48
Claims–NA   Miscellaneous Records #94, "Adjudication of Claims, 1855"
                RG 48

Unpublished Reports, Papers, and Recollections

Brown, Mary Jane. "Memoir." 1929.
Chambers, Andrew Jackson. "Recollections." 1904.
Lane, Barbara. "Political and Economic Aspects of Indian-White Culture Contact
    in Western Washington in the Mid-19th Century." Paper Delivered at Oregon
    Historical Society, May 10, 1973.
Tilden, Charles. "William C. Ralston and His Times." 1938.
Van Nostrand, Maren. "Miller Park Neighborhood: A Community History." Draft.
    1994.

Newspapers

Beardstown (Illinois) *Gazette*
Columbian (Olympia)
Commercial Age (Olympia)
Illinois Daily Journal (Springfield)
Olympia Transcript
Oregon Spectator (Oregon City)
Oregonian (Portland)
Pacific Tribune (Olympia & Tacoma)
Pioneer and Democrat (Olympia)
Port Townsend Weekly Message

Puget Sound Courier (Seattle)
Seattle Gazette
Seattle Intelligencer
Territorial Republican (Seattle)
Washington Standard (Olympia)
Weekly Argus (Port Townsend)

Government Documents

Allen, John B. *Reports of Cases Determined in the Supreme Court of the Territory of Washington, from 1854 to 1879.* Olympia: C. B. Bagley, 1879.

Furste, Edward, ed. *Messages of the Governor of Washington Territory, Also the Correspondence with the Secretary of War, Major Gen. Wool, the Officers of the Regular Army, and the Volunteer Service of Washington.* Olympia: Edward Furste, 1857.

Kappler, Charles J., comp. *Indian Affairs, Laws and Treaties* Vol. 1. Washington, D.C.: GPO, 1904.

U.S. Congress, House. *Claims Growing Out of Indian Hostilities in Oregon and Washington.* 35th Cong., 2d sess., 1858, H. Ex. Doc. 51 (Serial 1006).

———. *Expenses of the Indian Wars in Washington and Oregon Territories.* 35th Cong., 1st sess., 1858, H. Ex. Doc. 45 (Serial 955).

———. *Letter from the Secretary of the Interior, Transmitting in Compliance with the Resolution of the House of the 15th Ultimo the Report of J. Ross Browne on the Subject of the Indian War in Oregon and Washington Territories.* 35th Cong., 1st sess., 1858, H. Ex. Doc. 38 (Serial 929).

———. *Memorial of the Legislature of Washington Territory, Paying An Appropriation to Defray the Expenses of the Existing War.* 34th Cong., 1st sess., 1856, H. Misc. Doc. 64.

———. *Memorial of the Legislature of Washington Territory in Relation to the Establishment of a Semi-Monthly Mail Between San Francisco and Puget's Sound.* 38th Cong., 1st sess., 1864, H. Misc. Doc. 58 (Serial 1200).

———. *Memorial of the Legislature of Washington Territory Asking for the Relief of Settlers on Railroad Lands.* 43rd Cong., 1st sess., 1874, H. Misc. Doc. 217 (Serial 2421).

———. *Report on the Condition of the Indian Reservations in the Territories of Oregon and Washington, November 17, 1857.* 35th Cong., 1st sess., 1857, H Ex. Doc. 39 (Serial 929).

———. *Report of the Superintendent of Indian Affairs for Washington Territory.* 37th Cong., 3d sess., 1862, H. Ex. Doc. 1 (Serial 1157).

U.S. Congress, Senate. *Papers Relating to the Proclamation of Martial Law in Washington Territory.* 34th Cong., 1st sess., 1856, S. Ex. Doc. 98 (Serial 823).

———. Report of the Secretary of the Interior Relative to the Indian Disturbances in the Territories of Washington and Oregon. 34th Cong., 1st sess., 1856, S. Ex. Doc. 46 (Serial 821).

———. *Report of the Superintendent of the Coast Survey, 1856.* 34th Cong., 3d sess., 1856, S. Ex. Doc. 12 (Serial 888).

Washington Territory. *Council Journal of Washington Territory, 1856–1857.* Olympia, 1857.

Books, Articles, Theses, and Dissertations

Allison, Elizabeth M., and W. A. Katz, "Thornton Fleming McElroy—Printer, Politician, Businessman." *PNQ* 54 (April 1963): 54–65.

Alta California Almanac & Book of Facts. San Francisco: F. McCrllish, 1874.

Anker, Roy M. "Popular Religion and Theories of Self-Help." *Handbook of American Popular Culture*, edited by M. Thomas Inge. Vol. 2. Westport, Conn.: Greenwood Press, 1980.

Bagley, Clarence B., ed. "Attitude of the Hudsons's Bay Company During the Indian War of 1855–1856." *WA Quart.* 8 (October 1917): 291–307.

Bancroft, Hubert Howe. *History of Washington, Idaho and Montana, 1845–1889.* San Francisco: The History Company, 1890.

————. *History of Oregon.* San Francisco: The History Company, 1888.

Barth, Gunther. *Instant Cities: Urbanization and the Rise of San Francisco and Denver.* New York: Oxford University Press, 1975.

Bates, Kate Stevens. "The Old Stevens Mansion." *WA Quart.* 19 (April 1928): 108–11.

Beider, Robert E. "Kinship as a Factor in Migration." *Journal of Marriage and the Family* 35 (August 1973): 429–39.

Benninghoff, Joe. "The Early History of Jefferson." *Marion County History* 4 (June 1958): 3–10.

Berkhofer, Robert F. "The North American Frontier as Process and Context." *The Frontier in History: North America and Southern Africa Compared*, edited by Howard Lamar and Leonard Thompson. New Haven: Yale University Press, 1981.

Bischoff, William N. "The Yakima Campaign of 1856." *Mid-America* 31 (1949).

Bischoff, William J., S.J., ed. *We Were Not Summer Soldiers: The Indian War Diary of Plympton J. Kelly, 1855–1856.* Tacoma: Washington State Historical Society, 1976.

Bishop, D. M. *California State Business Directory, 1875–1876.* San Francisco: D. M. Bishop, 1875.

————. *The New City Annual Directory of San Francisco.* San Francisco: D. M. Bishop, 1875.

Blankenship, George. *Lights and Shades of Pioneer Life on Puget Sound.* Olympia, 1923.

Blankenship, Mrs. George E. *Tillicum Tales: Early History of Thurston County, Washington.* Olympia, 1914.

————. *Old Olympia Landmarks.* N.p., ca. 1915.

Bogue, Allen G. *From Prairie to Corn Belt: Farming on the Illinois and Iowa Prairies in the Nineteenth Century.* Chicago: University of Chicago Press, 1963

————. "Social Theory and the Pioneer." *Agricultural History* 34 (Winter 1960): 21–34.

Bonney, W. P. "Marker for Camp Montgomery." *WA Quart.* 22 (October 1931): 293–95.

Bourke, Paul F., and Donald A. DeBats. "The Structures of Political Involvement in the Ninteenth Century: A Frontier Case." *Perspectives in American History*, New Series 3 (Cambridge University Press, 1987): 207–38.

Bowen, William. "The Oregon Frontiersman: A Demographic View." *The Western Shore: Oregon Country Essays Honoring the American Revolution*. Ed. Thomas Vaughan. Portland: Oregon Historical Society, 1975.

———. *The Willamette Valley: Migration and Settlement on the Oregon Frontier*. Seattle: University of Washington Press, 1978.

Bowles, Samuel. *Across the Continent: A Summer's Journey to the Rocky Mountains, the Mormons, and the Pacific States*. New York: Hurd & Houghton, 1865.

Camp, William M. *San Francisco, Port of Gold*. Garden City, N.Y.: Doubleday, 1948.

Clark, Malcolm, Jr. *Eden Seekers: The Settlement of Oregon, 1818–1862*. Boston: Houghton Mifflin, 1981.

Cline, Gloria Griffin. *Peter Skene Ogden and the Hudson's Bay Company*. Norman: University of Oklahoma Press, 1974.

Coleman, Edmund T. "Puget Sound and the Northern Pacific Railroad." *WA Quart.* 23 (October 1932): 243–60.

Cox, Thomas R. *Mills and Markets: A History of the Pacific Coast Lumber Industry to 1900*. Seattle: University of Washington Press, 1974.

Cronon, William. *Nature's Metropolis: Chicago and the Great West*. New York: W. W. Norton, 1991.

Crumin, Arthur, ed. *1840 Atlas of Cass County, Illinois*. Virginia, Ill.: Cass County Historical Society, 1984.

Darroch, A. Gordon. "Migrants in the Nineteenth Century: Fugitives or Families in Motion?" *Journal of Family History* 6 (Fall 1981): 257–77.

DeLorme, Roland L. "The United States Bureau of Customs and Smuggling on Puget Sound, 1851–1913." *Prologue: The Journal of the National Archives* 5 (Summer 1973): 77–88.

Dicken, Samuel N., and Emily F. Dicken. *The Making of Oregon: A Study in Historical Geography*. Portland: Oregon Historical Society Press, 1979.

Diggins, John Patrick. *The Lost Soul of American Politics: Virtue, Self-Interest, and the Foundations of Liberalism*. New York: Basic Books, 1984.

Doyle, Don Harrison. *The Social Order of a Frontier Community: Jacksonville, Illinois, 1825–70*. Urbana: University of Illinois Press, 1978.

Eaton, Edgar Eugene. "A History of Olympia Newspapers from 1852 to 1885." Master's thesis, University of Washington, 1963.

Eblen, Jack E. "An Analysis of Nineteenth Century Frontier Populations." *Demography* 2 (1965): 399–413.

Elder, Glen H. "Family History and the Life Course." *Journal of Family History* 2 (Winter 1977): 279–304.

Epler, Cyrus. "History of the Morgan County Bar." *Journal of the Illinois State Historical Society* 19 (October 1926–January 1927): 161–75.

Faragher, John Mack. *Sugar Creek: Life on the Illinois Prairie*. New Haven: Yale University Press, 1986.

Finger, John Robert. "Henry L. Yesler's Seattle Years, 1852–1892." Ph.D. diss., University of Washington, 1968.

Ford, Thomas. *A History of Illinois from Its Commencement as a State in 1814 to 1847*. Chicago: S. C. Griggs, 1854.

Galbraith, John S. "The British and Americans at Fort Nisqually, 1846–1854." *PNQ* 41 (April 1950): 109–20.

———. *The Hudson's Bay Company as an Imperial Factor, 1821–1869.* Berkeley: University of California Press, 1957.

Garretson, Charles Edwin. "A History of the Washington Superintendency of Indian Affairs, 1853–1865." Master's thesis, University of Washington, 1962.

[Gibbs, George, and H. A. Goldsborough]. *A Brief Notice of the Recent Outrages Committed by Isaac I. Stevens, Governor of Washington Territory.* Steilacoom, 1856.

Gibson, James R. *Farming the Frontier: The Agricultural Opening of the Oregon Country, 1786–1846.* Seattle: University of Washington Press, 1985.

Gilbert, James Henry. *Trade and Currency in Early Oregon: A Study in the Commercial and Monetary History of the Pacific Northwest.* New York: Columbia University Studies in History, Economics and Public Law, 1907.

Gochanour, Eileen, comp. *1850 Morgan County, Federal Census.* Springfield, Ill., 1983.

Gosnell, W. B. "Indian War in Washington Territory." *WA Quart.* 17 (October 1926): 289–300.

Gottlieb, Beatrice. *The Family in the Western World from the Black Death to the Industrial Age.* New York: Oxford University Press, 1993.

Gray, Mary A. "Settlement of the Claims in Washington of the Hudson's Bay Company and the Puget's Sound Agricultural Company." *WA Quart* 21 (April 1930): 95–102.

Gridley, J. N. "The County Seat Battles of Cass County, Illinois." *Journal of Illinois State Historical Society* 7 (October 1914): 166–94.

Hager, Judith E. "Mile Eighty-Eight: The History of Frontier Beardstown, 1818–1860." Master's thesis, Northern Illinois University, Dekalb, 1965.

Haines, Francis D., ed. *The Snake Country Expedition of 1830–1831: John Work's Field Journal.* Norman: University of Oklahoma Press, 1971.

Hareven, Tamara, and Maris A. Vinovskis, eds. *Family and Population in Nineteenth Century America.* Princeton, N.J.: Princeton University Press, 1978.

Hedlund, Gerald Curry. *Inland Cultural Sites at Connell's Prairie.* Auburn, Wash.: Green River Community College, 1973.

Hendrickson, James E. *Joe Lane of Oregon: Machine Politics and the Sectional Crisis, 1849–1861.* New Haven: Yale University Press, 1967.

Hicks, U. E. *Personal Recollections of Scenes, Incidents, Dangers and Hardships Endured During the Yakima and Clickitat Indian War, 1855 and 1856.* Portland: George Himes, 1885.

Himes, George H., ed. "Diary of Samuel Royal Thurston." *OHQ* 15 (September 1914): 150–70.

Hochspeier, Sherrill, and Ann Hochspeier. *Jefferson Cemetery, Jefferson, Marion County, Oregon, 1861–1990.* Salem: Willamette Valley Genealogical Society, 1990.

Holbrook, Francis X., and John Nikol. "The Navy in the Puget Sound War, 1855–1857." *PNQ* 67 (January 1976): 10–20.

Howard, Robert P. *Illinois: A History of the Prairie State.* Grand Rapids: Wm. B. Erdmans Publishing Co., 1972.

Hussey, John. "The Women of Fort Vancouver." *OHQ* 92 (Fall 1991): 265–308.

Iman, Margaret Windsor. "My Arrival in Washington in 1852." *WA Quart* 13 (October 1927): 254–60.

Jacksonville [Ill.] Genealogical Society. *Jacksonville Genealogical Journal* 3 (June-August 1975).

Jamison, Isabel. "Independent Military Companies of Sangamon County in the 30's." *Journal of the Illinois State Historical Society* 3 (January 1911): 22–48.

Johannsen, Robert W. *Frontier Politics on the Eve of the Civil War.* Seattle: University of Washington Press, 1955.

Johansen, Dorothy O. "The Oregon Steam Navigation Company: An Example of Capitalism on the Frontier." *PHR* 10 (June 1941): 179–88.

Johnson, David Alan. *Founding the Far West: California, Oregon, and Nevada, 1840–1890.* Berkeley: University of California Press, 1992.

Josephy, Alvin. *The Nez Perce Indians and the Opening of the Pacific Northwest.* New Haven: Yale University Press, 1965.

Katz, W. A. "Public Printers of Washington Territory, 1853–1863." *PNQ* 51 (July, October 1960): 103–41, 171–81.

Kingston, C. S. "The Walla Walla Separation Movement." *WA Quart.* 34 (April 1933): 91–104.

Kipp, Lawrence. "The Indian Council at Walla Walla, May and June, 1855." *Sources of the History of Oregon.* Vol. 1, Pt. 2. Eugene: Contributions to the Department of Economics and History of the University of Oregon, 1897.

Knight, N. R. "The Background of Early Washington Banking." *WA Quart.* 26 (October 1935): 243–63.

———. "Pioneer Private Bankers in Washington." *WA Quart.* 25 (October 1934): 243–54.

Lang, William L. "'Ambition Has Been My God': William Winlock Miller and Opportunity in Washington Territory." *PNQ* 83 (Summer 1992): 101–9.

———. "An Eden of Expectations: Oregon Settlers and the Environment They Created." *Oregon Humanities* (Winter 1992): 25–29.

Langley, Henry G. *The Pacific Coast Business Directory for 1867.* San Francisco: Henry G. Langley, 1867.

———. *The San Francisco Directory for the Year Commencing December 1865.* San Francisco: Towne & Bacon, 1865.

———. *The San Francisco Directory for the Year Commencing 1869.* San Francisco: Towne & Bacon, 1869.

Lee, Judson F. "Transportation: A Factor in the Development of Northern Illinois Previous to 1860." *Journal of Illinois State Historical Society* 10 (April 1917): 17–86.

Lokken, Roy N. "Frontier Defense of Washington Territory, 1853–1861." Master's thesis, University of Washington, 1951.

———. The Martial Law Controversy in Washington Territory, 1856." *PNQ* 43 (April 1952): 75–93.

MacColl, E. Kimbark. *Merchants, Money, and Power: The Portland Establishment, 1843–1913.* Portland: The Georgian Press, 1988.

Mann, Ralph. "Frontier Opportunity and the New Social History." *PHR* 53 (November 1984): 463–91.

Martin, Douglas Dale. "Indian Relations on the Pacific Slope, 1850–1890." Ph.D. diss., University of Washington, 1969.

Masterson, James R. "The Records of the Washington Superintendency of Indian Affairs, 1853–1874." *PNQ* 37(January 1946): 31–57.

Meany, Edmund S. "First American Settlement on Puget Sound." *WA Quart.* 7 (April 1916): 136–43.

———. "Newspapers of Washington Territory." *WA Quart.* 13 (July 1922): 181–95, 251–68, and 14 (January 1923): 21–29, 100–7.

Meeker, Ezra. *The Tragedy of Leschi.* Seattle, 1905.

Meinig, Donald W. *The Great Columbia Plain: A Historical Geography, 1805–1910.* Seattle: University of Washington Press, 1968.

Morgan, Murray. *Puget's Sound: A Narrative of Early Tacoma and the Southern Sound.* Seattle: University of Washington Press, 1979.

Moses, John. *Illinois: Historical and Statistical.* 2 Vols. Chicago: Fergus Publishing Co., 1892.

Nalty, Bernard C., and Truman R. Strobridge. "The Defense of Seattle, 1856." *PNQ* 55 (July 1964): 105–10.

Newell, Gordon R. *So Fair a Dwelling Place: A History of Olympia and Thurston County, Washington.* Olympia: Olympia News Company, 1950.

Oliver, William. *Eight Months in Illinois.* 1843. Reprint, Chicago: Walter M. Hill, 1924.

Peck, J. M. *A Gazeteer of Illinois in Three Parts.* Jacksonville: R. Goudy, 1834.

Perrin, William Henry. *History of Cass County, Illinois.* Chicago: O. L. Baskin & Co., 1882.

Pickens, William Hickman. "A Marvel of Nature: The Harbor of Harbors: Public Policy and the Development of the San Francisco Bay, 1846–1926." Ph.D. diss., University of California, Davis, 1976.

Pomeroy, Earl. *The Pacific Slope: A History of California, Oregon, Washington, Idaho, Utah and Nevada.* 1965. Reprint, Lincoln: University of Nebraska Press, 1991.

Prince, Carl E., and Mollie Keller. *The U.S. Customs Service: A Bicentennial History.* Washington, D.C.: Department of Treasury, 1989.

Prosch, Charles W. *Reminiscences of Washington Territory: Scenes, Incidents, and Reflections of the Pioneer Period on Puget Sound.* Seattle, 1904.

Richards, Kent. *Isaac I. Stevens: Young Man in a Hurry.* 1979. Reprint, Pullman: Washington State University Press, 1993.

Robbins, Roy M. "The Federal Land System in an Embryo State." *PHR* 4 (Fall 1935): 356–75.

Schlicke, Carl P. *General George Wright: Guardian of the Pacific Coast.* Norman: University of Oklahoma Press, 1988.

Sellers, Charles, Jr. *The Market Revolution: Jacksonian America, 1815–1846.* New York: Oxford University Press, 1991.

Shaw, Col. B. F. "Medicine Creek Treaty." *Proceedings of the Oregon Historical Society,* 1901. Portland: Oregon Historical Society, 1901.

Short, William F. *Historical Encyclopedia of Illinois and History of Morgan County.* Chicago: Munsell Publishing Co., 1906.

Scott, Franklin William. *Newspapers and Periodicals of Illinois, 1814–1879.* Springfield: Illinois State Historical Library, 1910.

Simmons, Katherine N. "The Cultural Beginnings of Olympia, Washington, 1850–1865." Master's thesis, State College of Washington, Pullman, 1948.

Smith, Marian W. *The Puyallup-Nisqually*. New York: Columbia University Press, 1940.

Splawn, Andrew Jackson. *Ka-mi-akin: The Last Hero of the Yakimas*. Portland: Kilham Stationery and Press, 1917.

Steele, Harvey. *Hyas Tyee: The United States Customs Service in Oregon, 1848–1989*. Washington, D.C.: U.S. Department of Treasury, 1990.

Stephenson, Charles. "Determinants of American Migration: Methods and Models in Mobility Research." *Journal of American Studies* 9 (August 1975): 189–98.

Stevenson, Shanna. *A History of Lacey and Olympia*. Norfolk: Donnelson Company, 1989.

Swan, John M. *Olympia, the Pioneer Town of Washington, Its Socialization, Origin and Early History from a Pioneer's Retrospection*. Olympia, n.d.

Thomas, William. *History of Morgan County, Illinois*. Chicago: Donnelley, Lloyd & Co., 1878.

Throckmorton, Arthur L. *Oregon Argonauts: Merchant Adventurers on the Western Frontier*. Portland: Oregon Historical Society, 1961.

Tolmie, William F. *The Journals of William Fraser Tolmie: Physician and Fur Trader*. Vancouver: Mitchell Press Ltd., 1963.

Trafzer, Clifford E., ed. *Indians, Superintendents, and Councils: Northwestern Indian Policy, 1850–1855*. Lanham, Maryland: University Press of America, 1986.

Trafzer, Clifford E., and Richard D. Scheuerman. *Renegade Tribe: The Palouse Indians and the Invasion of the Inland Pacific Northwest*. Pullman: Washington State University Press, 1986.

Unruh, John D., Jr. *The Plains Across: The Overland Emigrants and the Trans-Mississippi West, 1840–1860*. Urbana: University of Illinois Press, 1979.

Vance, James E., Jr. *Geography and Urban Evolution in the San Francisco Bay Area*. Berkeley: University of California Press, 1964.

Van Kirk, Sylvia. *Many Tender Ties: Women in Fur Trade Society, 1670–1870*. Norman: University of Oklahoma Press, 1980.

Vaughan, Thomas, ed. "The Round Hand of George B. Roberts." *OHQ* 63 (June-September 1962): 101–241.

Vindication of Governor Stevens, for Proclaiming and Enforcing Martial Law in Pierce County, W.T. Olympia: n.p., May 10, 1856.

Vinovskis, Maris A. "Family and Schooling in Colonial and Nineteenth Century America." *Journal of Family History* 12 (Spring 1987): 19–38.

Walters, Ronald G. "The Family and Antebellum Reform: An Interpretation." *Societas* 3 (Summer 1973): 221–32.

"Washington Territory in the War Between the States." *WA Quart.* 2 (October 1907): 33–39.

"Washington's War Governor." *WA Quart.* 8 (April 1917): 91–95.

West, Elliott. *Growing Up with the Country: Childhood on the Far Western Frontier*. Albuquerque: University of New Mexico Press, 1989.

Whitney, Ellen M. *The Black Hawk War, 1831–1832*. 3 vols. Springfield: Illinois State Historical Library, 1973.

Winkle, Kenneth J. "The Voters of Lincoln's Springfield: Migration and Political

Participation in an Antebellum City." *Journal of Social History* 25 (Spring, 1992): 595–612.

Winthrop, Theodore. *The Canoe and the Saddle, or Klalam and Klickitat.* Edited by John H. Williams. Tacoma: John H. Williams, 1913.

Works Progress Administration. *Told by the Pioneers.* Olympia, Washington, 1934.

Wylie, Irvin G. *The Self-Made Man in America: The Myth of Rags to Riches.* New Brunswick, NJ: Rutgers University Press, 1954.

Yates, Richard, Jr., and Catharine Yates Pickering. *Richard Yates: Civil War Governor.* Danville, Ill.: Interstate Printers, 1966.

Index